The Rhetoric of Mao Zedong

Studies in Rhetoric/Communication
Thomas W. Benson, Series Editor

The Rhetoric of Mao Zedong

Transforming China and Its People

Xing Lu

The University of South Carolina Press

Published by the University of South Carolina Press
Columbia, South Carolina 29208

www.sc.edu/uscpress

Manufactured in the United States of America

26 25 24 23 22 21 20 19 18 17
10 9 8 7 6 5 4 3 2 1

Library of Congress Cataloging-in-Publication
Data can be found at http://catalog.loc.gov/.

ISBN 978-1-61117-752-7 (cloth)
ISBN 978-1-61117-753-4 (ebook)

This book was printed on recycled paper
with 30 percent postconsumer waste content.

This book is dedicated to my father, Lu Rong 吕荣,
and my mother, Jiang Hong 江虹;
both are the sources of my inspiration and wisdom.

Contents

Series Editor's Preface

In *The Rhetoric of Mao Zedong*, Professor Xing Lu offers a wide-ranging history and criticism of one of the most important revolutionary and national leaders of the twentieth century. Mao Zedong (1893–1976) rose to leadership of the Chinese Communist Party, commanded party and army in revolution, war, and civil war, and assumed his role as unchallenged leader of China from 1949 until his death in 1976. A large part of his power, and a core element in Mao's transformation of China, stemmed from his education in Confucian and Marxist thought and his adaptation of that thought in a rhetoric of class struggle, Marxism-Leninism with "Chinese characteristics," and doctrines of serving the people, criticism and self-criticism, and Chinese nationalism. These themes, articulated in Mao's rhetoric, guided national policy and infused daily life and human relationships.

Professor Xing Lu is the author of *Rhetoric in Ancient China, Fifth to Third Century B.C.E.*, and *Rhetoric of the Chinese Cultural Revolution*, both published by the University of South Carolina Press. In *The Rhetoric of Mao Zedong*, Xing Lu traces the beginnings of Mao's rhetoric, his rhetorical theories, his rhetorical style, and his rhetorics of class struggle, construction of the new communist person, Chinese nationalism, and Chinese foreign policy, concluding with an extended discussion of the legacy of Mao's rhetoric in China after Mao Zedong. Professor Xing Lu, who was born in Mao's China in 1956 and who was also educated in China, later earned a doctorate in rhetoric and communication at the University of Oregon; she is currently a professor of communication at DePaul University in Chicago. She brings to her study of the rhetoric of Mao Zedong a deep personal history and an impressive mastery of two great cultural traditions.

THOMAS W. BENSON

Preface

I was born in 1956, when China was at the end of its first Five-Year Plan, a centralized economic endeavor based on the Soviet model for socialist development. Mao Zedong and his army had "liberated"[1] China from a three-year civil war, washing away a humiliating past of Western gunboat diplomacy and semicolonization by the Japanese, when he established the People's Republic of China on October 1, 1949. By 1956 China had reached its highest level of economic growth to date, with a 15 percent increase in GDP and a national income growth rate of 9 percent per year since 1952.[2] As the numbers indicate, Chinese living standards improved immensely as compared to those of previous decades, and citizens began to enjoy equal access to education, equal pay for men and women, and free medical coverage. Corruption was rare, and prostitution and drug-related crimes were entirely eradicated. People helped each other, had a great sense of national pride and social security, and exhibited high enthusiasm for constructing a new, socialist China. Chinese society was, at least comparatively speaking, both stable and thriving.

My mother always told me that "1956 was a good year." That year was Mao's launching pad for the rest of contemporary Chinese history. If he had not instigated the Anti-Rightist Movement the following year, if he had not inaugurated the Great Leap Forward in the year of 1958, and if he had not launched the Cultural Revolution ten years after 1956, China would have embarked on a trajectory toward economic growth and industrialization at least three decades sooner. Mao Zedong would have left the global scene as an unmitigated national and international hero. However, Mao's cult of personality, the Soviet model of one-party rule, and the dogma of class struggle combined with his despotic leadership ensured Mao's status as a powerful and yet deeply controversial twentieth-century world leader.

As I was growing up, I learned from my textbooks and teachers that Mao was the savior of China, that there would have been no new China without Mao, and that the Chinese people would still be suffering under a semicolonial rule of foreign powers and the feudal systems without Mao. Consequently I had great reverence for Mao. This veneration intensified in 1966, the first year Mao launched the Cultural Revolution. I was in the third grade. We ceased our usual studies and started reading Chairman Mao's quotations from the "Red Treasured Book" (known perhaps more widely as the *Little Red Book,* compiled in 1966).[3] We recited them every morning. Our teacher told us how to interpret Mao's words and instructed us how to apply them to our everyday lives.

The more quotations we could recite, the more revolutionary we proved ourselves to be. Passion among the Chinese people for Mao and his ideas was widespread and intense. I remember in particular one popular song that we sang all the time to demonstrate how much we loved Mao's works. One section of the lyrics follows:

> I love reading Chairman Mao's books the most.
> I have studied them thousands of times.
> I carefully decipher profound messages (in these books).
> I feel warmth in my heart (when reading them).
> I feel as if a timely rain was quenching drought-stricken land.
> Crops are drenched with dew.
> Chairman Mao's quotations have nourished me;
> I now have more energy to participate in the Revolution.
> Word by word, line by line,
> I read and think at the same time.
> Revolutionary truth shines through his words;
> Every word speaks directly to my heart;
> Just like a key that can open a thousand locks.[4]

During the Cultural Revolution, I carried Chairman Mao's *Little Red Book* in my pocket every day and everywhere I went, just like everyone else. I cut my hair short and wore a man's jacket with a Mao badge on it and soldier's shoes, as Mao expected young women to be masculine and militant.[5] In my family's small apartment (fifteen square meters for six of us), we hung twenty Mao portraits on the walls. This was not atypical of other Chinese families. My mother bought and traded over a hundred Mao badges of various designs. In my childhood diary, I quoted Mao's sayings ad infinitum, and I criticized myself for any thoughts or actions that deviated from Mao's teachings. In addition I would think of Mao's words when faced with challenging situations. I attended public rituals dedicated to the worship of Mao, and there we would dance and sing songs to worship him. I was ready to defend and fight for Mao; I would do whatever he asked the Chinese people to do, even if it meant sacrificing my life. I grew up in Mao's political and rhetorical culture, having inherited his romantic idealism, his speech, and his ways of thinking. As Qian Liqun (钱理群), an expert on Mao studies in China, has said, "Mao is my spiritual father" (2012, 17). Years later I now look back at my own fanaticism and marvel at my complete and utter indoctrination. It was not just me; it was widespread.

But in 1968, two years after the start of China's Cultural Revolution, Chairman Mao Zedong faced a formidable challenge. In the wake of crippling economic devastation and widespread closure of universities, it had become clear that higher education (or indeed even urban employment) was no longer a viable option for the majority of China's youths. Fearing that the younger urban generation might foment social chaos if they remained idle, Mao Zedong issued a call to action: On December 22, 1968, he published a directive in the *People's Daily* instructing all those who had graduated from middle or high school over the past three years (the majority of whom were Red Guards) to leave their homes and receive a "re-education" from the peasants in the countryside.

It was with little hesitation, then, that I joined the roughly sixteen million Chinese youths (between the ages of fifteen and eighteen), known as the "sent-down" or "educated" young people, who left their urban lives in exchange for hard rural labor. However, during the five years I worked tilling the soil to grow vegetables, I began to question Mao's claims that peasants were the best teachers and that knowledge gained from books had no use. I found myself desperately curious and eager to learn; but the schools were closed, teachers and intellectuals were denounced, and there were no textbooks with which I could satisfy my yearnings. In particular, I became enamored with the idea of someday becoming an interpreter, like those I had seen in the few documentary films we were allowed to watch at the time. It was this dream that would eventually drive me to study English on my own, in spite of Mao's directive.

I managed to borrow an old English textbook from a friend's father and started learning the English alphabet. Every day I wrote a few English words on a piece of paper and brought it to the fields, trying to memorize them while scraping weeds away from the vegetables with my shovel. As my English vocabulary grew, I found myself increasingly interested in language and literature. When the university entrance exams resumed in 1977—one year after Mao's death and the end of the Cultural Revolution—I immediately took steps to continue my formal education.

Even after I was admitted to a university in the spring of 1978, however, I found myself torn between admiring Mao as a great national hero and resenting him for trying to deprive me and millions of other Chinese youths of an education and for launching the Cultural Revolution, during which my family suffered.[6] Of course, I kept my thoughts to myself, if for no other reason than fear: I was terrified that my family and I might be branded as "counter-revolutionaries." Nonetheless the turmoil of my private thoughts continued.

Many years later, when I was finishing my doctoral program in rhetoric and communication at the University of Oregon, Mao's words continued to echo in my mind, shaping my thoughts and, albeit intermittently, guiding my behavior. Even though my blind faith in Mao had dissipated long ago, Mao's dialectical thinking, his determination, his sense of equality (especially between men and women), and his sympathy for disadvantaged people were still deeply ingrained in my value system. At the same time, I also came to the realization that Mao's polarized and radical ways of thinking and speaking have caused immeasurable harm to China's society and its people. These moral conundrums were not specific to me but rather were endemic in my entire generation.

Ever since I began studying the power of rhetoric in transforming individuals and societies, I have often asked myself, what exactly was it about Mao Zedong that imbued him with such remarkable powers to transform China and the Chinese people? From this central inquiry sprang a host of related questions: How was he so effectively able to persuade his comrades and members of the Chinese intellectual community to join him in the revolution? How did he rise from the ranks of a peasant's son to the most powerful leader in China? In what ways and to what degree did he do so through his rhetoric and discourse, and why does his rhetorical legacy still live on? Indeed, would Mao's rhetoric still have a place in Chinese thought and behavior? What is the connection between Mao's rhetoric and China's political discourse propagated by current Chinese leaders? What is the role of Mao's rhetoric for China in the twenty-first century on the world stage? Will it ever be possible for the Chinese people to break away from the shadow of Mao? Would they even be willing to do so? These are the questions that motivated me to embark on this book project. My background growing up during Mao's era positioned me to study Mao's rhetoric with a historical and contextual perspective. I hope to shed light on some of these questions by carrying out an exhaustive and careful analysis of Mao's rhetoric selected from his speeches and writings covering a period of sixty-two years, situating it firmly within the sociopolitical contexts that Mao was born into, lived through, and ultimately transformed.

Acknowledgments

This project would not have come to fruition without the generous assistance of a number of people. First and foremost, I would like to thank my adviser and mentor, David Frank, who encouraged me to take on this project. He listened to my initial pitches and offered great insight on the first two chapters of this book. I am grateful for his unfailing support of my research on Chinese rhetoric ever since I was in graduate school thirty years ago. I am equally grateful to Perry Link, a prominent China-studies scholar, who graciously agreed to read the draft of chapter 3 despite his busy schedule. His comments were extremely helpful, and his scholarly works on Chinese political language continue to be a source of inspiration. Moreover, I am indebted to a number of rhetorical scholars who have kindly provided helpful feedback on the manuscript. LuMing Mao read chapter 2 on Mao's theories of rhetoric; Herbert Simons read chapter 4 on Mao's rhetoric of class struggle; Mei Zhang read chapter 5 on rhetorical construction of a new Communist person; Michelle Yang read chapter 7 on Mao's foreign policy rhetoric; Donovan Conley and Stephen Hartnett read and edited portions of the conclusion. I benefited from the expertise and research of each of these scholars.

I am grateful for the generous help I received from a number of individuals on collecting sources on Mao. Shensheng Zhao, a well-learned friend, kindly gave me two boxes of books on Mao and encouraged me to pursue the project before he passed away five years ago. Aizhen Li and Zhihong Xia, dear neighbors and scholars, purchased a number of books on Mao in China for me. Bertrand Chung from Taiwan offered me several of his private collections on Mao published in Taiwan. Weidong Tan directed me to some online resources regarding Mao that I would not have found otherwise.

I have benefited from the two anonymous reviewers of this work. Their close and careful reading of the manuscript and their editorial suggestions for improvement were very helpful. The suggestion from one of the reviewers on the reorganization of the introduction helped unify the theme of transformative rhetoric in this book. I also extend my thanks to Jim Denton for his faith in me to complete this project and for his guidance in the review process.

Special thanks go to Judy Bowker, my guardian angel and beloved friend, who read through and edited chapters 1 through the conclusion. As a rhetorician herself, she asked thought-provoking questions, and her careful editing stimulated my thought process and improved the quality of the manuscript.

This project was supported by DePaul University's Research Council Paid Leave in 2013–14 and the College of Communication Summer Research Grant in the summer of 2011, which allowed me to be released from teaching and concentrate on research and writing.

I owe gratitude to my daughter, Wendi Lulu Gu, and my husband, Licheng Gu, my two favorite cheerleaders. Since she was a baby Wendi has always watched me research Chinese rhetoric. Now that she has graduated from college and works as a literary agent at a literary agency, she has helped me with edits and asked me intellectually engaging questions throughout the process. Licheng has sacrificed his own time to cook and shop for me so that I could have more time to write. He also made many trips to the Northwestern University library on my behalf for books, as he is a faculty member of the university. Finally, my parents, who are both in their late eighties, are a continuous source of inspiration to me. They have supported me in more ways than they will ever know. Their lifelong experiences before and after China's revolution in 1949 provide me with a real sense of China's modern history and motivate me to learn more about Mao's rhetoric. They both benefited and suffered under Mao's authoritarian rule, and consequently they have mixed feelings about Mao. They will not be able to read this book, as it is written in English, but this work is tangible proof of their memory. This book is dedicated to them.

Notes on Translation

I have used both English and Chinese sources for this study. I translated all the Chinese sources used in this study when the English translations were not available or were inaccurate.

Mao wrote many speeches and essays in different time periods, but the English versions of his selected works were published in later years. In each citation to Mao's speeches, I give two dates: the year of Mao's work and the year in which the English translation was published. For example, I use "Mao 1937/1967" to indicate that the speech was written in 1937 and the translation was published in 1967.

Introduction

Mao Zedong, the founder of the People's Republic of China, was revered as the "red sun" shining over China. He was widely eulogized for his contributions to establishing a new China that touted equality, unity, independence, and a better life. Before his death in 1976 books, films, songs, and theatrical performances adulated him. His portrait was in every household, and his *Little Red Book* was read every day and by everyone in China. Since Mao's death in 1976, China has moved toward Westernization and economic reform, which has resulted in a booming economy and rapid improvement in the living standards for the Chinese people.[1] However, at the same time, China has experienced alarming corruption, moral decline, and an increasing gap between the rich and the poor. In such contexts Mao has been resurrected in various popular cultural forums; a sense of nostalgia for Mao's era has prevailed, and "Mao fever" has escalated. Taxi drivers hang Mao's portrait in their cars; Mao's badges are again worn by ordinary civilians; and books, shows, and songs under the theme of "red classics" have again become popular. In the celebration of Mao's 120th birthday on December 26, 2013, thousands of people in Shaoshan (Mao's hometown) together ate noodles, a traditional birthday meal and symbolic event meant to represent Mao's spiritual longevity.[2] In addition the Chinese government media has published a large number of books and articles on Mao's life and his glorious deeds. A number of films and TV series that have been produced applaud Mao's infallible leadership during China's Anti-Japanese War and the Chinese civil war, all while extolling his personal charisma, wisdom, and eloquence.[3] As observed by Melissa Schrift, "Mao, in spirit if not in body (his crystal-encased corpse in Tiananmen aside), is, indeed, alive and well in contemporary China" (2001, 2).

It is safe to say that no Chinese leader in Chinese history has had more influence on Chinese culture, thought, and communication than Mao Zedong. Mao was a skilled orator and delivered many of his directives via public addresses. He was also the author of a large corpus of written works, which over time have taken on a biblical dimension as the official, canonical texts of the Chinese Communist Party (CCP). Mao's works have been heavily studied by the Chinese and non-Chinese over several decades,[4] as his works are key spiritual and ideological resources for the Chinese people. They are undoubtedly the most prominent and widely read and cited texts, serving as official encomiums that depict Mao as an infallible Chinese icon.

Mao's words represented what the CCP felt to be the highest truth and still serve as the foundation of political discourse in contemporary China. His rhetoric has fundamentally transformed China—from a Confucian society characterized by hierarchy and harmony to a socialist state guided by Communist ideologies of class struggle and radicalization. This transformation was made possible largely because of his ability to attract, persuade, and mobilize millions of Chinese people, who became devoted to his Communist cause and his utopian vision. Today, Mao's legacy lives on, and he continues to be revered as a hero.

Mao also fascinates the rest of the world. His influence has extended well beyond China's borders. He is admired by many world leaders for winning the 1949 revolution against the United States–supported Nationalist army despite the challenges of a comparatively weaker army base and poor living conditions. To others, he represents the promise of socialism as a way to overcome imperialism and colonialism, particularly in the Third World. His political success has inspired revolutions in Africa, Southeast Asia, and Latin America, along with internal resistance to the establishments in the United States and Europe. Mao's works, particularly his *Little Red Book,* have been translated into numerous languages and are read by many across the globe. Even today the theory of "Mao Zedong Thought" still stands as a pillar of revolutionary ideology.

Numerous books on Mao Zedong's biography, his political views, and his military strategies have been produced both in the West and within China. Most of these books focus on the assessment of Mao. A thorough review of literature on Mao studies reveals different assessments of the chairman. The first interpretation paints him as an evil megalomaniac who single-handedly caused some of the worst injustices in modern history. Jung Chang and Jon Halliday (2005), for example, depict Mao as a mass murderer from the first sentence of their book: "Mao-Tse-Tung [Mao Zedong], who for decades held absolute power over the lives of one-quarter of the world's population, was responsible for over 70 million deaths in peacetime" (1). In his book *The Private Life of Chairman Mao*, Li Zhisui (1994) portrays Mao as a man of cruelty and selfishness, a womanizer, and a monster incapable of human feelings. Mao is regularly blamed, both in academic texts and in more casual assessments, for China's economic collapse and the death of millions that resulted from the Great Leap Forward and the Cultural Revolution. In some Mao studies he is painted as a master manipulator who evoked fear and coerced victims into confessing their "anti-revolutionary" crimes. In American magazines Mao is often compared to Hitler and Stalin as one of the twentieth century's greatest monsters.[5]

Of course, not everyone concurs with this evaluation of Mao. For example, a number of prominent sinologists have called the validity of Chang and Halliday's research into question,[6] and many others have adamantly refuted those simplistic assessments of Mao that reduce him to an evil caricature on par with Hitler and Stalin. Indeed such depictions of Mao tend to miss the nuances and complexities of both his character and his rhetoric.

Additional Chinese authors are more critical of Mao. These authors tend to be independent, liberal public intellectuals who are not affiliated with the CCP or the Chinese government and are able to publish their works outside China. As such, they are comparatively freer to voice their criticisms of Mao, including their objections to his utopianism, "his personal despotism in politics, his political scheming, a narcissistic tendency in his psychology, and his political cognitive structure" (Xiao 2010, 277). Gao Hua (2002), for example, has subtly criticized Mao's radical views and senseless actions against intellectuals during the period of his Rectification Campaign in Yan'an in 1942. Li Rui, one of Mao's former secretaries, stated his belief that Mao made some serious mistakes over the course of his lifetime, including various crimes committed during the party's political campaigns and China's economic development (Li Rui 2005a). Qian Liqun (2012), another prominent Mao scholar, has written two volumes detailing Mao's legacy in China, revealing horrors caused by Mao's thought reform campaigns and criticizing his radical ideology. However, as these scholars' publications are frequently banned in China, their voices are not often heard by ordinary Chinese people.

In contrast, the second interpretation of Mao is decidedly favorable. When Mao was first introduced to the international community by the American journalist Edgar Snow, Mao's public image was bolstered with praise and merits. In his book *Red Star over China,* published in 1938, Mao is presented as a competent and charismatic Communist leader who has overcome formidable adversaries to establish a new, stronger China, largely as a result of his extraordinary political talent and cunning military strategies.[7] Subsequently Mao has been deified as "the savior, the rejuvenator, the remoulder of China" (Paloczi-Horvath 1962, 14). Mao's achievements between 1949 and 1956 have been recognized by Roderick MacFarquhar (2010), one of the premier experts on Mao's China, as "the fastest, most extensive, and least damaging socialist revolution carried out in any communist state" (348). As Philip Short (1999) writes, "Mao had an extraordinary mix of talents: he was visionary, statesman, political and military strategist of genius, philosopher and poet" (630). Mao has been praised as having "an extraordinary ability to think on several levels at once, and could grasp the central issues and the large concern" (Apter and Saich 1994, 109).[8] Schell and Delury (2013) applaud Mao for his ingenuity in changing the face of China: a leader who "managed not only to uproot society from its deeply rooted traditional past but also inject into it a certain new dynamic pragmatism that, going forward, allowed it to reimagine and re-create itself in surprisingly innovative ways" (255). In China the official media, and scholarly and popular accounts credit Mao with an impressive list of accomplishments: transforming China's economy and military; leading the nation's breakaway from the Soviets' control; campaigning against corruption and bureaucracy in the early 1950s; building an industrial foundation; working to educate and empower women and common people; instilling a deep sense of national pride in the Chinese people; and reaching rapprochement with the United States, as embodied in the iconic handshake with Richard Nixon in 1972.[9]

Those who worked for Mao as guards, cooks, nurses, and secretaries during his lifetime have offered more personal accounts of the chairman, portraying him as kindhearted, humorous, well learned, sensitive, charismatic, and strong willed. Speaking from their own observations and experiences living closely with Mao, these authors depicted him as an ordinary person who loved his family, exhibited sympathy toward the poor, was passionate about his nation, and lived a frugal life.[10] These books have been relatively popular, attracting readers who still adulate Mao and admire what he did for China. However, studies of Mao in China have been heavily politicized. Only those books that praise and pay tribute to Mao are allowed publication in China.[11]

A third approach, exemplified by Deng Xiaoping, a paramount leader of China from 1978 to 1992, seeks to overcome this dichotomized portrayal of Mao by conducting a cost-benefit analysis of Mao's life. In his meeting with the Italian journalist Oriana Fallaci in 1980, Deng Xiaoping said of Mao, "His contributions were primary, his mistakes secondary" (Deng 1994a, 353), which later was commonly interpreted as "seven parts good, three parts bad." Deng confirmed his assessment of the chairman officially in the Resolution of the Sixth Plenum of the 11th Central Committee of the Communist Party of China the following year. The document acknowledged that Mao made serious mistakes when launching the Cultural Revolution; in addition it criticized his policies as inappropriate and unrealistic to employ, and thus detrimental to the nation's development. Nonetheless the resolution ultimately hailed Mao as "a great Marxist and a great proletarian revolutionary, strategist and theorist.... His contributions to the Chinese revolution far outweigh his mistakes."[12] Accordingly Mao's achievements outweigh his failures; he is no one-dimensional hero, and yet we can nonetheless place him squarely in the category of "good."

A fourth way of thinking about Mao attempts to avoid the pitfalls of reducing him to a simple hero or a villain figure; as Liang Shuming, a prominent Chinese intellectual, writes, "There is not one Mao Zedong" but rather "many Mao Zedongs" (Zhu 2007, 5). Apter and Saich (1994) note that Mao had both a "hard" side and a "soft" side depending on which part of his life one looks at—his accomplishments or his failures (33). Even Mao admitted that he had a dual personality represented by both a tiger and a monkey, with a dominant tigerlike nature tempered by a secondary, monkeylike demeanor.[13] Lee Feigon (2002), among others, points out that it may indeed be impossible to determine any singular vision of Mao, given that "much of the Western view of him turns out to have been an extraordinarily sophisticated mix of theoretical fiction—inventions disguised as facts" (10). Thus, despite the tempting simplicity of polarized "god Mao" and "devil Mao" portrayals, most contemporary Western scholars seem to agree that there are multiple Maos and consequently multiple meanings and interpretations of him and his legacy (for example, Apter and Saich 1994; Cheek 2010; Lynch 2004). They tend to offer positive reports of his character and achievements but negative evaluations of his thought-reform campaigns and post-1956 economic policies (which were generally disastrous for China). There is, however, a certain degree of moral relativism inherent in any perspective that adopts such a multiplicity of views. Although this sort of pluralistic approach avoids simplistic moral assessments of Mao as sinner or saint, it nonetheless fails to provide any definitive conclusion about how we ought to view his legacy. Most important to note, there have been essentially no studies to date that treat Mao as a truly persuasive, contextualized figure while offering insights on his rhetorical power over China and the world.

In contrast to simplistic renderings of Mao as tyrant or savior, as seven parts good and three parts bad, or as a kaleidoscopic persona impossible to characterize, the approach utilized in this book roots him firmly in his time and his spoken and written discourse beginning in 1913 and ending in 1975, which maps the overall trajectory of his life and political career. Drawing on both Chinese and English-language documents, I look closely at the essential source of his power: his political rhetoric. I seek to capture the complexity and nuances of Mao's impact as a rhetorical figure situated in specific historical and cultural contexts of modern China. In short, this book examines a full range of Mao's discourse over a span of sixty-two years, identifies rhetorical themes and styles, and analyzes Mao as a symbolic power, a skilled rhetor, and a maker of myths who reshaped and transformed the minds of Chinese people. It was in precisely this capacity that Mao wielded the power of rhetoric, using it as a vehicle through which he would ultimately gain and secure his political and cultural power. I suggest that the arc of Mao's political career is tethered to the development of his command and manipulation of symbols, namely, his use of rhetorical strategies, modes of argumentation, generic antecedents, and stylistic devices. It is useful to trace the development, emergence, and evolution of Mao's ideas and arguments in response to changing rhetorical situations in modern China.

Rhetoric as defined by George Kennedy (1991) is "the energy inherent in emotion and thought, transmitted through a system of signs, including language, to others to influence their decisions or action" (7). Scholars generally agree that rhetoric functions to shape perceptions, foster collective commitment, and induce action (for example, Burke 1969; Farrell 1993). Effective rhetoric adapts to an audience and responds to the exigencies of a situation (for example, Perelman and Olbrechts-Tyteca 1969; Bitzer 1968). Rhetoric is "an ability, in each [particular] case, to see the available means of persuasion" (Aristotle 1991, 36). In his recent publication, James Crosswhite (2013) articulates the concept of what he calls "deep rhetoric," advocating for "the idea of a rhetoric that takes historically specific shapes, and which divides itself into forms of discourse, but which also has generative power that is in the process of exceeding those shapes and forms" (27). In other words, a view of rhetoric as "deep" presumes that it has the capacity to create consciousness and give rise to transformational change. Mao's rhetoric has generated power, created new consciousness among the Chinese people, and overwhelmingly transformed Chinese society. This work not only identifies and exemplifies Mao's persuasive and manipulative techniques but also examines how he adapted his rhetoric to different rhetorical exigencies and audiences throughout China's modern history and dynamics of international situations; how he appropriated Confucianism and Marxism and projected this hybrid ideology onto China and Chinese people; and how his rhetoric altered the perception of reality for the Chinese people and mobilized the Chinese people to follow his directives. In other words, Mao's rhetoric is treated here as transformative rhetoric—not simply as linguistic strategies or figures of speech but as symbolic capital, capable of bringing profound changes (as well as destruction) to individuals and societies.

By transformative rhetoric, I mean the use of rhetoric to move and mobilize a society toward a common goal, while also reconstructing the preexisting reality and reshaping cultural habits, institutional practices, and ideological beliefs. Transformative rhetoric unites constituents of various backgrounds, transcends ideological differences, and gives justification for demonizing enemies; it inspires passion and collective commitment for a cause, creates fantasy and illusion, and provides hope for a better future. It is important to note that it requires a powerful, persuasive speaker as well as a rhetorical audience or a collective that has experienced a state of crisis, demands a solution, and willingly takes action. Transformative rhetoric is often characterized by an inflexible posture of righteousness and the prophetic promise for a better future, similar to the process of a religious conversion. The power of transformative rhetoric in political contexts has been studied by many Western scholars in their analyses of President Lincoln, Martin Luther King Jr., Malcolm X, and President Obama, to name just a few.[14] Mao's transformative rhetoric is rooted in his deep-seated belief in moral integrity, his unswerving insistence on ideological correctness, and his strong sense of nationalism. In particular, Mao's rhetoric prior to 1949 is largely couched in the rhetoric of hope, which has served to bolster the spirit of the Chinese people and motivate them to rally behind him in order to reap the rewards he so convincingly promised. Despite the many and varied challenges that the CCP would face during his lifetime, Mao (1947/1967d) consistently offered an optimistic perspective: "when dark clouds appeared in the sky, . . . we pointed out that this was only temporary, that the darkness would soon pass and the sun break through" (159). Drawing from the ancient Chinese notion of "Mandate of Heaven," traditionally employed to legitimize dynastic rule, Mao reiterated in his speeches and writings that the CCP represented the majority of the Chinese people and that they were therefore on the right side of history; thus he contended that the CCP was capable of overcoming any difficulties and was predestined to win the revolution. This confident assertion of his party's righteousness along with his ability to paint a visionary picture of the nation's future positioned Mao as a reassuring beacon of hope amid uncertainty and hardship.

Part of what made Mao's rhetoric of hope so powerful was that it was woven into a mythic vision of what China, and the Chinese people, could be. Rowland and Frank (2002) state, "Myth speaks directly to questions of value, meaning, and purpose. Symbol systems must be grounded in myth. However, myths must fit the scene and the time in which they are used" (301). Mao was a master mythmaker, and he made use of this power to mobilize the people of China and harness their tremendous energies in the interest of building a socialist China, all the while aggrandizing himself as the helmsman of China.

It is not claimed here that Mao's command of rhetoric provides the only or even the most important explanation for his influence; certainly political, economic, military, and cultural factors all acted in concert to secure his legacy. Nonetheless rhetoric has a unique and undeniable capacity to create self-perception, solidify national identity, and induce action. In this way rhetoric serves as a foundation, an actuator, and an amplifier for the other sources of power Mao wielded. I posit that without his masterful deployment of rhetoric, Mao Zedong could not have made the mark he did on China and its people; thus, examining his use of symbolic resources and rhetorical appeals is key to understanding Mao's transformation of China in the twentieth century.

It must be noted that Mao's rhetoric is not internally consistent. In my reading of Mao's works, I have observed Mao's rhetorical capacities as they unfolded over the span of his lifetime, both shifting in their focus and evolving in their effectiveness. His political position morphed from anarchist to pragmatist, from reformist to revolutionary, and from Confucianist to Marxist, from a champion of democracy to an authoritarian ruler. Indeed much like his conflicting personae, Mao's rhetoric oftentimes contradicted itself, particularly when I assess the various positions he took throughout the course of his lifetime. For example, while at one point he had deemed intellectuals to be revolutionary allies, he later accused them of being bourgeois or class enemies. Before 1949 he demanded a free, democratic, coalition government; after he assumed power in 1949, however, his rhetoric took on a decidedly more dogmatic tone as he espoused a fierce commitment to "the proletarian dictatorship." Mao's rhetoric evolved into a constant theme of class struggle and ideological conversion; he called on his people to better themselves consistently through self-criticism and build their nation with pride and loyalty to the party. This vision of cultural and ideological transformations maps neatly onto Mao's ideological vision, which resulted in endless cycles of humiliating confession and merciless persecution. Schell and Delury (2013) have noted that "in Mao's ideological universe of ceaseless contradictions, protracted struggle, and permanent revolution, there were never real finish lines" (230). Thus processes of change—and turmoil followed by mercurial stability—formed an inextricable part of Mao's rhetorical vision.

The shift in his discourse as a new ideology took hold was profound: the oppressed became the oppressor, and the discourse that had once been revolutionary was now considered hegemonic. Yet in spite of these profoundly divergent ideological positions, Mao was nonetheless able to captivate his audience and offer a compelling vision of China's political future—even if that future looked markedly different from one moment to the next. Undoubtedly the changing political climate in China that was facilitated or exacerbated by Mao's rhetoric necessarily shifted across time, revealing his skill as a rhetor who was able adeptly to deploy the tools of discourse to meet and alter whatever rhetorical situation he faced.

As his ideological commitments and discursive strategies shifted, so too did his persona. In particular, 1949 was a watershed year that demarcated an especially notable change in Mao's image as he shifted his concerns from "the survival of the revolutionary movement" to "the more difficult ethical and political ones of preserving revolutionary identity" (Womack 1982, xiii). Before 1949 Mao was "a servant of the people, a military leader who lives, eats and dresses like the common soldiers, a student and scholar of frugal tastes" (Paloczi-Horvath 1962, 13). Snow (1938) even believed that Mao "had in his youth strongly liberal and humanistic tendencies" (95). Sidney Rittenberg, the first American to join the CCP, who lived in China from 1944 to 1979, testified that before 1949 Chairman Mao "was the best listener I've ever spoken with. He would focus the whole being on you; what you were saying became the most important in the world to him." Later, however, he would transform into "an imperialist" who "tended to penalize people who stood up against him on issues. He became someone who likes to hold force and wasn't a good listener."[15] Rittenberg's assessment painted a compelling picture of Mao's transformation from an empathetic and modest servant of the people to an intolerant and tyrannical figure when he became an exalted leader of one of the world's greatest powers.

When Mao became the supreme leader of China in 1949 and attained a nearly godlike status, his words became infallible as his leadership became increasingly authoritarian. He adopted an aura of omnipotence. This drastic shift—in ideology, public identity, and rhetorical style—is at the crux of Mao's reputation as one of the most controversial figures of the twentieth century. In the words of Li Zehou, a contemporary Chinese philosopher, "No matter if you love him or hate him, praise him or criticize him, Mao Zedong leaves a huge shadow in modern China far surpassing anyone else. This shadow has overwhelmed, dominated, and controlled the life, destiny, misery and happiness of millions and several generations" (2008, 12). An analysis of the symbolic resources with which he crafted his persona and made manifest his political perspectives, then, offers some insight into the various dimensions of his being and the ways in which he continually acted and evolved in response to changing conditions in modern China. This book maps various rhetorical strands both diachronically and synchronically, as they were woven together at particular moments in Mao's life. Here a historical perspective is uniquely helpful: in analyzing how Mao leveraged rhetorical resources to meet various ideological ends, I am able to chart how Mao used a host of appeals drawn from Chinese traditions, but also how he interpreted the discourse of Marxism-Leninism to serve his own revolutionary goals.

My background and previous work in both Western and Chinese rhetoric afford me a unique set of perspectives with which to understand how Mao crafted his rhetorical appeals and China's rhetorical identities. To begin with, Mao drew on and appropriated an ancient tradition of Chinese rhetoric, which I previously explored in my first book (Lu 1998). There, I have uncovered and analyzed historical Chinese texts that offer rich and varied persuasive strategies, rhetorical techniques, and forms of artistic expression that the rhetoricians of ancient China conceptualized and deployed in literary, philosophical, political, and psychological domains. Mao relied heavily on these Chinese symbolic resources in his own writing and speeches, not only in constructing rhetorical appeals to help him reach his persuasive goals, but also in formulating his own rhetorical theories and styles.

Of course, the impact of Mao's rhetoric cannot be understood solely in the context of ancient Chinese theory; it is also essential to understand the discursive environment that characterized China throughout the last half of the twentieth century, when powerful symbolic resources were as influential as any political or military campaign. My prior analyses of Chinese political rhetoric in the modern period, found in *Rhetoric of the Chinese Cultural Revolution* (Lu 2004b), provides a valuable backdrop for my current exploration of Mao's discourse. Specifically I previously examined the rhetorical power of political symbols and symbolically infused practices that characterized the cultism of Mao and types of symbolic activities, including slogans, wall posters, revolutionary songs and operas, loyalty dances, denunciation rallies, political study sessions, and criticism and self-criticism meetings during the Cultural Revolution. This revolutionary rhetoric damaged Chinese culture, and its negative influence on thought and communication can still be felt in today's China. More important, in the context of our present enterprise, the root of these rhetorical forms can be traced to the political culture and discourse that Mao created after becoming chairman of the Chinese Communist Party in 1943.[16] Examining the ultimate influence that Mao's discourse has had on China and the Chinese people sheds light on our present understanding of China's political rhetoric. These historical perspectives led me quite naturally to the framework I utilize in this study: one that seeks to contextualize Mao's discourse, analyzing texts as historically and culturally situated responses to specific exigencies.

I started collecting Mao's works and rereading his writings about ten years ago as a rhetoric scholar. My secondary sources are not limited to the publications in China but also expand overseas from both Chinese and Western scholars. However, my analyses of Mao's rhetoric are heavily based on the primary texts written or spoken by Mao. During my annual trips to China, I have had numerous conversations with my family and friends about Mao and have also made notes and observations on the public discourse on Mao in this post-Mao era.

The primary texts of my analyses include Mao's early writings before he became a Communist, a complete set of Mao's works (five volumes published in China), and a complete set of his manuscripts in the Chinese language (thirteen volumes published in China).[17] I have reviewed each of these texts in their original Chinese, translating into English as necessary when expert translations were unavailable or inaccurate. In addition I have examined English versions of Mao's texts translated by prominent Chinese scholars, along with ten English volumes of his writings edited by Stuart Schram. I have collected a set of Mao's speeches on tape (also available online), along with a large number of memoirs written by those who had close contact with Mao throughout his life; none of these materials have been translated into English. It is crucial to include the original Chinese texts alongside their English interpretations in any assessment of Mao's rhetoric, as translation cannot always capture the nuanced meanings embedded in Chinese writing.[18] I am grateful that my bilingual background and training in rhetoric allowed me to accomplish this. Similarly my secondary sources include both Western and Chinese scholars, as I seek a rapprochement between Eastern and Western understandings of Mao Zedong.

Mao's writings are both numerous and vast in scope, incorporating elements of Chinese history, philosophy, political science, military strategy, foreign relations, literary critique, and persuasion. His early works reflect his training in the classical Chinese language. As he grew older, Mao became an admirer of Hu Shi and Chen Duxiu, both of whom were vocal advocates for replacing the classical Chinese language with vernacular Chinese following the 1911 May Fourth Movement; thus, starting in 1917 Mao joined many of the Chinese intellectuals who wrote in the modern, vernacular language, called *baihuawen,* in the wake of the movement. He continued to write prolifically through the 1950s,[19] at which point his works shifted toward brief edicts and personal correspondence. After Mao's death, more of his works were published between 1992 to 1998, including a collection of his early essays immediately following his death and thirteen additional volumes (comprised of his writings after 1949).[20] My analyses of Mao's rhetoric are grounded in my reading and reflections of this full range of discourse.

Preview of Chapters

There are eight chapters in this book, in addition to this introductory chapter. Chapter 1 describes and analyzes Mao's early writings from 1913 to 1917, before he became a Marxist and a Communist. The three texts focused on here are written in classical Chinese and consist largely of class notes and comments on his school readings. Mao's writing from this period demonstrates a strong influence of Confucian teachings and Mao's commitment to the public good. It also shows him as an ambitious and patriotic young man who was well versed in Chinese classical works and yet also was inspired by socialist ideals when China was humiliated by the Western powers. When he was in his early twenties, he wrote that the people of China ought to strengthen their bodies—through exercise and physical education—as a prerequisite to strengthening the nation. On a cultural level, he pushed against China's traditional family-centric mind-set in favor of one that focused on the nation as a whole. He compared Confucian doctrines with Friedrich Paulsen's *A System of Ethics* in content and style. In these early works, Mao exhibited an ability to engage intellectually in arguments and a capacity to persuade his audience eloquently. These early writings also reveal the multiple sources of influence that shaped Mao's value system, philosophical orientations, and political views.

Chapter 2 entails a review of Mao's theories on truth, knowledge, and dialectics, which he borrowed from Marxist doctrines and classical Chinese philosophy. In particular, Mao codified his theory of rhetoric by addressing the issue of arts and literature in Communist-occupied territories. Specifically, during the time of the Anti-Japanese War, Mao established himself as an authority on Marxist and Leninist theories, but he also disseminated his own theories of rhetoric and persuasion that remarkably transformed the social consciousness of the Chinese elites who came to his revolutionary base in Yan'an. There, Mao taught his new followers that they were expected to represent the voices of the workers and peasants in the content and form of their literary and artistic work. Moreover he argued that ordinary people and their life experiences were the authentic sources of truth and knowledge. He helped them appreciate the power of words in condemning one's enemies and cultivated the use of persuasive language tailored to the interests of ordinary people.

Chapter 3 presents the rhetorical styles used by Mao throughout his writings. In particular, his use of metaphors and references to Chinese history and classical texts were most effective. His overall rhetorical style was largely influenced by

Han Yu, a classical Chinese writer, as well as by Liang Qichao, a reformist during the transition period between the Qing dynasty and the Republic of China. Moreover, Mao's rhetoric relied on common, simple language to explain abstract ideas. He effectively reached a mixed audience of illiterate peasants and well-educated intellectuals in his Communist base, helping both groups identify the pressing problems facing China while justifying the Communist path China ought to take. He was clear, passionate, compelling, and vigorous in his rhetorical style. He used concrete examples to bring home theoretical propositions to establish commitment to the Communist ideology through his emotional appeals. Mao also occasionally used curse words and sarcastic remarks when attacking his enemies. By doing so, Mao empowered the masses, creating a set of new rhetorical expressions that were foreign, militant, and ideologically driven and that maintained remnants of traditional Chinese rhetoric.

In chapters 4 through 7, Mao's rhetoric is examined in specific areas. Chapter 4 explores the ways in which Mao rhetorically promoted, modified, and appropriated the Marxist theory of class struggle. Legitimizing class struggle as a Communist concept, Mao employed the idea as the cardinal principle for his revolution and eventual rule over the nation. Mao radicalized the notion of class struggle, deploying it as a tool with which he mobilized the masses to condemn the bourgeoisie. He polarized the people's opinions and attitudes toward one another. His propagation of class struggle altered Chinese society in terms of human relationships, cosmology, and the traditional Chinese value of harmony.

Mao made extensive use of Marxist ideology in his rhetoric in order to both unify and motivate the Chinese people to participate in everlasting revolution. Many of Mao's speeches and essays were aimed at achieving the CCP's ideal vision of conformity by rallying the proletariat under the banner of class struggle. He spent his entire life convincing his party and the nation that the Marxist concept of class struggle was an issue of life and death. He warned that citizens would need continuously to cultivate a proletarian consciousness and remain on guard lest they fall prey to bourgeois influence. While other Marxists—namely Stalin—would simply execute or exile those who were accused of being "class enemies," Mao believed that class consciousness could be raised through political education and persuasion; thus his mission was not to purify the party by weeding out dissidents but rather to convert skeptics via rhetorical influence. Under this logic, Mao launched relentless ideological remolding campaigns, beginning in 1942, both within the CCP and beyond.

Just as the other threads of Mao's rhetoric evolved and adapted to meet changing political and cultural conditions, so too did Mao's ideological rhetoric morph in response to his needs. For example, the way he identified the "enemy class" changed at different moments in Chinese history, as did the degree of emphasis he placed on class struggle. Moreover he used the concept of class struggle to a number of different ends: to justify his theory of permanent revolution; to legitimize the CCP's rule; to demarcate friends and enemies; to induce compliance; to generate hatred; and to mobilize fanaticism. Ultimately, then, Mao rebranded Marxism not only to suit the Chinese situation but also to serve his own political needs. This trend only intensified after 1949, when he followed Lenin's footsteps by adopting an ever more radical ideological stance.

Chapter 5 identifies and analyzes Mao's rhetoric, mainly directed at CCP members, on the transformation of a new Communist person. Mao's idea of a new Communist person was based on the Confucian belief that humans are malleable. The notion also drew on the traditional expectation that a moral leader will serve as an exemplar. This emphasis on morality can be attributed to the role of Confucian influence in Mao's early life, as he grew up studying classical Confucian texts. While Aristotle, in his *Nicomachean Ethics*, views a virtuous disposition as the result of proper upbringing and the formation of appropriate habits, Confucian teaching emphasizes self-cultivation and self-criticism as the keys to moral refinement. In addition the Chinese sense of morals or virtue—which is rooted in Confucian tradition—outlines a number of core principles: the sacrifice of self-interest for the greater good; matching words with action; modesty; plain living; courage; perseverance; and a love of learning. Not only did Mao rely on these moral touchstones throughout his work, but he also employed them in a decidedly rhetorical fashion, binding them to his political goals and the identity he exhorted the Chinese people to adopt.

Mao adapted the traditional Confucian virtues to reflect what might be called "the Communist virtues": selflessness; servitude in the name of one's country and one's people; and a willingness to sacrifice one's own well-being for the sake of the party and the nation. To speak in this discourse was to indicate that one thoroughly embodied the proletarian consciousness and was thus a person of morality. By contrast, any selfish thoughts or behaviors were considered both sinful and bourgeois. By appropriating classical Chinese concepts of self-criticism and self-cultivation, Mao preached ardently toward a goal and process of transforming a selfish person into a person of proletarian consciousness. His rhetoric on cognitive, attitudinal, and behavioral change was predicated on absolute moralism (similar to Puritanism) and political correctness. Mao temporarily achieved his goal via several rectification campaigns.

Chapter 6 discusses Mao's rhetoric of nationalism. Because his rhetoric was heavily shaped by nationalist themes, he is and was, for many, the penultimate symbol of nationalism. Because he grew up in a period when China was invaded by foreign powers and humiliated into a series of unfair treaties, young Mao developed a sharp resentment toward imperialism, and concomitantly, he developed a distinctly nationalist set of ambitions. His rhetoric of nationalism championed three interconnected values that, in his view, would help bring about a strong and powerful China: national sovereignty; self-reliance; and independence. By repeatedly sharing stories of China's humiliating past and chastising foreign powers for their aggression, Mao crafted a narrative of victimization through which he reconstructed the Chinese identity. He employed rhetoric of denunciation, condemning Chiang Kai-shek's close ties with the United States to promote patriotic sentiment. Despite the fact that China is a country made up of disparate regions speaking different dialects, Mao claimed that his people were all citizens of one unified nation with a shared history and desire to liberate themselves from poverty and oppression. Nationalism was also propagated by means of Mao's predictions of—and promises to build—a strong, prosperous, and democratic China. Today nationalism has been instilled in the minds of the Chinese people, and it is regularly employed as a rhetorical strategy to help shape and justify China's economic, military, and international relations policies.

Chapter 7 offers a treatment of Mao's rhetoric on Chinese foreign policy, particularly with the United States, from his early revolutionary period up to the years preceding his death. China's relationship with the United States during this period went through a series of massive rhetorical shifts, positioning the two nations first as allies, then as ideological enemies, and finally as strategic partners. Accordingly Mao's rhetoric shifted from praising to condemning and ultimately to reconciling with the United States. In his anti-American rhetoric, Mao presented himself not only as a national hero but also as a world leader in the fight against imperialism. Conversely Mao's historical meeting with Richard Nixon in 1972 served as evidence that Mao was a flexible strategist when facing various rhetorical exigencies. His pragmatic concerns for China's future outweighed the ideological differences between the two countries. His coinage of the Three Worlds Theory inspired revolutions in colonized nations and enabled him to build alliances with developing countries throughout the world.

This book's concluding chapter summarizes Mao's rhetoric diachronically and synchronically over the span of his lifetime in the contexts of Chinese history and culture. It discusses the resurgence of Mao's legacy, especially in the years since his death. Currently Mao has been commoditized, culturally consumed, and politically appropriated. In particular, I trace the lingering echoes of Mao's rhetoric propagated in the political discourse of the current Chinese president, Xi Jinping. It is concluded that Chinese political and official discourse needs to break away from Mao's rhetorical legacy and adapt to increasingly more diverse and sophisticated domestic and international audiences.

Mao Zedong's legacy, both good and bad, is still alive, glorified by some Chinese people even as it continues to haunt others. Indeed the rhetor has in fact become the rhetoric, as Mao has slowly been transformed into a powerful symbol in his own right—a symbol of Communist China, an icon of Chinese heroism, a representative of the dispossessed, and a wellspring of Chinese spirit. By exploring the contours and implications of his rhetoric, then, we may understand not only China's past but also its present and future in the global context. It is my hope that this study makes a unique contribution to the corpus of literature on Mao's political influence in modern China, shedding new light on how he so profoundly was able to shape China's revolution, Chinese culture, and China's relations with the world through his rhetorical power. Moreover, we can better understand the role he played in the history of modern China and the world in the latter half of the twentieth century. In addition we can better understand the characteristics of Chinese political rhetoric in today's global context as China becomes an emerging economic and military power in the world. Although this book is not focused on comparative rhetoric, it nonetheless offers primary data for doing comparative studies on political rhetoric between China and other countries. In my recent publication in *Rhetoric Review* (Lu 2015), I point out the need to compare rhetoric between nations, especially between nations that traditionally have conflict for various reasons. Studying Mao Zedong's rhetoric helps us understand how Chinese political rhetoric differs or is similar to that of other nations in response to similar or different rhetorical exigencies.

ONE

★ ★ ★ ★

Rhetorical Themes in
Mao Zedong's Early Writings

Mao Zedong was born to a moderately well-to-do peasant family in 1893 in the village of Shaoshan in Xiangtan, Hunan Province. Mao's father, a successful farmer and businessman whom Mao found to be authoritarian and oppressive, sent his son to a private school hoping Mao would help the family with book-keeping and legal issues after receiving an education. Mao's mother was illiterate and a devout Buddhist, a kind and generous woman, always ready to help those in need. Mao attended the Buddhist temple in their village with his mother and even attempted without success to convert his father to Buddhism. Mao appeared to be resentful of his tyrannical father but maintained a strong and loving relationship with his mother.[1] Mao's own character manifested a combination of his parents' traits: dominating and dictatorial like his father; sympathetic for the poor like his mother.

Mao exhibited a rebellious spirit from an early age. Once when he was ten years old, he ran away from school after the teacher beat him. Fearing he would be beaten again by his father if he went home, Mao wandered in the wildness for three days before his family found him. His rebellion also prompted frequent heated arguments with his father, who accused him of laziness. Those arguments may have been instrumental in Mao's budding rhetorical skills of employing deductive reasoning as a means to win an argument. Edgar Snow writes of an instance in Mao's youth, for example, when Mao sought to invalidate his father's accusation of his laziness by arguing that older people should do more work than younger people. His father was three times older than he was, Mao argued, and therefore should do more work. Mao then assured his father that he, Mao, would certainly do more work when he reached his father's age. Unlike a typical, filial son who would never overtly challenge his parents, Mao sometimes cursed his father and once even threatened to commit suicide when his father became violent. Mao wrote that he realized after a few such instances with his father that "when I defended my rights by open rebellion, my father relented, but when I remained meek and submissive he only cursed and beat me the more" (Snow 1938, 133). Perhaps these abrasive episodes with his father instilled in Mao the fierce defiance later directed against his political enemies and against the international threats he deflected later in his life.

Mao's Early Readings and Influences

In addition to Mao's personal experiences with conflict, the social transition taking place in China during Mao's early life helped shape his thinking and writing styles. During his formative school years, Mao used his free time to further pursue topics from his formal education, such as the Chinese classics and Western socialist ideologies. Mao's rhetorical style incorporated those of classical and modern Chinese scholars. Moral and ethical appeals as well as a recurring, passionate call for building China into a strong nation wove through Mao's discourse. The young Mao Zedong desperately sought a solution to China's backwardness and searched for a path to China's modernization. Mao's political position shifted from one of anarchist to one of pragmatist, from reformist to revolutionary, from a disciple of Confucius to a follower of Marx. Mao developed his philosophical frame from readings in three compelling areas: 1) Chinese classics; 2) Western and reformist ideas; and 3) works of socialism and Marxism.

Influence of Chinese Classics

The first area of readings that shaped Mao's philosophies spanned a wide range of Chinese classics. Confucian classics constituted some of the key works, including *The Great Learning, Doctrine of the Mean,* Confucius's *Analects,* and the *Mencius* (together known as the "Four Classics"); and *Book of Songs, Book of History, Dao De Jing, Zhuangzi,* and the *Complete Collection of Han Yu* (Gong, Pang, and Shi 2009). Mao once said that he could recite these classics verbatim and was a fervent believer in Confucianism (Li Rui 2005b, 2). Moreover, Mao was familiar with secular Confucian values expressed through popular texts such as *The Three-Character Classic,* or *sanzi jing* (三字经),[2] and secular Chinese poems such as *Thousand Character Classic* (千字文)[3] and *Thousands of Poems* (千家诗), a collection of the best poems composed during the Tang and Song dynasties. Mao's favorite poet was Qu Yuan (屈原), whose *jiuge* (Nine Odes 九歌) and *lisao* (Song of Sorrow 离骚) contain messages of patriotism, heroic acts of soldiers with highly expressive and romantic styles. Mao could recite these poems even into his old age. His favorite book throughout his life was *Twenty-Four Histories,* which covers Chinese history from 3000 B.C. through the Ming dynasty (1368–1644).

These Chinese classics, particularly the Confucian texts, greatly shaped Mao's sense of morality and virtue. Mao's belief that moral thought would lead to moral words, which in turn would lead to moral action is extolled in Confucius's seminal work, the *Analects.* Moreover, Mao's rich knowledge of Chinese classics equipped him with a linguistic repertoire and a set of discursive resources in his writing and persuasive arguments. He was compelled to recite classical texts in school and was expected to reference aphorisms from these texts in his oral arguments and written essays. Mao employed numerous stories, characters, plots, proverbs, and statements from Chinese classics and literary works in his later speeches and writings. His remarkable memory allowed him to engage these discursive resources with ease. In Chinese culture, a well-learned person is often identified by his/her ability to memorize Chinese classical texts (history, poems, and philosophical concepts) and express them fluently and eloquently. Such a person is highly respected in society and tends to be equated with having a good character and a strong ethos.

Among the classical writers, Mao's rhetoric was mostly influenced by Han Yu, whose writings Mao studied intensively while he was in school. Han Yu (韩愈) lived between 768 and 824 during the Tang dynasty in China. He was a well-known essayist, philosopher, politician, and poet. He is the first listed among the "Eight Great Prose Masters of the Tang and Song [dynasties]" (唐宋八大家). Han Yu was a devout believer and propagator of Confucianism throughout his life; he pursued a mission to revive Confucian tradition and restore Confucian social/political order. Han Yu believed that Confucianism was the only school of thought that would unite China and create a strong central authority in politics and orthodoxy in cultural matters. Han vehemently opposed Buddhism, a religion imported from India that became popular in the imperial court and was favored by the emperor. Han Yu believed that a person's character was revealed through his writings. He championed "the old style prose" (古文) used during the pre-Qin (before 211 B.C.E.) period, a style employed in Confucian classics. Han's writing broke away from stylized formality with a focus on ornamentation, a characteristic of the prose during the Tang dynasty. Consequently Han Yu is known for initiating a new style of writing more suited to argumentation and the expression of opinions. Another characteristic of Han Yu's prose is that he addressed contemporary issues and linked the private and moral lives of an individual to the public welfare of the state. Han's writing is well known for its open, frank, humorous, sarcastic, daring, and forthright style manifested particularly in his denouncement of Buddhism.[4] According to Mao's classmate Zhou Shizhao, Mao seriously studied all of Han's essays until he could recite them fluently. He also devoted a major portion of his notebook to writing his interpretations and comments about Han's poems and essays (Zhou 1961). In his writing, Mao adopted Han's rhetorical features of mocking authority, using soaring innuendos and savage humor. Mao was particularly fond of Han's vigorous and belligerent verbal attack on a target enemy. Mao modeled these rhetorical styles of Han Yu for his own defense of communism and for attacking Chiang Kai-shek in later writings.

Mao's knowledge base of literature, government politics, and China's geography was expanded through his avid reading of a number of other important books, such as *Selections of Refined Literature* (文选), edited by Xiao Tong 萧统 (768–824).

An important anthology for any educated Chinese person to have read, this book compiled the literary writings from the late Warring States period (300 B.C.E.) to the early Liang dynasty (500 A.D.). *Zi Zhi Tong Jian* 资治通鉴 (Comprehensive Mirror to Aid in Government), edited by Sima Guang (1019–86), was another favorite of Mao's; it recorded Chinese history from 403 B.C.E. to 959 C.E., covering sixteen dynasties and spanning almost fourteen hundred years. Mao also gained information about the geography of China by thoroughly reading *Du shi fangyu jiyao* 读史 方与纪要 (Important Notes on Reading the Geography Treatises in the History), written by Gu Zuyu 顾祖禹, a scholar from the Qing dynasty. Further, Mao loved books written by Kong Rong 孔融 (153–208), renowned for his poetry and prose characterized by sarcasm and mockery,[5] and Chen Liang 陈亮 (1143–94), a well-known scholar in the South Song dynasty. Chen is well known for his use of compelling poetry, penetrating words, and a practical approach to politics and social transformation. In addition Mao's works reflect the influence of Ye Shi 叶适 (1150–1223), who advocated originality and creativity in using words and composing poems. Ye's political view resembled that of Chen Liang in that Ye rebuked empty talks and argued in favor of economic development.[6] Mao's own political thought and rhetorical styles as demonstrated in his later writing reflected varying influences of these scholars.

Mao's early writings demonstrated that he built a solid foundation from the Chinese classics from pre-Qin (before 221 B.C.E.) philosophy to Chu-style poetry,[7] from prose written during the Han dynasty (206 B.C.E.–220 A.D.) to the argumentative styles of the Tang dynasty (618–907). In his own early pieces Mao revealed a familiarity with the doctrines of Neo-Confucianism in the Song dynasty (960–1279) as well as with thinkers in the Ming and Qing dynasties (1368–1911). Furthermore, Mao's philosophical orientation was largely influenced by Gu Yanwu 顾炎武 (1613–82), Wang Fuzhi 王夫之 (1619–92), and Yan Yuan 颜元 (1635–1704), who advocated the integration of theory with practice, speech with action. Their pragmatic orientation of *jingshi zhiyong* 经世致用 (attending to the issues in the real world and solving social problems) had predisposed Mao's political orientation to pragmatism, taking action to solve real-life problems.[8] Mao was inspired by Gu Yanwu's famous saying "Every person has the responsibility to determine the fate of their state." Specifically Mao regarded Fan Zhongyan 范仲淹 (989–1052), Yue Fei 岳飞 (1103–42), Wen Tianxiang 文天祥 (1236–83), and Zeng Guofan 曾国藩 (1811–72) as his role models in moral standards, patriotism, and sacrifice for the country.[9]

In 1910, at the age of sixteen, Mao transferred to a school outside his village and left home for the first time. In the new school, which put more emphasis on learning modern ways of thinking than on Chinese classics, Mao was educated in natural sciences and English, but he was best known among his teachers for writing good, classic essays. Chinese language teachers used his essays as examples for other students in the school to emulate, circulating Mao's essays among students (Li Rui 2005b). Mao's classics teacher, who was nicknamed "Yuan the Big Beard," required Mao to read Chinese classics and write essays in classical Chinese. Therefore some of Mao's early writings were in the form of classical language. Mao became so knowledgeable and well versed in classical language that his classmates nicknamed him "genius Mao" and "think tank" (He Yi 2010, 96).

By his own admission, Mao disliked studying classics due to the rote learning methods and rigidity in content, even though his speeches and writings were filled with allusions, stories, and quotations from these classics. Mao found classical Chinese fiction more interesting and engaging. Within this category, Mao read at an early age *Yue Fei Chronicles, Revolt against the Tang, Romance of the Three Kingdoms, The Water Margin, Travel to the West,* and *The Art of War.* Mao was not allowed to read these books as they were not Confucian orthodox, so he read them beneath his quilt using candlelight at home and covered them with Confucian texts in the classroom. From these books he read about the heroic acts of individuals, patriotism, rebellions, and war strategies. In his subsequent writings Mao referenced many stories from these popular fictions as means of persuasion and employed ideas from these works in military strategies when he was commander in chief of the Red Army. Later, when he became a more critical reader, Mao began to notice that no representations of peasants appeared in these stories; characters were dominated by glorified warriors, rulers, and officials (Snow 1938, 134). This realization planted the seeds for his mission to transform Chinese culture into one that represented and spoke for peasants and the poor. At the same time Mao read about stories of ancient kings and emperors such as King of Yao, King of Shun, Emperor Qin Shi Huang, and Emperor of Han Wudi. Mao's favorite emperors were Emperor Qin Shi Huang and Emperor Han Wudi; both used military strategies and ordered brutal killings of the opposition to gain and maintain control.

Mao educated himself in ways other than through reading books. During the years while he was studying at Hunan Normal School, he traveled five counties barefoot with a classmate in Hunan. They did not have much money for food and lodging, so they decided to beg for food and shelter. Along the way they met some scholars of classics and had intellectual discussions on issues of money, morality, religion, Confucius, Laozi, Zhuangzi, political power, the Chinese family, and China's future (Siao-yu 1959). This traveling experience greatly enriched his geographical knowledge of Hunan and deepened his sympathy for poor peasants.

Exposure to Western and Reformists' Ideas

The second set of readings from Mao's early life consists of books written by Chinese reformists introducing the West and Western ideas. Mao read *Words of Warning in an Age of Prosperity* (盛世危言), authored by Zheng Guanying (郑观

应). In this book Zheng searched for causes of China's backwardness and argued that China needed to learn from the West to develop a capitalist economy in machine making, trading, and tariff protection. China also needed to borrow techniques from the Western parliamentary democracy, the constitutional monarchy, and the education system. Zheng's ideas were eye opening for Mao; they expanded his vision from one limited to Hunan Province to one that encompassed the world and from a narrow interest in classical stories to a dynamic investment in current social issues.

When he was at the Hunan Normal School, Mao was perturbed by some students' attitudes toward him. By his own account, he observed, "Many of the richer students despised me because usually I was wearing my ragged coat and trousers....I was also disliked because I was not a native of Hsiang Hsiang [where the school is located]....I felt spiritually depressed" (Snow 1938, 137). However, despite his feelings of exclusion, this school provided Mao with exposure to the outside world. One of his classmates lent him a book titled *Great Heroes of the World* (世界英杰传), from which Mao read biographies of Napoleon, Catherine of Russia, Peter the Great, Wellington, Gladstone, Montesquieu, Rousseau, George Washington, and Abraham Lincoln. Mao most admired Washington for his leadership in winning the war for America's independence.

It was also at Hunan Normal School that Mao first heard of Kang Youwei and Liang Qichao, the two leading reformists at the time,[10] and started reading their books on China's reforms. Mao fervently read *Journal of the New People,* a progressive magazine edited by Liang Qichao. The journal and the books written by these authors gave Mao the idea that individuals could bring changes to the world through political participation and leadership. Knowledge learned from books could be put into practice and could impact society. Mao was attracted to Kang and Liang's reform movement. In particular he was interested in Western political thoughts introduced by Liang and Liang's sharp critiques of feudalism. Mao was impressed by Liang's writing style and described it as "clearly reasoned, emotional appealing, and having a magic spell" (Li Rui 2005b, 4). Later, Mao wrote passionate essays that imitated Liang's writing style. Once he even used "Ren" from Liang's title name (Liang Ren Gong) to fashion for himself a pen name, Xue Ren, meaning "learning from Ren."

Mao learned about Sun Yat-sen and his revolution when he moved to Changsha, the capital city of Hunan. There, Mao was shocked to hear about the death of "Seventy-Two Heroes" in the Guangzhou Uprising against the Qing dynasty in 1911.[11] This massacre was a catalyst for Mao's transition from sympathizing with the reformers to supporting revolutionaries. Mao participated in student demonstrations and cut off his queue, a symbol of loyalty to the Qing emperor. Mao even wrote his first big-character essay.[12] In the essay Mao no longer romanticized about a constitutional monarchy but envisioned a new Chinese government with

Sun Yat-sen as the president, Kang Youwei as the premier, and Liang Qichao as the foreign minister. When the Wucang Uprising occurred,[13] Mao joined the army and served for six months.

After a failed attempt to be admitted to a more advanced school, Mao decided to teach himself and began to read translated books by Western authors in the Library of Human Province.[14] In this library Mao read Adam Smith's *The Wealth of Nations,* Darwin's *Origin of Species,* Thomas Huxley's *Evolution and Ethics,* Herbert Spencer's *The Study of Sociology,* John Stuart Mill's *On Liberty,* and works written by Rousseau and Montesquieu on law as well as world geography. These readings offered Mao a preliminary sense of social development and political and economic structures of a modern society in the West. Mao particularly learned how to study a society from reading Spencer's *The Study of Sociology.* Mao loved the book so much that he recommended it to his classmate Xiao Zisheng and described the book as the essence of everything (为学之道在是矣) (Li Rui 2005b). Mao was convinced that studying society and putting political theories into practice for social change were scientific endeavors.

In *Mao and China,* Stanley Karnow (1972) explains that "the years at the Hunan Normal School gave Mao the solid erudition that he displayed throughout the rest of his life" (35). Mao not only met his favorite and most admired teacher and future father-in-law, Yang Cangji, at this school but also made a number of friends who were interested in current affairs and the future of China. As he remembered, "My friends and I preferred to talk only of large matters—the nature of men, of human society, of China, the world, and the universe!" (Snow 1938, 147). Soon, Mao founded an organization called Xinmin Xuehui (New Citizen Association). Mao engaged in vigorous discussions on social issues with other, like-minded members. Sometimes he went to the teachers' homes to ask questions and write letters to well-established scholars in the country (Li Rui 2005b). Mao's favorite reading at this time was *New Youth,* a monthly journal edited by Chen Duxiu, the first chairman of the Communist Party. The journal introduced "Mr. Science" and "Mr. Democracy" to Chinese readers and took a strong anti-tradition/anti-Confucianism stand, calling for the abandonment of Confucian rituals, restrictions for women, and advocating for the use of vernacular language. From reading this journal, Mao further expanded his knowledge about liberal thinking, democratic ideas, and national crises. By his own admission, "At this time my mind was a curious mixture of ideas of liberalism, democratic reformism, and utopian socialism" (Snow 1938, 149). By reading articles written by Chen Duxiu in *New Youth,* Mao imbibed Chen's writing style, characterized by using exhortation and epigrammatic phrases, projecting hope for the future, talking directly to the reader, being concise and assertive, and calling for action (Payne 1950). At this stage of Mao's life, his political ambition and nationalism were very much shaped by Liang Qichao and Chen Duxiu. Mao's second set of readings, predominantly made up of Western books as well as books and articles by Chinese reformists on politics and social change, differed in style, tone, and content from the Chinese classics and introduced Mao to ideas beyond Chinese borders.

Works of Socialism and Marxism

Mao's third set of readings consisted of Marxist and socialist theories. When Mao graduated from Hunan Normal School in June 1918, he became actively involved in student movements. He shifted his reformist position to a revolutionary position, from offering a Confucian menu of individual transformation to a Marxist view of social transformation as a solution to China's problems. While working as a librarian at Peking University, Mao joined a number of organizations on campus, such as the Society of Philosophy and the Journalism Society.[15] During his time in Peking University, Mao met with Li Dazhao, the head of the Peking University library and a cofounder of the Communist Party. Mao followed the news on the Russian Revolution and began to be interested in Communist literature. Mao told Snow in 1938 that three books he read during this time converted him to Marxism: Karl Marx and Friedrich Engels's *The Communist Manifesto,* Karl Kautsky's *Class Struggle,* and Thomas Kirkup's *A History of Socialism.* Mao's correspondence with Cai Hesen, a good friend of Mao's who had joined the Communist Party in France, also had an impact on his adoption of Communist ideals (Karl 2010, 13).[16] In 1921 Mao officially became a Communist and attended the first meeting of the Chinese Communist Party in Shanghai.

Why was Mao attracted to Marxism given his Confucian training background? Scholars have explicated the similarities between Confucianism and Marxism: both emphasize ideological conformity and the moral integrity of individuals (Chu 1977; Fairbank 1976; Pye 1968). As Fairbank (1976) vividly describes, "There are Confucian overtones in the Marxist-Maoist orchestration. The crucial role of ideology under communism lends particular interest to China's ideological past" (59). Ironically Mao's training in Confucianism in his early years with an emphasis on personal morality/responsibility for the well-being of the state seems to have echoed with the Marxist notion of a utopian society. In addition the Marxist theory of historical progression from feudalism to communism may have been appealing to Mao as it gave him hope for China to move out of the semicolonial and semifeudal society. He might have easily accepted the Marxist notion of social change and dialectical materialism since Laozi and some other Chinese scholars had discussed similar notions of dialectics and change. Mao might have found a match between the Confucian teaching of sacrifice and serving the public with the Communist cause of achieving equality and creating the common good by liberating the poor and the oppressed people. Most tellingly Mao witnessed how Marxism brought revolution and positive change to Russia, which had a similar social and economic condition as China: a society that was underdeveloped and primarily agricultural with a large peasant population. At the same time Mao was also disillusioned with the reformists' failed attempts to change the country. In the view of Schell and Delury (2013), Mao's lifetime of conflict with his father paved the way for Mao's embrace of the Marxist notion of class struggle and triumph; thus they contend that "Mao's conversion to communism was initially motivated less by a belief in Marxism than by his frustration with the agenda of earlier reformers and revolutionaries" (208).

Analyses of Mao's Early Writings

I consider Mao's writings from 1912 to 1920 as his early works. Mao used the classical style in his writing from 1912 to 1917; starting in 1917, he began to use vernacular, or *baihua wen* 白话文, in his writing. Fortunately most of Mao's early writings have been translated into English and are available to English-speaking readers today. These early writings are in the formats of personal letters, class notes, essays, editorial commentaries, declarations, and announcements. They cover a range of topics: from discussing Confucian values to China's social problems; from advocacy for Hunan (his home province) independence from the rest of China to petitions of expelling a ruthless warlord from Hunan; from defending women's rights to condemning the ills of China's feudal practices. Since it is impossible to analyze all his early writings, three pieces were chosen: "Classroom Notes"; "A Study of Physical Education"; and "Marginal Notes to Friedrich Paulsen: *A System of Ethics.*" These three pieces are written in the classical Chinese language and provide more textual evidence in terms of Mao's character development, his concerns for China, and the influence he received from Confucian education and Western ideas. These pieces also show a trajectory of Mao's rhetoric and thought development in his youth.

"Classroom Notes" (讲堂录)

This piece consists of the class notes that Mao took from October to December 1913 when he was a student in the preparatory class at Hunan Normal School in Changsha.[17] The notes have two categories, language arts and self-cultivation, taught respectively by two teachers: Yuan Zhongqian, who taught language arts with a particular focus on Han Yu's writing; and Yang Cangji, who taught ethics and self-cultivation. The notes are largely summaries of Yuan's and Yang's lectures with specific names of people, places, and their views. In his notes Mao listed a number of Westerners and their achievements: Columbus, Newton, Franklin, Watt, Spencer, and Benjamin Kidd (Schram 1992, 33–34, 39), indicating his knowledge of the Western world.

Note taking is a habit and tradition of Chinese learning. Notes, or *biji* (笔记), not only record what one has learned but also record the reflections and inner thoughts of the learner. These notes can be taken alongside a book or article, or they may be written in a separate notebook. Scholars have the tradition of exchanging their notes among peers. Study notes taken by emperors and prominent intellectuals are also taken seriously and treated as national treasures in Chinese history. Mao had a habit of taking such study notes on numerous books he had read throughout his life, many of which have been collected and studied by party officials and intellectuals.[18]

"Classroom Notes" consists of forty-seven pages and over ten thousand words. The first eleven pages are Mao's copy of Qu Yuan's poems *lisao* (离骚) and *jiuge* (九歌). The remaining pages cover Chinese classical works from Pre-Qin (before 221 B.C.E.) to the Qing dynasty (1644–1911), ranging from philosophy to various literary and ethical works. Mao's notes are a mixture of verbatim notes and his own comments and elaborations on certain concepts. These notes provide information about the formal topic Mao had been taught and also interpretations about what he gleaned from his course; they provide a basis for ascertaining what modes of thinking modified Mao's value orientation and honed his political ambition. Further, these notes indicate Mao's love for the Chinese classics, works he frequently sought out for inspiration and strategic design until the last years of his life. From a careful reading of the notes, three rhetorical themes emerge that illustrate the strong influence Mao received from Confucian teaching.

Rhetoric of Confucian values on self-cultivation and moral standard. In these notes Mao referenced Confucius, Mencius, and Neo-Confucian scholars on learning, diligence, cautious speech, and the virtues of being thrifty. Confucian teaching emphasized the achievement of gaining these virtues through self-cultivation and by learning from role models. Mao agreed that "all men seek to follow the examples set by the wise and virtuous in order to learn filial piety, righteousness, and a sense of honor and shame" (Schram 1992, 16). Mao noted Confucius's comment on the love his student Yan Hui had for learning and good temperament when conducting his studies: "He did not transfer his anger, he did not repeat a fault." Mao continued to note, "Only those who are content with poverty can achieve things. Therefore, it is said, 'If you can chew on vegetable roots, you can do all things'" (23–24).[19] Parallel to this saying, Mao copied these words by Confucius: "With coarse rice to eat, with water to drink, and my bended arm for a pillow—I have still joy in the midst of these things. Riches and honors acquired by unrighteousness are to me as a floating cloud."[20] These notes demonstrate Mao's endorsement for plain living that often was the foundation for cultivating a high moral standard, a strong character, and determination to cope with adversities. Mao quoted from *Yi Jing* (Book of Changes 易经) that a morally superior man stands tall, shows dignity and spiritual independence, and has neither fear nor sorrow for what he believes is the right thing to do. Moreover, Mao chastised laziness as the biggest enemy to self-cultivation. One must overcome lethargy and eliminate idleness, he noted, which only lead a person to his grave (Schram 1992, 15). Another quality Mao cited as characteristic of a self-cultivated person was to be meticulous. Mao wrote, "If a man does not over-look anything of which he is capable, and if he carries this through from small things to greater things, it will not be hard for him to be a sage" (38). Mao cited Julius Caesar as an example of a person overlooking one small thing that ultimately led to his own assassination (38).

The person Mao mentioned many times in these class notes was Zeng Guofan 曾国藩 (1811–72), a commander of the Xiang army for a Qing emperor. Mao acknowledged Zeng's two life principles: magnanimity and sincerity (Confucian principles). In Zeng's explanation, "To be magnanimous means not to be envious; to be sincere means not to boast, not to covet undeserved reputation, not to do overly impractical things, and not to talk about ideals too loftily" (Schram 1992, 10). Zeng was, in Mao's notes, a devout Confucianist and a supreme example of self-cultivation revealed through his diaries and his family letters. Another moral exemplar Mao admired was Yi Yin 伊尹, a leading statesman of the early Shang dynasty. Mao described Yi Yin as representing "perfect moral character, scholar-ship, economics, and practical achievements. . . . His heart was truly impartial. He has great insight and an important manner" (18). It is evident that as a young man Mao wanted to model himself after these two figures. He copied from Wang Chuanshan (1619–92) 王船山 (also known as Wang Fuzhi 王夫之), a well-known Confucianist between the Ming and Qing dynasties, that some "moral standards were valid for all time, such as benevolence, righteousness, the rites of proper conduct, wisdom, trust, providence, and the will of the people" (36). Mao coveted these core Confucian values and attempted to put them into practice. In addition to notes on Confucian sayings and values, Mao took notes on Mencius and other Confucianists such as Xunzi 荀子, Zeng Can 曾参, Han Yu 韩愈, Zhu Xi 朱熹, Cheng Yi 程颐, Wang Yangming 王阳明 (also known as Wang Shouren), and Wang Chuanshan, explaining their concepts and agreeing with them on how to build moral character.

Like a model Confucianist, Mao never stopped learning; he read all his life until the day he passed away. He lived a simple life; he remained independent in his thinking; he demonstrated extraordinary vigor in pursuing his revolutionary goals; and he achieved remarkable political successes by paying attention to things big and small. By modeling himself after Confucianists such as Zeng Guo-fan and Yi Yin, Mao set a high standard for himself and for others. He never gave up moral absolutism as a construct in his life. He strongly believed that a person could be remolded and transformed through self-cultivation and modeling after good examples. This strong sense of ethos had been his core ideology and was the nexus of all the political campaigns he launched during his lifetime.

Rhetoric of the sage in political ambition and strategic thinking. Mao's notes are filled with heroes he admired: from sage kings such as Tang and Yu in the Xia, Shang, and Zhou dynasties to ministers such as Zhuge Liang 诸葛亮, Guan

Zhong 管仲, and Fan Zhongyan.[21] Like many educated Chinese at the time, Mao wanted to model himself after sages. A sage, suggested through Mao's notes, not only focuses on self-cultivation but also performs heroic acts for the sake of the community. Mao referenced Wang Chuanshan (1619–92), a patriotic Confucian scholar in the late Ming dynasty: "There have been heroes who were not sages, but there have never been sages who were not heroes" (Schram 1992, 19). Mao explained, "Sages are those who are perfect both in virtue and in accomplishment; heroes lack virtue, but have great achievements and fame. Napoleon was a hero, not a sage" (19). Mao quoted Confucius on virtues of will, duty, righteousness, and moderation of expression as criteria for becoming a sage. Moreover, Mao commented that a sage must have lofty ideals and an ideal character. To do so, a person must think not of himself but of the universe. Mao quoted Mencius: "The individual self is the small self; the universal self is the great self. The individual self is the physical self; the universal self is the spiritual self" (21).

It is clear that Mao's highest goal was to achieve the universal self and a sage status. Throughout his notes Mao frequently quoted scholars who expressed a universal outlook and a determination to serve the people. For example, he quoted Zhang Zai 张载 (1020–10): "Our goals are to establish a common mind for the whole world, to establish the way for the people, to restore and continue the teachings of ancient sages, and to open the way to the great peace for all future ages" (Schram 1992, 22–23). Further, Mao copied from his teacher Yang Cangji: "A benevolent man looks at the whole world and the whole of humanity as his body, and considers one individual and one family and as his wrist. . . . If he can save the whole world, even if it costs his low life and that of his family, he is at peace about it" (22). Mao mentioned Jesus and Socrates, both of whom sacrificed for a just cause to save the world, calling them sages together with Confucius (22). It is apparent that Mao was greatly enticed by the thought of becoming a sage who served the people and sacrificed for the country. In fact Mao not only sacrificed several of his family members for China's revolution but also called for every Chinese person to abandon his or her individual interests and sacrifice for their country.

Mao understood that it was not easy to be a sage as one might be slandered or be misunderstood by his or her own people. But Mao believed that a true sage would stand firm on his position and listen to his own conscience. Mao quoted Zhuangzi and Confucius to support his view: "He refused . . . to be deterred though the whole world blamed him" (Zhuangzi); and "The more they are slandered, the more steadfast they will be" (Confucius; Schram 1992, 27). Mao offered the example of Shang Yang, who was much hated by noble families but whose reform brought prosperity to the state of Qin and eventually unified China. Mao had personal experiences of being criticized, excluded, and demoted by officials at the Communist Party headquarters four times while he was the leader of the

Red Army from 1928 to 1932. He had been accused of being "rightest," "authoritarian," or "opportunist" during this time period. However, Mao never capitulated; each time his military strategies proved right in hindsight, one reason Mao built his reputation and gained support within the party.

In running state affairs Mao had learned dialectical and strategic thinking from Laozi and Sunzi. Mao quoted Laozi: "In the world, there is nothing more submissive and weak than water. Yet for attacking that which is hard and strong nothing can surpass it" (Schram 1992, 30). Mao may have learned strategic thinking and intrigues from reading *Sunzi* as he quoted, "To win one hundred victories in one hundred battles is not the acme of skill. To subdue the enemy without fighting is the acme of skill...therefore, the victories won by a master of war gain him neither reputation for wisdom, nor merit for valor" (30). Thus Mao had learned that "military force was the last resort, that it was not fitting to wage war for a long time and kill many people, and that awful military triumphs were shameful" (30). The idea of winning the war by wisdom rather than by force guided Mao's military strategies against the Nationalists and the Japanese and won him support from his comrades. In another place, Mao showed being influenced by Zhuangzi when he paraphrased an analogy of the big bird and the small bird: "Once the big bird takes off, it will not rest until it reaches the Heavenly Lake half a year later. As for the little bird, it will take only half a day to dash to the elm and sandalwood. If you compare their capacities, there is a gap, but each acts according to its nature" (48). By quoting Zhuangzi, Mao demonstrated his belief that everything has its own merits and that it is important not to use the same criteria to measure things of different natures in the same way. This philosophical outlook prepared Mao for strategic thinking in military maneuvers, state affairs, and foreign relations later in his life.

Rhetoric rooted in Chinese tradition. From Confucius, Mao picked up the notion of *shenyan* 慎言, or cautious speech. In the *Analects,* Confucius spoke of the cautious use of words as an indicator of a gentleman. Mao further elaborated: "To be discreet in what you say and what you do is to have gained learning" (Schram 1992, 16). Mao also quoted from Han Yu: "The superior man remains in his own place, and thinks of his appointments; if he is not appointed, he thinks of cultivating his speech, in order to enhance his virtue" (Schram 1992, 43). This message echoes Confucius's teaching that a person speaks in the manner that fits his position in the social hierarchy (Lun Yu 1992, 3:13). Otherwise the person's discourse would be perceived as offensive and intruding, and likely would bring trouble to the speaker. Mao was also aware that speaking provocatively in an immoral and chaotic society would incite people but would likely sow seeds of grievance as warned by Han Yu (Schram 1992, 42). Mao was definitely in favor of Confucian writing, as he said, "The writings of the Confucian scholars were different from those of the men of letters. The former were translucent and pure, but the latter, unrestrained and argumentative" (Schram 1992, 33). Mao regarded Confucian writing as conveying morals for character building, while those who spoke and wrote eloquently may not be superior in moral character.

In Mao's own writing, he demonstrated rhetorical features of Confucianism and of "men of letters." In the section of composition, Mao filled his notes on the effectiveness and techniques of writing. He quoted from Pan Lai 潘来 (1646–1708), a student of Gu Yanwu (1613–82), who identified many topics concerning the art of writing: "Of all the classics and history and the hundred schools of thought, the natural and human science, regulations and institutions, anecdotes and legends, grasses and trees, insects and fishes, is there anything which is not material for writing? As for editing, adaptation, climaxes and anticlimaxes, openings and closings, and changes and intrigues, are there any of these which do not constitute techniques for writing?" (Schram 1992, 44). A good writer, according to Pan Lai, is critical of himself, is humble, and uses translucent and elegant diction; "his writing skills and content complemented each other. His craftsmanship was extraordinary and endlessly refined" (44). Mao also quoted Wei Bozi 魏伯子 (1620–77), an essayist from the Qing dynasty: "A masterpiece's remarkableness lies in its commonness, its subtlety in its breadth. As for its ins and outs, and the relation between the whole and the parts, its splicing and transformations lie in its straightforwardness, its rich taste lies in its blandness, and its glamour lies in its modesty" (45). Further, Mao noted an inscription on Wei Bozi's desk, which read, "Be neat, profound, generous, and even [in writing]. Neat means to be simple and clean in heart, profound means to do things with sincerity and firmness; generous means to give when one has more than enough, and even means to be calm and at ease in deeds" (45). Mao then wrote himself a note: "Avoid writing awkwardly, or in too labored a style" (45). Mao's writing did not show him as a humble and modest man, but it indeed demonstrated a rich employment of diction as well as a lucid and straightforward style with profound meanings and climax.

Mao's "Classroom Notes," revealed him as a diligent and ambitious young man. He was well learned and well versed in Chinese classics and was influenced by Confucian values on morality and character building. He adopted various rhetorical styles and strategic thinking from the antiquities. Moreover, these notes demonstrated Mao's ability for independent thinking and his practical orientation for making connections between theoretical concepts and real-life situations. In the West, Aristotle's notion of ethos is about moral character exhibited through knowledge, competence, and goodwill. Further, ethos can be manipulated, as it is the perceived credibility and trustworthiness conferred by the audience. In the Chinese tradition, especially in Confucian teaching, the ethos or moral character of a person refers to the inner quality of benevolence, magnanimity, and sincerity achieved through learning, self-cultivation, following examples of the sage, and plain living. Mao attempted to model after those who possessed these moral qualities. His reflections indicated his patriotism for China and his ambition of devoting his life to the public good.

"A Study of Physical Education" (体育之研究)

When Mao was studying at Hunan Normal School, this article was published in *New Youth* on April 1, 1917, under the pseudonym "Twenty-eight Strokes" (the name Mao Zedong in Chinese takes twenty-eight strokes). The motivation for writing the article was triggered by the death of seven students at the school who had succumbed to an epidemic. This tragedy shocked and saddened young Mao, who attributed the deaths of his schoolmates to a lack of physical education. Mao wrote the article in classical Chinese.

Mao started the article with the rhetorical exigency of the nation: "Our nation is wanting in strength; the military has not been encouraged. The physical condition of our people deteriorates daily" (Schram 1992, 113). Mao found these conditions "disturbing" and called for a change in attitude toward physical education. Traditionally, Chinese education placed much emphasis on rote learning and on the mental grasp of knowledge. Spending hours and hours of studying was encouraged and praised. There was little mention of strengthening the physical body in Chinese education. Mao raised this issue and considered it a serious matter in modernizing China, linking physical weakness with the weakness of the nation.

Mao defined physical education as a "simple way for preserving life" (Schram 1992, 114) and followed his definition with examples of Confucius's archer and charioteer practices, the German sport of fencing, and Japan's *bushido* (武士道). Mao then expounded on the importance of physical strength in connection with virtue and the mental grasp of knowledge. He used a metaphor to illustrate the relationship: "The body is the chariot that contains knowledge, the chamber that houses virtue" (115). He stressed that "physical education really occupies the first place in our lives. When the body is strong, then one can advance speedily in knowledge and morality and reap far-reaching advantages" (115). For Mao, physical well-being was the prerequisite for moral development and intellectual education. This view challenged the traditional Chinese view of ranking intellectual activity above physical exercise.

In the article Mao provided the benefits of strengthening the body through exercise and expounded on the harms of not doing so as seen throughout Chinese history. He offered convincing examples to illustrate his argument. Particularly he mentioned Yan Yuan 颜渊 (Confucius's student), Jia Yi 贾谊 (a politician of the Han dynasty), and Wang Bo 王勃 (a poet in the Tang dynasty), who were all highly intellectual and moral exemplars but who all died young. In contrast, Yan Xizhai 颜习斋 (1635–1704) and Li Gangzhu 李刚主 (1659–1733) from the Qing dynasty were both well-educated and physically strong and therefore able to win battles.

Mao criticized those who treated physical education superficially. He warned that to be aware of the significance of having a strong body was vital. To accomplish that goal, Mao discussed the dialectical relationship between *jing* 静 (quietness) and *dong* 动 (movement). He acknowledged that Laozi, Sakyamuni, and Lu Jiuyuan 陆九渊 (1139–93) all advocated a quiet mind through contemplation and meditation. But Mao disregarded these methods, calling them insufficient. Mao argued that *dong,* or movement, was fundamental in being a human; a person could slow his aging process by doing physical exercise, or *dong*. Even a person born with a weak body could be improved through exercise. Mao gave the examples of American president Theodore Roosevelt and Japan's Judo founder, Jigoro Kano, both of whom started their lives with weak bodies but became healthy and strong through physical exercises (Schram 1992, 118).

Mao further developed his argument on the benefits of teaching physical education in schools by emphasizing that "physical education not only strengthens the body but also enhances our knowledge.... It also harmonizes the sentiments" (Schram 1992, 119). These benefits are accrued, Mao contended, because "physical strength is required to undertake the study of the numerous modern sciences, whether in school or through independent study" (119). If a person is physically weak, Mao argued, the person will likely be overtaken by his emotions and be less likely to use reason. Moreover, Mao posited that physical exercise would strengthen the will and cultivate heroism. To support his argument, Mao cited a famous poem composed by Xiang Yu 项羽, a Chinese household hero: "My strength uprooted mountains, my energy dominated the world" (120). Mao also provided an example of a physically fit general who accomplished a military mission overseas. In addition Mao stated that exercise would bring joy and a sense of personal worth, which helps with intellectual growth and moral cultivation (123).

To answer the question of why people tended to resist physical education, Mao gave four reasons: (1) lack of awareness; (2) old habits; (3) lack of advocacy; and (4) feeling shamed. Mao addressed the flaws and misperceptions of each cause and recommended methods of exercise such as walks, games, and military training. Particularly he pointed out the regimen used by Zeng Guofan, a well-known household name, including walking, a light diet, and feet washing, as a means of strengthening the body and preventing disease. Mao suggested exercising twice a day either in the nude or wearing light clothes, asserting that these exercises should be "savage and rude" (Schram 1992, 124). He borrowed from Chen Duxiu's slogan "Civilize the mind and make savage the body" (119) and finished the article by describing a set of physical exercise that he had designed himself. He called it "the six-section system of exercise" that covered the movement from head to trunk. Mao maintained a strict exercise regimen throughout his life, such as walking, mountain climbing, and swimming. He swam numerous times in the Yangtze River until he was seventy-three years old. Mao's passion for physical exercise may have helped him survive malaria a few times during his years in the mountains and caves of his revolutionary base.

In this article Mao used a number of rhetorical techniques to present his argument. He first put forward the urgent situation facing the nation, making an analogy between the physical body and the corpus of the nation. He then provided good and bad examples from Chinese classical thinkers and national heroes to support his argument. He addressed the opposing views by discrediting their reasons for not doing physical exercise. He elaborated benefits and harms, identifying cause and effects, and he finished the article by proposing specific actions. Mao's article challenged the traditional Chinese view of "studying first" and criticized the old habits and attitudes toward physical education. His manual of exercise was similar to workout plans advocated by modern practitioners as central to healthy living. In Karl's (2010) observation, the style of directly posing the problem and then proposing the uncompromising statement of a solution was "Mao's quintessential mode of public address" (11).

"Marginal Notes to Friedrich Paulsen: A System of Ethics" (伦理学原理批注)

If "Classroom Notes" demonstrated Mao's interpretation of what he learned from his teachers on Chinese classics, "Marginal Notes to Friedrich Paulsen: *A System of Ethics*" revealed his grasp of Western philosophy. This work showed Mao's reflections and critical and original thinking on a broader range of issues, and it elevated Mao's knowledge base and intellectual sharpness to a higher level. During Mao's years studying at Hunan Normal School, Friedrich Paulsen's *A System of Ethics* was the assigned reading by Professor Yang Cangji, whom Mao admired most for his moral standards and sense of justice.[22] The book was published in 1913 in China and was translated by Cai Yuanpei 蔡元培, who was the chancellor of Peking University.[23] Mao read the book and wrote lengthy notes of twelve thousand words on it. Written in 1917 when Mao was twenty-four years old, Mao's notes summarized key points of Paulsen's arguments and conveyed Mao's opinions, analyses, explanations, and comments in the margins of the book. In addition the notes contained brief inscriptions of agreement or disagreement with Friedrich Paulsen, such as "an excellent point," "true statement," "I strongly support this view," "it does not make sense," and "I have doubts on this passage." More important, Mao offered thought-provoking comments on the issues of morality, political power, the relationship between theory and practice, the relationship between self and society, the role of conscience, the sense of duty, and the meaning of death. In many places Mao challenged Paulsen's views, making connections to Chinese classics and China's political situation. The themes that follow have emerged from Mao's notes.

Rhetoric of moral philosophy. Throughout the notes, Mao compared Eastern and Western philosophical concepts as he read along. He agreed with Paulsen's discussion of conscience and intuition as a priori for ethical imperative. He found Paulsen's concepts of conscience and intuition similar to Mencius's notion of "internal righteousness" and Wang Yangming's 王阳明 concept of "principled mind" (Schram 1992, 178). In other words, ethical behavior is driven by an inner sense of justice, and this understanding of ethics is not absent in Chinese tradition. Mao also found Paulsen's views on self-sacrifice for the sake of promoting interests for others similar to the Confucian theory of ethics and Mozi's notion of mutual love (289, 290) in that serving the public good is the ultimate goal of a person's life. On Paulsen's point that "goodness brings happiness and evil brings misfortune," Mao wrote next to it, "There is a similar saying in our country: 'On the good-doer He sends down all blessings, and on the evil doer He sends down all miseries'" (292).

Further, Mao identified similarities between Kant's rational-based morality and the Neo-Confucian concepts of *li* 理 (reason) (Schram 1992, 187, 261). Paulsen's discussion of ideals and social development reminded Mao of Liang Qichao's article on the relationship between present and future (222). While Paulsen stated that "the perfect life is one in which our spiritual abilities are developed to their highest where thought and imagination and action are developed to the highest degree" (227), Mao concurred that a spiritual life of the human race was the ultimate goal and pointed out that Paulsen's view was in line with the Neo-Confucian doctrines in the Song dynasty (227). Based on his readings, Mao concluded that "Paulsen is a supporter of idealism" (231). Mao seemed to comprehend Paulsen's theories of ethics easily, as he had found similar concepts in works by Chinese thinkers. In some ways Paulsen's idealism echoes Mao's early training in Confucian ethics.

In addition to these areas of agreement, Mao agreed with Paulsen on moral relativism. He concurred that moral standards change over time and vary in different societies and in different persons. His agreement with this position shows that young Mao seemed to be in favor of practical morality rather than moral absolutism. Practical morality contradicts Mao's stated views on morality from his "Classroom Notes," in which Mao treated moral standards as absolute. In Mao's later writings he exhibited both absolute and relative orientations toward morality. For example, he defended Marxism as the only, absolute correct political theory for social change and demanded that the Chinese people conform to Communist ideology as the only moral compass. Simultaneously, Mao rhetorically modified Marxism to suit the Chinese situation, such as seizing power from a rural base and relying on peasants rather than relying on factory labors from the city. Mao's definitions of friends and enemies also changed over time based on rhetorical situations rather than on principles.

Rhetoric of self and human nature. On the topic of individual self, Paulsen defined egoism as focused on self-interest and altruism as unselfish. Mao argued, however, that the two cannot be strictly separated because by nature everyone, even the altruist, has self-interest. People seeking their own interests should not be considered unworthy as long as they do not harm others. On the surface Mao seemed to accept the idea that "ultimately the individual comes first" (Schram 1992, 201). But then Mao asserted that sometimes self-interest can even benefit others. He mentioned Confucian values of self-discipline and self-cultivation as doing good not only for oneself but also for others. Moreover, Mao argued that serving and helping others is part of human nature. He listed Chinese filial sons, faithful widows, loyal ministers, and devoted friends as examples (204–5). He declared, "My desire to fulfill my nature and perfect my mind is the most precious of the moral laws" (205).

Mao might have misunderstood the distinction between self-interest, which seeks benefits only for the self, and self-cultivation, which aims at benefiting others and society through perfecting oneself. It is also possible that Mao lived by the moral principle of serving others and the state, as he was influenced by Confucian teaching. In Mao's later writings he condemned any form of self-interest in thought, attitude, and action and used self-cultivation as a cultural and moral appeal to transform a selfish person into an altruist. Mao retained that position from the 1940s until his death in 1976 through endless mind-reform campaigns. Mao might have been influenced by Paulsen's point that humans can become vicious if they are not controlled or restricted. As much as he wrote that he believed in nature, Mao may have had more faith in humans to change or modify nature, as he said, "I still suspect that human beings are powerless from beginning to end.... Nature has the power to define us, and we have the power to define Nature. Although our power is very small, it cannot be said to have no effect. Nature without us would be incomplete.... This basic nature that is capable of being molded, I call our potential nature, and it is to this nature that I have responsibility" (Schram 1992, 308–9). Throughout his life Mao attempted to command nature by making efforts to create extraordinary yields from grain growth during the period of the Great Leap Forward and by remolding the nature of his people through constant thought reforms. Mao's well-known essay "The Foolish Old Man Who Removed the Mountains," written in 1945, was a story about an old man who was determined to move two mountains that blocked the doorway of his house, where he lived with his sons and grandsons. God was touched by the old man's unshakable conviction and sent down two angels, who carried the mountains away. Mao praised this act and used it as an analogy for overthrowing the mountains of imperialism and feudalism in China (Mao 1945/1967c, 272).

Rhetoric on dialectical thinking. Mao's fondness of dialectics seems to have been much informed by the Chinese cosmology and Daoist perspective of interconnections between things in the universe. At times Mao disagreed with Paulsen and presented his own counterarguments. For example, Paulsen stated that the increase of military and intellectual power would lead to the decrease of obstacles and avoidance of mistakes. Mao countered, "This is not true. As mankind's powers increase, external obstacles also increase.... For example, a great new continent to the West confronted Columbus, Yu was faced with the great flood, and a host of European nations rose up to surround Paris and defeat Napoleon" (Schram 1992, 235). This dialectical relationship between force and counterforce had been the source of Mao's strategic thinking. Similar to Hegel's theory of thesis and antithesis and Foucault's theory of power and empowerment,[24] Mao believed that power is not absolute; it is relative and relational. Power dynamics change over time, he argued, and dialectical tension always exists between force and counterforce. Change or "synthesis" takes place as the result of such dynamics. His famous saying "Whenever there is oppression, there will be confrontation" was a revolutionary slogan ingrained in the minds of Chinese people.

Mao continued to show his dialectical thinking on the topic of social change. Paulsen made a point that if a society has strong military power and strict rules, that society will reach peace and all evils will disappear. Mao disagreed. He contended that a society of great harmony is not sustainable because once harmony is achieved, competition and friction are inevitable. He referenced Laozi, Zhuangzi, and Tao Yuanming 陶淵明, all of whom imagined an ideal society, but also warned that the ideals could be either false or unrealistic. Mao further asserted that there is a "natural alternation between order and disorder, and the cycle of peace and war" and thus that "chaos too is part of the process of historical life, that it too has value in real life.... When they [people] come to periods of peace, they are bored.... It is not that we like chaos, but simply that the reign of peace cannot last long, is unendurable to human beings, and that human nature is delighted by sudden change" (Schram 1992, 238). This dialectical view of society was the guiding principle throughout Mao's life in that he created one political campaign (chaos) after another and used them as justification for launching the Cultural Revolution during peaceful times. Mao referred to himself as possessing the spirit of the Monkey King in the Chinese classic novel *Journey to the West* (Mao 1998a, 71). This assessment of himself implies that Mao liked to stir things up, that disorder was normal for him. Toward that end, Ying-shih Yu (1993) has claimed that "Mao Tse-tung [Mao Zedong] may well be interpreted as Chinese Marxist radicalism incarnate. He was a genius in destruction but wholly incapable of constructive work" (135).

This dialectical thinking corresponds with Mao's view on death. Paulsen discussed that aging and death are part of natural law and should not be despised. Mao took the point further by stating that "our death is not death, but simply a dissolution. All natural things are not destroyed. Not only is death not death, life too is not life, but simply a uniting" (Schram 1992, 245). To Mao, death was a natural phenomenon, simply a part of the transformative process in that a person enters the natural world and experiences change. In this sense death should not be perceived as painful and fearful, he maintained. He concluded that "all phenomena in the world are simply a state of constant change for which there is no birth and death, no formation and demise.... So birth is not birth and death is not destruction" (249). Mao's view of death sounds similar to the Buddhist view of reincarnation in that there is no end to life, except that Mao did not believe in soul. He claimed himself as an unequivocal materialist. In 1956 Mao signed a proposal for cremation along with 151 other high-ranking officials. According to hearsay, Mao wrote in his will that he wanted to be cremated after his death. Ironically his successors decided to keep his dead body on display for the nation to pay its respects.

Rhetoric on social change. Mao agreed with Paulsen regarding how the cycle of natural phenomena can also be applied to social change. Paulsen wrote, "History proves that all nations inevitably go through the stage of old age and decline, of withering and contraction. As the fixed habits of thought and action, the historical stock of ideas, of structure and authority, increase with time, tradition acts as an obstacle to the forces of renewal, and the past oppresses the present, opposing the powers of the new age, gradually grinding them down, until this historical organism inevitably collapses. At this time, do the individuals have the ability to give life to the basic elements of the old civilization and create a new historical reality?" (Schram 1992, 249). In the margins beside this statement Mao noted that "this is precisely the position of the Republic of China" (249). When Mao wrote these notes, China was undergoing a radical social transition from an imperial monarchy that had ruled China for over two thousand years to a republic. Old thinking and old habits were being challenged and criticized, and new ideas and behaviors were emerging. For example, men no longer wore queues and women abandoned foot binding. New vocabularies in science, democracy, and nationalism filled the public discourse. Paulsen's view on social change might have influenced young Mao as Mao pushed for replacement of the four olds (old ideas, old customs, old habits, and old culture) with new alternatives for a radical change of Chinese culture and tradition.

Paulsen's view of social change gave young Mao hope for China and a realization that a national character could be changed through destroying the old system and establishing a new system. As Mao noted, "I used to worry that our China would be destroyed, but now I know that this is not so.... I very much look forward to its destruction, because from the demise of the old universe will come a new universe, and will it not be better than the old universe?" (Schram 1992, 250). Paulsen may have been the most influential voice to Mao, especially considering Mao's radical view of social change in nineteenth-century China. The vision

Mao developed in part from these readings was realized when Mao obliterated traditional Chinese culture and replaced it with revolutionary and politicized party culture during his reign.

Rhetoric on being a great man. Mao shared with Paulsen the belief that a great man should not be constrained by a sense of duty or external laws and that instead a great man should act based on his own judgment and on the impulse of his feelings. Mao called this the spirit of a sage and made a connection to Mencius's concept of *haoran zhiqi* (vast flowing energy) and *da zhangfu* (grand gentleman)[25] (Schram 1992, 264). Mao also echoed Paulsen's messages that a true moral leader should not be influenced by his party or any external pressure when making a decision. Mao concurred, "Even though his words may not be believed and his action may not be effective, he simply does what is right" (266). When in 1949 Mao became China's paramount leader, this description of the qualities that constitute a "great man" bestowed Mao with the legitimacy to exercise despotism. His economic policies and political purge had been proven unrealistic, disastrous, and too radical; however, Mao refused to listen to any opposing views and insisted on pushing the country even further toward radicalization, with the eventual launch of the Cultural Revolution and the belief that he was doing the right thing for China.

On writing. On the topic of writing, Paulsen used the example of German philosopher Christian Wolff's writing process in the consideration of his international readers in the seventeenth century. Mao, in contrast, believed that good writing comes from the free thinking of the writer, independent of the reader's acceptability. He commented, "When engaged in writing, the writer is oblivious to both the past and the future, concentrating so intently on the writing that he is unaware of anything or anyone else except himself and his writing. This is the way it must be if the writing is to be true and honest, and not false and superficial" (Schram 1992, 285). For Mao, good writing came from the writer's inner feelings and sense of presence: Mao made this argument in another place: "Words are the sounds of the heart, and the sounds of the heart are the expression of the inherent capacity of the basic nature of the heart" (Schram 1992, 300). According to Mao's guards, when Mao was writing an article or a speech, he had no books or any other materials by his side for reference or support. From their perspectives, Mao's ideas emerged only from thoughts and information Mao had collected or from feelings he had experienced. He would not stop in the middle of his writing and always finished writing an article in a single, sometimes sustained effort (Xu Yuanhong 2013). Mao's view of writing changed drastically over his lifetime; in 1942 he wrote "Talks at the Yan'an Forum on Literature and Art," in which he stressed that a writer must have in mind the lives and perspectives of workers, peasants, and soldiers when he or she was writing. Writing must have a target audience, he asserted, and a clear political goal that served the interest of the proletarian class.

In addition to beliefs about the appropriate perspective to take as a writer, Mao exhibited a preference regarding style of writing. In Paulsen's *A System of Ethics,* for example, Mao wrote the marginal notes in a semiclassical Chinese language format. The notes indicated Mao's familiarity with Chinese classical works and Chinese situations as well as a willingness to learn about new concepts and ideas from the West. As Rebecca Karl (2010) points out, "Mao's marginal notes ... demonstrate his lively engagement with the unfamiliar terms and ideas" (12). Mao consistently compared Paulsen's Western ideas with those of Chinese classics. Through these comparisons, Mao conveyed a sense of pride for Chinese culture and demonstrated his acute ability to make cultural and philosophical comparisons (for example, Kant's moral philosophy with the Neo-Confucian concept of *li,* or reason, and Paulsen's notion of the great man with Mencius's concept of *da zhangfu,* or grand gentleman). Although an argument can be made that Mao was influenced by Chinese classical notions of morality such as Confucius's notion of righteousness and self-cultivation and Mencius's concept of a great man, nonetheless Paulsen's work reinforced these moral conceptualizations for Mao and broadened his intellectual horizon. Moreover, Paulsen's writing helped Mao develop his dialectical thinking on issues of self, society, and death; Paulsen's ideas provided Mao with a framework from which to view the relationship between an individual and her society; Paulsen pushed Mao's thinking to a more radical outlook on social change; and Paulsen's words provided Mao with an idea of what a great politician should look and act like. Mao's attraction to Paulsen's positions was evidenced when Mao wrote "Quite true, quite true!" alongside Paulsen's statement that "the goal of my will is the common shared welfare of the individual and of society" (Schram 1992, 203).

Mao's style of writing in these notes exhibited chain reasoning,[26] comparison and contrast, references to authoritative works, and the use of analogies. Most strikingly Mao was fond of reconciling contradictory oppositions, a characteristic of his rhetorical maneuvering and a technique quintessential to his mind-set. Mao's critiques of Paulsen's work were intellectually vigorous and challenging; when Mao agreed with Paulsen, he wrote enthusiastic and engaging reactions. As Ross Terrill (1980) observes, "Mao's style was to be a clarifier, and to be against any whiff of self-indulgent complacency. He was the knife in any situation. He would challenge and probe and test and defy" (34).

In conclusion, Mao demonstrated his political ambition from his early years as influenced by both the Chinese classical works and Western reform ideas. He established his ethos as a knowledgeable person of Eastern and Western philosophy, a person of integrity and morality, and a person with a strong will to save and serve his country. The rhetorical meanings Mao articulated and the devices he used throughout his early writings were consistent. In both "Classroom Notes" and "Marginal Notes to Friedrich Paulsen: *A System of Ethics*," Mao emphasized the moral character of the speaker/writer drawing from Western and Chinese ethical values and classical thinkers. His knowledge of history and interpretation of the current situation led him to the ambition of saving China from its backwardness. Even though he never claimed himself as a sage, his early writings showed his desire to emulate them and follow their moral compass. Moreover he engaged his readers through rational appeals by presenting evidence, providing examples, analyzing the cause and effect, and proposing new actions, as he did in "A Study of Physical Education." Evidently at this early stage of his life Mao was determined to become a great man by actively engaging in social issues and participating in social change in China.

TWO

Mao Zedong's Theories of Rhetoric

Mao Zedong claimed to be a Marxist and was recognized for his "sinification of Marxism."[1] That is, Mao is known to have successfully applied Marxist-Leninist theories of epistemology and social change to the conditions of China's revolution. However, Mao's exposure to Marxism was limited because he lacked direct translations of Marxist works from German to Chinese. Scholars who have studied Mao generally agree that Mao's knowledge about Marxism largely came from Chinese translations of Soviet philosophical sources from which Mao drew categories and concepts of Soviet Marxist in his own philosophical writings (Knight 1990; Schram 1969; Wittfogel 1960). Specifically Mao learned about Marxism secondhand from Stalin's *History of the Communist Party of the Soviet Union, Short Course*. He considered the book "the best synthesis and summing-up of the world communist movement" and "the only comprehensive model in the whole world" (Mao 1967c, 24). Moreover, by his own admission, Mao said on June 4, 1958, at a conference in Wuhan that he "likes to read Lenin's works, especially his works produced during the Soviet revolutionary period. This is because Lenin writes in vivid and vigorous language; he reasons things out for his audience; his words are heart-felt, and he speaks the truth" (Yi Yan 1998, 81). According to Sun's 1993 study, Mao read Lenin's works such as *The State and Revolution, Left-Wing Communism,* and *Two Policies in 1932* when he was able to have access to the translated versions of these texts.

China may not have a set of rhetorical theories per se in its tradition by the Western standard, but it does have senses and conceptualizations of rhetoric that can be traced to the Spring–Autumn and Warring States period (770 B.C.E.–221 B.C.E.) (Lu 1998). A rich collection of studies on classical Chinese rhetoric has been produced since the 1970s and was pioneered by Professor Robert Oliver (1971). Scholars in general agree that Chinese rhetoric is not as explicit as Western rhetoric due to the highly contextualized nature of Chinese culture; Chinese rhetoric is embedded in Chinese literary, historical, ethical, and philosophical texts. In particular, philosophy and rhetoric are inseparable and interdependent (Garrett 1991; Jensen 1992; Lu 1998).

This phenomenon has continued in the modern era. Among modern Chinese thinkers and political leaders, Mao Zedong was one of the most eloquent writers and speakers. He wrote a number of articles and speeches that addressed ethical issues of the speaker, audience adaptation in speaking and writing, and the construction and presentation of messages. Mao did not name any of his works "rhetorical theories," but his theories of rhetoric were embedded and intertwined within his political and philosophical views. Mao's rhetorical theories can be divided into four arenas: 1) those on truth and knowledge (epistemology); 2) those on dialectics and contradiction; 3) those on art and literature; and 4) those on persuasion. An examination of Mao's writings reveals that Mao's philosophical views and rhetorical concepts exhibited significant influence issuing from Marxist-Leninist Communist ideology as well as influence stemming from traditional Chinese ontology and epistemology.

Mao's Theories on Truth and Knowledge

Robert Scott (1999) has claimed that rhetoric "is a way of knowing; it is epistemic" (138). He explains that rhetoric is not only a method to convey truth; it is also a process of generating truth and knowledge. Scott contends that through speaking and writing, humans come to know social norms and draw rational conclusions. As a means for humans to address the many versions of truth contesting with each other, then, rhetoric functions to present and unify different perspectives. "Rhetoric is thus not a deficient purveyor of technical knowledge, but rather the only proficient supplier for the knowledge that makes social interaction possible" (Lucaites, Condit, and Caudill 1999, 126).

Although Chinese rhetoric has a tradition of rational argument from the schools of Ming and Mohism (Lu 1998), the common assumption of Chinese culture made by early sinologists is that Chinese thought is characterized by intuition and lack of logical thinking (for example, Lin 1962; Northrop 1944). Also due to the influence of Buddhism, Chinese people place more emphasis on direct experience such as sudden enlightenment as the source of truth and knowledge (Li Zehou 1986; Oliver 1971) than on logical thought.

Although Mao's mother was a Buddhist and may have taught Mao from the perspective of that religion, Mao did not follow Buddhist beliefs; Mao was an atheist. He may not have believed in sudden enlightenment as a way of gaining knowledge, but his view of epistemology was close to the Chinese pragmatic tradition in that he argued that truth and knowledge are first drawn from one's experience and then processed through rationalization.[2] Mao espoused his theory of truth and knowledge in his seminal article "On Practice." The piece was published in July 1937, when Japan launched a large-scale war with China at the same time that political conflict intensified between Mao and Wang Ming, the former CCP leader.[3] Mao wrote the essay to challenge what he perceived as the increasing dogmatism and subjectivism within the Chinese Communist Party. At the time the CCP had established its own youth training workshops in Yan'an and invited Mao to give lectures on philosophy. Mao initially wrote the essay as lecture notes, so his direct audiences were young party members, but his target audience also included his political opponents, such as Wang Ming and Bo Gu, Soviet-trained CCP leaders who issued military orders without considering China's practical situation. Mao's essay established him as a credible Marxist theorist and elevated his reputation among party leaders. The essay is treated here as a rhetorical text not because Mao discussed truth and knowledge in it, but because the rhetorical implications of the essay in prescribing a formula for gaining truth and knowledge suited the Chinese context, guided the Chinese revolution, and transformed the Chinese way of thinking.

Mao's theories on truth and knowledge were formulated based on his experiences with external and internal enemies. From 1931 to 1934 Chiang Kai-shek, the president of the Chinese Nationalist government, launched five encirclement campaigns against the Chinese Red Army. The Red Army successfully defended its territory in the first four campaigns by employing Mao's guerrilla military strategies, but efforts failed during the last campaign. As a result the Red Army was forced to retreat and started what is historically known as the "Long March."[4] After the Long March, the Red Army had been significantly reduced in size, and the Communist Party was on the cusp of being defeated by Chiang Kai-shek's offensive forces. Mao was the chairman of the "Soviet government" in Yan'an, but he did not wield real, enforceable powers, and many of his comrades did not agree with his military strategies of guerrilla fighting. Mao attributed the failure of the Red Army and the weakening of the CCP to the narrow thinking of a few top Communist leaders, such as Wang Ming and Bo Gu, who were trained in the Soviet Union and were guided by the Comintern and the military adviser Otto Braun (Chinese name Li De).

Mao accused Wang and Bo of acting in dogmatic and subjective ways in their applications of Marxist-Leninist theories, ways that failed to consider China's situation.[5] Mao treated this ideological division as a philosophical issue of epistemology. In this essay Mao proposed the epistemology of dialectical materialism, which is predicated on the integration of theory and practice, and of subjectivity and objectivity. Mao argued that the epistemology of dialectical materialism was the true, correct, and Marxist approach to how humans view, know, and change the world. While known as a romantic revolutionary, Mao in this essay sounded rational and practical in his approach to solving China's problem. As Womack (1982) points out, "Interaction of theory and practice with the goal of effective revolutionary action is the basic characteristic of Mao's own pattern of development and the main trait of his political thinking" (188), despite the fact that Mao's view on this topic drew heavily from Joseph Stalin's *Dialectical and History Materialism* (Knight 2005).

Knowing through Practice

The first question for Mao was determining the source and process of gaining truth and knowledge. Mao did not provide anything new but rather parroted what Marx and Lenin had claimed on this point. As a self-claimed devout Marxist, Mao believed that a person's perception is strongly influenced by his/her material conditions, political situations, and cultural life in a society. While Marx posited that the material condition of industrial workers shaped their social consciousness and Lenin professed that practical knowledge "is higher than [theoretical] knowledge" (Mao 1937/1967a, 297), Mao further elaborated on this process: "Man's knowledge depends mainly on his activity in material production, through which he comes gradually to understand the phenomena, the properties and the laws of nature, and the relations between himself and nature . . . between man and man" (295). In Mao's view, social activities included production, class struggle, political life, artistic pursuit, and scientific experiment, all of which were interrelated and dependent on one another. He believed moreover that humans' perceptions of these activities took place and developed from a lower to a higher level and "from the shallower to the deeper, from the one-sided to the many-sided" (296). Put another way, a person's perception and knowledge of the world are restricted by the mode of production (handcrafted or machine-made) and stages of the society (capitalism or socialism). When the mode of production is at a small scale and when the ruling class is exploiting people (such as in the early stage of capitalism), a person's knowledge is limited and biased. When the mode of production turns into a large-scale assembly line and the proletariat class emerges (as occurs in the early stages of an industrialized society), a person's knowledge becomes much more comprehensive.

Mao named such a process of gaining knowledge "the science of Marxism" (Mao 1937/1967a, 296) and referenced works of Marx and Lenin to support his point.[6] "Scientific Marxists," as defined by James Arnt Aune (1999), "stress a deterministic view of ideology, devalue individual experience and action, and emphasize the law-like character of historical change" (541). Indeed, Mao treated this process of gaining truth and knowledge as the absolute approach that helps achieve the "proletarian consciousness," a level of consciousness characterized as the most moral, advanced, and selfless state of mind.

While Mao viewed epistemology as a dynamic process of defining and redefining truth through practice, truth has to be tested after being gained through certain material conditions and changes of productivity. For Mao, the sole criterion for testing truth was repeated practices or activities. In his words, "The truth of any knowledge or theory is determined not by subjective feelings, but by objective results in social practices. Only social practice can be the criterion of truth" (Mao 1937/1967a, 297).[7] Mao augmented his claim by quoting from Stalin that "theory becomes aimless when it is not connected with practice" (Mao 1942/1967c, 40). For Mao, after a person gained rational knowledge (or conceptual and theoretical knowledge), it was important to apply such knowledge in the practice of revolution to verify the truth of such knowledge.

To Mao, one cycle of theory testing was not enough. Instead, "practice, knowledge, again practice, and again knowledge. This form repeats itself in an endless cycle, and with each cycle the content of practice and knowledge rises to a higher level" (Mao 1937/1967a, 308). Mao called this endless cycle "the dialectical-materialist theory of knowledge" or the "law of epistemology" (308). In Mao's view, this process of practice-theory-practice in obtaining knowledge was the law of epistemology that served as guidance for change, class struggle, and scientific and social experiments. To some degree Mao's view was the next step to Aristotle's notion of inductive reasoning in that conclusions drawn from examples (practice) will function as concepts or theories and can be used as premises for the application of new practice, and so on.

In the name of scientific Marxism, Mao illustrated a two-stage process of how humans come to know what they know and believe to be true. The first stage was "the perceptual stage of cognition" or "the stage of sense perceptions and impressions" (Mao 1937/1967a, 297). Mao used observations and visitors' first impressions when they went to Yan'an (the CCP's revolutionary base) as an example: "In the first day or two, they see its topography, streets and houses, meetings, hear talks of various kinds and read various documents" (297). During this time visitors formed their first impressions or initial perceptions of Yan'an.

The second stage was "the stage of rational knowledge" (Mao 1937/1967a, 298). This is the stage when a person begins to make a link between a concept and what he/she has observed and experienced. In making the link, the person will infer and draw logical conclusions about Yan'an. Mao purported that when visitors came to Yan'an and saw how prepared the Communist Party was in forging an alliance with the Nationalist Party in the fight against Japan, visitors would form conceptions, make judgments, and draw conclusions about the Communist Party more favorably.[8] Mao called this "the rational stage" of knowledge. To help his audience understand what he meant by "rational," Mao referenced a famous Chinese novel, *Romance of the Three Kingdoms,* and to illustrate his point he quoted a familiar phrase from the novel: "knit the brows and a stratagem comes to mind" (298). This means that eyebrows will tighten up when one is in a thinking mode, and through the thinking process, an idea or strategy will arise. This simple explanation was much easier for a Chinese audience to understand. But at the same time, Mao's simplification of the "rational process" brushed away a logical and critical engagement of the issue, making the process sound more like an intuitive awakening.

A Critique of Traditional Chinese Perceptions Regarding Epistemology

Most Mao scholars consider Mao to have been a disciple of Lenin and Stalin as he inherited their works. This conclusion is only partially true. Mao's theory on truth and knowledge also evolved from and was a critical response to indigenous Chinese philosophy on epistemology. In *Da Xue,* one of the Confucian classics, the concepts of *ge wu* 格物 (to study the world) and *zhi zhi* 致知 (to reach perfect knowledge) are raised as foundations for achieving a peaceful and harmonious society.[9] The philosophers Zhu Xi 朱熹 and Cheng Yi 程颐 from the Song dynasty (960–1279) discussed four processes of gaining knowledge: study; distinction; questioning; and reflection. They assumed that one must know first before they can act. In other words, a person's action is guided by what he or she knows. From there the process of knowing is moved from superficial to profound, from crude to refined, from accumulation to enlightenment (Wu 1990). In other words, the Neo-Confucian model of epistemology placed thought and consciousness before material condition and practical experience in gaining truth and knowledge.

The Neo-Confucian view of epistemology was challenged by later scholars. For example, Wang Yangming 王阳明, a well-known philosopher in the Ming dynasty (1368–1644), believed that knowledge and action are integrated—that only through simultaneous action could one gain knowledge (Wang, 1992). Another philosopher from the Qing dynasty (1644–1911) named Wang Fuzhi 王夫之 further developed this notion by stressing the need for both experience and reason in gaining truth and knowledge 知行合一, in that humans first gain their knowledge through senses and then reason carefully about what they have sensed. These philosophers challenged the traditional Chinese Daoist and Buddhist notions of intuition and sudden enlightenment as means to achieving truth and knowledge. However, these views of epistemology were not popularized in China as they were written in the classical Chinese language and only a few educated elites could read and understand them.

Mao seemed to have read the works of Wang Yangming and Wang Fuzhi since he referenced them in his study notes. Mao was one of the earliest persons in Chinese history to explain these epistemologies to the Chinese people in clear, vernacular terms—that all knowledge first comes from experiences and then becomes conceptual knowledge that in turn serves as a guide for further action, action that also will be tested and contested in practice and experience. Mao prescribed this "logical" process of epistemology for the Chinese people. This "new" way of thinking quickly became popularized, fundamentally challenging traditional Chinese beliefs about truth and knowledge that gave preeminence to conceptual knowledge, not empirical experience.

Mao did not believe that knowledge can be gained only from reading books. He criticized the traditional Chinese saying that "without stepping outside his gate, the scholar knows all the wide world's affairs" as pedantic and senseless. For Mao, knowing came from practice. Mao used an analogy to illustrate his point: "If you want to know the taste of a pear, you must change the pear by eating it yourself" (Mao 1937/1967a, 300). That is, if a person wants to get conceptual knowledge of the taste of a pear, he or she must physically eat it, which implies that no one could "know" anything he or she has not experienced. Mao made it clear that "anyone who thinks that rational knowledge needs not to be derived from perceptual knowledge is an idealist" (唯心论者) (302). He further explained that rational knowledge without sense perception (practice and experience) is like "water without a source, a tree without roots" (302). Mao deemed the philosophical label "idealist" as a negative term in Chinese political discourse. He associated idealism with subjectivity in perceiving and gaining knowledge. The term "idealism," for him, was moralized and politicized to refer to someone whose thinking not only was inaccurate and misguided but also brought negative consequences to social and cultural life. During the Chinese Cultural Revolution, if someone were labeled an "idealist," this person would also be deemed a class enemy. However, Mao did not follow his own theory regarding epistemology after the founding of the People's Republic of China. His economic policies were based not on practice or social reality but on his own idealistic and utopian views of China's economic development. Ironically he ceased his quest for an objective reality and became an idealist, manifesting a way of thinking that he had once vehemently criticized.[10]

Womack (1982) observes that Mao placed more emphasis on practical effectiveness than on abstract theories. Mao certainly did not have faith in formal education as the only source of knowledge. Additionally he reversed the conventional belief that the educated know more than the uneducated. In his words, "Intellectuals are the most ignorant and the workers and peasants are the most knowledgeable" (Mao 1958/1992c, 236). Starting in 1958, Mao sent many members of the educated elite to rural areas, factories, and military bases to learn from peasants, workers, and soldiers. Reeducating these intellectuals by immersing them in the mass population reflected Mao's ideological belief of epistemology (learning knowledge from experience), but an argument can be made that his actions revealed a political strategy he used to punish the arrogance of intellectuals and to compel them to obey his rule.

In summary, Mao's theories on truth and knowledge may not have been original since he studied Marxism secondhand from the Soviet Marxists. His contribution in the world of rhetoric is his employment of Marxist-Leninist theories to address contingent situations in China. He introduced and explained complicated and abstract Western philosophical concepts by writing in a vernacular Chinese that his audience could understand and to which they could relate. Most Chinese, including my own generation, learned about Marxist dialectical materialism from Mao's works. Although early Chinese Marxist writers such as Li Da and Ai Siqi wrote books introducing Marxism to Chinese audiences,[11] Mao was the first person in modern Chinese history to popularize Marxism in terms of how truth and knowledge were derived. Knight (1990) credits Mao for his remarkable rhetorical ability to surpass Lenin and Stalin, saying that Mao's philosophical essays are "more tightly argued and complete than the Soviet sources, in terms of content and many of his formulations, and much of his analysis and explanations, are clearer, more concise, systematic, and profound than the Soviet texts on philosophy" (45). Indeed, Mao's rhetorical shrewdness lay in his employment of the Marxist-Leninist framework and in his references to Lenin and Stalin to justify his own approach to China's revolution. This rhetorical strategy serves to secure Mao's ideological correctness since both Marx and Lenin are worshipped by the Chinese Communists as the beacons of communism, Marx being the founder of communism and Lenin putting communism into practice in the successful Russian Revolution. By using Marxism-Leninism for his ideological argument, Mao presented himself as an expert on the theories of Marxism/Leninism, which made his views harder to refute because Marxism-Leninism was regarded as the ultimate truth for Communists. Further, Mao presented himself first as the voice of the people, genuinely concerned with their emancipation from oppressive forces, and second as a realist who intended to address practical problems in China. Mao deliberately avoided acknowledging the possible influence on him of Wang Yangming's and Wang Fuzhi's notions of integration between experience and reason. This subterfuge was another strategic choice by which Mao set himself apart from any connection to "old China" so that he might create a new Chinese identity under the banner of socialism/communism.

Mao's Theory of Dialectics and Contradiction

The concept of dialectic (Greek: *dialektike*) was first employed by Greek sophists as an argumentation technique in their teaching. By arguing for and against an issue, students would learn how to "make the worse case appear the better" by manipulating probability in a judicial context (Kennedy 1980, 27). Aristotle considered dialectic as the counterpart to rhetoric (Aristotle 1991, 28) and treated dialectic as a form of reasoning or a logical method. In this method one would start with a widely accepted proposition and then move to the application of the proposition to the proposed problem (to avoid self-contradiction in the process of argumentation) (Aristotle 1941, 198). Plato invented and applied this method first in his "Socratic dialogues" with sophists in *Gorgias*. This dialectical process of reasoning allows a critical examination of arguments and counterarguments of an issue, a test of old propositions and a discovery of new ones in the process.

The meaning of "dialectic" has evolved in reference to history and the human condition since the nineteenth century. According to Hegel, "dialectic" consists of thesis, antithesis, and synthesis in the progression of ideas that push history forward, leading to a perfect world (Hegel 1989). This dialectical process of history was appropriated by Karl Marx and Friedrich Engels into "materialist dialectic," which references a world that is interconnected, contradictory, and dynamic based on the material conditions of social-economic class (Marx 1906). Marx and

Engels expanded the idea of dialectic to include how humans perceive and understand the material world. According to Grossberg (1979), Marxist dialectics is "a mode of understanding and interpretation" (235). The understanding of a phenomenon is achieved through application to particularity, interconnection with another phenomenon, and the sign of negation or contradiction (236). This Marxist concept of dialectic, especially the concept of contradiction, predominantly influenced the thinking of Communist leaders such as Lenin and Mao.

Accordingly, being dialectical requires the ability to identify contradictions and, by seeing things in opposing terms, ascertain how they relate and then configure ideas to induce change. Mao's view on contradiction was guided by dialectical thinking that drew heavily from his readings of Lenin.[12] For Plato and Aristotle, contradiction was logically unacceptable as it indicated ambiguity and paradox in things. Mao, in contrast, saw contradiction at the ontological level as inevitable and embedded in everything in the universe. In his words, "Contradiction is present in the process of development of all things and permeates every process from beginning to end" (Mao 1937/1967a, 318).[13] Contradiction was a natural phenomenon manifested in everything ranging from natural science to social movements. Mao applied this view of contradiction to war strategies, perceptions, and the conflict within the CCP in the Chinese context. Moreover, Mao used the concept of contradiction to explain his theory of class struggle: the state of conflict in a society resulting from differences and confrontations between the rich and the poor. For Mao, as long as differences existed in thought, social status, and worldviews, contradictions and confrontations would reside among them. Like Lenin, Mao believed that contradiction was the impetus for social change.

Mao identified the unity of opposites as the fundamental characteristic of contradiction. He credited this idea to Lenin and considered this unity as "the basic law of materialist dialectics" (Mao 1937/1967a, 311). Mao explained Lenin's concept in plain and clear language: "No contradictory aspect can exist in isolation. Without its opposite aspect, each loses the condition for its existence.... Without life, there would be no death.... Without misfortune, there would be no good life.... Without the bourgeoisie, there would be no proletariat" (338). Mao concluded, "It is so with all opposites; in given conditions, on the one hand they are opposed to each other, and on the other they are interconnected, interpenetrating, interpermeating and interdependent" (338). Interestingly this view is similar to the Daoist notion of yin and yang in that each presents the opposite of the other, but the opposing forces are simultaneously integrated to create equilibrium. Mao even borrowed the Daoist concept of *xiangfan xiangcheng* 相反相成 (things that are in opposition are also complementary) to illustrate that both conflict and unity exist between the two opposing aspects of a contradiction.

For Mao, contradiction equated with a problem or challenge that human beings faced in life. Contradiction could have internal and external constraints. Mao called these constraints internal contradiction and external contradiction, respectively. Mao asserted that the internal contradiction functions as the fundamental cause for change while the external contradiction functions as the secondary cause (Mao 1937/1967a, 313). Mao gave an example to explain his point: "Countries with almost the same geographical and climate conditions display great diversity and unevenness in their development. Moreover, great social changes may take place in one and the same country although its geography and climate remain unchanged. Imperialist Russia changed into the socialist Soviet Union, and feudal Japan, which had locked its doors against the world, changed into imperialist Japan, although no change occurred in the geography and climate of either country" (312). Here the people of each country were the internal cause (internal contradiction) while the geographical elements of each country were the secondary cause (external contradiction).

For any social change to take place, Mao explained, the will of the people is the decisive factor. To make his point clearly understood, Mao used an analogy of an egg hatching: "In a suitable temperature an egg changes into a chicken, but no temperature can change a stone into a chicken, because each has a different basis" (Mao 1937/1967a, 314). Mao justified his point by reviewing why the Communist Party liquidated individual opportunism within the party in order to lead China's revolution in a correct direction. In Mao's thinking, it was that correct political line (internal contradiction) within the party that would secure the success of revolution. Mao closely monitored the internal contradictions within the party and launched several political campaigns in his lifetime to silence voices he considered incorrect or harmful to revolution.[14]

Mao also divided contradictions into those of universality and those of particularity. In Mao's view, contradictions of particularity dealt with individual or particular characters that were conditional, temporary, relative, and subject to change. According to this point of view, types of contradictions can change, and different types of contradictions require different approaches to induce change. Mao called this tenet "the principles of Marxist-Leninism" and "the living soul of Marxism" (322–23). Mao used this view of contradiction to justify the three stages of the CCP's relationship with the Nationalist Party. In the first stage (1924–27), the CCP remained involved in China's revolution and was an ally to the Nationalist Party, but the CCP was a nascent organization and essentially silenced by the Nationalist Party. In the second stage (1927–35), the CCP and the Nationalist Party became enemies. The CCP suffered a tremendous loss in its military force due to the CCP leaders' strategic mistakes. Not until 1935, during the so-called third stage, when the Communist Party corrected its errors and formed a new united front with the Nationalist Party in resistance against Japan, did the CCP set out in the right direction. During this third stage the CCP matured after learning lessons from the past. In Mao's justification of the three stages, he treated the cause of each stage as the internal contradiction and considered the contradiction in each stage of alliance with the Nationalist Party as different, conditional, temporary, and relative; thus the relationship with the Nationalist Party was subject to change. Mao explained that the contradiction of particularity was the reason the CCP and the Nationalist Party had become enemies and friends at different points of history. These differing circumstances indicated that no definite answers exist to any problems because situations and issues at hand are contingent upon different circumstances and provide different rhetorical options and strategies. Mao's view was rhetorical in nature as rhetoric addresses contingent issues and is characterized by the process of weighing options.

Grossberg (1979) states that Marxist dialectical thought aims at producing change: "History is a battle of the new against the old in which the new stage could not have arisen except out of and in opposition to the old" (240). For Mao, change was inevitable, and his revolutionary goal was to replace the semicolonial and semifeudal China with a socialist China. Mao was convinced that a society would inevitably transform from a feudal society to a capitalist one, as had happened in Europe. Citing Lenin, Mao said that contradictions or unity of oppositions induce change; therefore, "the human mind should take these opposites not as dead, rigid, but as living, conditional, mobile, transforming themselves into one another" (Mao 1937/1967a, 340). Borrowing from Marx and Engels (*The German Ideology, The Communist Manifesto*), Mao believed that the ruling class of the bourgeoisie would eventually be replaced by the proletariat; a capitalist society would be inexorably replaced by a socialist society, as had taken place in the Soviet Union. Based on this logic, a socialist China was inevitable. Mao used the rhetoric of inevitability throughout his writings as a rational appeal for the Communist revolution.

In addition to referencing Lenin, Mao relied on traditional Chinese symbolic resources to support his argument for change. He used a traditional Chinese saying, "the new superseding the old" (Mao 1937/1967a, 333), and provided examples from traditional Chinese mythology such as Kua Fu's chasing the sun in *Shan Hai Ching*, Yi's shooting down of nine suns in *Huai Nan Tzu*, and episodes of ghosts and foxes metamorphosed into human beings in the *Strange Tales of Liao Chai*. Mao also used stories from popular Chinese literary texts such as *Journey to the West, Romance of the Three Kingdoms,* and *Water Margin.* Here, Mao mixed Chinese mythology with social change, as these anecdotes indicated that social transformation was possible. Through references to Marx and Lenin and examples in Chinese texts, Mao established himself as an expert on Marxist-Leninist theories. Mao's interpretation of historical progression toward social transformation was lauded as the absolute truth and a Communist dogma. His integration of traditional Chinese mythology and Leninist theories created a language easily understood by the public, a language that gave hope to the CCP and ultimately to the Chinese people. This view of history was the guiding principle for the CCP and an enthymemic[15] device to persuade the Chinese people that Mao and his party would lead China out of poverty into a bright future. Mao's use of Chinese examples demonstrated his remarkable rhetorical dexterity of turning Lenin's abstract ideas into digestible and relatable discourse that resonated with his Chinese audience.

Mao also applied Lenin's theory of dialectics to the socioeconomic structure of a society—that is, the contradiction between the economic base and its superstructure. Mao recognized, as discussed by Marx, that the productive forces and the economic base generally play the principal and decisive roles in a society. Mao took this point even further, stating that in certain conditions such aspects as the relations of production and the superstructure in turn manifest themselves in the principal and decisive role. He asserted, "When the superstructure (politics, culture, etc.) obstructs the development of the economic base, political and cultural changes become principal and decisive" (Mao 1937/1967a, 336). At this point Mao altered Marx's original social theory on the relationship between the economic base and the ideological superstructure. In Mao's belief, the forces of the superstructure (ideas, culture, and minds) in Communist China risked the danger of becoming bourgeois, which would lead China into a capitalist society (in economic form) and turn history backward, based on the Marxist prediction of the five stages of historical progression (from slave society to feudalism, capitalism, socialism, and then communism). This mind-set dominated Mao's thinking during his leadership within the Communist Party after he became the ruler of the People's Republic of China in 1949. This was evidenced by his consistent purges of high-ranking officials and endless political campaigns to reform the Chinese mind and culture, culminating in the launch of the Cultural Revolution.

Mao's rhetoric of change not only was influenced by Leninist thought but also manifested an apparent trace of Daoism in his interpretation of dialectics and contradiction. In his writing and speeches, Mao referenced ample examples and citations from Laozi and Zhuangzi. For instance, in his speech from the second session of the Eighth Communist Party Central Committee, Mao referenced Zhuangzi's saying "the shadow of a flying bird is in motion" (Mao 1956/1977, 332). Mao used the saying as an example of dialectics in that a thing can be moving and not moving. There is no absolute act of moving, nor is there an absolute act of not moving. All issues are temporary and conditional. In his "Correct Handling of Contradictions among the People," Mao quoted Laozi's saying "Good fortune lieth within bad, bad fortune lurketh within good" (Mao 1957/1977, 416). Mao used this saying to illustrate his point that anything good can turn bad and anything bad can turn good. Schram (1974) has observed that "the Chairman's understanding of contradictions was inspired not so much by Marxism as by the old Chinese dialectic of waxing and waning, decline and renewal, the yin and the yang" (26). Thus, Mao was not afraid of chaos. He believed that chaos would lead to stability, as contradictions are just a sum of interrelated parts and will ultimately reach a lofty, elevated conclusion to the benefit of all parties.

To some degree Mao's theory of contradiction resembles Kenneth Burke's notion of identification and alienation, but it contrasts with Burke's ideas regarding the purpose of rhetoric. For Burke (1969), identification is the key factor in persuasion; an orator may elect to speak in a way that appeals to the audience's core values, using manners such as gestures, tonality, order, and images with which the audience is familiar. However, at the same time, when an orator identifies with an audience, he or she simultaneously alienates or disassociates with others. "A person is both joined and separate" (Burke 1969, 21). That is, identification is rooted in alienation as well as division. Alienation and division are in conflict (contradiction) but also interrelated (a dialectical thought). In these ways Mao's theory resembles Burke's. With regard to the purpose of rhetoric, however, Burke and Mao differ. The purpose of rhetoric for Burke was to achieve peace, while for Mao rhetoric created contradiction, which in turn facilitated change in society and consciousness, eventually leading to revolution.

Mao's theory of contradiction is also similar to Michael Billig's theory of logic and antilogic in rhetorical argument. In his book *Arguing and Thinking* (1996), Billig observes that human thought is characterized by rhetorical oppositions, which he names "logic" and "antilogic." Billig argues that because of these oppositions, humans have the capacity for contradictions, a theoretical position similar to Mao's. As humans argue for one position, Billig asserts, they simultaneously are engaging in counterargument of the opposing position. Undoubtedly Mao was not an original thinker on dialectics and contradiction, although he was described as a good teacher and clarifier of the abstract and foreign ideas contained in Marxist-Leninist doctrine to the Chinese audience.

Mao's "sinification of Marxism" as a recognized contribution may actually have been Mao's rhetorical appropriation to suit his own revolutionary goals, rhetoric as a weapon created to help defeat his political opponents within the party. The appropriation blended the political ideology of the West with the Chinese intellectual tradition and cultural resources and linguistic repertoire. Joseph Esherick (1995) describes Mao's writing as "imbue[d] Soviet Marxism with a distinct Chinese style" (52). It is difficult to discern whether Mao's dialectical thinking was primarily influenced by Marxist-Leninist theories or by traditional Chinese indigenous philosophy. It seems, however, that Mao's familiarity with Daoist thinking paved the way for his acceptance of Marxist-Leninist theories on dialectics and contradiction. In this sense, Mao not only further rebranded or subverted Marxist-Leninist philosophical ideas into ideological orthodox but also put them into practice within an indigenous Chinese context. He successfully integrated foreign philosophies (in Marx, Engels, Lenin, and Stalin) with Chinese traditional thinking and cosmology in his rhetorical argument.

Mao's Theories on Art and Literature

While Mao preached dialectics and favored contradictions, Mao's revolutionary rhetoric could also be identified in his theorization of art and literature. Mao expounded the essence of his theory on art and literature in his speech "Talks at the Yan'an Forum on Literature and Art." In the speech Mao painted the world in two camps: the proletariat and the bourgeoisie. A person's thinking and actions were guided either by the proletarian worldview or by the bourgeois worldview. For Mao, a proletarian worldview was to accept Marxist theories of class struggle and the utopian vision of realizing a Communist society. The bourgeois worldview was to maintain the status quo of inequality; a person with such a worldview tended to have an orientation of subjectivism.[16] It is ironic that while, on the one hand, Mao believed that experience and practice shape consciousness, on the other hand, he gave more weight to the power of consciousness in guiding a person's attitude and actions. For Mao, maintaining a proletarian consciousness or a consciousness of class struggle meant constantly to obliterate any bourgeois thought. The alleged "bourgeois thought," as perpetuated by many intellectuals at the time, was broadly defined and yet condemned as a sinful thought.

Background and Audience of the Speech

Mao delivered "Talks at the Yan'an Forum on Literature and Art" on May 2, 1942, a few months after he launched the "Rectification Campaign." The claimed purpose of the Rectification Campaign was to teach party members and young intellectuals in Yan'an revolutionary ideas based on Marxist-Leninist theories and help them gain the correct proletarian consciousness. The hidden motive of the campaign "was to build on the accomplishments of Mao's success in military and political leadership and gain control of ideological leadership over the intellectuals of both Russian and Western training" (Wang 2000, 182). The Russian-trained intellectuals were targeted because they were the most perfidious of Mao's political opponents.[17] According to Vladimirov's observation (1975), the sole purpose of the Rectification Campaign was to establish loyalty to Mao and to enhance Mao's authority among party members through the mechanisms of fear and thought reform.

Mao delivered his speech late in the evening outside on a flat stretch of land in front of the cave dwellings in which the enthusiastic Communists lived and worked. While the Russian-trained intellectuals may have experienced tension during the speech, many audience members fondly remembered the scene of that night. For example, Huang still remembers, "Without any sign of fatigue Chairman Mao spoke on. It was already past midnight. The moon overhead made the night as bright as day. Under the moon and the stars, hills nearby and distant were darkly silhouetted. Not far away, the Yenhe River flowed merrily, its surface shot with silver" (in Melvin 2012).

The speech was delivered during the time period when China was engaged in the Anti-Japanese War (1937–45). At the start of the war, the Communist Party and the Nationalist Party formed an alliance after ten years of civil war. The Communist Party had established its base in Yan'an, Shanxi Province, and had attracted many left-wing writers, artists, and intellectuals with utopian ideologies and with determination to fight against the Japanese and build a new China.[18] The artists considered Yan'an an ideal place for individual freedom and social equality. They even called Yan'an "China's Moscow" and a "paradise described in Dante's *Divine Comedy*" (Gao 2000, 287). These young artists had contributed significantly to the dissemination of the CCP's policies and ideology. They had created various artistic forms such as poems, paintings, slogans, choirs, music, and dances. They had written articles, novels, and plays to praise the CCP and to criticize the Nationalist Party (Gao 2000, 283).

However, because many of them were Western educated and from wealthy families, they had revolutionary zeal but little contact with workers, peasants, and soldiers, who were the basis of the Communist Party. Mao initially welcomed these young intellectuals and praised them for their courage and talent. However, Mao fundamentally did not trust them and labeled them "petite bourgeoisie" who needed to adjust their worldviews. These "petite bourgeoisie" therefore were also the target audience of Mao's speech.

The Goals of Art and Literature

Mao started his speech by establishing a common ground with his audience: "Our aim is to ensure that revolutionary literature and art follow the correct path of development and provide better help to other revolutionary efforts in facilitating the overthrow of our national enemy and the accomplishment of the task of national liberation" (Mao 1942/1967c, 69). Then Mao charged his audience with an honorable mission to support the cause of national liberation by calling for the need to have "a cultural army," an army that would use pens instead of guns to defeat the enemy. To Mao, this cultural army "is absolutely indispensable" (69) to winning the cause.

Mao even made a link between the significance of winning this war and the cultural movements in China. This connection was rhetorically effective, as his audience was largely composed of young intellectuals who had been influenced by the spirit of the May Fourth Movement, which was characterized by anti-Confucianism, democratic ideals, and nationalistic sentiments.[19] For Mao, winning the war involved winning the hearts of the Chinese people, changing the ways that arts and literature traditionally were expressed in China, and therefore changing the ways they functioned in China. In this sense Mao attempted to re-create the Chinese culture often characterized by harmony into a culture of revolution and radicalization.

Traditionally speaking, China had been a high-learning culture, producing scholars and writers who received Confucian educations. Some of these scholars were also influenced by Western culture in modern times. Their literary and artistic works had been serving the elites and the wealthy in Chinese society for centuries. A vast majority of Chinese people (in Mao's estimate, 90 percent) still belonged to the peasantry class and still received little formal education. However, Mao believed that practice or direct experiences were the sources and testing grounds for truth. This belief meant that workers, peasants, and soldiers or the masses held more truth and knowledge about life, but their lives were not represented in traditional Chinese literary works. (Mao had made this observation when he was reading Chinese classics at school.) Those writers and artists who came to Yan'an had artistic talent and skills but did not possess the experience of peasants. The artists lacked a common ground with and an empathy for the masses. (Mao used the word "masses" as an equivalent to "working-class people.") This lack of common ground hindered the communication between the two groups and even bred resentment toward each other.

Therefore for Mao, "Talks at the Yan'an Forum on Literature and Art" aimed at identifying the challenges that these writers and intellectuals would face in integrating with the masses and setting up new goals regarding who would be served by their literary works and how artists would adjust their work to appeal to and serve a mass audience. Mao announced that the goal of his speech was to use art and literature as weapons to unite people and attack their enemies. He then listed three challenges that writers and intellectuals would face: the problem of class status; the problem of attitude; and the problem of audience.

In terms of class status, Mao requested that these writers and intellectuals adopt the mind-set of the proletariat as the correct form of consciousness.[20] The problem of attitude involved a choice of extolling the good deeds of the masses and condemning the evildoings of the enemy. Mao made it clear that writers and artists must choose to praise the party, the masses, and the people's army while at the same time exposing the duplicity and cruelty of Japanese imperialism and class enemies. He directed that in addition to creating expressions of anti-Japanese sentiments through the arts, artists needed to use their talents to expose the "feudal evils" and eulogize the heroes (Birth 1960). Emulating lofty heroes had been a long-standing approach of the CCP to inculcate values of courage, selflessness, and loyalty to the party. The practice of reporting only good news and blocking out bad news was a quintessential principle of CCP propaganda from the time Mao promulgated these theories.

Mao pointed out that the attitude toward the urban, petite bourgeoisie should be patience and tolerance. The goal of writers and artists was to educate the bourgeoisie and turn them into revolutionaries in heart and mind (Mao 1942/1967c, 71). With respect to the audience, Mao reminded the writers and artists that their primary audience in the revolutionary base consisted of workers, peasants, and soldiers, as well as some cadres and students. Mao declared that "all our literature and art are for the masses of the people, and in the first place for the workers, peasants and soldiers" (84).

To Mao, all forms of literature and art were inherently related to class and served certain political interests. There were no works of literature and art that were independent from class and politics. Moreover, Mao claimed, "Literature and art are subordinate to politics.... Revolutionary literature and art are parts of the whole revolutionary cause" (Mao 1942/1967c, 86). He cited from Lenin that proletarian art and literature "are indispensable cogs and wheels in the whole machine, an indispensable part of the entire revolutionary cause" (86). Thus the tasks of these writers and artists were to garner popular support for the CCP government, incite hatred among the masses for the landlord (class enemy), cultivate a proletarian consciousness, and fulfill the CCP propaganda commitment. In calling for these actions and inciting artists to comply with his mandate, Mao successfully politicized Chinese art and literature. Wang (1997) argues that Mao's vision of political power was not just about policy and government control but rather had become "a form of sublime art" (193). It was "a form of power implanted and operative in the inner sphere of the individual's mind, feelings, and tastes, power embedded in the symbolic activities and perceptual patterns by which we generate meaning and evolve culture" (Wang 1997, 15).

Mao recognized the intellectual gap between the rural peasants and the urban, educated backgrounds of young writers and artists; however, more of his concern was the psychological or emotional distance between the two groups that would make the task of fusing them challenging. He anticipated obstacles and even resistance to his call. He required the writers and artists to abandon their petit bourgeois class consciousness and reform their thoughts and feelings to those that would emulate the consciousness and thoughts and feelings of the masses. To persuade the writers and artists to undertake such a thought transformation, Mao used himself as an example.

Mao shared his own experience of transforming himself from a member of a petit bourgeois class to a member of the proletariat:

> Here I might mention the experience of how my own feelings changed. I began life as a student and at school acquired the ways of a student; I then used to feel it undignified to do even a little manual labour, such as carrying my own luggage in the presence of my fellow students, who were incapable of carrying anything, either on their shoulders or in their hands. At that time I felt that intellectuals were the only clean people in the world, while in comparison workers and peasants were dirty. I did not mind wearing the clothes of other intellectuals, believing them clean, but I would not put on clothes belonging to a worker or peasant, believing them dirty.

But after I became a revolutionary and lived with workers and peasants and with soldiers of the revolutionary army, I gradually came to know them well and they gradually came to know me well, too. It was then, and only then, that I fundamentally changed the bourgeois and petty-bourgeois feelings implanted in me in the bourgeois schools. (Mao 1942/1967c, 73)

Mao used his personal example and experience to illustrate that the only way to fuse oneself with the masses and transform one's class consciousness into a pro-letarian type was to mingle with the masses, even if this process could be long and painful. Mao's hope was that when these writers and artists transformed themselves into proletarian revolutionaries, the masses would be correctly served. In Mao's words, "If our writers and artists who come from the intelligen-tsia want their works to be well received by the masses, they must change and remold their thinking and their feelings. Without such a change, without such remolding, they can do nothing well and will be misfits" (73). To achieve this goal, he argued, the intelligentsia needed to live with proletarians, think like them, and speak their language. In later years Mao launched campaigns, sending the edu-cated urban youths to the countryside and forcing many intellectuals to labor in "May Seventh" labor camps for reeducation.[21]

Content and Form of Art and Literature

To meet the goal of serving the revolutionary cause, writers and artists were required to abandon arts and literature that contained feudalized and bourgeois ideas; these artists were expected to produce artistic works that represented the lives and interests of the proletariat class. Mao encouraged writers and artists to find sources of and inspiration for such works from the masses. Mao stated, "The life of the people is always a mine of the raw materials for literature and art, materials in their natural form, materials that are crude, but most vital, rich and fundamental" (Mao 1942/1967c, 81). In Mao's view, only works of such nature could serve the revolutionary function of educating the masses and therefore propel history forward. By concentrating on everyday experiences of exploita-tion, oppression, and suffering of the masses, the works of literature and art functioned to "typify the contradictions and struggles within them and produce works which awaken the masses, fire them with enthusiasm and impel them to unite and struggle to transform their environment" (82).[22]

Mao indicated that drawing sources from real life was not enough; the story must be elevated above life in its themes and representations in order to create a persuasive effect and a transformative experience. In his words, "Life as reflected in the works of literature and art can and ought to be on a higher plane, more intense, more concentrated, more typical, nearer the ideal, and therefore more universal than actual everyday life" (Mao 1942/1967c, 82). Ban Wang (1997) observes, "Communist culture courts exuberant passions rather than rejects

them" (123) and that "emotion can be appropriated to enhance rather than dimin-
ish political identity and effectiveness" (124). It was Mao's belief that through
dramatic and exhilarating spectacles, the political consciousness of peasants and
the writers and artists themselves would be morally elevated and Chinese culture
would be transformed. This transformative process is close to the persuasive
effect of Aristotle's notion of "catharsis" and the outcome of using St. Augustine's
"grand style."

Another point Mao made regarding the works of proletarian art and literature
was the unity of standard and taste. Most of these writers and artists had written
and produced works in the past for the sake of art, using aesthetics that appealed
to the elite class. Mao directly instructed them: "Your work may be as good as 'the
spring snow" [a Chinese metaphor for highbrow art], but if for the time being it
caters only to the few and the masses are still singing the 'song of the rustic poor'
[a Chinese metaphor for low-taste art], you will get nowhere by simply scolding
them instead of trying to raise their level. The question now is how might artists
bring about a unity between 'the spring snow' and the 'song of the rustic poor,'
between higher standards and popularization" (Mao 1942/1967c, 85).[23]

Mao's message meant that artistic and literary works should appeal to the
masses without compromising artistic merits. Mao set up two criteria for evalu-
ating literary and artistic works: the political criterion and the aesthetic criterion.
To Mao, the best works of literature and art manifested the integration of both
the correct political content and the finest artistic form. In his words, "What we
demand is the unity of politics and art, the unity of content and form, the unity
of revolutionary political content and the highest possible perfection of artistic
form. Works of art which lack artistic quality have no force however progressive
they are politically. Therefore, we oppose both the tendency to produce works of
art with a wrong political viewpoint and the tendency towards the 'poster and
slogan style' which is correct in political viewpoint but lacking in artistic power"
(Mao 1942/1967c, 90).[24]

Here, Mao demanded from the artists a perfect union of the correct political
content with the highest art form. Presenting political messages in the finest art
forms has become the sole criteria for Communist arts and performances ever
since Mao made these assertions. "The Eight Model Plays" produced during the
Cultural Revolution under the supervision of Jiang Qing (Mao's wife) exemplified
this unity of politics and aesthetics. These "red classics" are still popular in China
even though the contents of the play are irrelevant to today's less politicized
situation in China. Wang (1997) points out that aesthetic appeals often have "hyp-
notic and seductive power" as they are "oriented to the viewers' taste, penetrated
into their feelings, and shaped by their aesthetic judgments" (213). As Burke (1968)
states, "Form *is* the appeal" (138) because form serves to arouse and fulfill desires,
create needs, whet the appetite, and provide satisfaction in the minds and hearts

of the audience (31, 124). The Communist propaganda has used grandiose epic, heroic narrative, and subliminal forms to exhort emotion and mass hysteria. Such artistic forms have proven extremely effective, especially when the audience is uncritical and unsophisticated.

Refutation of the Opposing Views

In response to potential resistance to his requirements, Mao targeted the possible moral and logical flaws emerging from those who would oppose his ideas. Among the seven claims he refuted in the speech, three were closely related to rhetoric and deserve some attention. In refuting the claim that "literature and artistic works have always laid equal stress on the bright and the dark, half and half" (Mao 1942/1967c, 91), Mao used the Soviet Union as an example to develop his argument, contending that Soviet literature and art depicted only the positive elements of the Soviet people and government while writers of the bourgeoisie portrayed the masses as mobs. Thus, he argued, no "half-and-half" in art and literature exists. He wrote, "Only truly revolutionary writers and artists can correctly solve the problem of whether to extol or to expose. All the dark forces harming the masses of the people must be exposed and all the revolutionary struggles of the masses of the people must be extolled" (91). From the time of Mao's declaration to the present, CCP propaganda has reported only good news; bad news is swept away. In reporting and commenting on the CCP's top leaders, only praise, not criticism, is voiced.

Another position Mao refuted was "I am not given to praise and eulogy. The works of people who eulogize what is bright are not necessarily great and the works of those who depict the dark are not necessarily paltry" (Mao 1942/1967c, 92). Mao countered, "If you are a bourgeois writer or artist, you will eulogize not the proletariat but the bourgeoisie, and if you are a proletarian writer or artist, you will eulogize not the bourgeoisie but the proletariat and working people; it must be one or the other" (92). Mao denounced the type of writer who was not interested in the proletarian cause because, he said, that writer was not motivated to eulogize the deeds of the revolutionary people. Mao called such types of persons "termites" (93). By doing so, Mao moralized and politicized works of art, and he divided writers and artists into two classes: supporters of the proletariat and supporters of the bourgeoisie. Those with the proletarian cause in mind were motivated to praise the masses, and those who still held on to the bourgeoisie stand were deemed to be class enemies.

Some writers and artists claimed, "It is not a question of stand; my class stand is correct, my intentions are good and I understand all right, but I am not good at expressing myself and so the effect turns out bad" (Mao 1942/1967c, 93). This is a scenario when an artist has a good motive but does not have the talent or skill to render appropriately a desirable effect. Mao responded by illustrating the relationship between motive and effect with an analogy: "A person who acts solely by motive and does not inquire what effect his actions will have is like a doctor who merely writes prescriptions but does not care how many patients die of them" (93). For Mao, a revolutionary motive was not sufficient; persuasive effect was the ultimate measurement of what an ideal literary and artistic work was. Only those who considered the effects of their actions and insured that those effects would bring changes in people were deemed truly admirable and politically correct. Through techniques of refutation and by effective use of metaphors and logical, emotional, and ethnical appeals, Mao "skillfully alleviates the resistance on the part of his audience" (Wang 2000, 189).

In the "Talks," Mao redefined the goals of art and literature for the revolutionary cause and for ideological conformity. He explicated a new moral/ethical standard and required a change of attitude for the rhetor who must conform to Marxist ideology and produce artistic works for the interest and consumption of the proletariat. Mao specified the content and form of revolutionary art and literature and the audience for which the art production was created. Mao established a mode of rhetorical criticism that must examine both political implications and artistic merits in artwork. In this speech Mao employed rhetorical techniques of metaphor, analogy, refutation, examples, ethical appeals, and deductive and inductive reasoning. He used young intellectuals as agents of change in the cultural transformation while also requiring them to change themselves in their own political consciousness and cultural orientation. Mao subverted traditional Chinese values surrounding education by giving eminence to the uneducated masses. His instruction for party propaganda advocated for a combination of politically "correct" content displayed through artistic form to produce the best persuasive effect. However, Mao's adherence to positive content that praised the party restricted alternative productions of art and silenced dissenting voices. Karl (2010) writes, "The Party came to control and enforce what was defined as revolutionary. It was also the Party that came to define and enforce what was culturally appropriate to the moment" (65). With these requirements, Mao began the work of replacing the "old culture" with a "party culture" that politicized art and literature; he subordinated art and literature to ideological dogma. Intellectuals from this point forward had to reform themselves in the prescribed manner for fear of being accused of having "bourgeois thoughts."

Mao's "Talks" had an epochal influence on Chinese practices of literature and art. The speech and the proclamations within it fundamentally changed the relationship between the educated and the masses; Mao persuaded to his position a large number of left-wing and radical writers while silencing dissenting voices. Mao's style of refutation set an example for Chinese political writing and changed the style of big-character posters during China's Cultural Revolution.[25] Moreover, his "Talks" had a significant impact on China's cultural policy, a policy still practiced today.

Under Mao's regime, educated intellectuals were the primary targets for political campaigns and were forced to conduct self-criticism in both spoken and written form as ways to prove their loyalty to Mao. Mao used these persons for propaganda purposes, but at the same time he did not trust them politically and ideologically. Even if Lu Xun had lived through Mao's era, he would not have been able to survive Mao's series of thought-reform campaigns.[26]

Mao's Theory on Persuasion

For Mao, the role of propaganda was absolutely essential in creating a revolutionary culture, educating the peasant constituency and transforming the minds of the intellectuals into a proletarian consciousness.[27] But who would create the propaganda, and how would their work achieve the desired outcome or persuasive effect? Mao relied on the educated, although he did not trust those who criticized him or his policies on arts and literature. Mao said that propagandists "include not only teachers, journalists, writers and artists, but all our cadres" (Mao 1942/1967c, 60). To facilitate and expedite the process, Mao called for language reformation and rhetorical modification in both oral and written communication.

In traditional Chinese culture, written language was highly literary, distinctive from spoken Chinese in structure and vocabulary. Known as classical Chinese, the written form was concise, compact, and condensed in meaning. Literary references were not always acknowledged; educated Chinese readers were expected to know the sources.[28] Thus the ability to read and write literary classical Chinese was reserved for the educated elite in imperial China. Not until the early twentieth century was classical Chinese replaced by vernacular Chinese—language similar to modern spoken Mandarin both in structure and in vocabulary. This language reform was initiated by Hu Shi, a student of John Dewey from the school of pragmatist philosophy; Dewey visited and lectured in China between May 1919 and July 1921. In one of his lectures, Dewey called for a bridge of the gaps between written and spoken language to facilitate the spread of democratic ideas and to achieve associated living in China (Dewey 1973).[29] Hu Shi applied Dewey's concepts to China's situation and called for an implementation of "a national speech" or vernacular speech to replace the antiquated classical/literary written Chinese. Hu (2002) argues, "Those who use a dead classical style will translate their own ideas into allusions of several thousand years ago and convert their own feelings into literary expressions of centuries past" (360). To Hu, such a way of writing would stifle expression of new ideas and impede communication.[30] With the support of other Chinese intellectuals, language reform, formally referred to as the "Vernacular Movement" in the early twentieth century, enabled more people to read and write and expedited the Chinese public communication process. Moreover, as Chang (2002) states,

"Baihua [vernacular] served as a tool for the dissemination of new ideas essential for the creation of new culture" (53). As a strong proponent and skilled practitioner of vernacular Chinese, Mao was keenly aware that to educate the masses and transform China, vernacular Chinese language must be used in a way that was understandable to the masses.

In his speech titled "Rectify the Party's Style of Work," presented to students at the opening ceremony of the party school in 1942, Mao identified three main problems in the party propaganda on writing: namely, subjectivism, sectarianism, and stereotyped party writing (Mao 1942/1967c, 36). Among the three problems, Mao showed a strong dislike of "stereotyped party writing" and accused such writing of being "a vehicle for filth, a form of expression for subjectivism and sectarianism. It does people harm and damages the revolution, and we must get rid of it completely" (49). Stereotyped party writing is an appropriation of the classical Chinese "eight-legged essay," which requires a particular format and eight sections in a complete essay.[31] In the speech Mao condemned stereotyped party writing and used the term "eight-legged essay" as a metaphor to refer to those writings that still contained traces of antiquated writing style and failed to conform to the ideology of Marxism-Leninism. Mao particularly criticized the Confucian writings and other classical texts that served only the ruling class. Mao considered such writings old dogma and credited the May Fourth Movement for eradicating such writings, although he had learned Confucian teachings through classical language. Mao directed eight indictments against the "eight-legged style" or "the stereotyped party style" of writing, as he used the two terms interchangeably.

The First Indictment

Mao charged that stereotyped party writing or eight-legged writing lacks substance in that "it fills endless pages with empty verbiage.... Those who write long articles with no substance are like the foot-bonding of a slattern, long as well as smelly" (Mao 1942/1967c, 56). Mao further qualified his statement by saying that the problem was not length but the lack of substance: "Articles devoid of substance are the least justifiable and the most objectionable. The same applies to speech-making; we must put an end to all empty, long-winded speeches" (57). This point on substance in writing was first raised by Hu Shi in his 1917 essay "A Preliminary Discussion of Literary Reform." Hu pointed out that the old classical form of writing placed too much emphasis on form instead of substance, a practice that created barriers to communicating emotions and ideas. Mao adopted Hu Shi's point to suit the need of ideological control. He expected Communist writers to explain Marxist-Leninist ideological concepts, express revolutionary ideas, and convey passion for revolutions. Writings that emphasized only style would fail to achieve these goals.

The Second Indictment

Mao was concerned that stereotyped party writing or eight-legged essay writing was "pretentious with the deliberate intention of intimidating people" (57). Mao argued that such writings would have no effect on defeating the enemy but would hurt the proletariat class. In Mao's view, the audience could be pulled away because of the writer's pedantic style, which was often difficult for the masses to comprehend. Mao noted that some audiences easily could be put off by the harsh criticisms, and thus it was necessary for the propagandist to "speak warmly and sincerely with a desire to protect the cause of the people and raise their consciousness and must not indulge in ridicule and attack" (Mao 1957/1977, 431). It is ironic that both Mao and Lu Xun used satire and profanity in their own writing to attack their opponents.

The Third Indictment

Mao pointed out that stereotyped party writing or eight-legged writing failed to adapt to the audience. He was concerned that "we do not always know how to speak simply, concretely, in images which are familiar and intelligible to the masses. We are still unable to refrain from abstract formulas which we have learned by rote" (Mao 1942/1967c, 65). Mao was undoubtedly an advocate for using vernacular and simple language to communicate complicated ideas. He advised the propagandists to bear their proletariat audiences in mind and avoid "playing the lute to a cow" (59). Mao then used another analogy to illustrate his point further: "When shooting an arrow, one must aim at the target; when playing the lute, one must consider the listener; how, then, can one write articles or make speeches without taking the reader or the audience into account?" (59). Hu Shi offered advice on eight areas of how language should be used effectively, but he did not speak specifically about audience adaptation.[32] In the classical tradition, writings and speeches were circulated only among the educated elites. With the influence of Mao and Hu Shi, the Chinese audience had been expanded to include peasants, workers, and soldiers; reaching this new audience called for a change of writing style and a shift in what would constitute clarity in writing. Mao often demonstrated his rhetorical talent in using plain language to explain abstract concepts or introduce new terms. Xu (2013) provides two examples. When he was the organizer of an evening school in his hometown, Mao told other young teachers to use the term "foreign landlord" to explain to peasant students what "imperialism" meant. Another example is that Mao used the term "butt" to explain to his peasant soldiers what a revolutionary base meant. Just as a "butt" is required for a person to sit and rest, so is the function of a military base.

Mao's sense of audience adaptation was also influenced by Lenin and other socialist revolutionary leaders. For example, Mao referenced how Lenin wrote the first leaflet of agitation in plain Russian language, language with which Russian workers were familiar. This use of simple language may have played a significant role in persuading Russian workers that socialists could bring goodness to their lives. Mao told his Chinese comrades that "we must work in the spirit of Lenin. That is, we must do as Lenin did and not fill endless pages with verbiage, or shoot at random without considering the audience, or become self-opinioned and bombastic" (Mao 1942/1967c, 65). Moreover, Mao referenced Georgi Mikhaylov Dimitrov (1882–1949), a Bulgarian Communist politician, and his speech at the Seventh World Congress of the Communist International as another good example of how to speak to the masses: "We must learn to talk to the masses, not in the language of book formulas, but in the language of fighters for the cause of the masses, whose every work, whose every idea reflects the innermost thoughts and sentiments of millions.... The masses cannot assimilate our decisions unless we learn to speak the language which the masses understand" (65). Here, Mao advised his party propagandists to seek identification with the masses through appealing to the audience's values and using their language for effective persuasion.

The Fourth Indictment

Mao used the slang *biesan* (a term used in Shanghai for extremely thin and wretched-looking people who live by begging or stealing) to describe the lack of vividness in stereotyped party writing or eight-legged writing. In Mao's words, "If an article or a speech rings the changes on a few terms in a classroom tone without a shred of vigor or spirit, is it not rather like a *piebsan* [*biesan*], drab of speech and repulsive in appearance?" (Mao 1942/1967c, 59). Mao lamented, "At present many of our comrades doing propaganda work make no study of language. Their propaganda is very dull, and few people care to read their articles or listen to their talk" (59).

Mao encouraged these comrades to enrich their vocabularies and develop their language skills, drawing from three sources. The first source was from the masses, whose vocabulary "is rich, vigorous, vivid, and expressive of real life" (Mao 1942/1967c, 60). The second source came from foreign language, but the choice of vocabulary should be selective and should suit the needs of revolution. The third source was from classical Chinese language that was still alive and useful for revolutionary purposes (60). In this sense Mao did not object completely to the use of classical language and foreign words as long as they were vivid, rich, and effective. Mao's own writing style had been influenced by Han Yu, Zeng Guofan, Liang Qichao, and Lu Xun, all of whom were known for writing in vivid language.

The Fifth Indictment

Mao had disdain for the eight-legged writing style because of its convoluted arrangement, which often confused an audience. Mao used the analogy of Chinese medicine to illustrate his point:

Go and take a look at any Chinese pharmacy, and you will see cabinets with numerous drawers, each bearing the name of a drug—toncal, foxglove, rhubarb, saltpetre...indeed everything that should be there. This method has been picked up by our comrades. In their articles and speeches, their books and reports, they use first the big Chinese numerals, second the small Chinese numerals, third the characters for the ten celestial stems, fourth the characters for the twelve earthly branches, and then capital A, B, C, D, then small a, b, c, d, followed by the Arabic numerals, and what not!...For all its verbiage, an article that bristles with such symbols, that does not pose, analyze or solve problems and that does not take a stand for or against anything is devoid of real content and is nothing but a Chinese pharmacy. (Mao 1942/1967c, 60–61).

Studies on Chinese rhetoric by both Chinese and Western scholars have indicated that the Chinese use a variety of argumentative techniques and structural devices in their writing (for example, Garrett 1993; Hu 1993; Kirkpatrick 2002; Lu 1998). However, because Chinese is a high-context language and because Chinese thinking patterns tend to be circular (Kaplan 1966), some writing can be indirect when presenting an argument. Chinese rhetoric also places more responsibility on the audience to decipher meanings and less emphasis on the clarity of the speaker. Mao intended to change this rhetorical practice. Mao maintained that clear organization and effective structure in writing and speeches made the talks easier to follow and understand, especially when the audiences were less educated. Mao set an example for this straightforward style in his own writing.

The Sixth Indictment

Mao considered stereotyped party writing or eight-legged writing irresponsible and harmful to the audience. He criticized writers who did not understand the issue at hand before they wrote. They may be talented writers, Mao contended, but they did not take responsibility for what they wrote if they did not do the preparation work and did not proofread what they had written with the care with which "they would examine their faces in the mirror after washing" (Mao 1942/1967c, 62). Consequently bad writing may look like a "thousand words from the pen in a stream, but ten thousand li away from the theme" (62). Mao required writers to work hard in preparing and polishing their writing, and he exhorted them to develop a habit of examining themselves. Writing was a social and moral responsibility for the society, Mao explained, and it had an impact on the readers.

The writer must have knowledge in breadth and depth to produce good writing that brings a positive influence. Specifically Mao required that writers be familiar with the topics they wrote about so that they could make their points more persuasively. He referenced the Confucius saying "think twice" and Han Yu's words "A deed is accomplished through taking thought" (Mao 1942/1967c, 66) to make his point. Particularly Mao referenced Lu Xun's guidance in writing:

"reading it over twice after writing"; and "striking out non-essential words, sentences and paragraphs" (66). Mao recommended four readings as examples to follow for responsible writing: *The History of the Communist Party of the Soviet Union;* Dimitrov's statements at the Seventh World Congress of the Communist International; *The Complete Works of Lu Xun;* and the report from the Sixth Plenary Session of the Sixth Central Committee of the Communist Party of China.

The Seventh and Eighth Indictments

Mao accused stereotyped party writing or eight-legged writing of "poisoning the whole Party and jeopardizing the revolution" (Mao 1942/1967c, 62). The final indictment of such writing was that it "would wreck the country and ruin the people" (63). Mao's strong warning about the dangers of stereotyped party writing was linked to the life and death of the Communist cause. It is apparent that Mao recognized the significant role of rhetoric, both in form and content, in promoting, popularizing, and implementing his Communist ideology and political agenda. Mao's own writing on rhetoric was vehement, sarcastic, and scathing. His use of metaphors, analogies, quotations, and cultural references set up good examples for writing that would be clear, vivid, and persuasive.

Mao gave preeminence to the CCP's propaganda as it concerned the success or failure of the Communist cause in China. Mao's theory of persuasion aimed at rectifying the writing style of the party propagandists who were still influenced by traditional Chinese classical writing. Because of his strong belief that language shaped thought and action (similar to the linguistic relativity theory), Mao was extremely concerned with how language was used and how rhetoric functioned to adapt a message to an audience of common people, largely composed of uneducated peasants. For Mao, the topic of the writing must have substance of Marxist ideology and revolutionary content. The organization of the writing must be clear and straightforward; the language must be clear and vivid. A good rhetor must be responsible for what he or she was writing and must know how to adapt to the audience. Mao's list of indictments covered three rhetorical canons out of the five conceptualized by Cicero. Mao's prescription for rhetorical effectiveness identified him as keenly aware of the rhetoric used in modern China.

However, Mao did not quite reach his goals successfully. Stereotyped or pedantic party writing continued to plague the party propaganda. After he had firmly established his authority in China in 1949, Mao was still concerned that "some of the articles appearing today are extremely pretentious but empty, without any analysis of problems or reasoned argument, and they carry no conviction" (Mao 1957/1977, 430). Mao reiterated a message and warning in his speech at the National Propaganda Working Conference of the Chinese Communist Party in 1957 similar to the one he had given fifteen years earlier. Mao made it clear that propaganda was the work of persuasion, aiming to transform the Chinese mind to believe in the

Marxist theory of class struggle and to cause Chinese people to become loyal to the party instead of to their families and friends. Mao advised writers, "When writing an article, one should not be forever thinking, 'how smart I am!' but should put oneself on a completely equal footing with one's readers....The more you put on airs, the less people will stand for it and the less they care to read your articles. We should do our work honestly, take an analytical approach, write convincingly and never strike a pose to overawe people" (430–31).

Mao was caught in an irony. On one hand, he had to rely on the educated intellectuals to create and engage in the work of propaganda by calling them "educators" or "intellectuals." On the other hand, Mao did not trust these educated intellectuals because they belonged to the bourgeois class and needed to be reformed and "reeducated." Mao's perception seems to have been that in comparison to the working-class people, intellectuals were too arrogant, conservative, unstable, and undependable, not willing to shift their class consciousness to a proletariat one. Thus, Mao requested that they mingle with workers and peasants so that the intellectual might learn from their language and way of living.

In his *Marxism and Philosophy of Language,* Mikhail Bakhtin (1973) claims that language is inherently ideological. Words humans use reflect one's ideological position and serve the function of constructing the world. Mao's theory of persuasion was strictly explicated for the purpose of reinforcing Communist ideology and strengthening the leadership of the Communist Party. However, Bakhtin questions monolithic knowledge of truth and doubts if there is any correct view. Mao, in stark contrast, advocated the use of language for establishing ideological conformity and totalitarian control. Bakhtin proposes multiple voices or *hereroglossia* to allow diversity of expressions and perspectives. Mao restricted the use of language in such a way that silenced opposing voices and stifled freedom of expression.

Some intellectuals had to modify their aesthetic standards and fake their ideological guise to adapt to the knowledge level of the masses. They took these actions for the sake of ideological correctness and to avoid being persecuted as class enemies. Many writers had been criticized for not praising the party and masses enough and also were accused of having ulterior motives of opposing the masses and overthrowing the CCP. Many writers stopped writing after 1949 under the Communist rule because of such political suppression. The masses, in contrast, were easily persuaded and became blind followers of Mao's revolutionary rhetoric. As language was simplified, cognitive complexity was reduced, and the ability to think critically was deprived. Mao's rhetoric exhorted followers and destroyed enemies, but it also created dichotomized and radical thinking among the Chinese people.

In conclusion, Mao's theories of rhetoric were rooted in his philosophical views of epistemology and dialectical materialism informed by the secondhand Soviet-expressed Marxism. Mao believed that knowledge came from experiences and practice, requiring that educated intellectuals learn from the experiences of peasants, workers, and soldiers. Mao was convinced that contradiction, struggle, and conflict were imminent and inevitable in the process of achieving revolutionary goals. Arts and literature should serve the masses and the transformation of the Chinese mind and culture. Good writing should have substance, be well organized, use simple and vivid language, and adapt to the audience. Educated intellectuals were responsible for clearly and plainly explaining and expressing Marxist-Leninist ideologies; they also were expected to align their ideas with the CCP's political agenda and propaganda commitment.

Mao claimed to be a true Marxist, but his reading of Marx's works was limited. Nevertheless it is apparent that Lenin's and Stalin's works had major impacts on Mao's philosophical orientation, political ideology, and theories on art and literature. Mao's doctrine that art and literature should be subordinate to politics was a direct influence from the Soviet Union. Mao's advocacy for a cultural army to defeat dogmatic tradition and purge antiquated habits of writing established Mao as a vanguard for continued radicalism toward eliminating traditional Chinese culture since the May Fourth Movement.

Yet it is evident that Mao's theories of rhetoric also were influenced by Confucian thought, Daoist epistemology, and other Chinese intellectual traditions. Mao was well versed in Chinese classics and extremely knowledgeable about historical figures and events, legends and myths, war strategies and governing tactics. Mao made numerous references to these classical and popular symbolic resources throughout his writings. Thus it is not surprising that Mao was eloquent and persuasive as he appealed to traditional Chinese values using popular examples to illustrate his messages and as he appealed to the Soviet leader explaining Western Communist principles to justify his arguments for China's revolution. The hybridity of the Chinese tradition and foreign ideas had provided for Mao not only ethos, pathos, and logos in his arguments but also the basis from which his revolutionary rhetoric was derived, ultimately leading to what he hoped would be the transformation of the Chinese society and the Chinese mind. Ironically Mao's theories of rhetoric appeared to champion subaltern studies and give voice to ordinary Chinese people. While this positive aspect of Mao's rhetoric can be acknowledged, such rhetoric could also be perceived as serving to strengthen his authoritarian rule and stifle freedom of speech among Chinese intellectuals.

THREE

★ ★ ★ ★

Mao Zedong's Rhetorical Styles

Foreigners who have met and spoken with Mao Zedong were impressed by his charisma and eloquence. Edgar Snow met Mao in 1936 and recorded this first impression: "Mao seemed to me a very interesting and complex man. He had the simplicity and naturalness of the Chinese peasant, with a lively sense of humor and a love of rustic laughter.... [H]e combines curious qualities of naiveté with incisive wit and worldly sophistication.... He was a good speaker, a man with an unusual memory and extraordinary powers of concentration" (Snow 1938, 92–93). Twenty-six years later when Richard Nixon traveled to Beijing, he observed that Mao "has a remarkable sense of humor" and that "despite poor health, he [Mao] was sharp from an intellectual stand point" (Nixon 1978, 561, 621).

Ordinary Chinese people had little opportunity to create impressions about Mao based on face-to-face interactions. Although records show that Mao delivered many public speeches during his political and military career, Chinese people rarely heard Mao speak after 1949 because he gave speeches only at the CCP congregations after that date. The people could see pictures of Mao giving speeches, pictures which indicated Mao's intense facial expressions and forceful use of gestures. Recordings of his speeches demonstrated his use of vocal variation, emotional tone, and strategic pauses. Mao spoke with a strong Hunan accent but was understandable to most Chinese. His delivery was eloquent by both Chinese and Western standards. Many of his speeches, in fact, were later revised into essays.[1]

Rhetorical Influence from Chinese Scholars

Two scholars in Chinese history had the most impact on Mao's rhetorical style: Han Yu (韩愈) and Liang Qichao (梁启超). Han Yu (768–824) was an eminent Confucian scholar from the Tang dynasty (618–907). He was vehement about eradicating Buddhism, even at the risk of offending the emperor, a practicing Buddhist. The problem with Buddhism, according to Han Yu, is that it rejects the state, shows no respect for the rulers, and does not care about the well-being of families and society. Han Yu called Buddha "a man of the barbarian who did not speak the language of China.... He understood neither the duties that bind sovereign and subject nor the affections of father and son" (De Bary and Bloom 1999,

584).[2] Confucianism, in contrast, considers individuals' moral perfection as the impetus for a good family, social harmony, and a strong state. For Han Yu, the Confucian sense of humaneness was the only moral way that provided inner power for virtuous acts that benefited society. Compared with Confucianism, Buddhism would not bring any concrete benefits to improving the standard of living for the people, as its ultimate goal is to achieve enlightenment of individuals through meditation. Han obstinately spoke against Buddhism and clearly identified its harms to Chinese society with words of sarcasm and antagonism. Han praised Confucianism and extolled its value in building a moral and prosperous society. He also was an advocate for returning to what he considered to be the simple and straightforward "classical style" (the style of the Qin dynasty, 221–201 B.C.E., and the Han dynasty, 206 B.C.E.–220 C.E.) of writing. Han Yu wrote a number of prominent essays using this classical style.

Han's writing was characterized by straightforward statements and a forceful tone. In his essays defending Confucianism and condemning Buddhism and Daoism, he redefined the philosophical concepts of *ren* (benevolence) and *dao* (the way), referred to Confucian texts to enhance the historical prominence of Confucianism in Chinese culture, used evidence to demonstrate the economic benefits of Confucianism, and pointed out the absurdity of Daoism and Buddhism.[3] Han Yu's use of language was considered forthright, unconstrained, shocking, and free-spirited.[4] His rhetorical style marked a milestone in Chinese history and impacted Chinese culture and the Chinese people's thought pattern for generations after his death. Li Rui, the author of *Mao's Reading Life in His Early Years,* observes that Mao's writing shows traces of Han's influence. Not only is Mao's style similar to that of Han's in expression and sentence structure, but also his phraseology reflects Han's work; in fact, many phrases used by Mao in his five volumes of selected works are verbatim from Han's essays (Li 2005a). Similar to Han Yu's, Mao's acclaimed life goal was to build a strong and prosperous China without oppression and inequality—ultimately, a moral society. The difference between Han Yu's and Mao's beliefs is that Han promoted Confucianism and envisioned using the values of *ren* and the wisdom of *dao* to achieve prosperity without inequality, while Mao defended Marxism instead of Confucianism, redefined words such as "people" and "revolution," used evidence of the CCP's achievement, and condemned Chiang Kai-shek.

Mao's writing and liberal thoughts also were much influenced by Liang Qichao (1873–1929), a prominent scholar and reformer who led the intellectual discourse on modernity and nationalism when China was transitioning from the Qing dynasty to the Republic of China (1912–49) after centuries of being ruled under an imperial system. Liang was a prolific writer on Chinese culture, Chinese history, and comparisons between Chinese and Western cultures. Liang founded and was the chief editor of a biweekly journal, *Xinmin Congbao* 新民丛报 (*New*

Citizen) founded in 1902. The journal covered a variety of topics on social and political issues, both domestic and foreign. The journal was aimed at awakening Chinese people about these issues by using a style of writing that was both semi-classical and semivernacular Chinese. Liang's writing and reform ideas inspired Mao. Mao was a devout reader of every article Liang published in the journal and could even recite some of his articles (Li 2005b).

Liang's writings were characterized by his commitment to building a national consciousness among the Chinese people. Joseph Levenson (1959) summarized Liang's writing as "documents of acculturation, the process of displacement or modification of the techniques, institutions, values and attitudes of one culture by those of another" (34). Liang was a strong advocate for nationalism. In his view, the main reason for the fall of imperial rule was not internal corruption but rather that the Chinese people lacked a sense of citizenship and responsibility for their own society. A new country, argued Liang, needed its people to have a unified outlook on perpetuating the well-being of their nation as a whole (Levenson 1959). Under Liang's influence, Mao organized a New Citizen Association (新民学会), founded in 1918 and serving the purpose of reforming the minds of the Chinese people. Mao's mission for the New Citizen Association was to educate the Chinese people by using simple language and by transforming their characters from what Lin Yu-tang (1962) described as "family-oriented, passive, self-content, mild, patient" (chapter 2) into active citizens of the state with feisty and revolutionary spirits.

Liang is the most influential writer in Chinese modern history, in terms of both quantity and eloquence. The renowned scholar Yan Fu (严复) (1854–1921) praised Liang for "using a magic pen to shake society" (1986, 632, 646). Liang's advocacy for a "new style" became the model of writing throughout China. Liang's writing has been characterized as "clear and well organized, flowing with emotions and enthusiasm, casting a spell over the readers" (Li 2005b, 4). Those who read Liang's works often found themselves "shaken by the words either to great anger or with tears in their eyes" (Wu 2009, 29). Moreover, Yu Xilai (2009) credits Liang Qichao for his "authoritarian tone and charismatic persona." He describes Liang's speeches and writings as characterized by optimism, progress, and inspiration, aiming to boost national self-esteem and confidence. In terms of style, according to Yu (2009), Liang tended to present his view with an imposing manner in writing political commentaries, using an excess of prophesy and parallelism. Mao Sheng once commented that Liang's writing style was "sharp in presenting an argument, clear in reasoning, impassioned and untrammeled, forthright and forceful....He was the most charismatic political commentator at the time" (Mao Sheng 2011).[5] Mao Zedong's writings show strong traces of Liang's influence in the use of language, argumentation styles, and perceived rhetorical effect. In July 1919 Mao established the journal *Xiangjiang Pinglun* 湘江评论 (Xiangjiang Commentary). These traces of Liang's influence in rhetorical style are evident in the number of his editorial commentaries.[6] Furthermore young Mao wrote a manifesto for the journal in vernacular language, the use of which helped him reach ordinary Chinese readers who were not able to understand classical Chinese language.

Mao's shift from writing in classical Chinese language to writing in vernacular was fundamental in creating a persuasive effect on his readers. The vernacular movement (or *baihua* movement) was initiated by Hu Shi 胡适 (1891–1962), a writer, educator, and philosopher and a doctoral student of John Dewey.[7] Hu first published an essay in a liberal journal, *Xin Qingnian* 新青年 (*New Youth*), in the January 1917 issue proposing the replacement of classical language (*guwen* 古文) with vernacular language (*baihua* 白话) in writing.[8] Chen Duxiu 陈独秀, the editor in chief of *New Youth*, supported Hu's proposal and began to publish articles in vernacular language. Other prominent intellectuals such as Qian Xuantong 钱玄同 and Lu Xun 鲁迅 followed suit in their own writing. It was Hu's hope that this drastic change in written communication would revitalize the Chinese language and signify a literary revolution so that new thoughts could be communicated to ordinary Chinese people and a modern culture could be created as a result. Hu Shi was influenced by his teacher John Dewey, who proposed that China's modernization must be based on a transformation of the Chinese culture and mind. He purported that such a transformation could be facilitated through the use of a common language to affect consciousness, communication, and action (Dewey 1981). As Chang (2002) notes, the *baihua* movement "swept the nation like a wild fire and became the most intriguing cultural phenomenon in twentieth-century China" (50).

No clear evidence has emerged that Mao attended Dewey's lectures, but Mao supported the *baihua* movement and started writing his own essays in vernacular language. Moreover, Mao spent much of his life attempting to transform the Chinese culture, the minds of Chinese people, and the way Chinese people communicated. In his manifesto of the journal, *Xiangjiang Ping Lun* (Xiang Jiang Commentary), Mao used vernacular language in a way that was close to the spoken word, and he remained incisive and to the point. He called the reader's attention to China's problems through a question-and-answer form: "What is the biggest problem in the world? Putting food on the table is the biggest problem. What is the most powerful strength? A united front of all people is the most powerful. What [is not to be feared]? Do not be afraid of heaven; do not be afraid of ghost[s]; do not be afraid of dead people; do not be afraid of bureaucrats; do not be afraid of warlords; and do not be afraid of capitalists" (Mao 1919/1995, 292). These simple terms demonstrate Mao's pragmatic orientation as well as his spirit of audaciousness in solving China's problems. As Mao was at this point in his life a young man with a passion to save his country, his rhetoric seems to have been genuine and straightforward.

Mao's multifaceted writing targeted different types of audiences at different times in history. Some sections of his writings appeared logical, abstract, and filled with historical knowledge and the mastery of classics that appealed to educated readers. Other sections revealed his style as down to earth and much more acceptable to ordinary people. In some of his writings Mao presented himself with the rhetoric of a teacher, educating his readers about history, philosophy, and Chinese classics. In other writings Mao was a storyteller, narrating China's history and using metaphors to illustrate a point of view, moving and pleasing his audience in the process. He exhibited a fondness for using chain reasoning, allusion, slogans, historical references, quotations from literary texts, and words of condemnation when attacking his political enemies. Mao's rhetorical styles and strategies can be identified and analyzed in light of four recurring elements in his discourse: 1) the use of metaphors and analogies; 2) the use of history and Chinese classics; 3) the redefining of revolutionary terms; and 4) the use of profanity, emotive words, and violent language.

Use of Metaphors and Analogies

In their book *Metaphors We Live By,* Lakoff and Johnson (1980) argue that metaphors do not simply function as linguistic decorations but rather reflect, structure, and instigate thoughts and actions. Ultimately these authors argue that people think metaphorically and are persuaded by metaphors because metaphors reside in a person's conceptual system. Foss (2009) explains, "A metaphor joins two terms normally regarded as belonging to different classes of experience" (267). These two terms are the tenor and the vehicle. "The tenor is the topic or subject that is being explained. The vehicle is the mechanism or lens through which the topic is viewed" (267). Metaphors carry implicit meanings and values, paint pictures of reality, and serve to present arguments. Metaphors also can contribute to miscommunication of a message, creating a false sense of reality and presenting a biased perspective on issues and people. The effects of metaphors are directly related to the cultural values and experiences of the listeners. Decades of studies have demonstrated that Chinese rhetoric is characterized by the use of metaphors and analogies as sources of proof and argumentation (Jensen 1992; Lu 1998; Oliver 1971). Mao's writings are no exception.

Mao lived in a period of a drastic social transition in China, and he appeared to be a vanguard of Marxist ideology.[9] He undertook the task of explaining new ideas and arousing a new level of consciousness among the Chinese people, including the educated elites. Mao skillfully employed rhetorical resources from Chinese language and culture, filling his writings with metaphors and analogies with which most Chinese people were familiar. In his writings three major types of metaphors that demonstrated intensity and frequency were employed: nature metaphors; animal metaphors; and metaphors involving moving objects.

Nature Metaphors

After the "Mari Massacre," in which hundreds of Communist Party members were killed and arrested by Chiang Kai-shek's military forces on April 12, 1927, the CCP's numbers were greatly reduced and morale was low. Mao analyzed the situation and presented an optimistic prediction for the fate of the party. He used an old Chinese saying, "A single spark can start a prairie fire," to title his essay, implying that the burgeoning revolution would spread and ultimately make a lasting impact on the nation. Mao used the saying to encourage those who felt beaten down by oppositional forces to have hope and confidence. Mao explained, "Our forces, although small at present, will grow very rapidly" (Mao 1930/1967a, 119). He envisioned a "high tide of revolution," attainable and inevitable. He used vivid and poetic descriptions for this future vision by saying, "It is like a ship far out at sea whose mast-head can already be seen from the shore; it is like the morning sun in the east whose shimmering rays are visible from a high mountain top; it is like a child about to be born moving restlessly in its mother's womb" (127). The sea, the morning sun, the mountaintop, and the child in the mother's womb were vehicles through which a bright future of China's revolution (tenor) was painted. Ralph Mueller (2010) calls such a use of metaphor "creative metaphor" that employs literary expressions in political speeches to persuade. Such use of metaphor combines ethical and aesthetical evaluations in communicating and constructing an optimistic outlook of reality.

Toward the end of the Anti-Japanese War, Mao promoted a policy of "better troops and simpler administration" (Mao 1942/1967c, 99), which meant the reduction of personnel and the shrinking of war apparatuses. Mao anticipated some resistance to this policy among his comrades, but he argued that the current situation necessitated and justified the change of policy. To insure that his readers understood his point, Mao used several analogies in his arguments. One was the weather-changing analogy, which included a metaphor about changing clothes. Mao wrote, "When the weather changes, it becomes necessary to change one's clothing. Each year as spring turns into summer, summer into autumn, autumn into winter and winter into spring, we have to make this change. But owing to the force of habit people sometimes fail to make it at the proper turn and they fall ill. Present conditions in the base areas already require us to shed our winter garments and put on summer clothing so that we can move about nimbly to fight the enemy, but we are still heavily padded and weighed down, and quite unfit for combat" (101).

Mao used this clothes metaphor to justify the "better troops and simpler administration" policy under his leadership. For him, policy change was natural and inevitable, like the cycle of seasons. People needed to conform to the new policy like they needed to adapt to different weather conditions by changing clothes for each season. The changing of seasons and consequent adaptation of clothing constituted a familiar conceptual framework for the mass audience. This metaphorical view trivialized the impact of policy change and minimized any resistance to it; adapting to policy change was depicted as a matter of adjustment rather than of forced action.

In a similar way Mao used a metaphor of a peach tree to persuade his audience to scorn Chiang Kai-shek. By 1945 the Japanese had surrendered, and the whole Chinese nation celebrated in victory. Mao claimed the victory in the Anti-Japanese War as the Chinese people's victory, not as a victory belonging to Chiang Kai-shek. Mao accused Chiang of not expending enough effort to fight the Japanese and deemed Chiang Kai-shek shameful for taking all the credit for Japan's defeat. Mao used the peach tree metaphor to denounce further what he believed to be Chiang's dishonorable actions. Mao's charge was framed by asking a set of rhetorical questions:

> To whom should the fruits of victory in the War of Resistance belong? It is very obvious. Take a peach tree for example. When the tree yields peaches they are the fruits of victory. Who is entitled to pick the peaches? Ask who planted and watered the tree. Chiang Kai-shek squatting on the mountain did not carry a single bucket of water, and yet he is now stretching out his arms from afar to pick the peaches. "I, Chiang Kai-shek, own these peaches," he says. "I am the landlord, you are my serfs and I won't allow you to pick any...." We say, "You never carried any water, so you have no right to pick the peaches. We, the people of the Liberated Areas, watered the tree day in and day out and have the most right to gather the fruit." (Mao 1945/1967d, 16)

Mao presented a simple logic: only those who labored were entitled to reap the harvest. Such a farming metaphor was particularly apt since Mao was speaking to an audience supportive of the proletarian class. By using the metaphor about growing peaches, rhetorical questions, and imagined answers, Mao pointed to Chiang's character flaw of evading responsibilities during the war and then claiming victory at its end. First, Mao argued, not fighting in the war demonstrated Chiang's lack of patriotism. Second, Mao asserted, Chiang wanted to claim credit for winning the war, proving that Chiang was a man without integrity. Mao presented as common sense the idea that whoever planted seeds and took care of the growing process of the peaches (vehicle) deserved to reap the harvest of this great victory (tenor). Historical documents have shown that Chiang Kai-shek's army was ultimately the major military force in defeating the Japanese. While Mao's army mostly engaged in guerrilla warfare, Chiang's troops fought the main battles. Yet when this historical event was reduced to peach picking, Mao was able to deny Chiang's efforts and overlook American support in winning the war. Using this metaphor allowed Mao to engage his audience and gain their compliance to his argument while avoiding having to present a wholly honest portrayal of contributions from Chiang Kai-shek and the Nationalist army during the Anti-Japanese War.

Whether or not Mao's anti-Japanese rhetoric was a genuine indication of his patriotism can be questioned. On January 24, 1961, Mao met a Japanese Socialist Party delegation. When a member of the delegation said, "We are very sorry that Japan invaded the Chinese," Mao responded, "If Japan did not invade China, we [would] be still hiding in the mountains. Because the Japanese army occupied most parts of China, we did not have another choice, but we built anti-Japanese bases and engaged military battles which paved the way for our victory in the Civil War against the Nationalists. In this sense, we should thank Japanese war-lords."[10] Mao's remarks were edited out of his thirteen volumes of works written after 1949, but they were released by the *dagong* 大公报 newspaper Web site stationed in Hong Kong on February 28, 2014. This example shows the inconsistency and multifaceted persona of Mao: a suspicious gap appears between Mao's public rhetoric and what Mao proclaimed in private with a Japanese audience. Mao may have used anti-Japanese and anti–Chiang Kai-shek rhetoric to mobilize the Chinese people and galvanize support for the CCP. Such actions were consistent with his strategic schemes for gaining power and for elevating his reputation among the Chinese people through these ethical/moral appeals. It can also be argued that with the passing of time and changes in contexts, Mao adjusted his rhetoric in an attempt to save face for his Japanese guests.

Mao used another nature metaphor when Chiang Kai-shek launched a civil war in 1946, a year after the end of the Anti-Japanese War. However, even with the full support of the United States, Chiang's army began losing battles, forcing the Nationalist army to change from offensive military strategies to defensive ones. Mao wrote an essay analyzing the ongoing situation, predicting that Chiang would be defeated and a new China under Communist rule would emerge. Mao used nature metaphors to boost the morale of his troops: "When dark clouds appeared in the sky, we pointed out that this was only temporary, that the darkness would soon pass and the sun would break through" (Mao 1947/1967d, 159). Mao again painted a rosy picture of China's future through poetic natural metaphors. Nature metaphors often construe inevitability; Mao's use of nature metaphors brought hope for the CCP troops, confidence that they could defeat Chiang Kai-shek's military force, and a promise for a better future for China.

Mao also used a metaphor of growth to promote party building. One reason for the success of the CCP resulted from party members' willingness to travel to rural and poor areas to mingle with ordinary people, often quite poor peasants. To motivate party members to proselytize in this way, Mao referred to them as "seeds" of the revolution. Through these "seeds," he explained, Communist ideas and ideals would be disseminated, the mobilization of political campaigns would take place, and the reputation of the party would be built. Mao taught party members to be "mentally prepared, once there [with the peasants], to take root, blossom and bear fruit" (Mao 1945/1967d, 58). Mao then pictured the ordinary people as soil in which the CCP members (the seeds) could grow. Such a nature metaphor identified the seminal role that CCP members played in the revolution and described their inter-dependent relationship with the masses, thus encouraging CCP members to "build good relations with the masses, be concerned for them and help them overcome their difficulties" (Mao 1945/1967d, 59). As Lakoff and Johnson (1980) state, meta-phors create social reality and become guides for action. The "seed" metaphor generates a social reality of growth promoted by sowing seeds. One of the reasons the CCP succeeded, particularly in comparison with Chiang Kai-shek's National-ists, was the "mass line," the action of integrating party members with ordinary people. During this integration party members were directed to learn the people's concerns and help people solve problems while educating them by raising their so-called "proletarian consciousness" through propaganda work about Mao and the party. Mao's use of nature metaphor had been effective in linking and strengthening the relationship between the party and the Chinese people.

Animal Metaphors

Perhaps because of his peasantry background or perhaps because his audiences were largely peasants, Mao was fond of using animal metaphors. For example, he employed an animal metaphor to illustrate how learning took place. Mao discred-ited the old Chinese saying "Without stepping outside his gate the scholar knows all the wide world's affairs" as "mere empty talk in past times when technology was undeveloped" (Mao 1937/1967a, 299). Mao believed that no one could have knowl-edge without practice or experience in the real world. He asked a metaphorical question to illustrate this point further: "How can you catch tiger cubs without entering the tiger's lair?" (300). Using the vehicle of a tiger, Mao brought the tenor of "learning" to his audience. Mao was explaining that one could reach the interest-ing and provocative qualities of life (the tiger cubs) only by risking uncertain con-frontation with dangerous forces (the tiger in the lair). Using this animal metaphor to argue about the general experience in the real world, Mao helped his readers see the importance of learning from practice and experience, which may entail facing difficult ideas and uncomfortable circumstances; simultaneously Mao discounted the value of the passive experience of learning from books.

Mao's use of persuasive animal metaphors extended through a variety of top-ics. In his discussion of different types of democracy in the world, for example, Mao pointed out that some so-called democratic governments actually did not practice the tenets they espoused with regard to their treatment of the people. He used an animal metaphor to illustrate his point: "Their talk of constitutional gov-ernment is only 'selling dog-meat under the label of a sheep's head.' They display the sheep's head of constitutional government while selling the dog-meat of one-party dictatorship" (Mao 1940/1967b, 412). Mao used this animal metaphor to discredit Western democracy, which claimed to guarantee freedom by a constitution while in reality, Mao contended, people in a democratic society did not have freedom. Mao argued that the hypocrisy of democracy was like selling dog meat in the name of sheep. In traditional Chinese culture, a dog is a vicious animal and dog meat is naturally despicable. A sheep, in contrast, is a gentle animal symbolizing softness and goodness. The irony of Mao's metaphor is that after he became the leader of China, his one-party political system promoted his increasingly authoritarian leadership instead of promoting a transition into the democracy he had promised. Moreover, since the economic reform in the 1980s, the CCP had become so corrupt that it changed its mission, which originally was to serve the people truthfully. An argument can be made that Mao's metaphor of using a sheep's head to sell to an audience the dog meat of a one-party dictatorship could be used to characterize Mao's own actions and the actions of his party by the end of his reign.

In another realm Mao drew an animal metaphor from a Chinese classic. Since at the beginning of the Anti-Japanese War Mao's army was poorly equipped, Mao needed to address the question of how his small and weak force might deal with the enemy's enormous presence and teeming equipment. Mao used a legendary Chinese figure: the Monkey King in *Journey to the West*. In the story the Monkey King appears to be less powerful than Princess Iron Fan, his enemy. In fact, "the Princess was a formidable demon and was hard to conquer in a face-to-face fight. . . . The Monkey King made his way into her stomach and overpowered her by changing himself into a tiny insect" (Mao 1942/1967c, 101). Mao called on Communist soldiers to learn from the Monkey King's tactics in dealing with a more powerful enemy. His story meant that the size of military ordnance was not the indicator of success: victory was based on cleverly employed military strategies.

However, when the Nationalists called for negotiations toward establishing a coalition government with the CCP in 1945, Mao was cautious and suspected deception from his enemy; he suspected that Chiang would use trickery to trap the CCP. In this case Mao used the same story of the Monkey King and the Princess of the Iron Fan to make his point. But this time the Monkey King was the symbol of the Nationalists and the Princess of the Iron Fan represented the CCP. In Mao's words, "We should be prepared for the many troubles which will arise after the success of the negotiations, and we should be ready with clear heads to deal with the tactics the other side will adopt, the tactics of the Monkey who gets into the stomach of the Princess of the Iron Fan to play the devil" (Mao 1949/1967d, 372). In this version of the story, the Monkey King was transformed from a good animal to a harmful animal with devilish features, one that posed a threat to the Communists. In these two presentations, Mao manipulated the metaphor to fit his needs. The Monkey King was used in the first case to indicate benefits for the CCP and the people and in the second to indicate harm to the Communist Party.[11]

As the civil war turned in Mao's favor, he selected an animal metaphor to foreshadow postwar cautions to citizens. When he saw imminent victory over the Nationalists, Mao's rhetoric became tougher, more forceful, and more aggressive. In his essay "Carry the Revolution through to the End," Mao scorned as deceitful the peace efforts made by the Nationalist Party and the United States. He used an ancient Greek fable to illustrate his point: "One winter's day, a farmhand found a snake frozen by the cold. Moved by compassion, he picked it up and put it in his bosom. The snake was revived by the warmth, its natural instincts returned, and it gave its benefactor a fatal bite" (Mao 1948/1967d, 304). Mao compared the Nationalists with the snake and the CCP with the farmhand. Mao argued that if the members of the CCP were kindhearted toward the Nationalists, the Communists would be eaten up by the venomous Nationalist snake and would deeply regret their act of compassion.

Mao extended the metaphor to raise the level of vigilance: "Moreover, the serpents infesting most of China, big or small, black or white, baring their poisonous fangs or assuming the guise of beautiful girls, are not yet frozen by the cold, although they already sense the threat of winter" (Mao 1948/1967d, 304). This analogy served as a warning to the CCP: their enemy still lurked among them and had not yet surrendered to the truth that they had lost the war, although by now enemy combatants might be more dangerous because they would be aware of that inevitability. This enemy, Mao said in his metaphor, would not back down and, as is the character of snakes, would not change their evil nature. Mao used this fable to admonish his comrades to be aware of the potential danger of showing sympathy to the enemy. Mao directed his followers not to take pity on these snakelike scoundrels, not to be gullible about the peace rhetoric, but to carry on the revolution to the end. Mao used this animal metaphor to present an argument that the CCP should not abandon its position or cooperate with the Nationalists to form a coalition government.[12] Mao skillfully employed animal metaphors to present his argument on the best approach to learning, to smear Western democracy, to boost the morale of his army, and to caution his comrades about the traps of the enemy.

Moving Objects as Metaphors

Mao used common references when he constructed metaphors, tailoring his language to rely on concepts familiar to his audiences. Even as he dealt with philosophical and political topics, Mao chose items such as arrows and targets, chariots, and sailboats—references likely known to the proletarian class—to locate his audience in the vehicle of the metaphor (for example, a target) toward his goal of moving them to accept the tenor (that is, the Chinese revolution). For example, Mao claimed himself to be a true Marxist, and a true Chinese Marxist would be able to integrate Marxist-Leninist theories with the Chinese revolution. Mao used the metaphor of archery to characterize the relationship between Marxist/Leninist theories and the Chinese revolution. The target, as the vehicle, in his metaphor corresponded to the Chinese revolution, which was the tenor; the "arrow" was Marxism-Leninism. Mao claimed that "we Chinese Communists have been seeking this arrow because we want to hit the target of the Chinese revolution and of the revolution of the East. To take such an attitude is to seek truth from facts" (Mao 1941/1967c, 22). Here Mao used the vehicle of "arrow" and its relationship with the "target" to explain that Marxism-Leninism could be used in China's situation to arrive at the desired objective of China's revolution. For those who doubted the application of a foreign theory to the practice of China's revolution, this metaphorical link may have had a persuasive effect.

About those who refused to accept these Marxist views of epistemology, whom Mao considered to be reactionary, Mao wrote, "Their thinking is divorced from social practice, and they cannot march ahead to guide the chariot of society: they simply trail behind, grumbling that it goes too fast and they are trying to drag the chariot back or turn it in the opposite direction" (Mao 1937/1967a, 307). Here Mao used the vehicle metaphor of the "chariot of society" to indicate the progressive force, thereby distinguishing that group from the reactionary force he disdained. He linked the refusal to accept Marxism with an attitude of resisting the progression of history, leaving little room for the audience to doubt or take a middle position. That Mao really understood Marxist epistemology or privately believed Marxism was, in fact, applicable to China's situation is questionable. His demand for his followers to conform to Marxism, however, was categorical. The meaning of his chariot metaphor could be interpreted as a command to conform to the party line and demonstrate loyalty to Mao. If his intent was to insure conformity and coerce allegiance, the chariot metaphor may have been effective as a rhetorical device, but it was ethically deceptive.

In 1942 the war with Japan entered its fifth year, which Mao considered the "darkness before the dawn" (Mao 1942/1967c, 99). In his essay "A Most Important Policy," Mao emphasized the importance of making policies that met the challenges of this "darkness" (difficulties). To draw this point to the attention of his audience, Mao used the metaphor of sailing to describe the potential difficulties the Communist Party would face; he also criticized those who underestimated the difficulties: "They are unable to anticipate that the ship may encounter submerged rocks or to steer clear of the rocks with cool heads," he wrote. "What are the submerged rocks in the path of the ship of the War of Resistance? They are the extremely grave material difficulties of the final stage of the war. The Central Committee of the Party has pointed them out and has called on us to be on the alert and steer clear of them" (100). Mao used this metaphor of submerged rocks to refer to potential dangers or treacherous obstacles that might thwart victory in the war. Mao also suggested that leaders with cool heads were needed to "steer clear of the rocks." That is, patient and thoughtful navigators were needed to assure smooth sailing to the war's end. While Mao did not suggest in the writing that he was that great navigator, he was indeed worshipped as "the great navigator" for China during China's Cultural Revolution.

In summary, metaphors often functioned as techniques to enhance persuasion in Mao's speeches and writings. In these examples of writings prior to 1949, Mao used metaphors of nature, animals, and moving objects to explain war situations and strategies, justify his policy changes, issue warnings and condemn enemies, demand conformity, and boost the morale of his army. Some of his metaphors— such as the chariot metaphor—included the construction of a harsh reality faced by his party while also indicating a promising future for China. His metaphors conveyed messages of both caution and optimism, suggesting both his strong will and his dexterity with strategic moves. When the Chinese people were studying Mao's works during the Cultural Revolution, these metaphors were instrumental in helping them remember Mao's words. Mao's metaphors, memorized and recited repeatedly, were remembered and used by ordinary Chinese in dealing with everyday lives. As a result, these metaphors along with multiple other techniques and vestiges of Mao became part of Chinese political discourse and a symbolic resource of the CCP.

References to History and Chinese Classics

Scholars of rhetoric have concluded that ancient Chinese rhetors used authority to justify their arguments; the rhetors searched for wisdom by using established cultural values and by citing sages (Garrett 1991; Jensen 1992; Lu 1998; Oliver 1971). As Levenson (1959) notes, "It was in the nature of Chinese thought, historically oriented, to sanctify practice in terms of precedent" (34). In a similar way, Mao adhered to the rhetoric implemented by these ancient Chinese texts. His references to the past and to Chinese classics can be classified into two categories: 1) dealing with enemies; and 2) strengthening the Communist Party leadership.

Dealing with Enemies

Mao was known as a master of military strategy among his comrades after he was proved right in many battles against the Nationalist army. Since he was familiar with Chinese classics, he often used them to illustrate his war strategies. In his essay "Problems of Strategy in China's Revolutionary War," Mao referenced a story in *Shui Hu Zhuan* (*Water Margin*), a Chinese classic, to make a point about how strategic retreat is crucial toward winning any battle. The story goes, "In the *Shui Hu Chuan,* the drill master, Hung, challenges Lin Chung to a fight on Chai Chin's estate, shouting, 'Come on! Come on! Come on!' In the end it is the retreating Lin Chung who spots Hung's weak point and floors him with one blow" (Mao

1936/1967a, 211). Mao then told a story from *Zuo Zhuan* (*Zuo Tradition*): "During the Spring and Autumn Era, when the states of Lu and Chi were at war, Duke Chuang of Lu wanted to attack before the Chi troops had tired themselves out, but Tsao Kuei prevented him. When instead he adopted the tactic of 'the enemy tires, we attack,' he defeated the Chi army. This is a classic example from China's military history of a weak force defeating a strong force" (211). Both stories suggest that the best war strategy is for leaders to wait for the right moment to attack, especially if he or she is in a disadvantaged situation. Mao referenced these stories to make a point regarding the attitudes and tactics that a small and weak army could use to defeat a strong enemy. Drawing from these Chinese classics, Mao coined the famous sixteen-character formula for his military strategy in guerrilla warfare: "The enemy advances, we retreat; the enemy camps, we harass; the enemy tires, we attack; the enemy retreats, we pursue" (213). Mao's guerrilla strategy saved his army, avoided its elimination by Chiang Kai-shek's troops, and won Mao the reputation of being the military genius of the CCP.

In dealing with enemies, Mao borrowed heavily from ancient Chinese military strategists, particularly from their wisdom and abilities to analyze all factors in a situation. Mao was familiar with Sunzi's *The Art of War*, which placed an emphasis on strategies rather than on force in winning a war. Mao cited a number of historical figures and their strategies in his writings. He even compared Sun Tzu and a story in *Shui Hu Zhuan* with the Greek example of the Trojan horse:

> When Sun Wu Tzu said in discussing military science, "Know the enemy and know yourself, and you can fight a hundred battles with no danger of defeat," he was referring to the two sides in a battle. Wei Cheng of the Tang Dynasty also understood the error of one-sidedness when he said, "Listen to both sides and you will be enlightened; heed only one side and you will be benighted." But our comrades often look at problems one-sidedly, and so they often run into snags. In the novel *Shui Hu Chuan*, Sung Chiang thrice attacked a Chu Village. Twice he was defeated because he was ignorant of the local conditions and used the wrong method. Later he changed his methods; first he investigated the situation and familiarized himself with the maze of roads, then he broke up the alliance among the Li, Hu and Chu Villages, and finally sent his men in disguise into the enemy camp to lie in wait, using a stratagem similar to that of the Trojan Horse in the foreign story. And on the third occasion he won. (Mao 1937/1967a, 323–24)

Mao used these historical examples to illustrate the importance of knowing the enemy and the necessity of a careful analysis of the situation to win a battle. He wanted to remind his comrades to learn from the past and other people's mistakes so that similar failures could be prevented and victory was more assured. As the Chinese people have the cultural habit of learning from the past, this rhetorical technique was more likely to be effective.

Mao used the past in other ways as well, and some were less forthright. During the Anti-Japanese War, for example, Stalin's Soviet army provided military support to the CCP. On Stalin's sixtieth birthday, Mao wrote a letter entitled "Stalin Is a Friend of [the] Chinese People." In the letter Mao referenced a poem from the *Book of Odes,* which reads, "A bird sings out to draw a friend's response" (Mao 1939/1967b, 335), describing how Chinese people were longing for friendship and to emphasize how grateful the Chinese people were to Stalin for his friendship and support. At the same time, Mao distinguished Stalin from imperialists (the United States) who also were considered friends of China at the time. Mao described the latter type of friend as with "honey on his lips and murder in his heart" (335), as these friends did not display any genuine sympathy because their real intention was to conquer China. While the United States did provide financial, material, and military support to China during the Anti-Japanese War, Mao deliberately chose not to acknowledge these contributions.[13] Many young Chinese people were unaware of the U.S. support to China and the sacrifices of the Nationalist army in the war against Japan during Mao's era. The truth was gradually revealed after Mao's death in 1976.[14]

Strengthening the Party Leadership

When Japan invaded China in 1937, the Nationalist Party temporarily ceased fire with the Communists. Mao had to persuade his comrades that the Nationalist Party was no longer the enemy and that the peoples' true enemies were the Japanese and those who accepted the Japanese occupation. Mao made a point that "we should support whatever the enemy opposes and oppose whatever the enemy supports" (Mao 1939/1967b, 272). Mao augmented his point by referencing a sentence in a letter written by a historical figure in the Eastern Han dynasty: "Whatever you do, you must be sure that you do not sadden your friends and gladden your enemies" (272). Mao lauded this tenet as a clear-cut political principle that loyal Communists should follow. In this example Mao demonstrated not only his historical knowledge but also his rhetorical skills of using such knowledge for persuasive purposes to address the changing situation in China.

Not only did Mao strengthen his leadership by citing and promoting effective military strategy, but he also used the classics to promote himself as the leader of both the military and the masses. He cited Mencius's phrase "invincible under heaven" to describe his army (Mao 1943/1967c, 154). For the legitimacy of this mandate, Mao called upon party members to go out and mingle with Chinese people, to build ties with the masses. Mao was fully aware that the victory of his revolution would be founded on the support of the majority of the Chinese people. Such support would allow him to be "invincible under heaven." This Confucian appeal would resonate with the Chinese audience favorably with regard to their judgment of the legitimacy of the government he espoused. Mao's fear was that if party members lost contact with the Chinese people, the party would lose its legitimacy to lead. Mao's trust in the masses continued after the founding of the People's Republic of China (PRC). He relied on the masses to launch political campaigns and to tear down bureaucracy in the government.

Moreover, Mao believed that the Chinese people had immense creativity waiting to be discovered by the Communist leaders. He used the common Chinese saying "Three cobblers with their wits combined equal Chukeh Liang [Zhuge Liang], the mastermind" (Mao 1943/1967c, 158). Zhuge Liang is a well-known chancellor for Liu Bei in the novel *Romance of the Three Kingdoms,* a famous Chinese classic. Mao claimed that "the masses have great creative power. In fact, there are thousands upon thousands of Chukkeh [Zhuge] Liangs among the Chinese people; every village, every town has its own" (158). Mao used this claim to motivate the Chinese people to engage in creative and innovative activities by working in groups; these efforts among those who complied boosted the communal spirit and increased enthusiasm for productivity not only during the war but also during periods of peace.

Mao was the paramount leader of the Communist Party during the period 1949–76. In his works he taught party members how to think and lead. In his essay "Methods of Work of Party Committees," Mao spelled out twelve ways to lead; three of them employed vivid rhetorical techniques. The first two methods focused on keeping committee members informed among themselves. Mao used Laozi's saying to criticize those who "do not visit each other all their lives, though the crowing of their cocks and the barking of their dogs are within hearing of each other" (Mao 1949/1967d, 379). One purpose of staying informed was to avoid a lack of shared discourse among high-ranking party officials, which Mao claimed was a source of the problems in the past. For the third method, Mao explained the correct means for retrieving information from lower levels by citing Confucius, soliciting readers not to "feel ashamed to ask and learn from the people below" (379). Mao referenced Confucius, Mencius, Laozi, and Zhuangzi throughout his writings to illustrate his points and present his arguments.

As the CCP became stronger and grew in influence, Mao cautioned his comrades not to become conceited; he told them never to look down on others who were lesser in class origins, age, education, or length of service to the party. He considered those who harbored arrogant attitudes toward the masses as "carrying an encumbrance or baggage on their backs" (Mao 1944/1967c, 173). He advised party members that such an attitude would restrict their abilities to think critically. Mao was famous for "getting rid of the baggage and starting up the machinery" (175). After giving a lengthy account of the history of the Communists to support his view, Mao explained what he meant by "starting up the machinery": it "means to make good use of the organ of thought" (174), the organ being the brain. To substantiate his argument further, Mao cited Lenin and Stalin on the importance of using the brain and quoted from Mencius's notion that "the office of the mind is to think." Mao used the phrase to encourage active and critical thinking not to challenge authority, certainly, but to create a better understanding of any situation so that sound judgments could be made. As he concluded, "Much thinking yields wisdom. To get rid of the practice of acting blindly which is so common in our party, we must encourage our comrades to think, to learn the method of analysis and to cultivate the habit of analysis" (174–75). Ironically, while Mao encouraged his comrades to use analysis and method in their thinking, he suppressed dissenting views of intellectuals within the party, coercing those members to conform to the ideology of Marxism-Leninism. Therefore, although Mao made statements encouraging his comrades to avoid "acting blindly," he restricted their choices and accepted only a single method of analysis, the method of class struggle.

Redefining Revolutionary Terms

In *A Rhetoric of Motives,* Kenneth Burke (1969) explains that "you persuade a man only insofar as you can talk his language by speech, gesture, tonality, order, image, attitude, idea, identifying your ways with his" (55). To identify with the audience, a rhetor oftentimes names or defines a situation by choosing a particular set of words or a vocabulary that serves to help the audience interpret the situation as well as guide their thoughts and actions. Burke calls this rhetorical function the "terministic screen" that paints reality in a particular manner through certain words or vocabulary. Moreover words that occur with frequency and intensity in a text can reveal the rhetor's motive. Three key terms were used by Mao as "terministic screens" throughout his writings as part of his revolutionary rhetoric: *renmin* (people); *geming* (revolution); and *minzhu* (democracy). These three terms were used with greater intensity and frequency than any other terms in Mao's discourse and had the greatest impact on the political life of the Chinese people.

Renmin (People)

The literal translation of "people" is *renmin,* which is composed of two characters, *ren* and *min.* The word *ren* means "humans" and first appeared in *Shi Jing* (Book of Poetry), the oldest Chinese written text. The original version of *min* is *baixing* 百姓, which appeared in *Shang Shu* (*Book of History*) and in *Zuo Zhuan* (*Zuo Tradition*) in ancient China. This word means "ordinary people," or people of lower social-economic status who have little or no education. The related word, *zimin* 子民, is used as a humble self-reference to mean the subjects of kings and emperors in imperial China. Thus people in ancient times had no voice or agency. *Renmin* is a modern term imported from Japan and evolved from Liang Qichao's journal *xinmin Congbao* 新民丛报 (New Citizen) and Mao's organization *xinmin xuehui* 新民学会 (New Citizen Association).

In Mao's writings *renmin* referred to working-class people such as workers, peasants, soldiers, and the petite bourgeoisie, whom Mao considered the basis of the proletarian class (Mao 1942/1967c). *Renmin* was sometimes used interchangeably with *qunzhong* or *dazhong* (the masses). In 1944 Mao delivered a tribute to Zhang Side, an ordinary Communist soldier, and he later titled the speech "Serve the People." In this speech *renmin* became a generic term referring to the Chinese people. The word "people" was used together with "interest" and "liberation" as Mao claimed that the Communist cause was "wholly dedicated to the liberation of the people" and that the Communist Party "work[ed] entirely in the people's interest" (Mao 1944/1967c, 177). Here the category of *renmin* was expanded and the party's mission was elevated for the interest of the masses.

Mao used *renmin* in different ways to best serve his political goals. At the end of the Anti-Japanese War, for example, Chiang Kai-shek attempted to form a coalition government with the CCP on the condition that the CCP's army would be placed under the command of the Nationalist Party. Mao was enraged by this request and wrote a long essay called "On Coalition Government." In the essay Mao reminded Chiang Kai-shek and those who still did not have faith in the CCP that the CCP had taken on the cause of liberating the Chinese people and that its achievements in this area could not be ignored. Mao claimed that "the Chinese Communist Party is the most faithful spokesman of the Chinese people, and whoever fails to respect it in fact fails to respect the Chinese masses and is doomed to defeat" (Mao 1945/1967c, 258). Here, Mao again changed the meaning of *renmin,* from "masses" to "Chinese people." Since he had raised the status of the CCP to that of representative of the Chinese people, anyone who acted against the CCP was acting against the Chinese people; anyone who acted against the Chinese people would lose the "Mandate of Heaven" and thus would fail to rule. The meaning of "people" had come to mean those who were on the side of the CCP; later the word evolved into meaning those who supported and followed Mao. The CCP and Mao's enemies, such as Chiang Kai-shek, American imperialists, and those who opposed Mao, became nonpeople. The term was undeniably politicized by Mao.

Chiang Kai-shek started a civil war in hopes of eliminating the Communists once and for all. Mao wrote an essay entitled "The Situation and Our Policy after the Victory in the War of Resisting against Japan" in which he denounced Chiang's act of war as "killing *people* with swords" (Mao 1945/1967d, 14). In this way Mao implied that the civil war was not a fight between two parties for control of China but an assault against the Chinese people because the term "people" carried moral legitimacy. Chiang meanwhile was demonized for violating the moral legitimacy of the party and the Chinese people.

In 1957, after Mao had consolidated his power as the supreme leader of China, he again redefined *renmin,* this time to incorporate a broader sense and to function in opposition to *diren* (enemy). "We must first be clear on what is meant by 'the people' and what is meant by 'the enemy,'" Mao asserted. "The concept of 'the people' varies in content in different countries and in different periods of history in a given country" (Mao 1957/1977, 385). Mao then announced that *renmin* during the Anti-Japanese War period referred to those who fought in the war for China; *renmin* were those who resisted American imperialism and feudalism as represented by Chiang Kai-shek during the civil war. Previously, during the socialist construction period, *renmin* had referred to those who supported the Communist cause and *diren* referred to those who opposed and sabotaged the socialist construction.

Here, however, *renmin* became a code word for the CCP and a term to demonstrate political identity and the ideological orientation of a person. It no longer meant "people" or "humans" but rather referred to a certain kind of people who ideologically aligned with the CCP. The slogan "serve the people" had become a code phrase for serving the party. Those considered members of the proletarian class, such as workers, peasants, soldiers, the urban poor, and reformed intellectuals, all were qualified to be named *renmin;* those who disagreed with the party and Mao and those who belonged to the bourgeoisie, such as landlords, capitalists, and criminals, were deemed enemies. Young (1991) has noted, "The 'either-or' terminology occurs in Communist literature almost with the regularity of a pulse beat"; throughout the world it was typical to hear a Communist spokesperson using the words "two roads," "two paths," or "two forces" in his or her speeches (137). Such rhetoric, however, ignores the complexity of human nature and multiple perspectives of reality.

Yu Hua (2011), an author who grew up during the Cultural Revolution, tells readers that *renmin* was the first term he learned at school; in his mind, "*renmin* is Chairman Mao; Chairman Mao is *renmin* (1)." Yu admits that he never truly understood the meaning of *renmin* even though he used the term all the time. Perry Link (2013) discusses the ambiguous and abstract nature of the Chinese official language; he explains that the nature of the language allows the option of migrating the meaning of a word to a new meaning and accommodating different interpretations of a word (246–47). *Renmin* is such an ambiguous and abstract word that it can refer to human beings or revolutionary masses or the CCP or even Chairman Mao. Link points out that like China, other totalitarian societies as well have used abstract and ambiguous words in their official languages—for example the Nazi regime and the Khmer Rouge.

Geming (Revolution)

The term *geming* first appeared in *Yi Jing* (Book of Changes), one of the Chinese classics. The term refers to using force to overthrow a ruthless king and establish a new dynasty (汤武革命，顺乎天而应乎人). *Geming* consists of two Chinese characters that were borrowed by the Japanese, who matched its meaning with the English word "revolution" in translation. Liang Qichao first introduced the term to China from Japan, and Sun Yat-sen adopted it while he was in exile in Japan. Finding the term agreeable, he named his party the "Revolutionary Party." Later he changed the name to the Nationalist Party.

As early as 1927, when Mao witnessed a peasant uprising and wrote a report on that revolt in Hunan, he defined the revolution as a violent movement. In his words, "revolution is not a dinner party, or writing an essay, or painting a picture, or doing embroidery; it cannot be so refined, so leisurely and gentle, so temperate, kind, courteous, restrained and magnanimous. A revolution is an insurrection, and [an] act of violence by which one class overthrows another" (Mao 1927/1967a, 28). Mao also endorsed the role of peasants by instigating revolution; he asserted that "without the poor peasants there would be no revolution. To deny their role is to deny the revolution. To attack them is to attack the revolution. They have never been wrong on the general direction of the revolution" (33). Mao perceived peasants as the base and driving force in revolution as they were poor and lived at the bottom of society. They would be easily persuaded and showed more motivation than any other social group to participate in overthrowing the authority for hopes of a better life.

Mao did not settle on the meaning of "revolution" only as a violent movement. He used the term to classify people into friends and enemies. However, his revolutionary thought was not radical at its inception. He referred to Japanese imperialists and Chinese traitors as "counter-revolutionaries" and was willing to build alliances with rich peasants and national bourgeoisie (Mao 1935/1967a, 153–70).[15] As his political career grew after 1949, however, his notion of "counter-revolutionary" was expanded: "Whoever sides with the revolutionary people is a revolutionary. Whoever sides with imperialism, feudalism and bureaucrat-capitalism is a counter-revolutionary. Whoever sides with the revolutionary people in word only but not in deed is a revolutionary in word. Whoever sides with the revolutionary people in deed as well as in word is a true revolutionary" (Mao 1950/1977, 38). When Hu Feng, a prominent intellectual, challenged the uniformity of the party's discourse in 1955, Mao labeled him a "counter-revolutionary" (Mao 1955/1977, 172). In another essay, published in 1956, Mao defined "counter-revolutionary" as any negative elements that opposed positive elements (Mao 1956/1977, 298). "Negative element" was a euphemism for dissenting voices, and "positive element" was a code phrase for the party line. Thus "counter-revolutionary" no longer identified a specific social or political group but became a term that could be used loosely to refer to various patterns of thought and behavior, subject to interpretation.

By 1949, when the CCP took power, Mao had proposed a transition from a peasant revolution characterized by seizing social, economic, and political power to a socialist platform focused on economic development. Mao claimed that he would like to see "a bloodless transition" (Mao 1956/1977, 290). On the surface, Mao was advocating a peaceful transition and the end of violent revolution. In reality, millions of remaining Nationalists and their sympathizers were executed after the 1949 revolution under the banner of *zhenfan* 镇反 (cracking down on counterrevolutionaries). Mao justified his launch of the Cultural Revolution by his theory of permanent revolution.[16] In his speech at the Second Plenary Session of the Eighth Central Committee of the Communist Party of China, Mao told his comrades that the term "revolution" was still necessary in the act of overthrowing imperialists and class enemies as long as a contradiction existed between the superstructure and the economic base (338) and that "there would still be revolutions ten thousand years from now" (344).

Thus, Mao had added a new meaning to his earlier definition of "revolution": the revolution of thought and culture. According to Mao, the means of the Cultural Revolution no longer required military force but needed "a new form of revolution…namely, speaking out freely, airing views fully, holding great debates and writing big-character posters" (Mao 1957/1977, 484). Such revolution still entailed a life-and-death struggle between the proletariat and the bourgeoisie. Mao's continued revolution in the cultural and thought aspects was cruel. Millions of innocent people were charged as "counter-revolutionaries" and persecuted in the name of this continued revolution. In this sense, the term "revolution" no longer meant the overthrow of a ruthless ruler or a corrupt government; it meant the constant exercise of a dictatorship over so-called class enemies.

Minzhu (Democracy)

The Greek term δημοκρατία, or *demokratia* (*demos* means "people"; *kratein* means "rule"), means to rule by the people as a way to restrict the privileges of the Greek aristocracy. In contrast, the original meaning of the term *minzhu* first appeared in the *Book of History* (around 900 B.C.E.) to mean "the ruler of the masses" (for example, 简代夏作民主、天惟时求民主、其语偷不似民主) in China. This meaning of *minzhu* lasted until the end of the Qing dynasty (1911). Not until the start of the New Cultural Movement (1911), following the collapse of the Qing dynasty, did Chen Duxiu introduce the terms Mr. Democracy (or 德先生) and Mr. Science (or 赛先生) to China through his journal, *New Youth*. Chen introduced "Mr. Democracy" as a term to encapsulate human rights in all sectors of social life. Later China adopted Japan's translation of *minzhu* as "democracy."

Mao used the term *minzhu* throughout his writing. He proposed two types of *minzhu* in his polemic response to Chiang Kai-shek's government in 1937: one was reform in the political system; the other was reform in the freedom of speech. According to Mao, the "Kuomintang [the Nationalist Party] dictatorship of one party and one class must be changed into a democratic government based on the co-operation of all parties and all classes" (Mao 1937/1967a, 268), and conversely, the democratic process should include elections and freedom to assemble, conduct meetings, and speak freely. Mao pointed out that among the many qualities that China lacked, the two main qualities were independency and democracy, and it was necessary to achieve both through China's revolution (Mao 1940/1967b, 407). To build an independent, free, democratic, united, prosperous, and powerful China was Mao's purported goal and also his promise to the Chinese people (Mao 1945/1967c, 229). In this sense, Mao's interpretation of *minzhu* was close to the Western sense of democracy.

When Mao appropriated *minzhu* for internal party building, he proposed the concept as "democratic centralism" (Mao 1945/1967c, 230), a word coined by Lenin (Aune 1999, 542) as a means of gaining control within the party. "Democratic centralism," Lenin wrote, is a two-step process of decision making. The first step is to hear the voices of the subordinates; the second step is to make the decision by the leaders (based on the opinions of the subordinates). This process appears to give the opportunity to ordinary people to express their ideas just as citizens do in other democratic processes, but the ultimate decision in democratic centralism is made by top-level party officials who may or may not consider the opinions from below. However, as he gave instructions to his party members, Mao stated that democracy within the party was essential to party building because it allowed initiatives. Mao encouraged party members to exercise democracy. At the same time, however, Mao warned that party members must be clear on the relationship between democracy and centralism. "Only in this way can we really extend democracy within the Party and at the same time avoid ultra-democracy and the laissez-faire which destroys discipline" (Mao 1938/1967b, 205). Here the exercise of democracy was restricted and "centralism" was a code word for obedience to authority and top-down leadership.

In 1956, when Mao was facing criticism from intellectuals who demanded a "great democracy," he made a public distinction between "the bourgeois parliamentary democracy system of the West" and the proletarian great democracy in socialist countries. Mao charged that "the advocacy [of Western democracy] is wrong, for they lack the Marxist viewpoint, the class viewpoint" (Mao 1956/1977, 343). Mao then went on to argue that "democracy is a method, and it all depends on to whom it is applied and for what purpose" (343). Mao reiterated his point of combining democracy and centralism as the format for political deliberation and decision making. In his words, "Our aim is to create a political situation in which we have both centralism and democracy, both discipline and freedom, both unity of will and personal ease of mind and liveliness" (Mao 1957/1977, 473). While he attempted to strike a balance between too much freedom and too much control, criticism from intellectuals and resistance from other party officials on his economic policies posed threats to his credibility and his moral legitimacy to rule China. Instead of adhering to what he had promised regarding democracy within the party apparatus, Mao redefined and equated *minzhu*/democracy with mass movement and mass mobilization. By this time the term had become an abstract and empty word that lacked specific meanings about how democracy would be practiced.

While rejecting the Western form of democracy, Mao advocated for a so-called proletarian democracy characterized by "speaking out freely, airing views fully, holding great debates and writing big-character posters" (Mao 1957/1977, 484) in dealing with conflicts between party officials and the masses, especially when party officials became bureaucratic and corrupt. In 1957 Mao launched the Anti-Rightist Movement to silence dissenting voices toward him and the party in the name of this "great democracy" 大民主. In 1966 Mao launched the Cultural Revolution, which exercised "great democracy" in the form of speaking and debating freely and writing big-character posters that were publicly placed by the masses. Mao used this mass form of democracy to pull down his political opponents such as Liu Shaoqi and other top-ranking party officials. The exercise of such a form of democracy brought the country to chaos and to widespread violations of human rights.

Using Profanity, Emotive Words, and Violent Language

From 1933 to 1934 the Nationalist Party waged five onslaughts against the Red Army, led by Mao and other CCP leaders, aiming to annihilate the CCP once and for all. However, by the end of the fifth onslaught, Japan had invaded China. Mao and the Red Army called for a cease-fire and built an alliance with the Nationalists so that they might fight against the Japanese. Regardless of the cease-fire, Chiang Kai-shek still sent troops to attack areas occupied by the Communists. Chiang's justification was that Mao's government was illegitimate and that Mao's army consisted of "bandits." Mao wrote "Some Pointed Questions for the Kuomingtang [the Nationalist Party]," in which he denounced the Nationalists and called their rhetoric "plague," "bedbugs," "dog's droppings," and "rubbish" (Mao 1943/1967c, 128). He condemned Chiang Kai-shek for indulging in a domestic power play in the midst of a national crisis.

Mao's style of questioning was biting and filled with accusations. He told the Nationalists directly that they should not attack the Border Region (occupied by the Communists) and followed his assertion by referencing two famous Chinese sayings: "When the snipe and the clam grapple, it is the fisherman who profits"; and "The mantis stalks the cicada, but behind them lurks the oriole" (Mao 1943/1967c, 125). His message meant that the Communists and the Nationalists should join together to fight the Japanese, the common enemy of the Chinese people; otherwise the beneficiary would be the Japanese. Mao exclaimed, "How painful! How disgraceful!" at the end of the paragraph, denouncing the Nationalists' action of attacking the Communist-occupied territories rather than the Japanese-occupied territories. Mao presented himself and his party as the guardians for the nation, willing to put aside the ideological differences with the Nationalists when the nation was faced with a common foreign enemy. Mao and his party won the support of the Chinese people and also won sympathy from foreign countries by this reconciliatory appeal for unity.

Mao's speeches were passionate and forceful through his use of vivid language and emotive words. For example, in "Address to [the] New Political Consultative Conference" on July 15, 1949, Mao reached an emotional crescendo when he asserted that "the Chinese people will see that, once China's destiny is in the hands of the people, China, like the sun rising in the east, will illuminate every corner of the land with a brilliant flame, swiftly clean up the mire left by the reactionary government, heal the wounds of war and build a new, powerful and prosperous people's republic worthy of the name" (Mao 1949/1967d, 408). Mao expressed his lofty goals with emotive appeal, sentimentally promising hope to the Chinese people with his favorite nature metaphors.

Mao also expressed his emotions by using superlatives, calling Lu Xun "the greatest and [most] courageous standard-bearer of this new cultural force ... the bravest and most correct, the firmest, the most loyal, and the most ardent national hero, a hero without parallel in our history" (Mao 1940/1967b, 372). In discussing what constituted truth, Mao claimed, "Marxism-Leninism is the most correct, [most] scientific and [most] revolutionary truth" (Mao 1942/1967c, 41). In this respect, Mao's rhetoric resembled that of the Nazis and that of the Soviet Union; all three favored monumental expressions and superlatives (Young 1991, 83–84, 130). Such rhetorical style reached a climax during the Cultural Revolution when the political discourse was filled with inflammatory, flamboyant, and superlative expressions when eulogizing Mao and condemning class enemies.

In volumes 3 and 4 of Mao's works, Mao increasingly used words of attack, dehumanization, and profanity. He described Chiang Kai-shek and his American supporters as "paper tigers" (Mao 1946/1967d, 100, 101), named Chiang Kai-shek a "running dog" of American imperialism (Mao 1947/1967d, 136), and accused Chiang's government of "nothing but a government of treason, civil war and dictatorship" (Mao 1947/1967d, 138). Mao claimed to "overthrow the arch-criminal of the civil war, Chiang Kai-shek" (1947/1967d, 147), calling Chiang Kai-shek and his army a "bandit gang" (Mao 1948/1967d, 286), the term Chiang actually had used in the past to describe Mao's army. In the essay "Carry the Revolution through to the End," Mao asked, "Have the Chinese reactionaries headed by Chiang Kai-shek and his ilk not given proof enough that they are a gang of blood-stained executioners, who slaughter people without blinking? Have they not given proof enough that they are a band of professional traitors and the running dogs of imperialism? Think it over, everybody!" (Mao 1948/1967d, 303).

Moreover, Mao described Chiang as having "lost his soul" and as "merely a corpse" (Mao 1949/1967d, 313). Chiang was gravely demonized by Mao's rhetoric and was targeted as "the most vicious enemy" (Mao 1948/1967d, 303). Such rhetoric of dehumanization depicted Chiang as a soulless entity and provoked much hatred toward him. The rhetoric of vilifying (and the rhetoric of hatred) toward Chiang fed the psychological and political drive of the CCP and its followers, motivating them to overthrow Chiang's government with moral legitimacy and elevating Mao's image as the sole savior for China. Moreover, use of such language encouraged a militant mentality and instigated radical thought. Mao continued to use the rhetoric of dehumanization in reference to domestic "class enemies" after he came to power. Words such as "ox ghosts and snake spirits," "devils," and "parasitic worms" were used in his writings and poems in condemning "class enemies." These words and phrases that Mao used to condemn Chiang also were used in the condemnation and persecution of intellectuals and party officials at political rallies and in big-character posters during the Cultural Revolution.[17]

Such a use of violent rhetoric has historical precedence and has been examined by scholars. Rhetoric in both Greek and Chinese traditions has been studied and taught as a language art as well as a study of providing political expediencies for resolving conflict and addressing contingent issues. However, at the same time, as James Crosswhite (2013) points out, "rhetoric has been widely suspected as being mostly nothing other than violence and domination and trickery disguised, violence masquerading as reason and language, but every bit as coercive and domineering as an armed interlocutor" (134). To some extent Mao represented Crosswhite's "armed interlocutor" in his use of militant rhetoric to condemn his enemies. Violent rhetoric had been very much accepted and employed by the CCP's propaganda since the Rectification Campaign in 1942. Cao Changqing (1992) contends that the history of Chinese Communist journalism is a history of the violent use of language. He argues that the CCP used violent rhetoric to exercise its power and control the minds of the Chinese people. "Violent language," says Cao, "is the necessity of a totalitarian society to scare and threaten its people.... Violent language creates fear and psychological press; its attack and humiliation on people has [*sic*] a devastating effect on the recipients."[18] Growing up during the Cultural Revolution, I personally witnessed how violent language led to violent actions, dehumanized people, and brought a country to the brim of collapse.

To conclude, Mao demonstrated a rich rhetorical repertoire throughout his writings and speeches. As in his calligraphy, Mao developed his own unique rhetorical style and persuasive techniques. By referencing history and classics, Mao presented himself as a good teacher, a knowledgeable scholar, and a well-informed politician, characteristics that greatly enhanced his ethos. Throughout his writings Mao also portrayed himself as the guardian of Marxism-Leninism who was on the right side of history and acted as a beacon of truth and knowledge for the Chinese people. This ethical appeal and rectitude created a moral plateau that seduced the listener/reader to follow Mao's logic and his rhetorical spell, thus reducing the audience's inclination toward refutation.

Qian (2012) notes, "Mao['s] style is a complicated phenomenon involving language, society, and psychology" (408). Mao's use of language through metaphors, superlatives, and profanity engaged the reader/listener emotionally and psychologically. His bellicose rhetoric posed a threat to his political enemies, intimidating them into reacting with a fear of striking back. Mao's skills and acumen in redefining terms at different times in history and for different purposes served him well for his revolutionary goals and political maneuvers. Such eloquence combined with his political wisdom and strategic military skills lofted him to become the most powerful and charismatic cult in China's modern history. Millions of Chinese people mindlessly followed him and became mental slaves of his rhetoric. Mao's rhetorical style profoundly influenced the way Chinese people talk even in modern times.

FOUR

Mao Zedong's Rhetoric of Class Struggle

As a guiding principle for Mao's revolution before 1949 and a justification for permanent revolution after 1949, Mao's rhetoric of class struggle transformed China from a Confucian society to a nation of revolutionary fanaticism. As the core of Mao's revolution theory, the rhetoric of class struggle not only mobilized the masses in the resistance against the Japanese and Chiang Kai-shek but also tightened the unity of the party while simultaneously justifying the persecution of millions of innocent people. Mao espoused class struggle both as the ideological doctrine for the party and as a political rationale for cracking down on dissenters. Permeating every aspect of Chinese life during the Cultural Revolution, the rhetoric of class struggle polarized the nation, destroyed traditional Chinese relationship values, and dragged China into an abyss.

Mao directly appropriated the ideology of class struggle from Marx and Lenin, adapted it to the Chinese political context, and radicalized the concept. It was used as a rhetorical strategy for accomplishing his revolutionary goals.

Background

Mao had read biographies of Peter the Great, Catherine the Great, George Washington, the Duke of Wellington, and Napoleon by the time he was seventeen. In his early twenties he read philosophical works of the ancient Greeks and of Spinoza, Kant, Goethe, Hegel, Rousseau, and others. While the writings of these historical leaders and intellectuals influenced his political ambition and modes of thinking, none of them were as compelling and powerful as Karl Marx's theories of communism even in the altered versions that Mao read.[1] Marx's theories on class struggle in particular had a lasting influence on Mao's political thinking and ultimately the utmost impact on China's revolution.

Having examined the ancient history of the West and the process of European modernization, Marx and Engels in their legendary *Communist Manifesto* (1848) claimed that "the history of all hitherto existing society is the history of class struggle" (57). The Marxist notion of class was defined by one's relationship to the means of production in the age of Western industrialization. To Marx and Engels, those who possessed the means of production and employed waged laborers belonged to the bourgeois class. Those who did not have property or means of production but could afford only to sell their labor were in the category of the proletarian class. Although the bourgeois class could make contributions to the economic development of a capitalist society, Marx and Engels argued, it would become increasingly exploitative and oppressive of the proletariat. Consequently the two types of classes would constantly oppose each other, engaging in fighting, antagonism, and hostility. Lenin further claimed that class struggle "is the struggle of some people fighting against other people; it is the struggle of the powerless, the oppressed labors against the privileged, the oppressor, and the parasites; it is the struggle between the labor or the proletariat and the capitalists or the bourgeoisie" (Lenin 1903, 169). Mao found the theory of class struggle inspiring and applicable to China's problems during the years of his youth. He devoted himself to propagating and practicing the ideology of class struggle when he converted to Marxism in 1919. As China's political situation changed, Mao's rhetoric of class struggle expanded to address domestic and international contingencies and exigencies as well.

A brief review of China's modern history and Mao's early thinking explains the reasons why Mao found the notion of class struggle attractive and applicable to China's situation. According to E. R. Hughes (1968), China and the West developed their cultures and economies throughout most of ancient history in a parallel fashion. However, when Mao was born in 1893, China was ruled by the increasingly weak and corrupt Qing dynasty. The country was divided by several Western powers. The nation's loss in the Opium War (1839–42) forced China to sign the Treaty of Nanking, thus ceding Hong Kong to Britain and opening five ports for trade with the West. Foreigners gained rights to reside in China, where they established churches and schools. A year after Mao was born, China was defeated by Japan, the rising military power in the East.

Internal efforts had been made to overthrow or reform the Qing dynasty, but each attempt had failed miserably. For example, the Taiping peasant uprising attempted to overthrow the Qing dynasty but was crushed with help from the Europeans. Persuaded by Kang Youwei, a leading intellectual and reformist, the young emperor Guangxu launched a nationwide cultural, political, and educational reform in 1898 that was known as the Hundred Days of Reform, hoping to establish a constitutional monarchy in China. Unfortunately the reform lasted only 104 days and was then sabotaged by the dowager empress Cixi. Leading reformists such as Kang Youwei and Liang Qichao escaped to Japan in exile, but six of the reformists were executed.

In 1911 the Qing dynasty was finally overthrown by a revolution led by Sun Yatsen (1866–1925), an action known as the Xinghai Revolution. The revolution brought two thousand years of Chinese feudal monarchy to an end. Western ideas of democracy and science were introduced to the country, and China sent the best minds overseas to study. When Sun Yat-sen established the Republic of China in 1911, he laid out three fundamental principles for China's future: nationalism; democracy; and livelihood. However, China was still in a chaotic situation with infighting among warlords and Western powers. The Chinese people were suffering from poverty, disease, and famine. In reality, the future of China was still uncertain.

Mao, like many other young intellectuals in his time, was searching for ways to solve China's problems and build China into an independent, equalitarian, modernized nation. Before he was introduced to Marxism, Mao had formulated his own philosophical view of the world based on his readings of the histories of China and the rest of the world. His early writings indicated that "Mao perceived the law of the universe as characterized by action, clash, struggle, and confrontation. Struggle would exist forever and the impact of it would not be diminished by any cause" (Li 2008, 130). Judging from his "Marginal Notes to Friedrich Paulsen: *A System of Ethics*," Mao believed that human nature necessitated a society to engage constantly in the struggle between peace and disorder (Schram 1992, 238). Mao also was convinced that engaging in struggle would bring enjoyment to one's life. A well-known saying by the young Mao Zedong was "To struggle against Heaven, what infinite joy! To struggle against Earth, what infinite joy! To struggle against Men, what infinite joy!" (Terrill 1980, 31). Hence, Mao considered the constant struggle with heaven, earth, and other people as a necessary means to achieving social ideals and self-actualization. Such a worldview in his early age prepared him for an easy acceptance of the Marxist doctrine of class struggle.

It is highly likely that Mao never systematically studied Marxism. His understanding of Marxism largely was based on interpretations by Li Dazhao and Chen Duxiu, who first applied Marxist theory of class struggle to conditions in China (Li 2008). Mao was inspired by the theory and was convinced by its ideological value through witnessing the success of the Soviet revolution led by Lenin in 1917. In 1921 the Communist Party was founded, and Mao actively involved himself in the party's efforts to revolutionize China. Marxist doctrines of class struggle energized Mao's revolutionary passion and gave Mao an ideological framework to diagnose China's problems and, in so doing, provide hope to change China for the better.

Applying Class Struggle to China's Revolution

Marx's theory of class struggle enlightened Mao, who took it as his lifelong ideological commitment and as the guiding principle for his revolution. Mao reinterpreted Marx and Lenin's view of class struggle by casting it as a battle to be won or lost by one class or the other, rather than, for example, a benign coexistence between different social classes. In Mao's words, "Class struggle: some classes triumph, others are eliminated. Such is history; such is the history of civilization for thousands of years. To interpret history from this viewpoint is historical materialism; standing in opposition to this view point is historical idealism" (Mao

1949/1967d, 428). Historical materialism, in Mao's view, represented truth, correctness, progress, and morality, while historical idealism stood for falsehood, incorrectness, backward thinking, and immorality. This conceptual bifurcation made class struggle a battleground, treating it as a moral choice instead of a social phenomenon.

Moreover, Mao considered class struggle as a method of differentiating between friends and enemies. In 1926 Mao wrote "Analysis of the Classes in Chinese Society," in which Mao asked, "Who are our enemies? Who are our friends? This is a question of the first importance for the revolution. The basic reason why all previous revolutionary struggles in China achieved so little was their failure to unite with real friends in order to attack real enemies" (Mao 1926/1967a, 13). Mao then used class analysis to categorize friends and enemies, dividing Chinese people into five classes: the national bourgeoisie; the middle bourgeoisie; the petite bourgeoisie; the semiproletariat; and the proletariat. Mao never trusted the national bourgeoisie, for he thought that they were interested only in making profits and tended to vacillate between disliking imperialism and fearing revolution (Mao 1935/1967a, 155). Accordingly Mao proposed a policy of condemning the nation's bourgeoisie as well as uniting with them (Mao 1939/1967b, 290). For Mao, uniting with the national bourgeoisie was necessary to build an alliance for fighting against foreign imperialists. But in ideological and cultural aspects of the Chinese society, the national bourgeoisie belonged to the wealthy social-economic class, which was inevitably in conflict with the proletariat. Additionally Mao did not trust intellectuals, grouping them with the middle and petite bourgeoisie and calling them "three-day revolutionaries" and "dangerous to recruit" (Mao 1935/1967a, 164). However, during the war period Mao considered them as "constituting one of the motive forces of the revolution" and "a reliable ally of the proletariat" (Mao 1939/1967b, 321). In this sense, the categories of friends and ene-·mies fluctuated; the classes considered enemies were treated as friends when Mao needed them to build a large alliance at the beginning of his revolutionary cause, when the CCP was still weak and unpopular.

By 1937, after ten years of class alliance, Mao had narrowed down the Chinese classes from five to two: the proletarian and the bourgeoisie. Mao claimed that the proletarian class was the ruling class and that the CCP was the leader of the proletarian class, carrying on the legacy of Marxism. Moreover, Mao asserted that members of the proletariat class were the most progressive. Members of the bourgeois class, on the contrary, exploited others and were by nature bad people. Mao was convinced that the materially rich people such as bureaucrats, warlords, and even the educated people with rich family backgrounds would inherently align with the national bourgeoisie, the class enemy. Their material condition predetermined their propensity for self-interest and opposition against "good people"— the proletariat/revolutionary class. In Mao's words, "In a class society everyone lives as a member of a particular class, and every kind of thinking, without exception, is stamped with the brand of a class" (Mao 1937/1967a, 296).

The division of the classes into the proletariat and the bourgeoisie originated from Marx, but Marx's concept of the proletarian class consisted of industrial laborers. China at the time was still largely an agricultural country, and the majority of Mao's followers were peasants whom Mao called semiproletarians.[2] For Marx, class status was based on the mode of production, but for Mao, class status was attached to moral right. New standards in China for differentiating class status included assessing a person's moral integrity and judging a person's political attitudes. Mao believed that a person's attitude and action reflected that person's class status. To achieve moral integrity and the correct political attitude, a person was to be selfless, loyal to the party, and willing to sacrifice for the Communist cause. Those party members who deviated from these standards would be considered as belonging to the bourgeois class or charged with "counter-revolutionary" activities, which should be condemned and eliminated. Mao used his class struggle rhetoric to justify his purge of the Anti-Bolshevik League in 1930 in the Futian incident[3] and subsequent political campaigns to eliminate ideological heretics or his political opponents.

Mao's outlook toward class issues was not without traditional Chinese origins. Tang and Zuo (1996) have made an interesting assertion that Mao's moralistic "approach of analyzing classes actually originated from some Chinese traditional viewpoints other than Marxism" (160). This statement has some elements of truth. In Chinese history the change of dynasties was characterized by peasant rebellions against feudal monarchies. There was a general resentment against rich people in Chinese history, which is reflected in the common saying *weifu buren* 为富不仁 (rich people are not benevolent). Mao's moralistic and dichotomized approach to class struggle had an enthymemic appeal to Chinese people. Mao's resentment toward the rich people also may have come from some of his early experiences when he witnessed starvation among peasants in his hometown while rich people in the cities had an abundance of food but refused to share with the poor. Another experience occurred when he was studying in a middle school where rich students despised him for wearing ragged clothes (Snow 1938, 135, 137). Mao told Edgar Snow that these experiences left lasting impressions on him.

Mao also justified the moral legitimacy of the proletarian class by using the rhetoric of the new and inevitable. In interpreting Marx's theory of social change, Mao explained that the bourgeoisie used to play a progressive role but had turned reactionary and had to be overthrown. The proletariat had become the new exalted class in the same way it had in the Soviet Union.[4] This process of social change was one that, in Mao's words, "all other countries will inevitably take" (Mao 1937/1967a, 334). Mao's ontological view of the world was that new forces inevitably would replace old forces in a cycle of societal evolution. Having suffered from humiliation imposed by foreign powers, physical and psychological wounds of war, and also poverty and starvation, many of the Chinese people had strong desires for social change. Mao's rhetoric of class struggle allowed them to distinguish between their friends and their enemies, provided them with clear direction, and gave them the hope and illusion of smashing the old society and fighting for a new society.

Mao's discourse on class struggle not only was predicated on a person's class background but also focused on a person's class consciousness as manifested through that person's attitude and behavior. From 1937 to 1949, while he was commanding his army to fight against the Japanese and the Nationalists, Mao never stopped his ideological efforts to convert the class consciousness of young intellectuals who tended to come from the rich families and who had traces of both bourgeois and Western liberal thinking. Mao believed that a person could rebel against or even denounce his or her own class. In fact, many Communist leaders, including Mao, had come from landlord or bourgeois backgrounds. By joining the Communist Party, they had abandoned their rich class identity and transformed themselves into members of the proletariat. To be qualified as a member of the proletariat, a person had to involve himself or herself in the denouncement of class enemies, engage in criticism and self-criticism, and show absolute loyalty to the party. Those seeking to transform themselves into this preferred class were required to read Marxist-Leninist works, study Mao's works, and speak the revolutionary language largely constructed by Mao in his writings. One conclusion that might be drawn from this examination of Mao's speeches and writings is that his rhetoric of class struggle prior to 1949 had been effective in uniting the party, transforming the ideological consciousness of intellectuals and party members, and pushing the success of Mao's revolution.

Class Struggle in the Post-1949 Period

In 1949 Mao's People's Liberation Army defeated the Nationalists and established the People's Republic of China, known as Red China by the West. In the first few years of the new republic, Mao seemed to focus on economic development and the elimination of corruption. However, he faced three challenges: resistance from the remnants of the Nationalist Party; skepticism from those who doubted the CCP's leadership ability to construct a viable economy; and unrest stemming from a fractioning party. Since the CCP had its roots in rural China and relied on peasants as its largest base of support, the party's legitimacy to rule was questioned. Fearing resistance from the bourgeois class and rebellions from those still loyal to the Nationalist Party, Mao launched the Campaign to Suppress Counter-Revolutionaries in 1950[5] and a Sufan movement in 1955[6] to purge hidden "counter-revolutionaries." Both movements aimed at eradicating Nationalist forces as well as political opponents within the party. Millions were arrested and executed, marking a period commonly known as "red terror."

Despite the domestic resistance and international isolation in the early 1950s, Mao was clear that he had to prove his party's legitimacy to lead the nation by improving the living standards of the Chinese people and by building a strong military defense. At the Eighth National Conference of the Communist Party of China held in September 1956, the CCP announced its central tasks for the next decade: economic and cultural reconstruction. The ideology of class struggle was put aside. The report containing this announcement was drafted by Liu Shaoqi, Deng Xiaoping, and Chen Yun; and was endorsed by Mao (Mao 1956/1992b, 144). However, Mao was still concerned about the petite bourgeoisie composed largely of intellectuals and some top-level party officials. Mao's distrust and suspicion of intellectuals can be traced to the criticism toward party leadership from young intellectuals back in the Yan'an period of the early 1940s.

From the late 1930s to the early 1940s, many young and urban intellectuals came to Yan'an to join the revolution. They were attracted to Communist ideals such as equality and plain living. However, after a while some of them began to criticize party officials for their ill behaviors and authoritarian styles. Mao was alerted to such criticism and felt that his leadership was threatened. In response to the threat, Mao launched the Rectification Campaign in 1942. This was aimed at eradicating dissenting voices and reinforcing loyalty to the CCP. During the campaign Mao overtly recognized the contributions and sacrifices by young intellectuals for the Communist cause. Even then, however, Mao still questioned the allegiance of this group, and he feared that their inner thoughts were not in line with party ideology. "They could be liberalists, reformists, and anarchists but using the name of Communist," he wrote; such a problem would "lead to class struggle within the party" (Mao 1945/1991, 993).

Mao's fundamental lack of trust of the petite bourgeoisie was largely derived from Lenin, who claimed that the petite bourgeoisie had "dual sides. On one hand, it leans toward the proletariat and democracy; on the other hand, it turns reactionary. The petty bourgeoisie would try to block the progression of history and easily could be seduced by the system of dictatorship. This group can act against the proletariat toward solidifying their own, small capitalist status" (Lenin 1897/1984, 436). While Lenin proposed the methods of "struggle, influence, and inducing" with this group (Lenin 1919/1985b, 277), Mao's relationship with intellectuals was ambivalent. On one hand, he had to rely on them for eulogizing the glory of the Communist cause to enhance a positive image of the CCP and his own popularity. On the other hand, Mao's suspicions of them never diminished.

Based on his distrust of intellectuals, Mao extended his criteria for a new kind of class enemy: the hidden enemy that indulged in thought crime. In his speech at the Second Session of the Seventh Central Committee on March 5, 1949, Mao warned his comrades, "After the enemies with guns have been wiped out, there will still be enemies without guns; they are bound to struggle desperately against us; we must never regard these enemies lightly" (Mao 1949/1967d, 364). These "enemies without guns," according to Mao, were more insidious and dangerous, and the struggle with them was more ruthless.

Mao's adherence to "class struggle" after the CCP took power was significantly influenced by Lenin. In Lenin's thinking, when the proletarian class took power and exercised its dictatorship, the former exploitive class including landlords and capitalists would fight back. The class struggle between the two groups inevitably would take place. In Lenin's words, "When the proletariat takes power, its class struggle with the bourgeoisie will not end. On the contrary, the class struggle will become even more comprehensive, severe, and brutal" (Lenin 1920/1986a, 184). Further, Lenin stated that the "proletarian dictatorship is not the end of the class struggle. The class struggle will continue in new forms... and the overthrown class will never stop resisting the proletarian dictatorship" (Lenin 1919/1985b, 363). Mao was convinced by Lenin's explanation that the bourgeoisie could not be completely eradicated either physically or spiritually after a revolution. Mao concurred that the bourgeoisie would still hold economic and cultural resources, they would continue to benefit from advantages in management and the arts, and they would retain influence on society that would enable them to fight back and resist the proletarian dictatorship in different sectors of life (Lenin 1919/1986b, vol. 37., 275–76). Moreover, in Lenin's view, the bourgeois class would "try ten times harder with fanatical enthusiasm and would double its increase of hatred, fighting back to recover their lost paradise and protect their sweet lives from the past" (1918/1985a, 255). Mao took Lenin's warning seriously and was suspicious and vigilant toward an overthrow by the bourgeoisie, an overthrow intended to "restore" capitalism and pull China back to its semicolonial and semifeudal past.

Mao also took another of Lenin's warnings seriously. That is, even when the bourgeois class was overthrown, a new type of bourgeoisie would grow to replace the old one. According to Lenin (1918/1985b), "We have indeed overthrown the landlord and the bourgeoisie, cleaned the path. But we have not built a socialist edifice yet. The old generation has been eradicated, but a new generation will grow in this soil which has bred many capitalists. Some would think 'capitalists have made themselves rich; now it is my turn [to get rich].' So there lies the root for a new, growing capitalism" (242). According to this logic, the class struggle would never end; one class always would find a class enemy in a society, whether that enemy was the old or the new bourgeois class. In this sense, it was Lenin who cemented the idea of class struggle into Mao's thoughts. Lenin pointed out to Mao the kind of class enemy he would face even after he took power.

Mao experienced a few incidents that reinforced his belief that the petite bourgeoisie/intellectuals posed potential threats to his legitimacy. Hu Feng

(1902–85), for example, a Chinese literary theorist and critic who established his reputation as a leading figure in the League of Left-Wing Writers, criticized Mao's politicized theory on art and literature during the Yan'an period. Hu published "Reports on the Practice and State of Art and Literature in Recent Years" in 1954. In the report Hu called for writers to use their subjective viewpoints in their writing, which directly challenged Mao's doctrine of heroic representation of the masses in art and literature. Hu Feng was accused of being a counterrevolutionary and was imprisoned for twenty-four years.

Other instances spurred Mao's suspicions. One was direct criticism of Mao from prominent intellectuals in response to Mao's famous slogan "One Hundred Flowers Bloom, and One Hundred Schools of Thought Contend."[7] Zhang Bojun 章伯钧 (1895–1969), chairman of China's Peasants and Workers' Democratic Party and vice chairman of the National Alliance, proposed a multiparty, shared leadership in national affairs. Luo Longji 罗隆基 (1896–1965), also vice chairman of the National Alliance, demanded the rehabilitation of the Elimination of Counter-Revolutionary Movement led by the CCP. Chu Anping 储安平, the chief editor of the *Guangming Daily*, accused the CCP of *dang tianxia* (control of everything). Because the top leader of every workplace was a CCP member, Chu Anping claimed that the CCP was not acting on its promise for a government with multiparty political alliances. Instead the CCP was the only ruling party for China.

When such criticism became harsh and threatening to Mao's power and the Communist Party's control over China, Mao considered the complaints as signs of a class struggle and as attempts by the bourgeoisie to take over China. To Mao, it was absolutely necessary for the proletariat class to exercise dictatorship over the bourgeois class; otherwise the bourgeois class would attempt to reinstate capitalism. This rationale gave Mao the justification to launch the Anti-Rightist Movement in 1957. The purpose of the campaign was to suppress critics (mostly intellectuals) both within and outside the party. Mao accused the intellectuals who challenged his CCP party rule to be rightists in the anti-rightist campaign.[8]

The mantra of class struggle was not simply promoting a political ideology; it was also a political strategy to eliminate dissenting views. Mao presented the political strategy as a stage of development, an issue in the process of "permanent revolution." In his words,

> In China, although socialist transformation has in the main been completed as regards the system of ownership, and although the large-scale, turbulent class struggle of the masses characteristic of times of revolution have in the main come to an end, there are still remnants of the overthrown landlord and comprador classes, there is still a bourgeoisie, and the remoulding of the petty bourgeoisie has only just started. Class struggle is by no means over. The class struggle between the proletariat and the bourgeoisie, the class struggle between the various political forces, and the class struggle between the proletariat and

the bourgeoisie in the ideological field will still be protracted and tortuous and at times even very sharp. (Mao 1957/1977, 409)

Here, Mao grouped the petite bourgeoisie with the landlord and bourgeois classes, suggesting that intellectuals were a new kind of class enemy and that class struggle with this group lay in the ideological differences between capitalism and socialism, between Western liberalism and the proletarian dictatorship.

By labeling intellectuals as class enemies, Mao dismissed the validity of their criticism and ignored the opportunity to reform his political policies. In one of his speeches in 1958, Mao dismissed the knowledge of bourgeois professors as a delusion of the world and called people to "despise it, loath it, and scorn it, just like the way we despise British and American forces and knowledge in the Western world" (Mao 1958/1992b, 118). Because of Mao's denigration of the intellectuals, the public attitude toward them changed; from being the most respected group in traditional China *chou laojiu* (stinking number nine),[9] a pejorative term for intellectuals used during the Cultural Revolution.

During the period of the Anti-Japanese War (1937–45) and the civil war (1945–49), Mao treated the middle and petite bourgeoisie as allies and classified imperialists and members of the comprador bourgeoisie as class enemies. But when the imperialists were driven out and the bourgeoisies were overthrown, what enemy remained? In Mao's thinking, the victory of the Chinese Communist Party in 1949 did not guarantee the elimination of the constant class enemy, the bourgeois class, nor did it guarantee the elimination of other enemies within the country. Three new kinds of enemies now posed threats to Mao's China. First were those individuals born to rich families, such as many of China's prominent intellectuals. In Mao's thinking, these people would inherently carry traces of their rich class backgrounds. Second were those people who came from poor families but had transformed into the new bourgeois class—typically the bureaucrats within the party—now living luxurious lives and deserting their obligations to self-criticism and self-examination. Third were those who expressed dissenting views and crusaded against Mao's economic policies, such as Mao's failed Great Leap Forward drive. Peng Dehuai was an example of the third type of class enemy. After failing in his Great Leap Forward and causing nationwide famine, Mao was criticized by Peng Dehuai, a CCP general and defense minister, for over-reporting grain production.[10] Mao accused Peng of being a class enemy, charging that Peng spoke for the bourgeoisie while posing as a representative of the proletariat. Instead of listening to Peng and learning from his failed policies, Mao treated Peng as a class enemy and claimed that a class struggle still existed within the party.

From 1958 to 1962 Mao became increasingly concerned with the emergence of "new bourgeois elements" in Chinese society. As Mao's fear of China turning into a capitalistic society increased, his suspicion of intellectuals and top CCP leaders deepened and his advocacy of class struggle escalated. In 1962 Mao issued his edict "Never forget the class struggle" at the Second Plenum of the Eighth Chinese Communication Party Assembly. In his speech at the Tenth Plenum of the Eighth Central Committee, Mao explained why class struggle still existed by quoting from Lenin: "Lenin said: 'After the victory of the revolution, because of the existence of the bourgeoisie internationally, because the existence of bourgeois remnants internally, because the petit bourgeoisie exists and continually generates a bourgeoisie, therefore, the classes which have been overthrown within the country will continue to exist for a long time to come and may even attempt restoration [to capitalism]'" (Schram 1974, 189). Based on this rhetoric of prophecy, Mao warned party members, "We must raise our vigilance and properly educate our youth as well as the cadres, the masses and the middle-and basic-level cadres.... We must talk about this [class struggle] every year, every month, every day" (189–90). In Mao's view, as long as class existed in a society, class struggle never ended. The class enemy—the bourgeois class, including the petite bourgeoisie—would take over power they had lost and would exploit the proletarian class. To Mao, class struggle was the law of society and history.

Mao's paranoia of being sabotaged and his vehement propagation of class struggle were compounded by international exigencies as well. In 1956 uprisings took place in Hungary and Poland against their respective Communist governments, and these escalated Mao's fear that an uprising would occur in China. On February 25, 1956, Nikita Khrushchev delivered a secret speech to the delegates at the Twentieth Communist Party of the Soviet Union Congress. The speech revealed the brutality of Stalin's bloody purge of millions of counter-revolutionaries and dissidents.[11] This report shocked the CCP and shook the godlike image of Mao in China, as Stalin was highly exalted in China as well. At the same time, China's foreign relations with the United States were frozen as the United States did not recognize the legitimacy of Mao's China. However, according to Mao's interpretation, the United States had not given up on China but rather had devised a "peaceful evolution" strategy aimed at combating communism not through warfare but through economics and the infiltration of culture and ideas.[12] John Foster Dulles (1888–1959), President Dwight Eisenhower's (1890–1959) secretary of state, gave a speech on China on November 18, 1958, claiming that as China modernized, the Chinese people and the American people would become friends, also hinting that China would gradually move to a democratic society (Mao 1958/1992d, 606).[13]

Mao allowed the whole speech to be published and circulated it the next day among party members. Mao also carefully studied Dulles's other speeches and concluded that the United States had an ulterior motive to sabotage China's socialism and hijack Marxist ideology through a "peaceful evolution."[14] Mao stated at the Tenth Plenum of the Eighth Central Committee that revisionism may emerge in the third generation of the CCP leaders. But, he argued, that change would not matter.

"When the grandson becomes a revisionist, the grandson of the grandson will want Marxism. This is the law of dialectics" (Pang and Jin 2003, 1245–46). As Mao faced these international challenges, it is not surprising that he tightened his ideological control for fear of losing his personal power, fear of turning China into a capitalist society, or fear of becoming a revisionist like leaders in the Soviet Union. Mao's rhetorical weapon of ideological control was class struggle.

Class Struggle as Everyday Life

For Mao, class struggle was both ontological reality and epistemological inquiry. In his words, "Class struggle is an objective reality, independent of man's will....Class struggle is inevitable. It cannot be avoided even if people want to avoid it" (Mao 1957/1977, 454). To Mao, everything should be perceived, analyzed, and evaluated through the lens of class struggle. For example, in offering advice to young people on how to conduct research on society, Mao said that "the only way to know the conditions is to make social investigations, to investigate the conditions of each social class in real life"; the survey must be conducted by using "the fundamental viewpoint of Marxism, i.e. the method of class analysis. Only thus can we acquire even the most rudimentary knowledge of China's social problems" (Mao 1941/1967c, 11). In this sense, class struggle was totalized and rendered a framework for political judgments and human relationships.

Mao stretched his evaluations about class struggle to the topics of love and human nature and how these topics were expressed in art and literature. Mao contended that "it is a basic Marxist concept that being determines consciousness, that the objective realities of class struggle and national struggle determine our thoughts and feelings....Now as for 'love' in a class society, there can be only class love" (Mao 1942/1967c, 73–74). His view became more absolute when he asserted that "there is absolutely no such thing in the world as love or hatred without reason or cause....There has been no such all-inclusive love since humanity was divided into classes....There will be genuine love of humanity— after classes are eliminated all over the world" (90–91). That is, love was possible only if two persons came from the same class background. During the Cultural Revolution, dating partners wrote their love letters filled with revolutionary slogans on class struggle rather than expressions of romantic feelings. For example, a man wrote to his woman lover, "Nowadays class struggle is extremely complicated. There are all kinds of people in this world. You should stand firmly on your revolutionary ground. Never trust glib tongues and do not let [the] class enemy take advantage of you. You should always tighten the string of class struggle when interacting with people at [your] workplace and in social contexts." The woman replied, "I pledge in the name of revolution that I will stand firmly on my ground in facing the complicated class struggle embedded in human relationships. I will handle well any kind of relationship. Please feel at ease."[15]

This kind of revolutionary letter was common during the Cultural Revolution. Writing letters with expressions on class struggle indicated a level of "proletarian consciousness" and, in turn, one's moral compass. Professor Qian Liqun (2012) from Peking University shared that during the 1950s Qian's father was accused of being a counter-revolutionary. When Qian applied to join the Communist Youth, he was told he had to denounce his father and sever their relationship. At first he refused to do so, but finally he was persuaded by Mao's rhetoric of class struggle. Mao's teaching made Qian choose between his father and the politically correct class stand. If his father was a counterrevolutionary, Qian was told, his father belonged to the enemy class. If his father was the enemy, the argument went on, then Qian could not love his father and instead must cast hate toward the man who raised him. Being fourteen years old at the time, Qian had no critical ability to challenge this logic. Qian (2012) lamented that "the blood relationship between father and son is based on natural love. It is absolute and unconditional. . . . If you hurt your father, you have overstepped the bottom line of being a human" (35). Sadly Qian's denouncement of his father was justified in the moral appeal of class struggle rather than the "natural love" Qian later defined.

Mao purported that all human behavior and thought processes were based on class status and consciousness. In his words, "In class society there is only human nature of a class character; there is no human nature above classes. We uphold the human nature of the proletariat and of the masses of the people, while the landlord and bourgeois classes uphold the human nature of their own classes" (Mao 1942/1967c, 90). Artists and intellectuals were instructed by Mao to praise the proletariat and condemn the bourgeoisie in their art productions and performances.[16] No art or literature was allowed to transcend class or be independent of politics. Mao stated, "If you are a bourgeois writer or artist, you will eulogize not the proletariat but the bourgeoisie, and if you are a proletarian writer or artist, you will eulogize not the bourgeoisie but the proletariat and working people; it must be one or the other" (92). During the 1960s a number of movies with the theme of class struggle were shown repeatedly; these films powerfully reinforced the Chinese people's class consciousness.[17] In these films the heroes were from the proletarian class representing Communist morals of sacrifice, hard work, frugality, and loyalty to the party. The villains lived or had a desire to live luxurious lives and refused to follow the party line. All human expressions became essentialized in class categories.

To Mao, the proletarian and the bourgeoisie were two opposing classes that maintained fundamentally different interests. Their conflict was irreconcilable; therefore the ideological struggle between the proletariat and the bourgeoisie would never end. For an artist or a writer, class status and consciousness would not change unless the artist remolded his or her thinking and feelings to align with the workers and peasants (1942/1967c,73). Mao's essentialist view of class struggle contradicted his dialectical stance that nothing was stable and that change inevitably would happen. If a movement developed too far in one direction, it would naturally swing back to the opposite direction. Mao wrote to his wife Jiang Qing a year after he launched the Cultural Revolution, which brought chaos to China: "I read materials [about the Cultural Revolution] every day and I am very interested in reading them. The great chaos in the world will bring great order" (Mao 1966/1998a, 71).

Mao showed his adamant obsession with class struggle again in his published talks with his nephew, Mao Yuanxin, in 1964.[18] He said, "To study Marxism-Leninism is to study class struggle. Class struggle is everywhere; it is in your institution; a counter-revolutionary has appeared in your institution. Are you aware of this or not?" (Schram 1974, 243). Not only had Mao reduced Marxism to a single doctrine of class struggle, but in addition his words encouraged coworkers, friends, and even family members to remain vigilant about potential class enemies. Soon the slogan "Never forget the class struggle" became popular and permeated public and private discourse. Any conflict of opinions could escalate to issues of class struggle between the proletariat and the bourgeoisie. This escalation of class struggle, however, was only a prelude for another revolutionary storm: the Cultural Revolution.

In 1966 Mao launched the Cultural Revolution in the name of eradicating residual bourgeoisie among members of the government and preventing China from becoming a capitalistic society.[19] During the Cultural Revolution (1966–76), the mantra "Never forget the class struggle" filled speeches, big-character posters, rallies, and pamphlets. In a Red Guard speech, Liang Xiaosheng wrote, "We revolutionary students fight with determination at the forefront of class struggle. We pledge to Chairman Mao to be the dare-or-die corps on the front lines of class struggle.... Victory belongs to us because we have the sharp weapon of class struggle from Chairman Mao's thoughts" (Liang 1998, 27). "Class struggle" had become a banal phrase that permeated Chinese political discourse and escalated a radical and dichotomized way of thinking. Many Chinese people, young and old, expressed in their diaries their determination to carry on Mao's call for class struggle. For example, a friend wrote in her diary in March 1972 that "struggle [class struggle] brings us joy and happiness; struggle [class struggle] is our ideals and future. We—the youth of Mao Zedong's era—achieve our revolutionary goals through class struggle, spending every minute and every second on the cause of class struggle for the humanity. Struggle! Struggle! Struggle for our entire life—the revolutionary youth!" (Li 1972). Using such compassionate language to demonstrate their loyalty to Mao and their high spirit for class struggle was typical among young Chinese during the Cultural Revolution. As Qian (2012) notes accurately, "Since 1957, Mao gradually pushed China into the chariot of class struggle, just as he did for the Great Leap Forward. Once the chariot started, no one could stop it. Mao's Cultural Revolution brought China into another catastrophe" (377).

The Cultural Revolution was instigated in the name of class struggle. Mao claimed himself as the representative of the proletarian camp and condemned Liu Shaoqi for embodying the evils of capitalism and the bourgeois class.[20] At the individual level, a person's class background became the sole criterion for identifying friends and enemies, good and evil. Class enemies were those with rich family backgrounds but also those who said words or took actions that diverged from Mao's thinking. It was not uncommon for people to disown their parents, divorce their spouses, or beat their teachers because these people had been accused of being class enemies. These accused class enemies, many of whom held influential positions, were sent to prisons and deprived of any political power. For ordinary people who were labeled "class enemies," Mao's solution was to reform and rehabilitate them through harsh physical labor and "thought reform" campaigns characterized by criticism and self-criticism.[21]

Since class consciousness was also determined by one's political attitude, anyone had the potential to become a class enemy; everyone had to remain vigilant about their own bourgeois/capitalistic tendencies; everyone had to speak Mao's revolutionary discourse; and everyone had to engage in repeated criticism and self-criticism to guard against becoming members of the bourgeois class. Moreover, violence against persons who were labeled as class enemies became sanctioned and legitimized. Many innocent people were persecuted and beaten; some committed suicide; homes were looted; and friends and family members betrayed each other. These acts allowed for deception, self-deception, dehumanization, and humiliation. Red Guards considered their violence as revolutionary acts conducted on behalf of the proletariat and in defense of Chairman Mao. The Cultural Revolution made class struggle a witch hunt, a ubiquitous phenomenon. The entire nation was politicized in almost every aspect under the banner of class struggle.

The Impact of Mao's Theory of Class Struggle

In his youth Mao witnessed the failed attempts to build a modern China with equality, self-reliance, and prosperity. Drawing from those experiences and influenced by Marxism and Leninism, Mao ardently believed that the progression of history was characterized by the struggle between the proletariat class and the bourgeois class and that such a struggle was embedded in every aspect of life. Mao defined class division not only by material possessions and socioeconomic backgrounds, but also by ideology, attitude, language, and moral stance. To Mao, the proletariat class was inherently good and the bourgeois class was inherently evil. The interests of both classes were irreconcilable. Mao was convinced that the proletarian class must defeat the bourgeois class in the struggle to maintain the control of the Communist Party and to push history forward toward an egalitarian, democratic, and prosperous China.

Mao followed Lenin in claiming that the proletarian class was the most moralistic and advanced while the bourgeois class was the most exploitive and insidious. His association of the proletariat class with good people and the bourgeois class with bad people created a moral dichotomy for the Chinese people. His theories about class struggle were made manifest in his orientation toward radicalism, essentialism, and reductionism. Mao claimed to be a voice for the proletariat class. Such assumptions gave him the legitimacy to condemn the so-called class enemies. Mao also claimed to be a defendant of true Marxism throughout his writings, which added to his ethos and enhanced his persuasive appeal. Moreover, Mao bestowed upon himself the roles of interpreter and creative practitioner of Marxism, which established his ideological authority in the party and among the Chinese people.

Mao's theories about class struggle also were imbued with an apocalyptic appeal. In illustrating his theory, Mao attempted to convince the Chinese people that the CCP was on the right side of history by embracing a socialist society and proletarian dictatorship. A capitalist society with a bourgeois rule would pull history backward; only when the proletariat was in control of political power could history move forward. Kluver (1996) deems this mentality to be China's "national myth." Mao's rhetoric of class struggle played this myth and offered a "prophetic voice" (Frank 2009) to the Chinese people.

In addition Mao's theories about class struggle capitalized wholly on fear. Mao asserted that if the bourgeois class became the ruling class, China would turn into a capitalistic society filled with social evils and the proletariat would once again be exploited, forced to endure poverty and oppression. The government repeatedly depicted the evils of the old China through arts, literature, films, and stage performances. All these art forms propagated the same message: if the old China came back, the Communist utopia would never be realized. The dream of an independent, egalitarian, democratic, and prosperous China would never come true.

This argument gave Mao the rationale for "permanent revolution"—the idea that class struggle would never end in China. Mao's class-struggle rhetoric also indicated his deep suspicion of intellectuals and their dissenting views within the CCP, as well as his own fear of being sabotaged. Mao's paranoia mentality contributed to his obsession with real or imagined "enemies." Moreover, Mao used class struggle as a political strategy to suppress dissenting views and eliminate his opponents. When he expanded his definition of a class enemy from "enemies with guns" to "enemies without guns," class struggle became an ideological struggle, ultimately turning into a weapon of violence.

The notion of class struggle politicized and polarized the thinking patterns of the Chinese people. The pervasiveness of the class struggle doctrine divided the Chinese people between proletariat and bourgeois classes and polarized their judgments of others. Everyday thought processes became wholly dichotomous—everything was rendered in black and white. Chinese people related to one another either as political comrades or as class enemies. The proletariat class became a political capital, while people who were labeled as the bourgeois class were deprived of their human dignity and civil rights. The traditional Chinese values of human relationship characterized by harmony, tolerance, and respect as propagated by Confucius and Mencius were replaced by confrontation and hostility driven by the mentality of class struggle. Millions of innocent people were alienated, persecuted, and tortured to death after being labeled as class enemies. Children of the class enemies were discriminated against in every aspect of their lives and became what Gao Hua (2004) calls "politically despicable people."

The hallmark of the traditional Chinese way of life was *zhongyong* 中庸 (the mean or middle way). Confucius considered *zhongyong* to be the highest virtue in a person because it maintains equilibrium by avoiding extreme thought and actions. Another core value in traditional Chinese culture is *he* 和 (harmony), while the guiding norm in interpersonal relationships is called *yiheweigui* 以和为贵 (valuing harmony). Tolerance and compromise were strategies taught in the practice of managing interpersonal conflict. The notion and implementation of Mao's class struggle, however, instigated interpersonal tension, hostility, and hatred among the Chinese people. Many Chinese people adopted the *dou* 斗 (fight, struggle) mentality, the opposite of *he*, as their guidance and value for human relationships. Consequently some Chinese people easily picked fights, quickly took sides, and were more likely to use verbal attacks in arguments (Chen 2007).[22]

Jerome Ch'en claims that Mao's obsession with class struggle actually stemmed from his resentful personality, which can be traced back to his resentment of his father's authoritarian parenting, his witnessing of injustice and poverty in China, and his readings of revolutionary literature by anarchists and Marxists (Chen 1969). Mao's personality was characterized not by *he* but by *dou*. Ironically Mao established his own absolute authority and instigated poverty in China through his efforts toward class struggle in the name of building a society with equality, democracy, and prosperity. Michael Lynch (2004) paints Mao with even more contradictory characteristics: "As a Chinese revolutionary, he rejected Western values but made it his mission to match Western achievements; he led a revolution against the world to join the world. His driving purpose was to liberate China from decades of foreign oppression, but to realize this aim he adopted a Western political theory—Marxism" (2). Mao appeared to be a full-blown Marxist and Leninist in interpreting and executing the doctrine of class struggle but also a man with the mentality to rule like a Chinese emperor. In the name of doing good for the Chinese people, he actually manifested a banality of evil[23] by adhering to a radical Western ideology combined with authoritarian characteristics rooted in Chinese tradition.

By propagating and executing the doctrine of class struggle, Mao drastically changed the face of China dominated by Confucian values into a Marxist state. In traditional Chinese culture, social structures were characterized by hierarchical relationships; in addition the main moral tenets for human conduct were benevolence, righteousness, rituals, wisdom, and trustworthiness. Those who wielded more power in these hierarchical relationships were expected to practice such moral tenets to insure a harmonious, or *he,* way of living for all. Mao's rhetoric on class struggle abandoned these traditional modes of societal organization and created a new system of analysis on the perception of reality and human relationships, and a new way of thinking and making judgment on people's political identity. In many ways class struggle was a failed ideological doctrine and practice in China as it brought destruction and misery to the Chinese people. Gao Hua (2004) makes a good point that using class struggle as the dominant ideology during the peaceful period of history in China inevitably hurt and discriminated against the Chinese people, delaying the establishment of laws and universal values that would protect people's dignity and equality toward achieving social justice.

Nevertheless some Chinese scholars in Mainland China speak positively about Mao's impact on the transformation of Chinese culture. In his summary of Mao's contribution to cultural change through his theory of class struggle, Li Pengcheng (1993) argues that Mao's theory of class struggle placed the masses in the forefront of importance. Those masses acted as the force that pushed history forward, bringing a more independent and equitable society to the country than had been in place during China's semicolonial past. Traditional Chinese, in contrast, valued *zhongyong* 中庸 and *hexie* 和谐 (harmony), which keep Chinese society static and repetitive. Under the banner of class struggle, the Chinese people went from living in a "harmonious stasis" to living with a more vibrant, enthusiastic, and optimistic outlook toward life.

I disagree with Li's evaluation of the positive impact of basing social action on an ideology of class struggle. As illustrated above, the doctrine and practice of class struggle is disastrous. However, Mao indeed reshaped the Chinese character from what Lin Yutang (1962) has described as patience, indifference, old roguery, contentment, and conservatism to a new character of contention, competitiveness, aggression, excitement, and ambition. During Mao's period, especially during the 1950s and early 1960s, Chinese people unleashed unprecedented enthusiasm in building the nation's economy. Mao's revolutionary romanticism, his advocacy of change and fighting spirit, had significant impacts on the transformation of Chinese culture and the Chinese character. It is not an exaggeration to attribute China's economic success in the post-Mao era to this reinvented Chinese spirit and character. In addition, to a lesser degree of evil, Mao did not resort to the extremes practiced by the Khmer Rouge in Cambodia[24] or by Stalin in the purge[25] during which millions of innocent people were executed.

Class Struggle in the Post-Mao Period

Mao died in 1976, and with his death came the end of the Cultural Revolution. After his death there was mass disillusionment toward Mao's precepts, especially his theories on class struggle. In 1978 the CCP announced the abandonment of the class-struggle precept and centered its task on economic development and modernization. In the post-Mao era, China also abandoned Mao's idealism and radicalization. With the economy in a state of despair, Mao's successors began publicly rejecting Mao's precepts about class struggle.[26] Maurice Meisner (1989) observes that "perhaps the most telling symptom of the deradicalization of Chinese communism in the post-Mao era is the decline of revolutionary utopianism and the ritualization of socialist and communist goals" (358). Along with such a decline was the disappearance of a radicalized and revolutionary style of rhetoric. Post-Mao Chinese top leaders including Deng Xiaoping, Jiang Zemin, Hu Jintao, and Xi Jinping never used the term "class struggle" in their public speeches.[27] Workers who were formerly labeled as members of the proletarian class now were referred to as "ordinary labor" (普通劳动者).

Needless to say, China's economy boomed in the post-Mao era. It became the second largest economy in the world. Except for some decline in the past three years (2012–2015), the nation's GDP maintained an average of almost 10 percent for over thirty years since the launch of the economic reform in the early 1980s.[28] However, at the same time, internal conflicts between different interest groups intensified. The gap between the rich and the poor widened, and a new bourgeois class (people with extraordinary wealth) emerged. Jiang Zemin, the president of China after Deng Xiaoping, allowed the new bourgeoisie to join the Communist Party. Many children of the old revolutionaries held the financial and material resources of China, widening the class division between the "haves" and "have nots."[29] Workers and peasants, once treated by Mao as the proletarian class and the leading class of Chinese society, were being dispossessed and disadvantaged by the new economic policies that favored capitalists and foreign investment. In his book *Analysis of the Classes in Chinese Society* (2006), Jisheng Yang (杨继绳) identifies the new rich and new poor since China's economic reform in the early 1980s.

Ironically Mao's prediction of class struggle has become more evident in the post-Mao era. If Mao lived to see today's China, he would be saddened that his fear had become true—that the bourgeois class has beaten out the proletariat. China has become a state of semicapitalism under the leadership of the CCP. During Mao's era there was no class distinction in terms of material possessions.

Equality in salary, gender, education, and health had been largely achieved. Now, at the superficial level, China no longer champions the mentality of class confrontation, but the real class struggle has begun with the increasing gap between the new rich and the new poor. In his recent book *The Price of China's Economic Development,* Hong (2015) presents a compelling argument that the polarizing wealth/power, lack of an equitable social and legal system, and poverty of rights in China have resulted in social injustice, an abuse of power, and dreadful conditions for the poor and powerless—a heavy price that the Chinese people have paid for "economic miracles."

★ ★ ★ ★

FIVE

Mao Zedong's Rhetorical Construction of a New Communist Person

Belief in the malleability of human beings and their ability to change is recurrent in human history. Fukuzawa Yukichi (1835–1901), a Japanese Enlightenment writer, believed that Japanese people could become civilized if they were taught public virtue. Friedrich Nietzsche's (1844–1900) invention of Übermensch, or superman, painted the ideal goal of humanity through self-transcendence. In the history of communism, Lenin proposed the concept of "the new Soviet man" after establishing the Soviet Union.[1] Similarly Mao dedicated his life to cultivating the "new Communist person," someone who embodied a proletarian consciousness, showed loyalty to Mao and the Communist Party, was hardworking, and was willing to sacrifice for the country.

Mao spent his younger years emulating what he believed to be moral exemplars. Although he admired foreign leaders such as George Washington and Abraham Lincoln, Mao was more influenced by legendary Chinese heroes and nationalists such as Qu Yuan 屈原, Fan Zhongyan 范仲淹, Gu Yanwu 顾炎武, Zeng Guofan 曾国藩, and Liang Qichao 梁启超. All these Chinese legends shared in some part similar moral characteristics measured by traditional Chinese standards. These legends were industrious, strong-willed, plain-living, well-learned, courageous, and willing to sacrifice for the state. Mao drew inspiration from them for his own political ambition and spiritual nourishment.

John Fairbank (1972) observes, "Marxism, which grew out of the European experience, has a considerable degree of resonance with the Chinese experience" (31). According to Donald Munro (1977), the writings of Marx and Engels provided a philosophical base of malleability for Chinese communism, as they "are replete with references to personal reform" (392). Mao's desire to change the mind-sets of the Chinese people drew upon the Marxist theory of identity change as well as on the ideas of reformers such as Liang Qichao and revolutionaries such as Sun Yat-sen, both of whom used their writing and actions in part to change the passive character of the Chinese people.

In Mao's mind, a Marxist or a Communist person overlapped with the Confucian standard of a moral person, even if he would not openly admit it. Not surprisingly, Mao's notion of the new Communist person was couched in the Confucian concept and approach of moral teaching and learning. A Confucian belief holds that individuals can cultivate virtuous minds, compassion, and good qualities through learning from moral exemplars and that attitudes can be inculcated, the mind can be transformed, and behavior can be modified. Through self-cultivation and the imitation of virtuous models, then, moral perfection can be achieved. Personal transformation is made possible through self-awareness, self-evaluation, and comparison with role models. Accordingly Mao's rhetorical construction of a new Communist person was a hybrid of Marxist ideology and Chinese Confucian tradition. However, Confucius placed individuals' efforts as the main approach to becoming moral persons; Mao, in contrast, made model emulation an enterprise of nationwide persuasion for the purpose of ideological or thought control.

Traditional Chinese Conceptualization for a Moral Person

Largely due to the influence of Confucianism in Chinese society, an educated Chinese person is expected to cultivate self, manage the family well, sacrifice for the state, and bring peace to the entire empire (修身, 齐家, 治国, 平天下).[2] A moral person is expected be loyal to his superiors, filial to his parents, faithful to his friends, and conscientious about maintaining harmony in relationships as well as maintaining moderation in expressing opinions.[3] A good Chinese person exhibits moderation, modesty, and tolerance (Lin 1962). In Chinese literature scholars, ministers, and heroes with these qualities are highly praised and emulated.

Confucius coined the concept *ren* (仁 benevolence, loving, humanity) as the highest level of morality for both society and the individual. He mentioned *renren* 仁人 or *renzhe* 仁者 (a person with the quality of *ren*) many times in his *Analects* and often used *renren* and *junzi* (gentleman) interchangeably. For Confucius, a *renren* manifested three important qualities. First, a *renren* was concerned about the "Way" (the moral path to social order and individual perfection) and disregarded personal gain or wealth (Lun Yu 1992, 15:32). He could be entrusted with great tasks (15:34) and "does not seek life at the expense of his humanity; there are instances where he will give his life to fulfill his humanity" (15:9).[4] Second, a *renren* consciously and continuously cultivated virtues throughout life. Confucius believed that through self-cultivation, a person could gain respect from others and bring peace to those around him (14:40). Self-cultivation, for Confucius, was achieved through an assiduous study of formal rituals and the virtuous deeds of the past sages. A self-cultivated person did not impose upon others what that person did not wish for himself (12:2). Confucius considered a person's knowledge, credibility, and goodness important prerequisites for an individual's moral perfection. He also purported that anyone could gain moral qualities as long as they put in the effort (7:30). Subsequently a society composed of such individuals with moral attitudes and actions could be improved for the better. Third, a *renren* demonstrated the qualities of courage, bravery, resolution, and simplicity (13:27, 14:4).

In the *Analects*, Confucius gave two examples of *renren*: Yan Hui, his favorite student; and Guan Zhong, the chancellor for the king of Qi state during the Spring–Autumn period (770–476 b.c.e.). Confucius considered Yan Hui a model of self-cultivation and ranked him number one among his students (Confucius 1992, 11:3). Confucius praised him for his modesty, plain living, diligence, and moderation (6:3, 6:11). The second exemplar, Guan Zhong, assisted the king of Qi in governing the state and in handling foreign affairs with utmost dedication. Consequently the state of Qi became the most powerful state at the time (around 400 b.c.e.). Confucius applauded Guan Zhong for his humble upbringing, plain living, and selfless dedication to the well-being of the state (14:9, 14:16, 14:17). In summary, for Confucius, a renren, or a person of morality, was a virtuous, selfless, plain-living, and modest person. These qualities were Confucius's basic principles for building a moral society and have maintained their legacy for thousands of years throughout Chinese history. According to Yi Zhongtian 易中天 (2007), moral education has been an important ritual since the Zhou dynasty (1046–256 b.c.e.). For example, a typical ritual is called xiangyin 乡饮 (village drinking), in which every household is required to participate. The ritual covers singing, lecturing, decree announcements from the imperial court, and commending and criticizing local villagers. Participants are expected to reflect on their conduct and engage in self-criticism (Yi 2007, 136).

In his early years Mao's view of ordinary Chinese people was negative; he did not picture them capable of achieving high moral standards. In a letter to his friend Li Jinxi dated August 23, 1917, Mao wrote, "I feel that my countrymen have accumulated many undesirable customs, their mentality is too antiquated, and their morality is extremely bad" (Schram 1992, 132). Mao did not specify these undesirable customs, but he attributed them to moral problems rooted in Chinese history. Mao believed that these problems required "enormous force" to be removed and resolved. Because of the failure of the Hundred Days' Reform in 1898, Mao concluded that changes at the government institutional level—such as implementing a democratic system, drawing up a constitution, or creating a cabinet—would not benefit the Chinese people.

Instead, Mao believed that fundamental changes must occur within individual mentalities, changes including the development of sagelike qualities of morality, wisdom, and intelligence.[5] Mao used the concept of "ultimate principles" 本源 (Schram 1992, 132)[6] to name the qualities necessary for embodying a correct mental state. These ultimate principles are composed of correct philosophical orientations and ethical conduct. For Mao, philosophy would teach people truth and ethics would teach people moral standards. But first people had to be educated so that they would learn philosophy and ethics. Moral education with the correct philosophical orientation would mentally transform the Chinese people. Once they were transformed, they would speak moral language, exhibit proper behavior, and have broad perspectives. Without moral education, Mao believed, people would naturally lean toward evil.[7]

In his "Marginal Notes to Friedrich Paulsen: *A System of Ethics*," Mao expressed what he believed to be the ultimate goal of human life (Schram 1992, 193). He pointed out that motive and results are the two criteria for distinguishing between good and bad (Schram 1992, 195). A good person automatically would be motivated and would choose to do the right thing. No external pressure such as laws or regulations would have an effect on a good person's decision to perform good acts (Schram 1992, 205). "All values depend on the individual" (Schram 1992, 208), Mao said. In other words, the individual's will and determination decide the outcome of his or her action. In this sense, Mao drew closer to Confucianists who believed that "the perfection of the individual leads to the perfection of interpersonal relationships, which in turn leads to the perfection of family relationships, and so forth, ultimately creating a society in which it is possible for individuals to perfect themselves" (Kincaid 1987, 333).

Mao never lost faith in the ability of individuals' will power to affect social reality. As Meisner (1977) notes, "For Mao, the essential factor in determining the course of history was conscious human activity and the most important ingredients for revolution were how men thought and their willingness to engage in revolutionary action" (41). In this sense, Mao deviated from Marx, who claimed that economic structure is the basis for how people think and relate to one another. Mao believed the opposite, that thoughts and ideas impact the economy, not the other way around. This belief afforded Mao with a righteous justification to launch political movements, mobilize the masses, and persuade his comrades, the masses, and intellectuals to follow his revolution. However, his abandonment of democratic institutions to focus on moral teachings proved to be a fatal flaw in his revolutionary vision.[8]

In 1917 at the age of twenty-four, Mao already regarded himself as an educated, rational, compassionate, and sagelike person who was obligated to teach fellow countrymen to become moral persons. In his words, "If we go off by ourselves, they [peasants and uneducated Chinese] will sink lower and lower. It is better for us to lend a helping hand, so their minds may be opened up and their virtue be increased, so that we may share the realm of the sages with them" (Schram 1992, 135). Mao's claimed dream here was to create a harmonious society in which "all under heaven will become sages. None will be unenlightened" (Schram 1992, 135). In other words, Mao wanted to transform morally flawed individuals into "virtuous, meritorious, and eloquent" persons. In this sense, Mao attempted to imitate sages such as Confucius, who was not only pristine in virtue and accomplishment but also had the mission to convert others by changing the fabric of their thoughts and actions. Qian Liqun (2012) writes that "Mao's logic is that the masses (workers and peasants) granted him and his Party the mission of finding the Way (communism, socialism) to achieve peace for China. In the process, Mao left the legacies of virtue, achievement, and eloquence, thus turning himself into a communist sage" (175). This ideology was Mao's lifelong pursuit as well as his unshakable belief. Driven by this logic, Mao projected his moral standard onto the Chinese people, using constant thought reform and moral teaching in a lifelong pursuit of transforming traditional Chinese culture into a society of new Communist persons.

Remolding and Rectification

After Mao became the leader of China's revolution, he undertook the task of transforming the moral fabric of three groups of people. The first group was his peasant army. In October 1927, after Chiang Kai-shek's massacre of the Communists, Mao led the remnants of a defeated military force to Jinggangshan to join with Zhu De's forces. One major task Mao faced was to train his followers, largely composed of peasants and bandits, to become disciplined and morally conscious soldiers. To enlarge his military troops, Mao had to recruit peasant vagabonds and attract local bandit leaders, who tended to be lawless and had no sense of what Mao termed "proletarian consciousness" or "class consciousness."[9] These new Red Army "soldiers" were disobedient to the officers, stole from villagers, spoke profane language, and abused captives. These new soldiers were not educated and did not know how to discipline themselves. Mao feared that their behavior would tarnish the image of the Red Army among the Chinese people.

To solve these problems, Mao designed "Three Rules of Discipline and Eight Points for Attention" as mechanisms of behavior modification.[10] Any violation of these disciplines and attentions would be punished. These measures were successful for training a disciplined army force; however, behavior control by reward and punishment was not sufficient for Mao. He wanted internal change of these soldiers' minds and dispositions so that their good behavior would be natural and voluntary. To appeal to this audience, Mao wrote in vernacular Chinese, filling his works with metaphors and analogies for easy understanding of abstract and foreign ideas and his own proposed goals for Chinese revolution. For example, Mao described a revolutionary base as a "butt" on which the army could sit and rest; for his peasant army he used "foreign landlord" to refer to imperialism (Xu 2013). Mao seemed to know that winning over the masses by persuasion rather than by coercion was more effective in the long term.

The second group of people Mao faced was made up of young intellectuals[11] who had come to Yan'an after the start of the Anti-Japanese War (1937) and who were attracted to the Communist ideals of egalitarianism. These young intellectuals came mostly from wealthy family backgrounds. Their parents' and grandparents' generations were more likely to be educated in the Confucian tradition. Mao never truly trusted people from wealthy family backgrounds, believing that such people would always carry traces of self-interest and self-indulgence. In Mao's view, although these intellectuals might have been influenced by Western ideas and liberal thinking, they did not know much about the true essence of Marxism-Leninism, nor did they understand the experience of peasants, who made up the majority of China's revolution. In fact, some of the intellectuals might have been so influenced by Western individualism and liberalism that they had the potential to challenge and pose threats to the CCP's sole party rule.

Mao's doubts about intellectuals' loyalty to the party proved well founded during the movement of "a hundred flowers bloom, a hundred schools of thought contend," which was launched by Mao in 1956. In the spirit of democracy and egalitarianism, Mao initially solicited critical responses to government actions from people outside the CCP, especially from members of other puppet parties in China and educated elites. However, when some intellectuals voiced their criticism of the CCP and concerns about the one-party rule (such as Chu Anping's charge that Mao did not keep his promise to have a coalition government), Mao inevitably began to suspect the motives of these intellectuals and questioned their loyalty to the party. Seeing dissent of this kind voiced from intellectuals and non-CCP members, Mao felt intensified suspicion. He revealed his grave concerns at "Talks at a conference of secretaries of provincial, municipal and autonomous region party committees" in 1957: "There is queer talk among some professors too, such as the Communist Party should be done away with, the Communist Party cannot lead them, socialism is no good, and so on and so forth. Before, they kept these ideas to themselves, but since the policy of letting a hundred schools of thought contend gave them an opportunity to speak up, these remarks have come tumbling out.... Now they are coming out, probably with the intention of sweeping us away. Aren't they in fact attempting a restoration?" (Mao 1957/1977, 353–54). To discredit intellectuals, Mao reversed the traditional hierarchy of education by claiming that "the lowly are most intelligent; the elite are most ignorant" (卑贱者最聪明, 高贵者最愚蠢) (Mao 1958/1992b, 236). In Mao's judgment, this group was in the greatest need of thought reform and of being remolded.

The third group Mao sought to reform consisted of party officials and party members. Some party officials came from landlord, business, or urban petit bourgeois families, while others came from worker-peasant family backgrounds. Mao was concerned about the ideological correctness of these party officials or members of mixed backgrounds. In his words, "Although more or less tempered in long years of arduous struggle, quite a number have not acquired much Marxism, and thus ideologically or mentally they are apt to sway in the wind like rice stalks" (Mao 1957/1977, 355). Mao worried that once these party officials gained power, they would turn into bureaucrats and become dogmatic, ultimately losing their connections with the masses. In Mao's logic, a comfortable life would weaken a person's will and beget complacency and corruption. Mao saw that previous Chinese dynasties had all fallen due to their own internal corruption, and Mao feared that if the party became corrupt as had previous ruling institutions in China, the CCP would lose the legitimacy to rule China and the Chinese people would rise up against him and the party, as had happened with past rulers.[12]

To some extent the last two groups were more dangerous to Mao as they were covert and embedded among the people. Mao compared them to weeds in the fields that had to be constantly pulled out to secure a good harvest (Mao 1957/1977, 359). To prevent these groups from turning against the CCP, Mao believed that they needed to be constantly remolded through rectification campaigns or thought reforms. To convince people of the necessity for the thought reform, Mao used himself as an example of being remolded by Marxism: "For myself, I used to have all sorts of non-Marxist ideas, and it was only later that I embraced Marxism. I learned a little Marxism from books and took the first steps in remolding my ideology, but it was mainly through taking part in class struggle over the years that I came to be remolded" (403). Chinese people have a tradition of following exemplars. Mao believed that if he, their beloved leader, the ultimate symbol of morality, was willing to be remolded, then everyone else would follow suit. Mao's goal was to turn every Chinese person into a new Communist citizen.

Remolding the Chinese people, especially intellectuals, was single-handedly the most important facet of the CCP's ideological practice. This remolding was accomplished through a series of thought reforms. Mao launched several rectification movements or thought reforms to restructure the minds of party members and intellectuals.[13] Following Lenin, Mao believed in the idea of continuous, unmitigated reform because "the influence of the bourgeoisie and of the intellectuals who come from the old society, the very influence which constitutes their class ideology, will persist in our country for a long time" (Mao 1957/1977, 409–10). Thus a Chinese person was repeatedly to fight against any capitalistic ideas and reform himself or herself accordingly for the party. Mao wrote that "fighting against wrong ideas is like being vaccinated—a man develops greater immunity from disease as a result of vaccination" (410).

Mao continued to evoke the medical metaphor further by claiming that "a person with appendicitis is saved when the surgeon removes his appendix. So long as a person has made mistakes and does not hide his sickness for fear of treatment or persist in his mistakes until he is beyond cure, so long as he honestly and sincerely wishes to be cured and to mend his ways, we should welcome him and cure his sickness so that he can become a good comrade" (Mao 1942/1967c, 50). Mao called "wrong ideas" an "ideological and political malady" that must be cured with cooperation between the doctor (the party or Mao) and the patient (intellectuals and party officials). Through this process alone, anyone afflicted with an ideological disease could be cured and could become a productive member of society. Schurmann and Schell (1967) observe that "some aspects of thought reform are similar to practices in some Protestant sects"; these practices serve "as a channel for transmitting the new values and goals from the leaders to the people" (134). Reminders of thought reform were omnipresent, filling the public domain as well as the private domain. Popular political jargons such as "thought reform," "denouncing selfish thought," and "loyalty to the party" were endemic in all spheres of life—in the workplace, at home, and in social settings during Mao's era (1949–76). These slogans served as "ideographs" that embodied the values and ideology of a culture. They signaled a call for political commitment of the collective members to a normative goal (McGee 1980).

Mao's Rhetorical Construction of a New Communist Person

New Communist persons, according to Mao, must be "versed in Marxism-Leninism, politically far-sighted, competent in work, full of the spirit of self-sacrifice, capable of tackling problems on their own, steadfast in the midst of difficulties and loyal and devoted in serving the nation, the class and the Party" (Mao 1937/1967a, 291). Moreover, they "must be free from selfishness, from individualistic heroism, ostentation, sloth, passivity, sectarian arrogance, and must be selfless national and class heroes" (291). Taken together, a new Communist person was to 1) show ideological correctness and loyalty to the Party, 2) serve the people whole-heartedly, 3) engage in criticism and self-criticism, and 4) remain modest and live a plain life.

Showing Ideological Correctness and Loyalty to the Party

In his essay "Power of the Powerless," Vaclav Havel (1986) defines ideology as "a specious way of relating to the world. It offers human beings the illusion of an identity, of dignity, and of morality while making it easier for them to part with them" (42). Believing correct ideological thought to be the prerequisite for effective revolutionary action, Mao faced the formidable challenge of converting the Chinese peasants, who were mostly concerned with putting food on the table, and also the educated, who were often still embedded in the Confucian tradition and influenced by Western liberal ideals of democracy and freedom rather than Marxism and Communist ideology. For Mao, Marxism-Leninism was infallible and absolutely correct, but he was aware that Marxism and communism were foreign concepts. To make these concepts appealing and relevant to the Chinese, Mao appropriated certain tenets of Marxism and communism into basic and concrete moral values such as honesty, loyalty, and selflessness. More strikingly, Mao linked these values with ideological correctness.

For example, when Zhang Guotao (1897–1979), one of the top CCP leaders, took a different route during the Long March to claim independence from the party, Mao cast him as selfish. Mao proclaimed that "those who assert this kind of 'independence' are usually wedded to the doctrine of 'me first' and are generally wrong on the question of the relationship between the individual and the Party. Although in words they profess respect for the Party, in practice they put themselves first and the Party second" (Mao 1942/1967c, 44). Here, Mao disparaged Zhang's departure from the Communist Party as an act of self-interest and dishonesty. Mao chastised Zhang for the harm he had done to shake the morale of the party.[14] Further, Mao considered honesty an essential quality of a new Communist person. He named Marx, Engels, Lenin, and Stalin as honest people and regarded Trotsky, Bukharin, Chen Tu-hsiu (Chen Duxiu), and Chang Kuo-tao (Zhang Guotao) as dishonest people (44).[15] By aligning honesty with Communist theorists and leaders and by equating dishonesty with political dissidents within the party, Mao showed that the moral quality of honesty was not just a character trait but rather was a political demarcation and an ideological standpoint.

In 1942 Mao launched his first rectification movement in Yan'an among party members. He justified his action by claiming that contradictions abounded among party members in terms of their ideological orientations because they were born into different social backgrounds. Mao believed that even if party members living with these contradictions did have revolutionary zeal, their minds were still not aligned with Marxist or Communist ideology. In Mao's words, "the revolutionary fervor of these comrades was admirable. . . . but they had brought with them into the Party ideas which are out of keeping or not altogether in keeping with Marxism" (Mao 1945/1967c, 278). Mao was deliberately vague about the nature or specifics of these ideas. According to Gao Hua's (2002) research, these ideas were the demands for freedom of speech, the demands for equality between the officials and soldiers, and insistence on respect for democracy. Mao justified his launch of the movement by condemning these ideas as contradictory to Marxism.

The purpose of the rectification movement, according to Mao, was to spread Marxist education and solve these contradictions so that "our Party can go forward with great, firm strides in unprecedented (though not complete) ideological, political, and organizational unity" (Mao 1945/1967c, 278). Mao heralded Marxism as the theoretical guidance for China's revolution and lauded communism as the sole belief and value system for all. Those who refused to conform to the Marxist ideology and who expressed different views from the party line were labeled as morally defective people who were relentlessly suppressed and persecuted. This Rectification Campaign was the kickoff to China's continuous rounds of thought reform for the educated or bourgeois Chinese.

By 1956 Mao sensed resistance to his ideology from within and from outside the CCP. Once again he launched a rectification movement targeted at those who disagreed with his political views. For Mao, rectifying movements were effective in "curing" the moral defects of the dissidents. He used a weather metaphor and a health metaphor to illustrate his points: "From now on, all problems among the people or inside the Party are to be solved by means of rectification, by means of criticism and self-criticism, and not by force. We are in favor of the method of the 'gentle breeze and mild rain,' and although it is hardly avoidable that in a few cases things may get a little too rough, the over-all intention is to cure the sickness and save the patient, so we truly may achieve this end instead of merely paying lip-service to it" (Mao 1956/1977, 348). Here, Mao linked all his political exclamations and people's actions to ideological correctness, thinly disguising the mandate as a demand for a show of loyalty to Mao and to the party. Mao said that ideological conformity was a political task and the "life-blood of all economic work" (Mao 1955/1977, 260). Mao labeled Communist ideas and socialist practices as new and labeled thoughts and actions deviating from Communist ideology and socialist practice as old. Moreover, Mao associated "new" with "good" and "old" with "evil." Thus, he argued, it was natural and reasonable to abandon the old and establish the new, placing ideological differences on high moral ground. In doing so, Mao left little room for counterarguments and therefore began a rise to radicalism.[16]

Mao's rhetoric of progression ran through almost all his writings and justified the radical actions he took regarding the country's economy. For example, when Mao faced resistance against forming cooperatives in China's rural areas, he said, "From the start, the agricultural cooperative movement has been a severe ideological and political operative struggle. Before a new social system can be built on the site of the old, the site must be swept clean. Remnants of old ideas reflecting the old system invariably persist in people's minds for a long time, and they do not easily give way" (Mao 1955/1977, 260).

For Mao, peasants were to be educated with "political work" or "socialist ideology" to take on this new economic change.[17] Through cooperatives peasants could cultivate a socialistic consciousness that would allow them to devote themselves to the Communist Party and the country and to ultimately become selfless, new Communist persons. As Meisner (1977) writes, Mao's thought reforms "marked the appearance of a rigid ideological determinism that since has governed the history of Maoism" (185). Mao's success in establishing ideological conformity in China remains unprecedented in Chinese history and arguably is unsurpassed anywhere else in the world.

Serving the People Whole-Heartedly

After studying China for many years, John Fairbank went to China after Nixon's visit in 1972 and wrote his impression of the Chinese people at the time. He asserted that "Mao not only created a new society, but also a far-reaching moral crusade to change the very human Chinese personality in the direction of self-sacrifice and serving others" (Fairbank 1972, 37). Although China had never had any institutional caste systems, Chinese people even before Mao's era were quite class conscious. Confucius divided people into *junzi* (gentlemen) and *xiaoren* (small persons, base persons). *Junzi* symbolized the educated social elites, who possessed moral attributes, while *xiaoren* represented the uneducated masses, who cared only about pursuing material self-interests. In traditional China, *xiaoren* also were looked down upon for their participation in manual labor. Interaction between the two groups was limited.

Mao's revolution not only brought these two groups together but also reversed the social hierarchy and subverted traditional perceptions of morally desirable and undesirable people. Mao claimed that the proletariat class, which consisted of the uneducated masses such as peasants and workers, was the true emblem of morality. He called on intellectuals to learn from the humility of the masses as a way to dissolve their inherent hubris as members of the educated elite. Although Mao relied on the educated elite to propagate revolutionary theories and produce revolutionary art and literature, he also expected them to align with the interests of the masses and to demonstrate their devotion to Communist morals in the arts and literature.

Speaking to party members and intellectuals, who tended to come from wealthy family backgrounds, Mao faced the task of transforming their possible bourgeois worldview to a proletarian consciousness by mingling with and serving for the masses or the uneducated workers and peasants. The hallmark of the CCP, according to Mao, "is that we have very close ties with the broadest masses of the people. Our point of departure is to serve the people whole-heartedly and never for a moment divorce ourselves from the masses, to proceed in all cases from the interests of the people and not from the interests of individuals" (Mao 1945/1967c, 265). Throughout his life Mao emphasized this point of the party's necessity to integrate with the masses.[18] Mao's call for serving the people came partly from his ambition to save the Chinese people from suffering the humiliation they had suffered in the past, partly from a rhetorical strategy to win the support of the majority of the Chinese people and partly to maintain party legitimacy. To serve the people, he believed, every comrade must "love the people and listen attentively to the voices of the masses; to identify himself with the masses wherever he goes and, instead of standing above them, to immerse himself among them; and, according to their present level, to awaken them or raise their political consciousness" (Mao 1945/1967c, 265–66). Moreover, party members and intellectuals must physically live among the masses and learn from them as moral exemplars. Mao asked, "If our Party members spend their whole lives sitting indoors and never go out to face the world and brave the storm, what good will they be to the Chinese people?" (Mao 1943/1967c, 158). Accordingly party members had duel missions. They could learn from the masses through firsthand experiences and simultaneously disseminate Communist ideals among the masses. To Mao, this dualistic experience was the best way to "solve their problems and help them achieve liberation and happiness" (Mao 1943/1967c, 158). Integrating with the masses would allow party members, the new social elite, to imbibe "the proletarian consciousness" and remain connected with the real world.

Mao's success over Chiang Kai-shek was largely attributed to Mao's success in reforming, and continuously reforming, the moral character of the Chinese Communist Party. He set a high standard for party members, a high standard similar to the far-reaching standards of a Confucian persona. Strategically Mao asked party members to make allies with non-Communist members, claiming, "Communists must listen attentively to the views of people outside the Party and let them have their say. If what they say is right, we ought to welcome it, and we should learn from their strong points; if it is wrong, we should let them finish what they are saying and then patiently explain things to them" (Mao 1941/1967c, 33). Mao pointed to his belief that "the Communist Party is a political party which works in the interests of the nation and people and which has absolutely no private ends to pursue. It should be supervised by the people and must never go against their will" (33–34).[19]

Although Mao's requirements for party members were reminiscent of the Confucian teachings of modesty and collectivism, Mao aligned his party with the oppressed Chinese people, which gained him support and sympathy for his revolution. Confucius taught his students to put family duties first, be considerate of others, and sacrifice for the collective. Mao turned these traditional values of personhood into a secular dogma of serving the people and performing sacrifice for the party and the state. In her study of Chinese moral models selection, Rya Butterfield (2012) contends that Chinese rhetoric surrounding the selection and promotion of moral models in China plays an epideictic function and "provides symbolic equipment by which people can make sense of their community, engage in self-definition, [and] shape collective memory" for the service of the nation (100). Mao's approach to creating a new Communist person was based on a traditional Chinese approach of model emulation in moral teaching/learning; his approach exemplified this epideictic function for the Chinese people.

On September 8, 1944, Mao gave a eulogy in honor of Zhang Side, a soldier who died when a coal mine collapsed. Zhang was a Communist Party member and had participated in the Long March. Mao entitled the speech "Serve the People," which had become the motto and slogan of CCP members. In his eulogy Mao first characterized Zhang's death in the context of the CCP's fight against the Japanese, which aimed to "liberate people and work entirely in the people's interests" (Mao 1944/1967c, 177). Mao then claimed that Zhang died for the people. Mao referenced a Chinese writer, Sima Qian, who provided two views of death: one type of death weighs more than Mount Tai (a worthy death); and the other kind of death is lighter than a feather (a worthless death). Because Zhang's death was for the people, Mao concluded, "his death is indeed weightier than Mount Tai" (177).[20] In other words, dying for the people was the ultimate sacrifice for the Communist cause. In this sense Zhang was a moral exemplar to be emulated.

Serving the people also meant showing a willingness to listen to suggestions from anybody as a means to improve oneself. In the eulogy Mao referenced a man named Li Dingming, a non-Communist, who proposed the idea of "better troops and simpler administration." Mao endorsed his proposal and praised Li, essentially declaring that his party was committed to listening to and serving the Chinese people.

Another Communist role model eulogized by Mao was Doctor Norman Bethune, a Canadian Communist Party member who had come to Yan'an in 1938 to help the Chinese in their War of Resistance against Japan. Bethune died after contracting blood poisoning while operating on wounded soldiers. Mao called his sacrifice for the Chinese cause an example of "the spirit of internationalism" and "the spirit of communism" and asked every Chinese Communist to learn from him. In the eulogy to Bethune, Mao criticized those who "feel no warmth towards comrades and the people but who are cold, indifferent and apathetic" (Mao 1939/1967b, 338). Mao called such party members "non-Communists." A true Communist person, according to Mao, would be absolutely selfless and willing to sacrifice him/herself for the Communist cause.

Mao perceived altruism and self-sacrifice as crucial facets of virtue for a new Communist person. On March 5, 1963, Mao inscribed "Learn from Comrade Lei Feng" and launched a nationwide propaganda campaign to cultivate new Communists. Lei Feng (1940–62) was an ordinary soldier of the People's Liberation Army. After his accidental death his diary, which was filled with writing devoted to upholding the values of Mao and the party, was published. Lei Feng was exalted as a model new Communist person, a shining example of selflessness and modesty, and an exemplar of one who served the people. Mao called on the Chinese people to emulate his Communist spirit and moral integrity. Soon Lei Feng became a household name and a celebrity soldier. He has remained a cultural icon for decades.[21]

In serving the people, Mao demanded the deprivation of self. To Mao, selfishness was the kernel of the bourgeois world outlook while selflessness was the core quality of a Communist. In his essay "Combat Liberalism," Mao identified eleven types of selfish behaviors, among which were "to let things slide for the sake of peace and friendship when a person has clearly gone wrong" and "to indulge in irresponsible criticism in private instead of actively putting forward one's suggestions to the organization" (Mao 1937/1967b, 31). Other examples included showing no regard for the collective life, disobeying orders, and attacking others. Mao listed many common human flaws, but he said that these types of behavior stemmed from the selfish motives of the petite bourgeoisie. A true

Communist, according to Mao, must subordinate his or her own interests to those of the people and the revolution; a true Communist must value "the collective life of the Party and strengthen the ties between the Party and the masses" (33). In the name of serving the people, Mao denied that selfishness was inevitably a part of human nature and politicized the Chinese collectivistic cultural traits in ideological terms. Not until the end of the Cultural Revolution and after Mao's death was the question raised of whether or not a person could achieve a state of total selflessness.[22] There was no sense of self in Mao's teachings; the individual had to subjugate himself or herself to the prevailing political standard and party line.

Engaging Criticism and Self-Criticism

Mao claimed that the necessary tools for remolding oneself were criticism and self-criticism. He believed that using criticism and self-criticism was the most effective method for educating and transforming a person to the accepted Communist morality and proletarian consciousness. In Mao's words, "This is an excellent method, which impels every one of us to uphold truth and rectify error, and it is the only correct method for all revolutionary people to educate and remold themselves in a people's state" (Mao 1950/1977, 39–40). In every thought reform campaign, intellectuals and party members were expected to denounce their past "immoral behavior" (selfishness) and "erroneous views" (doubts about the party's leadership). They were to report how they would work hard to overcome their "ideological disease" and how they would move closer to becoming new Communist persons under Mao's guidance. This process exemplifies Burke's (1969) notion that people communicate in an attempt to eliminate alienation. Mao's followers strove to gain acceptance into the revolutionary family and regain their identities as new Communist persons by publicly confessing their flaws and aligning with the party.

Those who dissented from Mao's teachings drew Mao's attention. While Stalin launched ruthless purges in the Soviet Union, Mao was in favor of criticism and self-criticism as his primary method of challenging political dissidents. Mao believed that this method distinguished the CCP from other political parties, and he justified his position by evoking a hygiene metaphor: "As we say, dust will accumulate if a room is not cleaned regularly, our faces will get dirty if they are not washed regularly. Our comrades' minds and our Party's work also may collect dust, and also may need sweeping and washing" (Mao 1945/1967c, 267). Mao told his comrades not to fear giving and receiving criticism by evoking popular Chinese maxims: "Say all you know and say it without reserve" 知无不言, 言无不尽; "Blame not the speaker but be warned by his words" 言者无罪, 闻者足戒; and "Correct mistakes if you have committed them and guard against them if you have not" 有则改之, 无则加勉 (1945/1967c, 266). Mao concluded that criticism and self-criticism were "the only effective ways to prevent all kinds of political dust and germs from contaminating the minds of our comrades and the body of our

Party" (1945/1967c, 267). Mao reasoned that a true Communist person must acknowledge his or her own shortcomings and be willing to self-correct; the abilities to do so would demonstrate high levels of morality and self-cultivation (1944/1967c, 177).

The method of criticism and self-criticism was not Mao's invention. As an approach for self-cultivation, the word *fanxing* 反省 (self-examination, self-reflection) was a Confucian concept appropriated from a line in *Analects:* "I examine myself three times a day" (Confucius, 1:4). *Fanxing* was commonly practiced among ancient sages and *junzi,* and even today self-examination is embedded in the Chinese culture as it is a part of the Confucian tradition. Criticism and self-criticism provided an effective approach in bringing uniformity within the party during the Yan'an 1942 rectification movement. Mao requested party officials and intellectuals who were the targets of rectification to write self-criticism journals, reflect on their "incorrect" thoughts, and rectify their errors. Moreover, Mao ordered that these journals be screened systematically to keep tabs on the inner thoughts of party officials and intellectuals (Gao 2000, 326).

Many intellectuals and party officials were familiar with this approach as it was rooted in Chinese tradition, and they voluntarily cooperated in the process. For example, Wu Yuzhang 吴玉章, who went through the rectification movement in 1942, recalled that rectification was like self-cultivation (a familiar term to him), and thus it was not difficult to accept (Gao 2000, 327). Many offered confessions and self-criticism to demonstrate their "new birth" as new Communist persons.

Another example, Wang Ruofei 王若飞, one of the top leaders of the CCP, published his self-criticism report in the *Liberation Daily* on June 27, 1942: "I read books but do not explore the deep meanings of them. I am careless at work and not being thoughtful in handling problems. I bury myself in the work without realizing the loss. Strictly speaking, I lack the attitude of seeking truth from facts and revolutionary responsibility as a Communist Party member" (330). Wang Sihua 王思华, who studied Marxist political economy in Germany, published his confession in the *Liberation Daily* on August 23, 1942, in which he criticized himself: "thirteen years ago, I learned Marxist political economy and brought it back to China in its original form. By doing so, I committed dogmatism. I only thought about Greece and did not want to understand China" (331). He lauded Mao for his sinicization of Marxism. He denounced his German education and expressed his determination to remold himself through reeducation. Wang's self-criticism served as a model for many other top-level revolutionary intellectuals, who quickly followed suit.

After the founding of the People's Republic of China, Mao continued his rectification movement and his emphasis on the importance of criticism and self-criticism. Although he had defeated Chiang Kai-shek and ultimately had won the war, Mao was not confident that the Chinese people, particularly intellectuals and party officials, were truly convinced by the Communist ideology and supported the CCP's legitimacy to rule. In his report to the Third Plenary Session of the Seventh Central Committee of the Chinese Communist Party, Mao called for continuous thought reform and criticism to "raise the ideological and political level of cadres and rank-and-file Party members" (Mao 1950/1977, 31). At the same time Mao stated other purposes for doing so, including "correcting mistakes in work; overcoming the conceit and complacency of the self-styled, distinguished veterans; eliminating bureaucracy and commandism; and improving the relations between the Party and the people" (31). To prove the CCP's legitimacy, Mao focused on ideological uniformity as well as cultivated a good work ethic and increased the moral qualities among party members. Either by coercion or by willingness, once again some well-known intellectuals cooperated with Mao by publishing their confessions.[23]

During the Cultural Revolution, the process of criticism and self-criticism reached its climax. A typical self-criticism report, in either spoken or written form, began with a poetic eulogy of Chairman Mao and Mao's quotation and then moved to the confession of the writer's flaws and "incorrect" thinking. The deeper a person could dig into his or her "dark side," the more that person's confession proved his/her revolutionary passion. The practice was known as a "revolution in the deepest part of the soul." The confession was then followed by more quotations from Mao Zedong and then an application of Mao's quotations to the analysis of one's flaws and incorrect thought.

In their analyses people also had to express how Mao's teaching elevated their moral perceptions, which led them to act according to these moral guidelines. In their conclusions the self-criticizers had to admit that they still had room for further improvement and to express a willingness to engage in more self-criticism. The self-criticism concluded with adulation for Mao and an expression of determination to follow Mao down the revolutionary road.

For example, Hua Luogeng 华罗庚, a famous Chinese mathematician, wrote a self-criticism report following this format. In it he criticized himself as a "self-made man from the old society" and denounced his attachment to science without consideration for the interest of people. He thanked Mao and the Communist Party for helping him realize his moral defects and for guiding him in his scientific work. He expressed his admiration for those who worked selflessly and mingled with the masses, beginning his report with this line: "Had it not been for the guidance of the Thought of Mao Tse-tung, I dare say that I would surely have been contented with what I was" (Schurmann and Schell 1967, 163). Hua ended his report by writing, "Chairman Mao's thinking has stayed the sun for me. Under the brilliance of this sun that never sets, I will resolutely and ceaselessly walk on the road of revolution!" (166).

These examples exhibited a willingness to expose one's selfish motives and an ability to overcome one's own flaws, which signaled loyalty to the party and true political commitment to the Communist cause. Ip (2010) has aptly written that self-criticism had become "an institutional and moral obligation of all party members" (175). Those who were reluctant to engage in self-criticism were immediately cast as counter-revolutionaries. In fact, criticism and self-criticism had become political rituals that served to affirm a shared political identity and to communicate the myth of transcending to a new Communist person.[24] During the Cultural Revolution even teenagers had to find some personal flaws and selfish thoughts and acts in themselves and others so that they could engage in criticism and self-criticism during the times of "political studies" and prove their loyalty to Mao.[25]

Criticism was often put forth by one's peers, sometimes even good friends and family members in a public setting. Humiliation and ridicule were common. Lifton (1957) has noted that this process constitutes the manipulation of emotions. He writes that "it employs no theologians, but it closely resembles an attempt at inducing religious conversion—saving souls, stressing guilt and shame, demanding atonement, recantation, and rebirth. It makes use of no psychiatrists, but is certainly a coercive form of psychotherapy—focusing upon catharsis, analytic interpretations, and causative influence from early life" (reprinted in Schurmann and Schell 1967, 142). But Hu Ping (2007) makes a distinction between Christian confession and Communist self-criticism, in that the former takes place in private while the latter is entirely public. In self-criticism, the person's private thoughts are put on display for the public to judge. That judgment is considered crucial toward successfully conforming the person's ideals to the party line, a process reflected by the slogan "Communicate your heart (thought) to the Party," popularized in the early 1950s.[26]

In theorizing his rhetoric of redemption, Kenneth Burke (1966) postulates three steps: pollution; purification; and redemption. Although it is based on the Christian notion of soul cleansing, the process applies to physical, spiritual, and psychological states and patterns (Foss, Foss, and Trapp 1991). Pollution is the stage when a person feels guilty for having done something wrong as measured by the hierarchy or social order created by language or symbols. This guilt creates the need for redemption and purification. Purification can be achieved by finding a scapegoat (blaming others) or by self-mortification (blaming the self). By assuming guilt and then purging that guilt through either means, a community or individual can achieve a sort of vicarious atonement for sins and thus find redemption, remove the error, and experience a new birth (Burke 1984).[27] Thus the purification stage is the effort to cleanse the guilt, and redemption occurs when one has reached a new self. Mao's methods of criticism and self-criticism involved these stages. Through his speeches and writings, Mao established Marxism-Leninism and Mao-Zedong Thought as the moral and political hierarchy for Chinese people. A person had guilt if his or her thoughts, attitudes, or behaviors were not in alignment (or were accused of not being in alignment) with Marxism, Leninism, and Mao. The guilt would inevitably force the person conscientiously to self-correct by acknowledging the infraction publicly and by offering remorse.

Under the banner of criticism and self-criticism, the person accused of wrong-doing would have no option but to choose the route of mortification (blaming self, self-sacrifice, self-denial) for redemption to demonstrate that growth or change had taken place and to prove loyalty to Mao and the party. According to Burke, the individual or group experiencing guilt makes a symbolic offering to appease the authority or to achieve hierarchy. Once the person completes purification through confession and self-criticism, the person is redeemed and accepted by the party. Mao bestowed intellectuals with original sin since most of them had come from wealthy families and were often critical of the Communist Party's policies. As a result, the intellectuals had constantly to repeat the process of guilt, purification, and redemption or pollution, purification, and redemption. Because of the inherent nature of human imperfection, the cycle never ended (Rohler and Cook 1998). Even Ba Jin, a well-known Chinese writer, admitted that he genuinely felt guilty when he was denounced by the Red Guards. He was determined to transform himself, heart and soul, into a new Communist person (Ba 1987). In his book *The Captive Mind,* Czeslaw Milosz (1953) shares his experience with Polish Communist practices, which consisted of remolding a self into a "new man" who is "conditioned to think and act like others" (76). Over time this new man could "no longer differentiate his true self from the self he simulates, so that even the most intimate of individuals speak to each other in Party slogans" (Milosz 1953, 55). The independent thinking of Ba Jin and many other Chinese intellectuals was dissolved by the political ritual of self-criticism; the repetition facilitated their becoming slaves of party discourse.

Diary writing was a prevailing trend for self-criticism after the publication of *Lei Feng's Diary* in 1963. This "private" zone was invaded to drive out any faulty thinking that deviated from Mao's teaching. A thirteen-year-old teenager who was sent to labor in the countryside with her family wrote the following in her diary dated March 1970: "Because of the bourgeoisie trace in my mind and because of the feudal education in the old school, I look down upon the working class people; I want to avoid hard labor; I refused to use an oil lamp and sleep on an earth-made bed. When I talk with the peasants, I find them like country bumpkins. When I live with them, I find them dirty. In sum, I do not like anything in the rural area. I only think of myself and believe those who come from the city are noble people" (Li 1970). Li continued to criticize herself and expressed how much she had learned from the peasants and how Mao's words had enlightened her and made her aware of her wrong thoughts. Through diary writing, a person reflected on his or her "sins" and scrutinized any selfish thoughts and motives. It was expected that by repeatedly engaging in this kind of self-criticism, selfish thoughts would be cleaned up, loyalty to Mao and the party would solidify, and a new Communist person could be born.

Wang (1997) writes that "the transforming of the soul is carried out through the voluntary cooperation of the participant, who must learn to hate him- or herself for the slightest deviation from the party line and watch over his or her mind with utmost vigilance" (222). Indeed many people genuinely felt guilty about not living up to Mao's moral standards. Publicly or privately, exposure of their guilt was viewed as courageous, and they were seen as potential candidates for true, correct reform. This process of self-persuasion served as a powerful mechanism of control in thought and action.

Kenneth Burke (1969) suggests in his theory of identification that an essential part of identification occurs through self-persuasion. The above examples illustrate the relationship between identification and self-persuasion through the appeal of form (means to achieve identification). As Chinese intellectuals and party officials became familiar with the forms and practices of self-cultivation through self-reflection and self-criticism, the 1942 Rectification Campaign and subsequent thought reform rituals ceased to be new to the participants. Mao's moralistic rhetoric provided the participants with inferences, references, and logical reasoning that made them more willing and more motivated to participate in criticism and self-criticism. Moreover, such rhetoric served to induce participants' cooperation with and surrender to the process because they developed a desire to be enlightened and to transcend to the state of highly moral and ethical persons, new Communist persons.

Being Modest and Living a Plain Life

In his book *Marxism, Maoism, and Utopianism,* Maurice Meisner (1982) identifies some Maoist values: selflessness; hard work; frugality; self-discipline; diligence; and honesty (120). Meisner contends that these ascetic values are similar to Western bourgeois virtues and Protestant ethics of capitalism. However, for Mao, these were not just social and cultural values; they were also constituent parts of the Communist ideology and were appropriated as "socialist and Communist values." These values were derived from the Confucian tradition, consolidated during the Yan'an era, and characterized by ascetic and egalitarian practices.

Mao consistently emphasized building the ethos of party members on two aspects, plain living and modesty, two Confucian values coded in Communist terminology. He reiterated these two values in different time periods during his era. Upon his victory over the Nationalists in 1949, Mao's peasant-based army moved to the cities. Mao was concerned that his new government would be in danger of losing legitimacy if party members became weak willed, facing the temptation of a better material life. Mao cautioned party members in his speech at the Second Session of the Seventh Central Committee that "with victory, certain moods may grow within the Party—arrogance, the airs of a self-styled hero,[28] an inertia and unwillingness to make progress, a love of pleasure, and a distaste for continued hard living" (Mao 1949/1967d, 374). Mao was worried that such party members would be defeated by sugar-coated bullets rather than being conquered by enemies with guns. Thus, Mao advised the party that "the comrades must be taught to remain modest, prudent and free from arrogance and rashness in their style of work. The comrades must be taught to preserve the style of plain living and hard struggle" (Mao 1949/1967d, 374). Mao relied on the party members' discipline, resistance to materialistic temptation, and stoic living styles to build the new China. For Mao, it was essential for people to maintain plain living and modesty even after the CCP took power, and he called these values "intrinsic political qualities" (Mao 1956/1977, 349).

A few years after the CCP came to power, Mao was still deeply concerned about party members' moral integrity. According to Mao's own observations, some cadres "scramble for fame and fortune and are interested only in personal gain.... They vie with each other not in plain living, doing more work and having fewer comforts, but for luxuries, rank and status" (Mao 1957/1977c, 350). Moreover, Mao described party members who had become bureaucratic in their leadership styles and further created contradictions with their subordinates, such as workers and students. Mao saw this separation as a threat to the CCP's legitimacy and issued a warning for sanctions:

> There are several hundred thousand cadres at the level of the country Party committee and above who hold the destiny of the country in their hands. If they fail to do a good job, alienate themselves from the masses and do not live plainly and work hard, the workers, peasants and students will have good reason to disapprove of them. We must watch out lest we foster the bureaucratic style of work and grow into an aristocratic stratum divorced from the people. The masses will have good reason to remove from office whoever practices bureaucracy, makes no efforts to solve their problems, scolds them, tyrannizes over them and never tries to make amends. I say it is fine to remove such fellows, and they ought to be removed. (Mao 1956/1977, 345)[29]

In 1957 Mao announced that there would be another rectification movement. In his speech at the Party National Conference on Propaganda Work, Mao claimed that bureaucracy, sectarianism, and subjectivism would be corrected (Mao 1957/1977, 426). Another goal was "to carry forward our Party's tradition of plain living and hard struggle" (436). Mao criticized those party members for their purported dwindling revolutionary spirit, lamenting that "they are clamoring for position and for the limelight, becoming particular about what they eat and wear, competing for salary and scrambling for fame and gain" (436). Mao called on party members to "maintain the same vigor, the same revolutionary enthusiasm and the same death-defying spirit we displayed in the years of the revolutionary wars and carry our revolutionary work through to the end" (437). Mao demanded that party members maintain a plain lifestyle during the war period to demonstrate their devotion to the revolutionary cause. In Mao's logic, too much comfort would weaken one's spirit; hardship and suffering would render a person strong and enlightened.[30]

Modesty also was an essential attribute of the new Communist person. Mao began to notice that some party officials became opinionated or domineering. He cautioned them in one of his speeches by arguing that "only by guarding against conceit and complacency and continuing to learn tirelessly can you go on making outstanding contributions to the great People's Republic of China" (Mao 1950/1977, 41). During his speech at the National Conference on Financial and Economic Work, Mao brought this point up again, asserting that "we must study and must not become conceited or look down on others. Goose eggs do not think much of chicken eggs and the ferrous metals do not think much of rare metals— such a disdainful attitude is not scientific" (Mao 1953/1977, 110). Mao requested party members to "learn from the advanced countries, from the masses and from each other as to make fewer mistakes" (1955/1977, 155). In his article commemorating Dr. Sun Yat-sen, Mao described him as "a man with a receptive mind" (1956/1977c, 331), an example of modesty, learnedness, and selfless sacrifice for the nation.

Conclusion and Impact

Mao's efforts to transform China and the Chinese people were in some ways successful for the time period in which he lived, but these efforts utterly failed after his death. When Orville Schell visited China in the early 1970s, he noted a spirit of sacrifice among the Chinese people. In his comparison of China and the United States, Schell (1977) remarked that "to work and forget oneself is one of the leitmotifs of these young and politically ambitious workers. They seem to view sacrifice with the same relish that their Western counterparts view self-indulgence. They make sacrifices during the normal day which most men in our society make only at times of extreme hardship. They discuss sacrifice as a way of life for ordinary times, rather than as an unusual event" (183). This image of new Communist persons was the one Mao had wished for, rhetorically constructed and effectively remolded.

The Communist ideology had exerted extraordinary power in transforming Chinese society and the Chinese people. Mao had made the transformation possible by appropriating Marxist-Leninist theories of social change and combining them with Confucian values of human development. For Mao, politics and morality were intertwined. Transforming the Chinese people into new Communist men and women with desirable moral attributes put into practice Mao's ambition as a young man to change the cultural character of the Chinese people. He successfully directed the moral sense of the Chinese from a cultural orientation in the Confucian society to an ideological and political formulation in a Communist state. On the surface Mao's rhetoric toward the construction of a new Communist person appears similar to the Confucian concept of *renren,* while in fact he used Confucian moral doctrine in his persuasive appeals mainly for the ideological uniformity and legitimacy of the CCP's rule, which would ultimately consolidate his dictatorship.

Mao's rhetorical charisma, his moral argument for the necessity of thought reforms, and his brutal approach to ritualize and institutionalize them left little room for counterarguments and chances for resistance. As Ip (2010) points out, "when the top leadership of an authoritarian party pressed for changes that were unassailable in both ideological and pragmatic terms, the situation did not encourage others to question his decision, however unreasonable" (193). Rectification became a deprivation of individual freedom in thought and speech as everyone had to conform to the party line and infallible Mao Zedong Thought. Moreover, starting from the Yan'an period, thought reforms turned into witch hunts for those who refused or failed to conform to Mao's orthodoxies. Many innocent people were politically persecuted and deprived of their dignity and political freedom.

Out of fear or repeated inculcation, Chinese people, particularly Chinese intellectuals, were silenced. Some chose compliance over resistance, subjecting themselves to manipulation and coercion by political power. Some stopped speaking altogether, and their critical and reflective capabilities disappeared; some became cynical and disillusioned. Not until after Mao's death did some Chinese intellectuals again begin to play active roles in public and political life.[31]

Unfortunately Mao's efforts to create a new Communist person are seen by many Chinese people as propaganda, as the manipulation of fears, hopes, and passions of political participants. Mao's continuous thought reforms resulted in menacing emotional tension among intellectuals and party officials. People suffered traumatically as Mao divided them into "revolutionaries" and "counter-revolutionaries" based on how often and how willing they were to reform themselves to prove their loyalty and ideological conformity. The political ritual of criticism and self-criticism encouraged lies, personal attacks, self-denial, and self-humiliation. The publication of Lei Feng's diary permitted the intrusion of public/political discourse into the private domain of the inner self, politicizing private discourse. The emergence of Lei Feng and many other moral models was seen by Western observers merely as the product of Mao's propaganda tactics and mind control.

Ever since Deng Xiaoping launched the economic reforms of the early 1980s, China has become increasingly materialistic. Although government-controlled media still propagate the "Lei Feng spirit" to promote virtuous behavior, such a spirit is largely regarded by the average Chinese person as ex post facto. Based on Mei Zhang's (2000a, 2000b) research of model emulation in post-Mao China, the CCP continues to promote role models of altruism and self-sacrifice for the public good. Mei Zhang wrote, "The official stories of role models continued to function as Chinese political rhetoric designed to induce ideal citizen behavior in the reform era" (2000b, 148). However, the efficacy and impact of such models have become greatly reduced as the pursuit of money and self-interest has risen. Mao's political enterprise of remolding the Chinese people through ideological education has largely failed. China has experienced a moral vacuum and an ideological crisis since the economic reform. Ironically, in contrast to "a new Communist person," a face of "the exquisite egocentric person"[32] is emerging among young educated Chinese as the result of the one-child policy and the materialistic nature of the economic boom in today's China.

★ ★ ★ ★

SIX

Mao Zedong's Rhetorical
Constructions of Chinese Nationalism

Nationalism is traditionally associated with symbols, political leaders, and cultural values. In the past decade, scholars have examined nationalism from a variety of angles. Craig Calhoun (2007) treats nationalism as a process of "discursive formation"—"a way of talking" and "a cluster of rhetoric and reference" (151). According to Zheng (1999), Chinese nationalism is rooted in China's historical struggle against foreign powers and is "about China's sovereignty, independence, and its proper relations with other nation-states" (xi).

Mao's rhetoric of nationalism was characterized by constructing narratives. He effectively combined a morass of fear with a flame of hope and an image of a damaged past with the promise of a better China. His words were filled with nationalistic sentiments in the periods before and after he became the leader of China, most predominantly characterized by his condemnation of common enemies both foreign and domestic and by his projected vision of hope and optimism for China's future. Specifically I argue that Mao's rhetorical construction of Chinese nationalism was achieved through a narrative of victimization, a denouncement of Chiang Kai-shek and American imperialism, and a desire to build a strong and prosperous China. To Mao, China's sovereignty was defined in opposition to foreign enemies. His focus on China's victimization increased the peoples' fervor toward Mao's declarations of China's future prosperity. This national consciousness exuded by Mao served to reinforce his own political power and is believed to have gained China a respectable place in the world.

Historical Contexts of Mao's Nationalism

Mao was born on December 26, 1893, at a time when China was weak, having suffered multiple foreign invasions and chaotic periods of infighting. Toward the end of the Qing dynasty (1644–1911), China suffered a series of foreign assaults, resulting in treaties that disadvantaged the Chinese economy in favor of European interests. In 1842 British troops defeated the Qing imperial army to protect Britain's lucrative stake in the opium trade. The Qing government was forced to sign the Treaty of Nanking (August 29, 1842), by which China had to pay over twenty million silver dollars and cede Hong Kong to the British government. In June 1858 foreign powers imposed on China the Treaty of Tianjin, which allowed the Second French Empire, the United Kingdom, the Russian Empire, and the United States to trade, send Christian missionaries, and legalize the import of opium.

In 1895, following a pitiful defeat in the Opium War, China was overwhelmed by an attack from Japan, which had developed a powerful military during the Meiji Restoration (1868–1912). The Treaty of Shimonosek (马关条约) was signed on April 7, 1895, and stipulated that China was to pay two hundred million taels of silver, cede Taiwan and the Liaodong Peninsula to the Japanese, and open coastal cities to conduct free trade with Japan. Moreover, in 1898 Germany colonized the city of Qingdao, which was later occupied by Japan after 1914. From 1895 to 1914 Russia and Japan competed for control of Manchuria, the northeast region of China. In the midst of an already devastating period, China was further compromised when Russian forces took control of Lushun and Dalian, two important Chinese ports.

In response to this series of foreign invasions and inequitable treaties, the *yihetuan,* or Boxer Rebellion, took violent action against foreigners. The Boxers were mostly peasants from northern China who pledged to "support the Qing dynasty and exterminate the foreigners" (扶清灭洋). They terrorized foreign missionaries and destroyed stores with foreign merchandise, killing countless foreigners and Chinese converts.[1] Zhao (2004) refers to these antiforeigner movements as "nativist nationalism." The Boxers were ill-matched and were quickly defeated, but the United States and various European powers quickly took advantage of this defeat, implementing the Eight Power Expedition, or Eight-Nation Alliance, military action against China. The eight countries included the United States, Great Britain, Japan, Germany, Russia, France, Austria, Hungary, and Italy. In the summer of 1900 the allied forces defeated the Qing imperial army and pillaged Beijing. The Qing imperial government had no choice but to sign the Boxer Protocol of 1901, which paid an indemnity of 450 million taels of silver to the eight countries (amounting to one tael per Chinese citizen at the time). The expedition not only caused China's decline politically and economically but also inflicted wide-scale nationalistic humiliation.

Defeat by the Western powers gave rise to a unique Chinese nationalism. In the struggle for national survival, Chinese intellectuals realized that China's biggest weakness lay in its technological backwardness, that modernity not only was inevitable but also was the key to building a strong nation. To achieve modernity, China had to learn from the West. Represented by Kang Youwei and Liang Qichao, these intellectuals pushed the Qing government for reform. As a result Li Hongzhang (李鸿章) (1823–1901), a politician and general of the Qing Empire, pressed the Qing government to negotiate with the West and launched China's modernization process by building a navy and an army.

Between 1872 and 1875 the Qing government dispatched a total of 120 students to the United States to study science and technology. These students later became the precursors of China's modernization and Westernization. Terms such as "legal equality" and "national sovereignty" were introduced to China and frequently used in newspapers and journals (Zhao 2004, 48–49). Yan Fu 严复 (1854–1921), who studied at the Royal Naval College in England, returned to China and translated Thomas Huxley's *Evolution and Ethics,* Adam Smith's *Wealth of Nations,* John Stuart Mill's *On Liberty,* and Herbert Spencer's *Study of Sociology* into Chinese so that educated Chinese could become acquainted with Western thought.

The Chinese people, however, felt betrayed by the West after the 1919 Versailles Peace Conference, which transferred the former German concessions in Shandong Province to Japan instead of rightfully returning the land to China. On May 4, 1919, Chinese students and intellectuals took to the streets demanding the return of Shandong to China, instigating the antiimperialist May Fourth Movement. The movement condemned traditionalism, particularly Confucianism, as the major cause for China's backwardness. At this critical time China was exposed to Marxism-Leninism. In 1920 Chen Wangdao 陈望道, one of the first Communist Party leaders and a scholar of Chinese rhetoric, translated Marx and Engels's *Communist Manifesto* into Chinese from Japanese. Many radical Chinese intellectuals found the themes of Marxism-Leninism, antiimperialism, and nationalism attractive but most importantly applicable to China's weak situation.

This historical context had a lasting impact on Mao's notions of nationalism. According to Li Rui (1994), Mao's secretary of the 1950s, Mao had read *Words of Warning in a Prosperous Society* (盛世危言) by Zheng Guanying (郑观应) (1842–1921) when he was a teenager. This book proposed that Chinese leaders with a Western education could help China develop economically and militarily and ultimately improve Chinese standards of living. In his interview with Edgar Snow, Mao said that the book stimulated his desire to devote himself to China from a young age (Snow 1938, 134).

At the age of sixteen, Mao studied at a private school in Shaosan, his hometown, where he read a booklet titled *The Danger of Imperialism* (列强瓜分之危险). The booklet explained the circumstances surrounding how Japan had occupied Korea and Taiwan and how Vietnam and Burma/Myanmar had lost their sovereignty to the Western powers. Mao worried incessantly about China's future and felt responsible for the nation's well-being (Li 1994). Mao "liked to talk about current affairs with other students. He analyzed politics and military situations of the world. He was very clear. His points were based on evidence. Every time when he argued that China had failed to resist invasions by foreign powers and that young people should take responsibility for the country, he would become indignant with other students. He was sometimes excited, sometimes angry, and sometimes inspiring" (Li 1994, 118).

When Mao was a student at the Number One Teacher's College in Changsha, one of his teachers compiled a booklet called *Essay of Humiliation* (明耻篇), which was read widely among the students. The booklet was a response to Japan's Twenty-One Demands (二十一条), which were imposed on China after Japan soundly defeated the Chinese military. It was a recorded history of Japanese oppression over China and cited the various unreasonable treaties imposed on China during the previous ten years. A young Mao read the booklet and wrote on the margin, "May Seventh brought national humiliation; retaliation falls on the shoulders of our students!" (Mao 1995, 11; Schram 1992, 66).[2] In short, from a young age Mao was educated on China's history of foreign aggressions against it, which influenced the construction of his rhetoric during his rise to power.

The Chinese Concept of Family and Nation-State

The original tribes of ethnic Chinese lived in the middle and lower regions of the Yellow River before 221 B.C.E., but their ethnocentric view of the world, like those of many other ethnic groups, led them to believe that they lived in the center of the universe. In the Chinese classic *Shi ji* (史记) (Records of History), Sima Qian, the author, refers to China as *zhongguo* 中国, which translates as "the center of the world."[3]

Liang Qichao (1935) said, "For thousands of years, China remained in uninterrupted isolation. Chinese people refer to the land they live in as the universe (*tianxia* 天下) rather than a country (*guo* 国).[4] How can a people talk about patriotism if they have no concept of a nation?" (15). Liang was disappointed that China was so disjointed that its people did not even have a name for their own country; the English name China was given to the country by oppressive foreign nations (Liang Qichao 1935, 15). It was Liang who first introduced the Chinese term *minzhu*, or nation, to the Chinese people during the early twentieth century (Zhao 2004, 45; Hughes 2005, 5). Liang also proposed the terms for "new citizen" 新民 and "public virtue" 公德 (Liang Shuming 1987, 64). It was Sun Yat-sen who first called the Chinese people *guomin,* or national citizens, in his speeches as he launched his Nationalist Party, or *guomin dang.*

Although multiple peasant uprisings brought about a succession of dynasties, China was economically prosperous during most of its history since the Qin unification in 221 B.C.E. China's GDP in 1820 accounted for 32.9 percent of the world's overall GDP.[5] Culturally, Confucianism along with Daoism and Buddhism dominated much of China's moral sphere and spirituality. Confucianism taught Chinese people to place family first; thus of the "five cardinal human relationships" prescribed by Confucius, three point to family relationships.[6] Family, according to Confucius, provides individual members with emotional and financial support. Individual members, in turn, sacrifice for the family. As a result, cooperation and mutual assistance among family members were expected.

As Lin Yutang observed in 1938, "The Chinese are a nation of individualists. They are family-minded, not social-minded, and the family mind is only a form of magnified selfishness. . . . Public spirit is a new term—so is 'civic consciousness' and so is 'social service'" (164). Lin (1962) identifies fifteen Chinese characteristics, none of which reflects a level of social consciousness.[7] Lin concludes that China had not developed a sense of state or a sense of nationalism. The average Chinese individual, says Lin, cared only about his or her own self-interests; they were taught to be loyal to the emperor and obedient to people above them in the social hierarchy. Likewise, Liang Shuming's lifelong comparative study of Eastern and Western cultures concludes that the Chinese lacked a sense of publicness, habits of discipline, the ability to organize, and respect for the law. Specifically, "Chinese do not care about anything beyond their family. They have a very weak sense of nation" (Liang 1987, 68). Liang shares the view with Lin Yutang that traditional China lacked a national consciousness, as the Confucian tradition merely emphasized honoring the family.

Other Chinese scholars share similar views. Feng Youlan, a prominent Chinese philosopher, agrees that "in old China, the Chinese life is centered around the family, thus the Chinese have no sense of nation or patriotism" (Feng 1994, 186). Loyalty to the emperor or to their immediate superiors was at the very core of moral standards. Filial piety was exalted. In an essay titled "Chinese Dogs and Chinese People," Fu Sinian 傅斯年 (1919) describes seeing a police officer in Beijing training a foreign dog. He asked the police officer, "Why don't you train a Chinese dog?" The police officer answered, "Chinese dogs are too smart. Their sense of smell is better than foreign dogs, but they do not concentrate on the given task. When you send the dog to explore something, he will not do his task but will join other dogs if he sees a dog fight or sees a bitch." Fu uses this example to describe the Chinese people, who, he laments, have no sense of social responsibility. The author attributes this mentality to the oppression and authoritarian rule of the past three thousand years.

Chen Duxiu, one of the founders of the Chinese Communist Party, was even more explicit in his view of his fellow countrymen, stating that the "Chinese people only know their families. They do not know they have a country. . . . They only think about how to find a wife and have a son, and how to make money. They do not think about how they can make the country prosperous, stronger than other countries in the world. They do not think about how to eradicate evil for the benefit of the country. These things are not even in their dreams" (Chen 1993, 81). Chen attributes the humiliation suffered at the hands of foreign powers to this lack of national consciousness. The absence of public citizenship and lack of social consciousness echo Arthur Smith's account of China during his missionary period in the country. According to Smith (1894), the Chinese had no interest in what belonged to the "public" but that "the attitude of the government is handsomely matched by that of the people, who each and all are in the position of one who has no care or responsibility for what is done with the public property so long as she personally is not the loser" (109).

Influenced by Liang Qichao and Cai Hesen 蔡和森,[8] a young Mao Zedong shared the same perception that the Chinese people put too much emphasis on family and lacked an emotional attachment to the nation. Liang founded the *New Citizen's Journal* (新民丛报) and published a series of articles criticizing China's feudalism and introducing the Chinese people to the Western political system. Mao agreed with Liang's argument that only with new citizens could a new government take place. In one of his high school compositions, Mao wrote, "When I read in the *Shi Ji* [*Records of History*] about the incident of how Shang Yang[9] established confidence by moving the pole, I lament the foolishness of the people of our country. I lament the wasted efforts of the rulers of our country, and I lament the fact that for several thousand years the wisdom of the people has not been developed and the country has been teetering on the brink of a grievous disaster" (Schram 1992, 5). Inspired by Liang Qichao, Mao at the age of nineteen initiated and organized the New Citizen Association (新民学会) and launched his own journal, *Xiang Jiang Column* (湘江评论), in Hunan, his home province. He felt that China needed to change its mind-set and become a whole new nation altogether and define itself against foreign powers.

Mao's Rhetorical Construction of Nationalism

In her book *The Good Neighbor: Franklin D. Roosevelt and the Rhetoric of American Power,* Mary Stuckey (2013) traces and analyzes FDR's rhetorical trajectory in the construction of national power in the United States. Stuckey argues that FDR's rhetoric allowed him to unite the nation as one neighborhood and enabled him to facilitate a macro, national mind-set, rather than a micro, local orientation. According to Stuckey, "Presidents potentially possess enormous power over our national definitions; they help constitute us as a nation through the symbolic performance of their office; their rhetoric has instrumental effects on policy" (4). Stuckey's claims regarding the achievement of national solidarity provide the relevant framework in the case of modern China. Mao's rhetoric redefined China, mobilized Chinese nationalism, and affected government policy in economic development priorities. Based on my reading of Mao's writings, I argue that Mao used four rhetorical themes and strategies to cultivate nationalistic consciousness and to transform the collective mind-set of the family-oriented Chinese people: 1) a historical narrative of victimization and CCP victory; 2) the construction of a nationalistic identity; 3) the denunciation of Chiang Kai-shek and American imperialism; and 4) an expressed vision of a strong and powerful China.

A Historical Narrative of Victimization and CCP Victory

Rather than censor a humiliating history of victimization, Mao chose to lionize it. Mao and other "left wing" intellectuals and members of the Communist Party blamed Western imperialism for China's backwardness. Mao used a metaphor of "three mountains" to describe the oppression of the Chinese people: the mountain of feudalism; the mountain of imperialism; and the mountain of capitalism. Mao was not historically inaccurate in this analysis, as foreign powers such as Russia, Portugal, France, Britain, Germany, the United States, Italy, and Japan at some point in Chinese history had pillaged Chinese cultural treasures and natural resources, exploited Chinese labor, killed Chinese people, and taken over Chinese land as their residential and business concessions. Mao's emphasis on this specific historical narrative of victimization was not only crucial in creating national solidarity; it also shifted the blame of China's backwardness to an outside party and ultimately provided Mao with the opportunity to act as savior after an era of victimization.

When Japan invaded China and launched a full-scale Sino-Japanese war on July 7, 1937, Mao focused on the Japanese invasion as his rhetorical target. Japan initially occupied Manchuria (Northeastern China) in September 1931; consequently Manchuria became the colony of Japan. (My parents grew up in Manchuria during the Japanese rule. They told me that they had to learn the Japanese language at school and were treated as second-class citizens in their own homeland.) Japanese soldiers killed thousands of Chinese, burned their villages, and raped Chinese women.[10] The response from Chiang Kai-shek's ruling government was slow. In fact Chiang considered the CCP, not the Japanese, as his primary threat and implemented a policy of "internal pacification first and then external resistance" (Zhao 2004, 100). Mao, who was already a recognized leader of the CCP in 1937, responded to the Japanese invasion by condemning Japanese imperialism and calling for resistance. In his report to the Conference of Party Activities on December 27, 1935, Mao called out, "Comrades! A great change has now taken place in the political situation. Our party has defined its tasks in light of this changed situation. . . . Japanese imperialism wants to turn China into a colony, and we define ourselves against Japanese imperialism" (Mao 1935/1967a, 153). Mao then reminded his comrades of the history of foreign invasion and unequal treaties:

> As we all know, for nearly a hundred years, China has been a semi-colonial country jointly dominated by several imperialist powers. Owing to the Chinese people's struggle against imperialism and to conflicts among the imperialist powers, China has been able to retain a semi-independent status. For a time World War I gave Japanese imperialism the opportunity to dominate China exclusively. But the treaty surrendering China to Japan, the Twenty-One Demands

signed by Yuan Shih-kai—the arch-traitor of that time—was inevitably rendered null and void as a result of the Chinese people's fight against Japanese imperialism. In 1922 at the Washington Nine-Power Conference called by the United States, a treaty was signed which once again placed China under the joint domination of several imperialist powers. (Mao 1935/1967a, 153)

By citing historical facts to construct the national narrative of foreign invasion and humiliation during the past one hundred years, Mao made a rhetorical appeal that the Chinese people must fight against Japanese imperialism in order to gain China's independence from colonization and foreign power. Mao explicitly spotlighted China's most humiliating moments as a method of solidarity.

Avraham and First (2003) define nationalism as "a psychological phenomenon, involving needs and dispositions and its significance in the modern world" (284). The fear of China becoming a colony of Japan and Western powers was deeply rooted in the Chinese psyche, and Mao repeatedly painted a picture that the humiliation and ill-conceived treaties had deprived the Chinese of their dignity. By employing Japan as a common enemy and the ultimate reason for China's weaknesses, Mao made CCP followers and the general public receptive to his nationalistic appeals by rendering the Chinese people faultless.[11] After reviewing the history of oppression, Mao warned his audience that Japanese aggression at this point in history had been extended to other provinces and that Japan would soon colonize all of China (Mao 1935/1967a, 154). Mao declared that every Chinese person was facing the possibility of becoming a slave to a colonial power. Mao's response to this exigency was not only historically relevant but also emotionally escalating and provoking.

Given that China was still a semicolonized society, Mao prioritized a rhetorical shift in his vision for China. In 1940 he declared that China's nation building entailed two steps: "The first step is to change a colonial, semi-colonial and semi-feudal Chinese society into an independent, democratic one. The second step is to carry the revolution forward and build a socialist society" (Mao 1940/1967b, 342). According to Mao, the actions constituting the first step "began with the Opium War in 1840.... Then came the Movement of the Taiping Heavenly Kingdom, the Sino-French War, the Sino-Japanese War, the Reform Movement of 1898, the Revolution of 1911, the May Fourth Movement, the Northern Expedition, the War of the Agrarian Revolution and the present War of Resistance against Japan" (342–43).

This retelling of the major events in early twentieth-century China had appeared frequently in Mao's writing as justification for the necessity of revolution and nation building. In his article "On Coalition Government," Mao devoted an entire section, "History Follows a Tortuous Course," to describe in great detail the history of the War of Resistance against Japan to justify the CCP's leadership and to highlight their heroic acts during the war. Mao's repeated mention and condemnation of Japanese imperialism served to reinforce a sense of shame to remind the Chinese people of the devastating foreign invasions.

Facing stiff resistance to these themes and barraged by questions from all sides, Mao boosted the national spirit by referencing Wu Sung or Wu Song, a Chinese folk hero: "We must not show the slightest timidity before a wild beast. We must learn from Wu Sung on the Chingyang Ridge. As Wu Sung saw it, the tiger on Chingyang Ridge was a man-eater, whether irritated or not. Wu Sung's choice was to either kill the tiger or be eaten by him" (Mao 1949/1967d, 416). Here, Mao asserted that China's only chance to attain prosperity lay in defeating Japanese imperialists. Mao employed fear appeals and engaged his audience with a chain of reasoning to legitimize the CCP's leadership.[12] As Yingjie Guo (2004) has pointed out, "The inculcation of the sense of victimhood is coupled with efforts to create a sense of insecurity and danger" (34). Mao's call for resistance to military aggression and to a colonial culture further ignited the rise of Chinese nationalism and reaffirmed the legitimacy of the CCP's leadership in that resistance.

Ultimately Mao took advantage of these historical events and contexts to portray the Chinese people as victims of imperialism while simultaneously promoting his own ideological agenda of social change through rhetorical tactics of fear appeals, narratives, and chain reasoning. Mao's narrative was persuasive as it brought the Chinese people together by addressing the common problems that concerned the nation, problems that were faced by the imagined national community. Moreover, as Zhao (2004) points out, "This process had the effect of removing differences within the political community and replacing them with a common hegemonic order of signs, symbols, and values" (4). Mao's narrative on China's "century of humiliation" has become a way of talking among Chinese leaders and people to this day, as they recount Mao's rhetorical references to Chinese nationalism. Mao aligned the country toward a singularly nationalistic trajectory. This legacy remains.

The Construction of a Nationalistic Identity

Ironically Mao strengthened national morale by explicitly and repeatedly conjuring China's most humiliating historical moments in foreign relations. By thrusting all the blame for China's weak, semicolonial state onto foreign powers, Mao argued that China was merely a victim and not incapable of solidarity. The traditional Chinese lifestyle was centered around family, based largely on the Confucian value system of humanity and filial piety. This system closely examined familial consciousness but did not address a sense of national solidarity in China, which was a nation divided across regions, dialects, and various religious and political affiliations. Sun Yat-sen's famous saying that "the Chinese are like sand" implied that no cohesive force united the Chinese people. However, Japan's invasion of China provided an impetus for the development of cohesion. Nationalism began to permeate the Chinese mind-set after the defeats and subsequent humiliation imposed by imperialist powers. Mao's rhetoric of alliance paved the way for the construction of a nationalistic identity.

The alliance with the Nationalists gave Mao a broader platform for his nationalistic rhetoric. He began to use democracy as a rhetorical appeal to establish his ethos. He argued that "the key that will ensure victory for our armed resistance is the winning of political democracy and freedom," which required "domestic peace, unity, and the mobilization of people." He held the opinion that "without democracy, a genuine and solid national united front against Japan cannot be established in China and its goals cannot be attained" (Mao 1937/1967a, 267). To establish a democratic government, Mao called for change in China's political system: release political prisoners; remove the ban on multiple political parties; end the National Party's one-party dictatorship; and create a national government with the cooperation of all parties and all classes (268). He also advocated the founding of national assemblies and elections (268). He argued that "only thus can internal peace be truly consolidated, internal armed hostilities ended and internal unity strengthened, enabling the whole nation to unite and resist the foreign foe" (268). Mao asserted that China required a singular united front lest they fall victim to foreign powers yet again. However, during this time Chiang Kai-shek's Nationalist Party government demeaned the CCP by deriding them as "bandits."[13] In turn, by calling for national unity against the Japanese and demanding a democratic China, Mao gained for himself and for his party a certain moral integrity. In this sense Mao skillfully manipulated an international crisis to work in his favor.[14]

To gain recognition for the CCP and the support of the Chinese people, Mao referenced Sun Yat-sen's three principles—nationalism, democracy, and the people's livelihood—as the ideological legitimacy for establishing an alliance with the Nationalists and the democratic nation. Mao pledged to his Chinese audience that "we are ready to staunchly put them [the three principles] into practice; moreover, we ask the Kuomingtang [Nationalists] to implement them together with us, and we call upon the whole nation to put them into effect. We hold that the Communist Party, the Kuomintang, and the people of the whole country should unite and fight for these three great objectives of national independence, democracy and freedom, and the people's livelihood" (Mao 1937/1967a, 271). Here, Mao's vision of a democratic republic was an alliance among all revolutionary classes, or "a state based on the alliance of the working class, the peasantry, the petty bourgeoisie, and the bourgeoisie. Thus, although the future of the democratic republic may evolve in a capitalist direction, the possibility also exists that the republic will turn towards socialism. The party of the Chinese proletariat should struggle mightily toward the latter prospect" (275). Here, Mao emphasized the notion of national identity rather than a division between party lines that China's power lay with its masses. Instead of blankly calling for Communist rule, he called for an alliance toward common goals. He even envisioned the possibility of a capitalistic society; all these concepts deviated from Marxist-Leninist revolutionary theories that called for a proletarian dictatorship in a socialist/Communist society. Although Mao had, in this instance, rhetorically constructed himself as a moderate and a patriot, his real motive likely was to hinder Chiang's extermination campaigns and to gain support and moral legitimacy for the CCP.

Mao again identified a series of political events as the collective impetus for constructing a national identity: "There was first the Opium War against British aggression, then came the War of the Taiping Heavenly Kingdom, then the Sino-Japanese War of 1894, the Reform Movement of 1898, the Yi Ho Tuan Movement (Boxer Rebellion), the Revolution of 1911, the May Fourth Movement, the Northern Expedition, and finally the war waged by the Red Army. Although these struggles differed from each other, their common purpose was to repel foreign enemies or to change existing conditions" (Mao 1939/1967b, 243). While Mao credited Sun Yat-sen with leading the nationalistic movement, he also aimed to establish a "people's democracy" that broke away from what he saw as a "semi-colonial and semi-feudal" status. For Mao, the goal was to destroy imperialism and feudalism and transform "the old China into a new China" (248). By continuously and explicitly painting China's litany of failures in foreign relations, he was able to stress that China needed something as drastic as a revolution in governance.

In the name of defeating Japan and establishing a new society, Mao gave audiences the impression that he had put aside ideological differences with Chiang for the sake of national unity and a democratic China. Mao stated that the CCP and the Nationalist Party shared the common goal of "mobilizing and uniting all anti-Japanese forces of the Chinese people, completely wiping out the Japanese aggressors and building a new China that is independent, free, democratic, united, prosperous and powerful" (Mao 1945/1967c, 228–29). His nationalistic rhetoric fed a new patriotic national narrative and appealed to the mutual interest of peasants, capitalized on mass discontent, and demonstrated his ability to lead in times of war.

Further, Mao's nationalistic appeals demonstrated that he was willing to place the nation's political interests over his own political ambition. His nationalistic charisma attracted many young students as well as seasoned intellectuals to join the Communist Party during the Yan'an period. In the words of Zhao (2004), "The power of nationalism came from the fact that it locates the source of individual identity within a 'people,' which is seen as the bearer of sovereignty, the central object of loyalty, and the basis of collective solidarity" (4). In this sense, through his rhetorical construction of the Chinese national identity, Mao successfully established himself as China's moral beacon during this revolution. Sadly this exalted loyalty toward the nation later shifted exclusively toward the CCP, and then ultimately to Mao himself.

The Denouncement of Chiang Kai-shek and U.S. Imperialism

Ultimately Mao's emphasis on a historical narrative of victimization along with his public pleas for an alliance with Chiang and Chiang's subsequent rejection managed to paint Chiang and his party as disrupting the road toward a revitalized, independent China. On September 2, 1945, Japan surrendered unconditionally to the allied forces, bringing an end to World War II. In August 1945 Chiang invited Mao and CCP delegates to Chongqing, the headquarters of the Nationalist Party, for domestic peace negotiations. The negotiations ended with the Double Tenth Agreement issued by Chiang.[15] However, the two parties continued to fight over certain territories. In June 1946 Chiang launched an all-out attack on CCP-occupied areas, an incursion that instigated a civil war between the People's Liberation Army and Chiang, whose troops received military and financial aid from the United States.

Consequently Mao began to cast Chiang as a leader who rejected China's historical humiliation with no interest in defeating the Japanese. Mao denounced Chiang for starting the civil war and accused him of being a traitor. Mao also took the opportunity to elevate his party's moral legitimacy by juxtaposing the actions of the two parties: "We rely entirely on our own efforts and our position is invincible.... Chiang Kai-shek, on the other hand, depends entirely on foreign countries. We live plainly and work hard; we take care of the needs of both the army and the people," while in Chiang Kai-shek–controlled areas, top officials "are corrupt and degenerate, while the people under them are destitute" (Mao 1946/1967d, 91). Mao called for the Chinese people to take a side. In traditional China the concept of *tianming*, or a mandate from heaven, was used as a moral justification for rule. If the ruler was moral and brought benefits to the people, he had *tianming*, or the moral legitimacy to rule. If he was immoral and brought harm to the people, he would lose his *tianming*. Mao's remarks appealed to this traditional concept and painted Chiang as an illegitimate head of state who had exhausted his *tianming*.

Lucian Pye (1968) points out that "the dominant emotion of modern Chinese politics has been a preoccupation with hatred coupled with an enthusiasm for singling out enemies" (67). Mao rhetorically demonized Chiang. He depicted Chiang's government as the "running dog" of U.S. imperialism, equated Chiang with Japanese imperialism, and accused Chiang of allowing China to be colonized by Fascist Western powers. Mao charged that by launching the civil war the Nationalist Party had "declared themselves to be enemies of the entire Chinese people and had driven all strata of the people to the brink of starvation and death" (Mao 1947/1967d, 136). Mao depicted Chiang as an obstacle "for the establishment of a peaceful, democratic and independent new China" (1947/1967d, 136). Mao's other writings derided Chiang and his followers as "a gang of bandits" (1948/1967d, 286), "a blood-stained executioner" (1948/1967d, 302), "a professional traitor and running dog" (1948/1967d, 303), and a "war criminal" who "has lost his soul" and "is merely a corpse" (1949/1967d, 313). Mao wielded relentless verbal attacks on Chiang. Mao's aim was "to carry out the urgent demand of the people of the whole country. That is, to overthrow the arch-criminal of the civil war, Chiang Kai-shek, and form a democratic coalition government so as to attain the general goal of liberating the people and the nation" (Mao 1947/1967d, 147). To justify his point, Mao illustrated how in the past Chiang had disregarded Sun Yat-sen's calls for peace by cracking down on the CCP, carrying out a weak and passive resistance against the Japanese invasion, launching the civil war, and brutalizing people using foreign aid from the United States. Moreover, Chiang was portrayed as a traitor as he "has not hesitated to sell out our country's sovereign rights to foreign imperialism, to collude with the U.S. armed forces so that they should remain in Tsingtao and elsewhere and to procure advisers from the United States to take part in directing the civil war, training troops to slaughter his own fellow-countrymen" (Mao 1947/1967d, 149).

Toward the end of the manifesto, Mao made an emotional plea imbued with hopeful nationalistic sentiments: "All comrade commanders and fighters of our army! We are shouldering the most important, the most glorious task in the history of our country's revolution. We should make great efforts to accomplish our task. Our efforts will decide the day when our great motherland emerges from darkness into light and our beloved fellow countrymen will be able to live like human beings and choose the government they wish" (1947/1967d, 151–52). Although Chiang was still the president of the Republic of China, Mao rhetorically embodied head-of-state leadership by providing the impetus for change. In hindsight, Mao's motive for defeating Chiang both militarily and rhetorically—or reporting such a defeat—more realistically might have been designed to promote his own chances of becoming the leader of China. These possibilities make his account of history questionable.[16]

According to Mao, Chiang had also failed his country because he kowtowed to the United States. In his meeting with the American correspondent Anna Louise Strong, Mao simultaneously called the United States an imperialist nation and "a paper tiger." When it was clear that the CCP would win the civil war regardless of military and financial assistance from the U.S., Mao wrote an essay titled "Farewell, Leighton Stuart,"[17] which denounced the U.S. government for its military aid to the Nationalists. Mao claimed that the U.S. interests generated actions only for the purposes of colonizing China, and Mao condemned Secretary of State Dean Acheson's *The China White Paper* report.[18] Mao used empowering language by claiming that "we Chinese have backbone. Many who were once liberal or democratic individuals have stood up to the U.S. imperialism and their running dogs" (1949/1967d, 437). Mao again asserted Chiang's loss of *tianming* by claiming that Chiang had not only failed to strive for a national solidarity but also had relied on help from imperialist powers to strengthen his unfair dictatorship over China.

Further, Mao referred to the heroic deeds of the well-known poet Wen Yi-to, who "rose to his full height and smote the table, angrily faced the Kuomintang [the Nationalist] pistols and died rather than submit. Chu Tse-ching, though seriously ill, starved to death rather than accept U.S. 'relief food'. . . . We should write eulogies for Wen Yi-to and Chu Tse-ching, who demonstrated the heroic spirit of our nation" (Mao 1949/1967d, 437–38). In praising these two well-known public intellectuals, Mao sent messages to the Chinese people and to the U.S. government that the CCP would not yield to Chiang Kai-shek and that China's era of humiliation had ended. The Chinese people were of strong character and moral integrity, Mao contended, and were worthy of nationalistic pride. Further, Mao declared, "What matter if we have to face some difficulties? Let them blockade us! Let them blockade us for eight or ten years! By that time all of China's problems will have been solved. Will the Chinese cower before difficulties when they are not afraid even of death?" (438). Here, Mao redirected China's fear of U.S. sanctions against China into a rhetorical opportunity to promote nationalism among the Chinese people.

When the CCP defeated the Nationalists and established a new China, Mao was aware that the path to an independent nation would not be an easy one. In his "Address to the Preparatory Committee of the New Political Consultative Conference" on June 15, 1949, he warned his comrades, "I think it is necessary to call people's attention to the fact that the imperialists and their running dogs, the Chinese reactionaries, will not resign themselves to defeat in this land of China. They will continue to gang up against the Chinese people in every possible way" (Mao 1949/1967d, 407). Because of this continued perceived threat, Mao claimed that "the people all over the country must unite to smash resolutely, thoroughly, wholly and completely every plot against the Chinese people by the imperialists and their running dogs, the Chinese reactionaries. China must be independent, China must be liberated, and China's affairs must be decided by and run by the Chinese people themselves. No further interference, not even the slightest, will be tolerated from any imperialist country" (407).

Mao ended the speech by making the bold assertion that "the Chinese people will see that, once China's destiny is in the hands of the people, China, like the sun rising in the east, will illuminate every corner of the land with a brilliant flame, swiftly clean up the mire left by the reactionary government, heal the wound of war and build a new, powerful and prosperous people's republic worthy of the name" (Mao 1949/1967d, 408). Through these emotionally charged metaphorical appeals, Mao identified the potential enemy threats while also painting a bright future for China.

An Expressed Vision of a Strong and Powerful China

On October 1, 1949, Mao proudly stood on the top of the Tiananmen monument and declared to thousands of Chinese people, "The central government of the People's Republic of China was founded today." He delivered a speech ten days prior to the announcement on Tiananmen. He wrote in the speech that "The Chinese people comprising one quarter of humanity, have now stood up." This proclamation was meant to signify the end of imperialist aggression and a hundred years of humiliation and to condemn the corrupt government led by Chiang Kai-shek. Mao not only restored national pride to the Chinese but also offered the promise to build a strong, powerful, and prosperous nation.

As Mao wrote on September 16, 1949, "Of all things in the world, people are the most precious. Under the leadership of the Communist Party, as long as there are people, every kind of miracle can be performed.... We believe that revolution can change everything, and that before long there will arise a new China with a big population and a great wealth of products, where life will be abundant and culture will flourish" (Mao 1949/1967d, 454). With these words Mao proclaimed his confidence that the Chinese people would build a socialistic China. He also justified the Communist revolution and promised a better life for the Chinese people. Mao's nationalistic discourse began to shift away from a dour narration of China's victimization to the pronouncement of building a strong and powerful nation.[19]

By praising the greatness of the Chinese people and blaming foreigners for China's problems, Mao won the support of the Chinese people. But now Mao shifted the narrative of victimization to the rhetoric of reinvigorating China. In his rhetoric Mao no longer evoked images of the Chinese people as victims. Instead, Mao claimed that "the Chinese people have ceased to be passive in spirit and have gained the initiative. The period of modern world history in which the Chinese and Chinese culture were looked down upon has ended. The great, victorious Chinese People's War of Liberation and the great people's revolution have rejuvenated and are rejuvenating the great culture of the Chinese people. In its spiritual aspects, this culture of Chinese people already stands higher than any in the capitalist world" (Mao 1949/1967d, 458). Mao also anticipated that "an upsurge in economic construction is bound to be followed by an upsurge of construction in the cultural sphere. The era in which the Chinese people were regarded as uncivilized is now ended. We shall emerge in the world as a nation with an advanced culture" (Mao 1949/1977, 18). There were no Chinese leaders before Mao who had encouraged Chinese people to be proud of their culture and country, and few had given the Chinese people the hope for a better life as he did. Therein lay his effectiveness.

Nevertheless the culture that Mao referred to was not the traditional Chinese culture but a new national culture politicized under the leadership of the CCP. In many aspects Mao successfully transformed Chinese culture; party bureaucratic culture became characterized by an authoritarian rule, or a so-called proletarian dictatorship. In the name of building a socialist ruling structure, Mao purposefully destroyed traditional Chinese culture by removing any traces of the "four olds," which included old customs, old culture, old habits, and old ideas embraced in a Confucian China. Ironically, traces of a Confucian China were appropriated to suit the authoritarian government of a Communist China. For example, the traditional value of loyalty to the emperor and obedience to the elderly had been replaced by loyalty and obedience to Mao and to the party. However, it cannot be denied that Mao's revolution created a new national culture, uniting the nation under a new brand of self-respect. From Sun Yat-sen to Chiang Kai-shek to Mao Zedong, Chinese leaders in different time periods with different ideologies and political agendas had one thing in common: they were all nationalists. Zhao (2004) writes that "they shared a deep bitterness over China's humiliation and were determined to rejuvenate China . . . and they shared a strong sense of entitlement that China deserves a great power status as they believe China's decline is a mistake of history, which they should correct" (12).

Mao began to employ the symbol of the atom bomb to "correct" China's history of victimization and rejuvenate China's image in the eyes of the rest of the world. Mao was determined that China must have its own atom bomb, which would function as the best national defense. In a speech given in September 1945, Mao promised to build a strong army, air force, and navy for national defense. His concluding remarks were filled with nationalistic fervor: "Let the domestic and foreign reactionaries tremble before us! Let them say we are no good at this no good at that. By our own indomitable efforts, we the Chinese people will unswervingly reach our goal" (Mao 1949/1977, 18). Mao's use of repetition and exclamation served to reinforce determination and stir up patriotic passions. By exploiting the important national symbolism of China, Mao called on top Chinese scientists to develop atom bombs by relying on their own efforts. On October 16, 1964, China announced to the world that the country had successfully exploded its first atom bomb.[20]

China's development of the atom bomb posed a threat to Western powers. After 1949 the United States imposed economic sanctions on China, launched anti-Communist propaganda, and sent its Seventh Fleet to patrol Taiwan straits.[21] Mao combated this hostility by continuing to label the United States a "paper tiger" in order to trivialize American world dominance. Despite America's clear dominance on the world stage, Mao stressed that China would one day surpass the United States as a world power. In his speech at the first session of the CCP's Eighth Congress on August 30, 1956, Mao told the party representatives, "Given fifty or sixty years, we certainly ought to overtake the United States. This is an obligation. You have such a big population, such a vast territory and such rich resources, and what is more, you are said to be building socialism, which is supposed to be superior; if after working at it for fifty or sixty years you are still unable to overtake the United States, what a sorry figure you will cut! You should be read off the face of the earth. Therefore, to overtake the United States is not only possible, but absolutely necessary and obligatory" (Mao 1956/1977, 315).

In this speech Mao shifted the personal pronoun from "we" to "you" as a way to deflect the responsibility away from himself and toward the CCP members and to convince CCP members that China was capable of surpassing the United States. Mao also wanted to prove that the socialist system that China had undertaken was indeed superior to a capitalistic system. In his speech commemorating Dr. Sun Yat-sen on November 12, 1956, Mao made a claim that when the world entered 2001, China would become a "powerful industrial socialist country" (Mao 1956/1977, 330). Despite providing no backing for such a bold statement, his predictions and promises were rhetorically powerful because they boosted the morale of the Chinese people, motivated the Chinese people to engage in socialist construction, and painted an optimistic picture for the Chinese people and further reinforced their nationalistic sentiments.[22]

In summary, Mao sought a nationalism that not only was present as an institution but also constituted a collective identity. In other words, nationalism should not only offer the people faith in their sovereign government; it should also constitute how they viewed themselves as a nation. Rhetoric of a "strong state complex" was the source of Chinese nationalism, evident in Mao's early writings, his Great Leap Forward campaigns, and his investment in national defense and nuclear programs. Even today the ideas of a "great country" (*daguo*) and a "strong nation" (*qiangguo*) are prevalent in official and intellectual discourse.

China's Nationalism in Contemporary Times

Thanks to Mao's rhetoric of China's historical humiliation by the Japanese and Western powers and his promises of building an undefeatable nation, nationalism soared among the Chinese. In a desire to build a strong nation and uphold China's sovereignty, the Communist government employed patriotic political appeals to boost national pride against U.S. imperialism and Soviet revisionism through the government-controlled propaganda apparatus. The seed of Chinese nationalism planted and instilled by Mao is still evident in China today. Nationalism is part of the identity of the Chinese citizen rather than just a vehicle of national pride.

After Mao's death, China experienced an ideological crisis. Communist ideology, as the dominant CCP ideology, lost its appeal as citizens watched how other nations thrived under capitalist systems. The pervasive national optimism that characterized Mao's rhetoric died along with Mao. Therefore, without Mao the CCP began to see that it was losing its effectiveness and had to change how the party presented itself to the people. The CCP's political discourse abandoned Maoist rhetoric and launched economic reforms as a way to regain its legitimacy. Now the CCP positions itself as the representative of China's nationalist interest and the defender of Chinese national pride in its efforts to modernize. CCP leaders redirected Chinese nationalism, and the group now "portrays the Communist state as the embodiment of the nation's will" rather than the ideology of optimism. It phrases economic development as "a national cause" that would transform China "into a powerful and modernized country" (Zhao 1997, 732). Even in the absence of Mao, the remarkable rate of China's economic growth and the vast improvement of Chinese people's lives have fed national pride and confidence.

With the advent of the market economy since the 1980s, Chinese nationalistic discourse has become reemployed as a rhetorical strategy for the government to unify the nation and fulfill this post-Mao ideological vacuum. The spirit of nationalism has been inculcated through media, official discourse, the Patriotic Education Campaign, and the celebration of traditional Chinese values and contemporary achievements in economy, science, and technology. At the same time, as China makes its mark on international affairs during the twenty-first century, the world has witnessed a more valiant China. Despite China's sheer enormity in both population and geography, nationalism seems to be the one value shared most by the Chinese people and the government, triggered and reinforced by a set of high-profile demonstrations and protests: demonstrations against the United States for the accidental bombing of the Chinese embassy in Belgrade in May 1999; demonstrations against the United States for the collision of a U.S. spy plane with a Chinese jet close to the South China Sea in 2001; the boycott of the French supermarket chain Carrefour, which blocked the Olympic torch relay in Paris for the 2008 Beijing Olympics;[23] mass support for a series of satellite and rocket launches; and looting Japanese stores in Shanghai in protest of the dispute over Diaoyu Islands (钓鱼岛), also known as the Senkaku Islands. More notably, on September 3, 2015, China staged an enormous military parade to celebrate the seventieth anniversary of the victory of the Chinese people's resistance against Japanese aggression and the world anti-Fascist war. The parade was viewed as a projection of China's strength.[24]

Further, Chinese nationalism is now manifested in intellectual discourse and popular books. In spite of a history of being silenced and persecuted in Mao's China, Chinese intellectuals have in common with the CCP *qiangguo meng,* or the dream of a strong and powerful China. According to Suisheng Zhao (1997), Chinese intellectuals have been influential in mobilizing Chinese nationalism through their writings and publications, many of which engaged in discussions about achieving a strong and powerful China. Mirroring Mao's rhetoric, many intellectuals have condemned the United States for preventing China from reaching its true potential. For example, in national bestsellers such as *China Can Say No, China Can Still Say No,* and *China Is Not Happy,*[25] the authors accused the United States of being morally corrupt and aiming to connive and restrain China from economic development and keep China from achieving better living standards for its people. Accordingly, they argue, China should stand its ground and not bend to the imperialist impulse of the Western powers.

Meanwhile a number of television programs produced in the 1990s and 2000s about the Anti-Japanese War have been aired. These programs depict the brutality of Japanese soldiers, thus enflaming patriotic Chinese sentiment. Ying-shih Yu (2013) has observed that China's new nationalism has shifted primarily toward discourse against Japan and the United States. China's new nationalism is more outwardly aggressive rather than rhetorically polemic.[26] As Zhao (2004) clearly states, "The wars, unequal treaties, humiliations, and material and territorial losses suffered by the Chinese people during a century of contact with foreign imperialist powers were continuous sources of inspiration for Chinese nationalism" (50). In his rhetorical analysis of contemporary Chinese leaders' discourse on Google disagreements with China, Stephen Hartnett (2011) presents textual evidence to indicate that the trope of China-as-victim is used as a rhetorical strategy to defend China's cyberspace censorship policy. Hartnett calls such a rhetorical form "traumatized nationalism" (413), which breeds resentment and hostility toward Western countries, particularly toward Japan and the United States.

Nationalism has also been reflected in the "Mao fever" of the 1990s. Mao Zedong was praised in popular books as a "great patriot and national hero" because of his courage to stand firm against Western imperialism, and many of these books attribute the rise of China to Mao's resoluteness. Books featuring Mao's life once again became popular among Chinese youth. As a proponent of Mao's political legacy, Cui Zhiyuan argues that Mao's socialist ideals provided a model for China's modernization—that his invention of the commune system, his Great Leap Forward, and even his Cultural Revolution all had positive implications for China's economic development and the dream of a strong China (Zhao 1997, 737). Mao's legacy of proffering a strong nation lives on.

SEVEN

★ ★ ★ ★

Rhetoric of Mao Zedong's Foreign Policy

Although Mao Zedong did employ foreign policy advisers, records indicate that China's foreign policy in modern China was largely driven by Mao himself, especially in the last ten years of his life. Mao's rhetoric on foreign relations not only exhibited his devotion to the nationalist cause against Western imperialism but also painted Mao as China's savior from diplomatic isolation. In the early years Mao's revolutionary base and his political thought were little known to the world before Edgar Snow's publication of *Red Star over China* in 1938, a book based on Snow's interviews with Mao and other top Communist leaders. Once Mao consolidated his army force and his leadership in the CCP, he was eager to earn domestic and international support for his party. To do so Mao made contacts with foreign correspondents to whom he would present his plans for China's future, especially during the period of the Anti-Japanese War (1937–45), which attracted many international journalists. In his interviews he declared his party's resolve to fight for China's independence in order to win the sympathy and support of the United States.

Mao's rhetoric regarding the CCP's relations with the United States shifted from friendly to hostile when the United States decided to support the Nationalist Party during the civil war against the CCP. Mao's enmity toward the United States intensified after 1949 when the United States imposed economic sanctions on China and refused to recognize the People's Republic of China as a legitimate government. During his era, Mao's aggressive public rhetoric contradicted his private rhetoric and action, in which he used a more deferent manner toward the United States. For example, his public words of condemnation contradicted his surprising and private invitation to U.S. president Richard Nixon to visit China. Mao's rhetoric in foreign policy and his other strategic rhetorical moves reflected his shrewdness in both military and political tactics, his real or contrived contradictory personality, and his capricious disposition.

Further, Mao's success with China's revolution elevated him to the level of a model to be emulated by any nation in a struggle against colonialism and imperialism. He inevitably became revered as an inspiration for many other Third World leaders.[1] His works and writings became sources of inspiration and practical guides for resisting colonial power and military strategies.

Mao's Early Rhetoric on the United States: Shifting from Friend to Foe

Since his early years in Hunan, Mao had been troubled by China's poverty and inferior image as compared to that of a modernized Europe. In his speech "Strengthen the Party's Unity and Carry on the Party's Tradition,"[2] Mao painted a picture of the old China, lamenting that "China used to be stigmatized as a 'decrepit empire,' 'the sick man' of East Asia, a country with a backward economy and a backward culture, a place with no hygiene and where people were poor at ball games and swimming, where the women had bound feet, men wore pigtails, where eunuchs could still be found, and where the moon was inferior and did not shine as brightly as in foreign lands" (Mao 1956/1977, 313). Since the founding of the Communist Party in 1921, Mao and his comrades were determined to overturn China's inferior status on the world stage. Before 1936, however, little was known about Mao's revolutionary base. Chiang's government depicted Mao's Communist force as bandits. When he became the CCP's leader at Yan'an in Shanbei Province in 1935, Mao made a consistent effort to meet with foreign correspondents, disseminate his ideas about a democratic China to the West, and allow these journalists to visit Communist-controlled areas. Mao wanted to show foreign visitors his Communist communities, which he believed were characterized by equality, self-reliance, and the high spirit of people representing the hope of China's future.

The first U.S. reporter Mao invited was Edgar Snow, who interviewed Mao and Mao's close comrades in 1936 from July to October. Snow (1938) recalls, "They [Communist leaders] gave me a vast amount of their time and with unprecedented frankness provided more personal and impersonal information than any one foreign scribe could fully absorb" (16). In his widely acclaimed book *Red Star over China* (1938), Snow offered a sympathetic account of Mao's Communist beliefs and his revolution.[3] This publication marked the beginning of Mao's exposure to the world.

During the Anti-Japanese War (1937–45), the United States helped China defeat the Japanese with economic aid, weapons, and airpower. The war gave Mao the opportunity to build alliances with the Nationalist Party and win the sympathy and support of the United States. From 1936 to 1946 Mao met in Yan'an with over twenty foreign correspondents and delegates, most of whom were from the United States. From these meetings U.S. correspondents reported favorable impressions of Mao, describing his plain living, his political charisma, and what they saw as a genuine caring for improving the well-being of the Chinese people and creating a better China. Among these foreign journalists were Helen Forster Snow (Edgar Snow's wife); the U.S. journalists Agnes Smedley, George K. T. Wang, Robert Martin, and Anna Louise Strong; the British journalist James Bertram; U.S. brigadier general Evans Fordyce Carlson; U.S. delegations headed by Gunther Stein with members Israel Epstein and Harrison Forman; Maurice

Votaw; and an American Embassy employee, John Stewart Service. In addition Mao spoke about establishing a coalition government with Chiang Kai-shek with Patrick Jay Hurley, a U.S. brigadier general and personal representative of President Franklin D. Roosevelt; Col. David Barrett, the U.S. Army observation group leader; and George Marshall, a five-star U.S. general, chief of staff, secretary of state, and secretary of defense during World War II.

In each of these meetings Mao took the opportunity to introduce the CCP's political principles, presented himself as willing to build an alliance with the Nationalists against the Japanese, and expounded on his own war strategies against the Japanese. Evans Fordyce Carlson (1896–1947) wrote after meeting with Mao that "Mao is a modest, kind, and lonely genius. He is working hard in pitch dark nights to seek a peaceful and just life for his people" (Mao 1938/2012, 13). Likewise many other foreigners who met and talked with Mao have written books that expressed their favorable impressions of Mao and his promising revolution. Carlson predicted that the CCP would eventually rule China (15). Owen Lattimore, one of the three editors from *Pacific Affairs,* was reported as saying, "Mao Zedong is a person for the people—super intelligent but also apparently carrying the blood of a peasant."[4] Carlson left Yan'an with the impression that CCP leaders were serious about establishing a united front with Chiang's forces in the fight against the Japanese.

In 1935, before Mao established himself as the leader of the Communist Party based in Yan'an, the United States knew little about the CCP and was not interested in making contact with the party. According to Cohen (2000), the United States was more concerned about Soviet aggression than China because it believed that communism was unlikely to take place in China, as a dictatorship by the proletariat was not possible in a society so dominated by a rigid patriarchal family structure. But with all the new attention from U.S. journalists presenting a favorable impression of Mao and the CCP, Mao managed to gain new respect from the American populace. Presentations of Chinese people in American media showed more positive images.[5] For example, the movie *The Good Earth,* based on Pearl S. Buck's bestseller, was released in 1937 and offered a sympathetic account of Chinese peasants' struggles against poverty and harsh living conditions. The Chinese were depicted as courageous, dignified, and hardworking.

At this point in time, Mao saw the United States as a potential ally in the fight against Japan and maintained a favorable view of the country and its government. As Cohen (2000) notes, "After December 7, 1941 . . . the Communists became extremely friendly toward the United States. . . . In 1944, July Fourth was celebrated in Yenan [Yan'an] with tremendous enthusiasm and fulsome praise for Roosevelt, whose policies were lauded as expressions of the great tradition of freedom and democracy in the United States" (142–43). On the same day Mao entertained U.S. delegates and journalists with a banquet, and he had his secretary

Hu Qiaomu publish a commentary in the Communist newspaper *Liberation Daily* entitled "Celebration of American Independence Day—the Day of Freedom and Democracy." The commentary called the United States "the typical democratic country in the capitalist world," praised it for "having a glorious tradition of fighting for nationalism," and named Washington, Lincoln, and Roosevelt as great fighters in the name of democracy (Cohen 2000). On November 10, 1944, Mao wrote a letter to President Roosevelt claiming that "[the] Chinese people and American people have always had a profound friendship in our history and tradition" (Mao 1994, 39). Mao even requested a meeting with Roosevelt to plan the details of military cooperation between the United States and Chinese Communist forces (Cohen 2000, 147).[6]

Mao made himself an advocate of democracy who echoed American political values and practices. He condemned Chiang's one-party system and called for a multiparty political system. In doing so he placed himself closer to the American version of democracy and depicted Chiang's rule as a government of despotism. As Sheng (1998) points out, Mao's use of "democracy" in the U.S. connotation served to discredit the Nationalists' "one-party dictatorship" and "thereby legitim[ate] the CCP's political authorities in its territories" (181). Here, Mao's praise of the United States can be interpreted as a rhetorical strategy to alienate the Nationalist Party, rather than a genuine gesture and commitment to build China into a true democracy. His praise can also be viewed as a rhetorical strategy to undermine the U.S. alliance with the Nationalists. In fact, Mao's praise of the United States ended shortly after Patrick Hurley, the U.S. ambassador to China, announced on April 2, 1945, that the U.S. government would not recognize nor provide any assistance to the CCP and would instead assist Chiang's Nationalist Party.[7] Hurley's announcement enraged Mao, who responded with two commentaries published by the Xinhua News Agency. In the first Mao labeled Hurley as an "imperialist," calling Hurley's April 2 announcement a "nasty scheme" with "imperialist platitudes" for the purposes of denying the CCP's legitimacy, wrecking national unity, and sacrificing the interests of the Chinese people (Mao 1945/1967c, 282).

In the second commentary, Mao pointed out Hurley's contradictions: "When Hurley visited Yenan [Yan'an] as Roosevelt's personal representative in November 1944, he expressed agreement with the Chinese Communist Party's plan for the abolition of the Kuomintang [Nationalists] one-party dictatorship and the establishment of a democratic coalition government. But later he changed his tune and went back on what he had said in Yenan" (Mao 1945/1967c, 285). The United States was depicted as betraying the Chinese people because it had failed to keep its promise to the CCP. Further, Mao warned the United States that the action of betraying the CCP and supporting Chiang Kai-shek would infuriate the Chinese people and bring damaging consequences. In his words, "If the Hurley policy continues, the U.S. government will fall irretrievably into the deep stinking cesspool of Chinese reaction; it will put itself in the position of antagonizing hundreds of millions of awakening Chinese people and will become a hindrance to the War of Resistance in the present and to world peace in the future.... It will place a crushing burden on the government and people of the United States and plunge them into endless trouble" (286). Once again Mao presented himself as the voice of the Chinese people by condemning Hurley's statements as harmful to China's future and detrimental to the interests of the Chinese people as well as to the American populace. The U.S. betrayal of the CCP as depicted by Mao provided him with a legitimate reason to proclaim U.S. hypocrisy, condemn its pro–Chiang Kai-shek policies, evoke anti-American sentiment, and galvanize support of Mao's CCP by the Chinese people.[8] Mao was also able to unify the CCP further by establishing the United States as another common enemy.

Mao questioned the motives of U.S. policies to abandon the CCP. In his talk with A. T. Steele, an American correspondent, Mao charged that "judging by the large amount of aid the United States is giving to Chiang Kai-shek to enable him to wage a civil war on an unprecedented scale, the policy of the U.S. government is to use the so-called mediation as a smoke-screen for strengthening Chiang Kai-shek in every way and suppressing the democratic forces in China through Chiang Kai-shek's policy of slaughter so as to reduce China virtually to a U.S. colony" (Mao 1946/1967d, 109). This remark accused the United States of two crimes: 1) instigating a civil war; and 2) attempting to turn China into a U.S. colony. Mao's words resonated with the Chinese people's fears of internal chaos and their resentment about their colonial past regarding Western powers. To intensify his rhetoric against the United States further, Mao called its people "imperialists" and "reactionaries," comparing the U.S. government to Hitler and Japanese warlords and ultimately accusing the United States of desiring to colonize the world (98).[9] At the same time, Mao reiterated his unwavering stance, claiming, "All reactionaries are paper tigers"[10] (100). He evoked memories of the overthrown Russian tzar Nicholas and the defeat of Hitler, Mussolini, and the Japanese in World War II. Mao claimed that "Chiang Kai-shek and his supporters, the U.S. reactionaries, are all paper tigers, too" (101), suggesting that they would all be defeated by the CCP's army at the end.

Mao continued to contend that Chiang and his U.S. supporters appeared to have military strength that was used to frighten the Chinese people, "but history will finally prove that our millet plus rifles are more powerful than Chiang Kai-shek's airplanes plus tanks.... The day will come when these reactionaries are defeated and we are victorious" (Mao 1946/1967d, 101). These words served to boost the morale of Mao's army and undermine the morale of the CCP's enemies. Mao's prediction was proven to be true, as Chiang Kai-shek's U.S.-backed, well-equipped army was defeated by Mao's poorly equipped troops in the three-year civil war, which led to the establishment of the People's Republic of China in 1949.

In summary, Mao's rhetoric toward the United States was marked by fluidity. At first he attempted to use the political appeal of democracy to gain U.S. support for his party. However, Mao's attitude toward the United States became hostile when America began to support Chiang Kai-shek and his Nationalist Army with military supplies during the civil war (1946–49). Mao's rhetorical construction of the United States shifted from friend to enemy, from depicting the United States as a model of democracy to showing it as a model of evil imperialism. He used these powerful ethical and emotional appeals to blame the United States of America for impeding peace and the well-being of the Chinese people.

Intensifying the Rhetoric of Anti-Americanism in Regard to *The China White Paper*

By the end of 1948 it was clear that the CCP would defeat Chiang Kai-shek and his U.S.-supported army. In June 1949, because the United States refused to recognize the People's Republic of China as a legitimate state, Mao declared that China would lean toward the Soviet Union in its foreign relations.[11] Mao continued to intensify this anti-American sentiment through his public writings and declarations until the early 1970s.

In response to the fear of Communist domination in Asia and accusations that the United States had betrayed and abandoned Chiang Kai-shek, the Truman administration issued *The China White Paper* (1949) with an attachment of Secretary of State Dean Acheson's Letter of Transmittal to President Truman. *The China White Paper* documented U.S. policies toward China between 1844 and 1949 and was intended to rid the Truman administration of blame for the fall of Chiang Kai-shek and the victory of the Chinese Communists. Acheson stated in the letter that the Nationalists "had sunk into corruption, into a scramble for place and power" (vii). They were "weakened, demoralized, and unpopular" (x), and all the military aid and support given to them in the past had "been fruitlessly spent" (xvi). Further, Acheson's letter disclosed the massive amount of military aid given to Chiang Kai-shek's government, while also referring to the Chinese Communists as "ruthless" and "fanatical," serving "not their [the Chinese people's] interests but those of Soviet Russia" (xvii).

The China White Paper was published just as Mao had defeated Chiang Kai-shek and taken over China. To unite the entire nation under his Communist ideology, Mao took the opportunity to condemn the United States by writing a set of five essays between August 14 and September 16, 1949. In these essays Mao once again labeled the United States "American imperialists" and condemned the country's interference with China's internal affairs. He called *The White Paper* "a counter-revolutionary document which openly demonstrates U.S. imperialist intervention in China" and reframed its claimed humanity, justice, and virtue as merely "trickery and deception" (Mao 1949/1967d, 442).

Through the refutation to Acheson's charges, Mao rhetorically constructed the United States as hypocritical, evil, and the ultimate political and cultural enemy of the Chinese people. In response to Acheson's charge that the CCP was a "totalitarian government," Mao retorted, "Indeed this is absolutely true so far as the power of the people's government to suppress the reactionaries is concerned.... A government of the people's democratic dictatorship led by the Communist Party is not dictatorial or autocratic but democratic. It is the people's own government" (Mao 1949/1967d, 444). Mao argued that the U.S. government "exercises dictatorship over the people ... [and] practices so-called democracy for the bourgeoisie" (445). Here, Mao used the traditional Chinese rhetorical technique—"using poison to attack poison"—of charging an opponent with the same charge leveled against him.

Mao also redefined and reinterpreted the history of U.S.-China relations. In the *White Paper,* Acheson defined U.S.-China relations as "friendly," listing U.S. aid to China throughout history, including the use of the Boxer indemnity scholarship for the education of Chinese students.[12] Mao, however, called Acheson a liar and described U.S.-China relations as "a history of aggression against China by U.S. imperialism" (1949/1967d, 447). In Mao's recount, "The history of aggression against China by U.S. imperialism, from 1840 when the U.S. helped the British in the Opium War to the time it was thrown out of China by the Chinese people, should be written into a concise textbook for the education of the youth" (Mao 1949/1967d, 447). Mao continued his vehement charge, saying that "the United States was one of the first countries to force China to cede extraterritoriality.... The United States compelled China to accept U.S. missionary activities, in addition to imposing such terms as the opening of five ports for trade" (448). Mao argued that from religious indoctrination to philanthropic and cultural undertakings, including the use of "Boxer indemnity" for educating Chinese students, the United States aimed for spiritual aggression and cultural invasion of China.

Moreover, Mao accused the United States of being responsible for China's civil war and for the deaths of millions of Chinese people. In Mao's words, "The war to turn China into a U.S. colony, a war in which the United States of America supplies the money and guns and Chiang Kai-shek supplies the men to fight for the United States and slaughter Chinese people, has been an important component of the U.S. imperialist policy of world-wide aggression since World War II" (Mao 1949/1967d, 433). Here, Mao deliberately omitted discussing U.S. aid toward China during the Anti-Japanese War. Mao's anti-American rhetoric escalated the tension between China and the United States, further amplifying the ideological rift and intensifying the anti-U.S. attitude among the Chinese people.

In the essay "Farewell Leighton Stuart" (August 18, 1949), Mao refuted Acheson's explanation that despite U.S. support of the Nationalist Party, the United States was working toward a compromise between the CCP and Nationalist Parties. Acheson had argued that this option reflected the will of the American people and demonstrated America's responsibility to the world. Mao countered that the so-called "international responsibility" was actually an "intervention against China." Mao wrote, "Acheson defiles U.S. public opinion; his is the 'public opinion of Wall Street,' not the public opinion of the American people" (1949/1967d, 435). Here, Mao effectively used the rhetorical strategy of redefining and shifting the positive meanings of words and phrases to negative ones, evoking resentment among the Chinese people for foreign invasion and intervention in the past. To address those who still maintained positive views toward the United States, Mao used a sarcastic tone and said, "Acheson is giving you a lesson. He is a good teacher for you. He has made a clean sweep of your fancied U.S. humanity, justice and virtue. Isn't that so? Can you find a trace of humanity, justice or virtue in the White Paper or in Acheson's Letter of Transmittal?" (437). Again, Mao used moral and emotional appeals to condemn his enemy and awaken those who still had illusions about American democracy, leaving little room for his readers to question his argument.

With this rhetorical bombardment, Mao accused Acheson's letter of being a missive of moral defection. Here, Mao took advantage of the transparent U.S. politics of publicizing the White Paper to express his nationalistic stand and to spread anti-American sentiments among the Chinese. Mao's essays had indeed provoked anti-Americanism in China, resulting in further mistrust and antagonism between the United States and Chinese Communists for decades. A nationwide campaign vilifying the United States was staged; rhetoric of anti-Americanism was ubiquitous, giving the CCP opportunities to legitimize its rule and unite the Chinese people against the United States as the common enemy.

After the Communist takeover in 1949, the United States treated China as a "red terror" and a "communist menace," calling for isolationist policies against the country (Tao 1999). In the United States, McCarthyism intensified an anti-China sentiment, as evidenced by Secretary of State John Foster Dulles's famous refusal to shake hands with Premier Chou En-lai at the Geneva conference on April 26, 1954. While the Chinese government persecuted any citizens who had contacts or relatives in the United States, the American government conducted racial profiling and even imprisoned Chinese Americans who had contact with their families in China (Chang 2003). At this point in history, relations between the United States and China remained strained by animosity and ideological rift.

Interplay between Mao's Public and Private Rhetoric from the 1950s to the 1970s

U.S.-China relations during this time period were largely shaped by Cold War rhetoric. In Philip Wander's critique (1997), Cold War rhetoric is described as misleading and dangerously provocative; furthermore, "the rhetoric of American foreign policy lends itself to cynical and bitter commentaries based on lies, half-truths, and macabre scenarios" (175). The same can be said for the rhetoric of Chinese foreign policies during this time period. Both sides assumed the stance of moral righteousness; both characterized the other as dangerous enemies; both sides used dehumanizing terms and moralistic rhetoric to attack each other. Such rhetorical antagonism promoted fear, stereotypes, and isolation between the two peoples.

After the founding of the People's Republic of China, the United States refused to recognize its legitimacy, and U.S. fear of communism intensified. Further, the Eisenhower administration signed the Sino-American Mutual Defense Treaty with Chiang Kai-shek's government in 1954 to secure Taiwan from invasion by Mainland China and increased U.S. military bases in East Asia. When Chou En-lai, China's premier, offered to have informal contact with the United States, the gesture was rejected by Dulles, who also vehemently attacked the PRC and refused to compromise with Mao (Cohen 2000). According to Cohen (2000), "In practice, this policy [of containment] became increasingly anti-Chinese, an unprecedented campaign of opposition to the development of a strong, modern China. There was no longer any question of whether the United States would interpose itself between China and her enemies, for the United States had become China's principal enemy" (180). China's participation in the Korean War in 1950–53 solidified this image of China as an enemy.[13]

Influenced by their media, U.S. citizens viewed Mao's government as aggressive, irrational, and dangerous, while many Chinese, championed by Mao's anti-American rhetoric, regarded U.S. citizens as morally corrupt imperialists. Rhetoric in the 1960s in the United States described the Chinese as "ignorant," "warlike," "sly," and "treacherous" (Mosher 1990). According to Harry Harding (1992), "In 1967, more than 90 percent of the American public held unfavorable images of China, and about 70 percent saw China as the greatest threat to the security of the United States" (3). McCarthyism and the witch hunt for CCP sympathizers heightened U.S. fears. The U.S. State Department refused to issue visas for travel to China. Henry Luce, the son of a missionary in China and publisher of *Time, Life,* and *Fortune,* launched a tireless campaign against "Red China" in his magazines. Mao's portrait was on the cover of the February 7, 1949, issue of *Time;* the caption on the portrait read, "The Communist Boss Learned Tyranny as a Boy" (Perlmutter 2007, 34).

At the same time Mao continued his Cold War rhetoric against the United States. On November 6, 1957, Mao gave a speech at the ten-year anniversary celebration of the Russian Revolution, swearing that socialism would replace capitalism and condemning the United States for interfering with other countries' internal affairs. Mao was particularly pointed about U.S. involvement in Taiwan and U.S. blockades and sanctions against China. He declared that American imperialism "will not stop six hundred million Chinese people from taking the socialist path." He told the United States, "The imperialist jackals must remember that the days are gone when they order about humanity at their will; the days are gone when they dominate the Asian and African nations" (Mao 1957/1992e, 620). Mao also was encouraged by Soviet successes in the space program. He boldly proclaimed that "the imperialists are in decline as they are like the sun at six o'clock in the evening. . . . The Western countries have fallen behind. . . . The East wind was prevailing over the West" (636). This wind metaphor is a famous line in the Chinese classical novel *Dream of the Red Chamber* to indicate a macroshift in the status quo.

Mao's anti-American rhetoric had a profound effect on how the Chinese people perceived the United States. "Down with American imperialism" was the slogan employed in almost every political rally throughout China and frequently appeared in the media and in Mao's speeches. The *People's Daily,* the Communist mouthpiece, called the United States "the most dangerous enemy in the world" (April 28, 1969). Throughout the 1960s China and the United States verbally attacked each other with animosity and radicalized language.[14]

Yet, while Mao was bellicose and aggressive in his rhetoric against American imperialism in public, he also made covert remarks about hopes to normalize China's relations with the United States. In fact Mao's rhetoric toward America contained contradictory facets. In public his rhetoric was often characterized by aggressive remarks and flamboyant accusations, while in private he appeared to be friendly and conciliatory. For example, on January 27, 1957, Mao gave a speech to party secretaries at the provincial level in which he predicted, "There will be the day the U.S. wants to have a normal diplomatic relationship with us. By then when Americans come to China, they will regret [not having a relationship with China]. Because by then China will change; our house is clean, parasites are eradicated" (Mao 1994, 281). This showed that Mao never gave up the hope of normalizing diplomatic relationship with the United States. His definitions of friends and enemies would change based on circumstances. Another example of Mao's inconsistency toward U.S.-China relations was that after the implementation of the 1954 Sino-American Mutual Defense Treaty, which protected Taiwan from being invaded by the People's Republic of China, Mao decided to launch a massive bombardment against Jinmen (an offshore island of Taiwan) on August 23, 1958, as an act of retaliation. In one of the Politburo Standing Committee meetings, Mao told his comrades that "we must teach the Americans a lesson. America has bullied us for many years, so now that we had a chance, why not give them a hard time?" (Wu 1996, 209). But when Mao sent a team to negotiate with the United States on the issue at the ambassadorial level, Mao told the representatives of the negotiation team to "be moderate and cautious to avoid hurting American feelings and interests" (Hong 1998, 355).

Mao's anti-American rhetoric toned down after Sino-Soviet relations deteriorated in 1960. He began to look for opportunities to reach out to Washington through private channels. In June 1960, nearly twenty years after Edgar Snow left China in 1941, Snow visited China for the first time after the founding of the People's Republic of China. He was impressed by China's economic development and was invited by Mao to review the National Day (October 1) parade on the terrace of Tiananmen, followed by a meeting with Mao on October 22. The two old friends talked for about seven hours. In this meeting Mao told Snow that "China will shoulder the responsibility of world peace whether or not the United States recognizes us or whether or not we get into the United Nations" (Mao 2012, 198). Mao also told his old friend that everything between the United States and China was negotiable except the sovereignty of Taiwan. Mao even expressed his desire to swim in the Mississippi and Potomac Rivers before he became too old (Liu 1998, 193). Here, Mao altered his tone about the United States, hoping that his conversation with Snow would offer his conciliatory stance toward America. Snow's report, however, was rejected by major U.S. news agencies, and the U.S. government did not engage Mao's private message (Liu 1998).

Mao continued shifting between public condemnation of the United States and private negotiations for reconciliation with his former enemy in the early 1970s. For example, in response to the U.S. military action in Cambodia, Mao publically issued a statement on May 20, 1970, titled "People of the World, Unite and Defeat U.S. Aggressors and All Their Running Dogs." In the statement he labeled America a "monster" and a "paper tiger in the throes of its death-bed" and depicted it as "the enemy of the entire world." Mao called for "people of the world [to] unite and defeat the U.S. aggressors and all their running dogs" (Mao 1970/1998b, 96–97).[15] Mao's antagonistic rhetoric against the United States exerted a steady and embittering force on the Chinese people's attitudes toward America. However, Mao sent a different message to the United States through private channels. On October 1, 1970, just a few months after Mao's hostile May 20 statement, Snow and his wife appeared on the Tiananmen rostrum a second time alongside Mao Zedong watching China's National Day parade. This picture of Snow and Mao shocked the world and may have been intended to send a subtle message of reconciliation with the United States.

On December 18, 1970, Mao met Snow again for a long conversation, in which Mao told Snow that he (Mao) liked U.S. Republicans and wanted to see Richard Nixon elected president of the United States. Moreover he invited Nixon to visit China. Half jokingly he told Snow, "If he wants to come to Beijing, please tell him to come secretly.... We can talk, success or not. We do not have to be so rigid" (1970/1998d, 164–65). Mao said to Snow that "our current policy of not allowing Americans to come to China is not correct.... If President Nixon wants to come to China, I'd like to talk with him or even quarrel with him. He can come as a tourist or as a President" (166–67). Snow published his conversation with Mao in the April 18, April 25, and May 9, 1971, issues of the Italian *Time* magazine as well as in *Life* magazine in the United States. "The Conversation with Mao" also was reprinted in major U.S. newspapers.

The U.S. government was completely surprised by Mao's informal invitation. On April 26, 1971, a spokesperson for the White House stated at a press conference that President Nixon had noticed Snow's articles that conveyed Mao's desire to meet. The U.S. State Department made an announcement that the U.S. government had been hoping to improve its relationship with the PRC (Mao 2012, 246–47). A week later of Mao's meeting with Snow on December 18th, 1970, the *People's Daily* published a picture of Mao and Snow and quoted Mao as saying, "People from all over the world including American people are our friends" (December 25, 1970). U.S.-China relations took a dramatic turn afterward. Followed by what is now known as ping-pong diplomacy,[16] Henry Kissinger, President Nixon's national security adviser, secretly visited China from July 9 to July 11, 1971.

Mao's contradictions in his public and private rhetoric dealing with the United States appear to have been examples of either personality traits or cunning use of rhetorical techniques. It seems likely that the contradictions between his public rhetoric and actual implementation of diplomacy constituted a larger strategic plan regarding U.S.-China relations. His anti-American rhetoric served to promote nationalism and divert attention to domestic problems. But Mao was also aware that after a breakup with the Soviet Union, China would have faced diplomatic isolation from the Western world. His private meetings and remarks paved the way for negotiation and reconciliation between the two countries. By using private channels, Mao would not have to risk public rejection to an overt request to reengage political relations with the West.

Nixon's Visit to China and Meeting with Mao

On July 15, 1971, President Nixon announced in a televised address to the nation his acceptance of Mao's invitation to visit China. In his speech Nixon (1971) told his audience, "There can be no stable and endurable peace without the participation of the People's Republic of China and its 750 million people." He further reiterated, "I have taken this action because of my profound conviction that all nations will gain from a reduction of tensions and a better relationship between the U.S. and the People's Republic of China." The trip to China, Nixon assured the American people, "will become a journey for peace, peace not just for our generation but for future generations on this earth we share together." Nixon's rhetorical appeal for world peace brought him success in persuading the American audience to support his foreign policy moves toward China.[17] On February 1, 1972, President Richard Nixon changed the course of East-West relations with a landmark visit to China to meet with Mao Zedong. Both leaders touted the visit as a step toward normalizing relations between China and the United States. Relations that had been frozen between the two nations for two decades began to thaw.

Both Henry Kissinger, who accompanied Nixon on the trip, and Nixon recorded their meetings with Mao.

To Kissinger, Mao showed "a bantering and elliptical style" in the conversation. Kissinger observed, "Most political leaders present their thoughts in the form of bullet points. Mao advanced his ideas in a Socratic manner. He would begin with a question or an observation and invite comments. He would then follow with another observation. Out of this web of sarcastic remarks, observations, and queries would emerge a direction, though rarely in binding commitment" (Kissinger 2011, 257). To demonstrate further Mao's conversational style (Mao was seventy-eight years old at the time), Kissinger offered an example, a self-mocking remark by Mao: "I think that, generally speaking, people like me sound a lot of big cannons. (Zhou [En-lai, premier of China] laughs) That is, things like 'the whole world should unite and defeat imperialism, revisionism, and all reactionaries, and establish socialism'" (257). It could be that Mao's bombastic rhetoric against the United States was merely for show and that Mao did not take it seriously. Such remarks could also have been Mao's face-saving strategy for himself and American leaders. Further, Kissinger commented, "Mao laughed uproariously at the implication that anyone might have taken seriously a slogan that had been scrawled for decades on public surfaces all over China" (262). When Mao met Kissinger in October and December 1975, a year before Mao's death and when his health was in decline, Kissinger noted that "Mao conducted both conversations with extraordinary lucidity" (306). Kissinger remarked on Mao's "characteristic combination of whimsy, aloof patience, and implicit threat—at times in elusive, if not unfathomable, phrasing" (306–7).

When Nixon attempted to engage Mao on concrete issues of international relations regarding specific countries, Mao "preferred to talk about broad philosophical issues and to engage in light banter" (Yang 2011, 11). Mao joked with his American guests about girls in Paris, taunted Kissinger for not looking like a secret agent, and told Nixon that he (Mao) had voted for Nixon for his second term. Upon leaving that meeting, Mao told Nixon that his book *Six Crises* was not bad. When Nixon complimented Mao, saying, "You look very good," Mao replied, "Appearances are deceiving" (Nixon 1978, 564). These examples displayed Mao's erratic personality, his penchant for controlling rhetorical interplay, his intelligence, and his sense of humor. Kissinger's and Nixon's China visits of 1971 and 1972, respectively, transformed the character of U.S.-China relations from hostility to cooperation. By 1973 Kissinger had announced that the United States and China were not adversaries or friends but "tacit allies" (Goh 2005). After twenty-two years of nearly complete isolation, this rhetorical mending of relations not only acknowledged ideological differences but also emphasized peace and common interests.

Mao's aggressive and hostile rhetoric toward the United States in public discourse might have been exaggerated, but it functioned to unite China by targeting an enemy and evoking nationalist sentiments among the Chinese people. Mao's decision to invite Nixon to China signaled a shift in his stance from defending moral righteousness to seeking mutual benefits and from ideological dogma against the United States to pragmatic concerns in the contexts of domestic and international exigencies. Beer and Hariman (1996) consider using strategies and calculating advantages in the "game of nations" to be a realist rhetoric for practical political gains.

As China's relationship with the Soviets deteriorated, Mao seems to have fashioned a way to ensure China's national security by establishing normal relations with the United States. Kenneth Burke (1969) calls such rhetorical strategy the "operation of antithesis" as it creates identification by uniting two ideologically separate forces (China and the United States) against a shared adversary (the Soviet Union). In this sense Mao crafted a rhetorical scheme that opened the possibilities for other, acceptable rhetorical options both for himself and for Nixon, choices that benefited the political positions of both. The availability of those choices led to the meeting between Mao and Nixon in 1972 and eventually led to a reengaged relationship between the United States and China. In maneuvering this rhetorical situation and creating a pathway advantageous to both leaders, Mao left a foreign relations legacy and opened the possibility for future interactions between China and the United States.

Analysis of Mao's Public and Private Rhetoric

Mao's rhetoric in foreign policy, in particular regarding the United States, demonstrated a contradictory interplay between public and private domains. In public Mao's anti-American rhetoric in the 1950s and 1960s presented him as a belligerent hawk; in private he avoided personal confrontation and preferred light, friendly banter rather than substantive, political negotiation and discussion. In public Mao appeared to be dogmatic and stubborn; in private he employed light humor to restrict conversation to those topics with which he could display flexibility and adaptability. In public Mao's rhetoric was direct and antagonistic; in private his rhetoric was indirect and elusive, often shrouded in metaphors and analogies. In public Mao appeared to be xenophobic and hostile; in private Mao was taunting and self-deprecating, entertaining with intelligent humor peppered with elliptical and aphoristic comments. In public Mao condemned and denounced the U.S. government; in private he vacillated between musing about re-creating ties with the United States and avoiding direct confrontation with key figures about ways of coming to terms with the U.S. government.

These contradictory facets of Mao and his use of rhetoric manifested his two sides: *huqi* (tiger spirit) and *houqi* (monkey spirit). In a July 8, 1966, letter that Mao wrote to his wife Jiang Qing, he explained that "the tiger spirit is my main characteristic; the monkey spirit is my secondary characteristic" (Mao 1966/1998a, 72). A tiger spirit refers to strong-willed, principled, dominating personality traits, whereas a monkey spirit refers to flexible, strategic, and manipulative characteristics. Mao's self-description identified his tiger spirit as primary. During a meeting with Col. David Barrett, who negotiated with the CCP and Chiang Kai-shek on December 8, 1944, Mao was tough and unbending. He told Barrett firmly, "The Communists will not accept a demand for complete surrender. We'd rather fight to the last drop of our blood" (Mao 2012, 28). As Barrett recalled, "During the whole process of conversation, Mao's attitude was unyielding and difficult to deal with. He did not lose temper with me, but he was furiously shouting that we would not give in an inch and he cursed Jiang Kai-shek as a turtle egg" (28).[18] At other times Mao showed what he self-described as his monkey spirit—flexible and compromising when he felt cornered. His private talks with Edgar Snow in 1970 and his meetings with Henry Kissinger in 1971 and Richard Nixon in 1972 demonstrated his flexibility regarding ideology. In those instances Mao avoided the role of an ideological zealot, presenting himself as a leader to whom ideology was not particularly important but rather was just part of the political game. In his private meeting with Indonesian premier Ali Sastroamidjojo on May 26, 1955, Sastroamidjojo described Mao: "He does not put on an air showing that he is a people's leader who has transformed Chinese history, the Chinese nation, and fate. He is very easy going like an elder in a big family, just like a well-respected elder in the Chinese residential area in Indonesia" (Mao 2012, 73).

Mao's skillful shift between public and private rhetoric suggested an interplay between yin and yang dynamics rooted in the Chinese rhetorical tradition. Kirkpatrick (2012) has defined the Chinese yang style as direct, antagonistic, and authoritative while characterizing the Chinese yin style as indirect, oblique, and self-deprecating. Typically the yin style is used when the audience is more powerful and when strategic communication such as calculated insinuation is needed and perceived to be more effective.[19] However, Mao's private or yin style of rhetoric proved ineffective with the American government as his conciliatory message in the private conversation with Snow was ignored. This might have been caused by a two-decades-long anti-American public rhetoric by Mao that had constructed him as hostile toward the United States. American policy makers did not pay attention to his softened rhetoric and modified positions in private conversions, especially when Mao's public and private treatments of the topic were contradictory. This interpretation is supported by examining other topics raised by Mao for which his veracity was not called into question. Liu (1998) observes that "when Mao talked about peace and negotiation, no one in Washington believed him. When he lectured on national liberation and common struggle against the United States, he was taken very seriously" (194). The lack of open channels of communication between the two countries and Mao's antagonistic public rhetoric toward the United States made it difficult for U.S. leaders to decipher Mao's real intentions and strategic moves communicated through private channels.

Anti-U.S. Rhetoric with Third World Audiences

In the first eight years after the founding of the People's Republic of China in (1949–1956), Mao was focused on China's economic development. China's need to ameliorate foreign relations forced him to be less ideologically bound. On June 15, 1949, Mao delivered a speech at China's Political Consultative Conference, stating, "We are willing to discuss with any foreign government the establishment of diplomatic relations on the basis of the principles of equality, mutual benefit and mutual respect for territorial integrity and sovereignty.... The Chinese people wish to have friendly co-operation with the people of all countries and to resume and expand international trade so we may develop production and promote economic prosperity" (Mao 1949/1967d, 408). Based on Mao's directives, Premier Chou En-lai developed the "Five Principles" of China's foreign relations: mutual respect for sovereignty and territorial integrity; mutual nonaggression; noninterference in each other's internal affairs; equality and mutual benefit; and peaceful coexistence.[20] These principles served as strategies for reaching out to non-Communist countries and transcending social systems and ideologies.

On July 7, 1954, Mao gave a report on the international situation at the politburo, stating that countries with different social systems could coexist peacefully and that ideological conflicts should not be an obstacle for political and economic cooperation. U.S.-China relations, he reported, should be handled strategically but with flexibility. He welcomed people from the United States to visit China on the condition that U.S. visitors and politicians respect tenets regarding Taiwan and agree with the Five Principles[21] (Shanghai Mao Zedong Thought and Practices Studies Committee 1993, 165). These statements were not published and were inconsistent with his public, anti-U.S. rhetoric. The principles suggest that as early as the 1950s Mao was willing to express in an unpublished, uncirculated report that he did not want to isolate China from the Western world and may have favored diplomatic relations with countries across the ideological spectrum. The contradiction in Mao's rhetoric resided in his public statements to the contrary and his insistence that visitors to China conform to his Five Principles and his political preferences with regard to Taiwan.

However, as the Cold War escalated in the mid-1950s, Mao became entrenched in the dualistic international environment: the Communist camp led by the Soviet Union and the capitalist camp headed by the United States. On November 18, 1957, Mao delivered a speech at the World Conference of the Communist Party and the Workers Party Delegations held in Moscow. He referenced a Chinese saying from the famous Chinese novel *Dream of the Red Chamber*: "If the east wind does not prevail over the west wind, the west wind shall prevail over the east wind" (Mao 1957/1992a, 636). "The east wind" referred to China, the Soviet Union, and Eastern European Communist countries, and "the west wind" referred to the United States and Western European nations. Mao predicted that "countries like the Soviet

Union and China will prevail over the U.S. and Europe" and continued by claiming, "Our sky is bright and the sky of the west is clouded. We are optimistic; they are nervous. Two satellites were launched into the sky; they could not sleep"[22] (Mao 2012, 147). In his speech Mao abandoned the theme of flexibility in favor of a resolute, implacable claim. He embraced an ideological division of international politics that presented the world as black or white, good or evil. His remarks predicted uncontested victory for the Communist camp, and he portrayed himself as a leader of the Communist world.

On one hand, Mao pummeled the United States as the most egregious enemy of the Chinese people, presenting himself as a beacon of the Communist ideology. On the other hand, Mao declared that coalition building was of paramount importance, advocating alliances with peoples and regions in Asia, Africa, and Latin American—regions still colonized and oppressed by Western powers. Mao's definitions of old China as a semifeudal and semicolonial society were compatible with the political problems of sovereignty in these regions. Mao's success with his peasant revolution and his strong anti-U.S. stand won him a reputation for ideological clarity and political strength and shrewdness, a reputation that appealed to leaders of these regions.

On January 13, 1964, Mao published an article in the *People's Daily* declaring that "American imperialism is the most vicious enemy in the world." He called for unity in the socialist bloc and solidarity with others who had suffered from American invasion, control, and interference. Mao wrote that "the angry wave against American imperialism from the people of the whole world cannot be stopped. There will be great victory for people of the whole world in their struggles against American imperialism and its running dogs" (Mao 1964/1996e, 11:7). In a meeting with a delegation composed of African political leaders from Guinea, South Africa, Kenya, and the Congo on April 27, 1961, Mao reified links between his goals and those of other countries: "Chinese people take the victory of anti-imperialism won by the peoples of Asia, Africa, and Latin America as their own victory. We support enthusiastically and have sympathy for any anti-imperialism and anti-colonialism" (Mao 1961/1996c, 9:477–78). Mao attempted to build an alliance with these regions by targeting the United States as the common enemy and by denouncing U.S. imperialism as an iniquitous and evil force. A similar type of rhetoric appeared in Mao's declarations of support for the Congo (Mao 1964/1996g, 247) and Dominica (Mao 1965/1996i, 11:365), as well as in his responses to anti-U.S. demonstrations in Japan (Mao 1964/1996f, 11:10) and in his meetings with a delegation from Sudan (Mao 1964/1998c, 13:105).

Cook (2010) points out that "Maoism provided the ideological underpinnings and a practical blueprint for the struggle" occurring in Third World nations (288). Indeed, Mao's revolutionary success attracted leaders of the developing countries and set an example showing how a weak country could overcome obstacles and act in defiance of a superpower. As a self-appointed leader of the Communist world, Mao felt entitled to advise the leaders from Asia, Africa, and Latin America. On May 14, 1960, Mao told a delegation composed of journalists and political leaders from Cuba, Brazil, and Argentina, "Do not be afraid of imperialists. They are paper tigers. They are actually afraid of people from Asia, Africa, and Latin America. People have the real power. As long as we unite and build an alliance together, we can drive out the imperialists" (Mao 1960/1996a, 9:188). Similarly, on September 30, 1960, in his talk with Ferhat Abbas, the Algerian political leader and president of the Algerian provisional government from 1958 to 1961, Mao advised Abbas, "The U.S. appears to be powerful, but it controls too many places and has done so many bad things. People everywhere oppose them. You have the condition for persistence. As long as you have determination and a fighting spirit, you can keep your strength. Reduce your human cost as much as you can. In ten or twenty years—if the flag of your national liberation has not yet fallen—you will rediscover hope" (Mao 1960/1996b, 297). Mao's words helped reduce weaker nations' fears of more powerful countries such as the United States. Mao reminded these nations that their real power lay in the hands of their people. History was on their side, he told them, and they would inevitably defeat U.S. imperialists and win their independence if they maintained the will to do so. Mao rationalized that the United States could not sustain power and dominance if it spread its control too thinly.

Latin American leaders such as Che Guevara (1928–67), Fidel Castro, and Hugo Chavez (1954–2013) admired Mao's stance on America. Guevara applied Mao's guerrilla war tactics in the Cuban revolution and emulated Mao's desire to create the consciousness of a "new man" driven by moral rather than material incentives. Guevara even named his daughter "Little Mao." Chavez's speeches often were filled with Mao's quotations and poems, treating Maoism as the guiding light for Venezuelan socialism. Castro too studied Mao's work on guerrilla wars and printed Mao's military works for his army. Abimael Guzman, the leader of the Shining Path (the Communist Party of Peru), staged a Maoist insurgency and was a strong believer in and practitioner of Mao's theory of violence and armed struggle in Peru from the late 1970s through the 1980s. Mao sent the same message to his African friends, denouncing U.S. imperialism and boosting the morale of the oppressed. In his meeting with delegations from Tanzania and Zambia on July 11, 1970, Mao told his African friends, "Actually, imperialists in this world do not live easy lives. They are afraid of the Third World. . . . We must dispel the myth about imperialists' political and military power" (Mao 1994, 588).[23]

Mao understood that a direct confrontation with America was dangerous, and the majority of these Third World nations were not equipped economically or militarily to combat the West. Nevertheless, Mao offered African leaders an optimistic outlook. He continued to encourage them to recognize the power of their own people and not to be intimidated by their enemies. Mao's rhetoric of discrediting the United States was drawn partly from his own experiences defeating the stronger army with a weaker army and partly from his staunch belief that a just cause would prevail over an evil force. Mao's "people's war" doctrine was predictably popular among Third World nations, and Mao's statements empowered the leaders and peoples of those nations.

Mao's anti-American rhetoric also contained a denunciation of racism and expressed support for the civil rights movement in the United States. On August 8, 1963, Mao made a declaration of support for U.S. African Americans in their struggle against racial discrimination, calling them to action: "United workers; peasants; revolutionary intellectuals; liberal bourgeois of white, black, yellow, and brown colors of people! Oppose American imperialist racial discrimination. Support the struggle of American black people against racial discrimination.... American black people must win the victory of their just struggle. The extremely vicious colonialism and imperialist system started and thrived from slavery and from selling black people. It will end with the complete liberation of the black people" (Mao 1963/1996d, 10:337).

On April 16, 1968, Mao made another declaration of support, attributing the assassination of Dr. Martin Luther King Jr. to American imperialists. Mao wrote, "Closely united, the people of the whole world, vigorously and persistently attack American imperialists, our common enemy. [I am] certain that colonialism, imperialism, and the whole exploitation system will completely crumble. The day is not far when the oppressed people and oppressed nations in the world will be completely turned over [liberated]" (Mao 1968/1998a, 487). Robert Williams (1925–96), an American civil rights leader, considered Mao's revolution a great inspiration for the Afro-American struggle for freedom and equality. Williams wrote, "Chairman Mao was the first world leader to elevate our people's struggle to the fold of the world revolution" (1967, 1).[24] Leaders of the Black Panther Party and black radicals saw Mao's China as "the beacon of third world revolution and Mao Zedong thought as the guidepost" (Kelley and Esch 1999, 8). This was the first time that Mao had linked race issues with imperialism and had called on nonwhite people to unite against American imperialism. In doing so Mao expanded his ideological alliance to include African Americans. His bold, lofty, and passionate statements resonated strongly with some African Americans.[25]

Mao's Three Worlds Theory

Mao's unwavering support for oppressed regions and subjugated people led him to formulate the Three Worlds Theory. On February 22, 1974, Mao met Kenneth David Kaunda, the president of Zambia, and three days later he met Houari Boumediene, the chairman of the Algerian Revolutionary Committee. In both meetings Mao proposed the Three Worlds Theory: "In my opinion, the United States and the Soviet Union are the First World. Moderate countries such as Japan, countries in Europe,

Australia, and Canada are the Second World. We [China, Zambia, and Algeria] are the Third World....The Third World has the most population. All of Asia is Third World except Japan. The whole of Africa is Third World. Latin America is also a Third World" (Mao 1974/1998e, 379). Mao singled out the United States and the Soviet Union as superpowers and marked Third World countries as colonized, oppressed, and economically disadvantaged. The countries with moderate wealth and that generally allied with the superpowers comprised the Second World. Mao created a hierarchy of nations using politico-economic status and regions instead of dividing nations by ideological preference.[26]

This strategic move resembled the deliberate alliance he had made with peasants in his own revolution. As he had gathered peasants to his cause, he had gained power. Now at the international level he proselytized to economically deprived nations, thereby winning converts all over the world and substantiating his role as champion of the oppressed. In 1974 then Chinese vice premier Deng Xiaoping (1904–97) explained Mao's Three Worlds Theory in a speech at the United Nations, justifying China's cooperation with non-Communist countries. On November 1, 1977, the *People's Daily* published an editorial, "Chairman Mao's Theory of the Differentiation between the Three Worlds Is a Major Contribution to Marxism-Leninism." This article explained in more depth the implications of Mao's Three Worlds Theory. In the introduction of the article, the author wrote, "Third World people account for over 70% of the world's population and as a worldwide anti-imperialist force, they constitute the mainstream of the world's revolutionary struggle....Subjected as they are to the most ruthless oppression, these countries and peoples of the Third World have been the most resolute in their resistance. For a fairly long historical period, they will continue to wage a fierce struggle against imperialism and above all, the superpowers." The title of the article abandoned the Marxist-Leninist ideology of socialism versus capitalism and instead aimed at global alignment. Jiang An (2013) has made the point that this theory is "a hallmark achievement of China's diplomatic strategy and international relations" (35). Mao realized that foreign policy based on ideological boundaries had not acquired for him or for China reliable allies, an exchange of resources, or increased international standing. In the late 1960s China's international relations were limited to North Korea and Albania. Mao felt isolation not only from the United States but also from the rest of the world. The Three Worlds Theory seemed to open the possibility of entering a common ground from which developing countries in Asia, Africa, and Latin American could fight for national sovereignty and independence while Mao—and China—could occupy a central, international position among them.

The theory constituted a strategic move that ostensibly meant that poor nations could build alliances among themselves; however, the move also explicitly meant that Mao could then promote ideological influence in those countries and the rest of world. At a theoretical level, Mao had positioned himself to foster partnerships simultaneously among struggling societies while also promoting interdependence among those countries. At a practical level, Mao positioned himself as a principal advocate for these nations' revolutions against western colonizers and American imperialism. The Three Worlds Theory, according to Mao, was a powerful vision for the working-class and poor peoples of the world to unite in the struggle against imperialism and military aggression by the superpowers, an echo of his work to organize Chinese peasants to unite against the bourgeoisie. This strategy won China friends from Asia, Africa, and Latin America. According to Cook (2010), China in the 1970s established a cordial relationship with a diverse array of Third World monarchs and reactionaries. On October 25, 1971, Mao's strategy came to fruition when seventy-six countries voted to support the People's Republic of China as the only lawful representative of China to the United Nations, replacing Taiwan as the legitimate government for China.

From the late 1970s to the 1980s after Mao's death, the Third World Maoism movement continued. Based on Cook's (2010) historical research, Mao's influence was seen in the Communist Party of India, which seriously studied Mao's *Little Red Book* and even launched its own, small-scale cultural revolution. The Communist Party of Kampuchea (Cambodia) not only followed Mao's guerrilla war strategies but also adopted Mao's methods of criticism and self-criticism, persecution of intellectuals, and slaughter of anyone suspected of anticommunism.[27] The only surviving Maoist believers are members of the Communist Party of Nepal, who are referred to today as Maoists. The party led a prolonged, Maoist guerrilla war against the monarchy and finally agreed to end the war in exchange for participation in the election of the assembly of Nepal. In 2008 the party won the majority vote in the election and became the ruling party of the Nepalese Constituent Assembly.[28]

In Summation

Mao made his first contact with the world through his interview with U.S. foreign correspondent Edgar Snow. Mao's early rhetoric regarding the United States was favorable as he aimed to win sympathy and support in establishing a coalition government with Chiang Kai-shek. He then directed hostility toward the United States when America abandoned the CCP and supported Chiang Kai-shek. Starting in 1949, Mao vehemently and publicly condemned the U.S. foreign policy of isolation toward China, which ignited anti-U.S. rhetoric and anti-U.S. sentiment among the Chinese people. However, in private Mao made declarations and held conversations in which he expressed to certain individuals or small groups the need to reestablish ties with this former ideological enemy.

The goal of establishing an alliance with the United States became more pressing when Mao severed relationships with the Soviet Union, especially as Mao reached old age. His invitation for Nixon to visit China, haltingly triggered by a random event between U.S. and Chinese Ping-Pong teams, provided Mao with opportunities to announce his vision for future U.S.-China relations based, as he espoused, on cooperation, mutual benefit, and mutual respect. This move, shifting from ideology to pragmatism, not only released a measure of Cold War tension between the two nations but also paved the way for China's economic reform and its 1970s open-door policy launched after Mao's death. Mao demonstrated adeptness at managing an interplay between his public and private rhetoric and, as he grew older, between his rhetoric of ideology and a rhetoric of pragmatism in his discourse regarding China's relations with the United States.

Such skill also may indicate that Mao's rhetoric was often deceiving—privately and/or publicly—leading to misleading public perception and perhaps international interpretation. Mao's use of tactical rhetorical strategies, such as "elusive...unfathomable phrasing" (Kissinger 2011, 307), allowed him to make one proclamation in private, make a different declaration in public, and act on either statement with impunity; he could say one thing and act in an opposite way. His definitions of friends and enemies also shifted based on political expediency. However, when he needed the United States to save China's economy, Mao was willing to hold out an olive branch to America to make peace, further demonstrating his contradictory personality and his pliable rhetoric. Mao gained reputation as a Third World leader through his own revolutionary success as well as from his initially unsolicited and later unyielding advice to leaders of Third World nations. Mao alleged that his advice placed real power into the hands of the people and not into the hands of those with military strength—perhaps drawing from his own experience defeating Chiang Kai-shek. Mao worked to convince Third World leaders to seek courage, develop confidence, and act with audacity in fighting colonialism and imperialism in their own countries.

Conclusion
Mao Zedong's Rhetorical Legacy Lives On

Mao Zedong was no doubt a controversial figure in the twentieth century on the world stage. During his rule in China, Mao was elevated to the status of a living god, resulting in mass hysteria, blind faith, absolute obedience, and cultish behavior of all kinds among Chinese people. Fervent devotion to his teachings and eradication of any alternative views made Mao the final arbiter of truth and knowledge, which ultimately led to acts of destruction and cruelty in the names of the revolution and the permanent revolution. Ironically, and maybe inevitably, Mao successfully destroyed the revolutionary legacy he had painstakingly achieved; he created glory for China, but by the time of his death he had also brought the country to chaos and the brink of economic collapse.[1] In the words of Andrew Walder (2015), "Mao Zedong left China quite a crisis, an unsettled state and society very much in flux" (341).

Consequently many Chinese people resent Mao for the disaster of China's economy and blame him for their families' and individual sufferings during the Cultural Revolution. They still remember the experiences of being forced to confess and labor, being beaten and tortured, being separated from their family members, and being deprived of their education. They consider Mao to have been a brutal dictator who abused power and failed to deliver the better life he promised to the Chinese people. However, many other Chinese people still regard Mao as a cultural icon and national hero. They still show great respect for him for bringing China to independence and giving China a foundation for its socialist economy. Mao was also praised for making China one of the military powers in the world and for his fearlessness of Western sanctions and the Soviet pressure. Most importantly, Mao's teachings of serving the people, criticism and self-criticism, plain living, modesty, and devotion to the collective made him a symbol of morality for millions. The Chinese people have been dismayed over rampant corruption and alarming inequality since the economic reform in the 1980s, and nostalgia for Mao's era looms large among them.

In response to the polarizing perceptions of Mao, President Xi Jinping (2013) delivered a speech commemorating Mao's 120th birthday anniversary in which he credited Mao with his merits but also cautioned, "Revolutionary leaders are not gods, but human beings; we cannot worship them like gods or refuse to allow people to point out and correct their errors just because they are great; neither can we totally repudiate them and erase their historical feats just because they made mistakes. We should not simply attribute the success in historically favorable circumstances to individuals, nor should we blame individuals for setbacks in adverse situations; we cannot use today's conditions and the level of development and understanding to judge our predecessors, nor can we expect the predecessors to have done things that only successors can do." Apparently Xi wanted the Chinese people to take a contextual approach to their assessment of Mao, and he asked them to consider the constraints and conditions during the time period in which Mao lived in addition to Mao's own limitations as an ordinary human being who made mistakes. Xi attempted to demystify Mao and give more weight to historical conditions rather than to judge his acts as either absolutely right or absolutely wrong. In doing so Xi brought Mao's godlike stature down to that of an ordinary person with faults but also excused Mao from his wrongdoings. Xi's words implied that each generation of CCP leaders has its own missions and visions that cannot be judged out of context. Even this assessment is vague and ambiguous; it situates Mao and his rhetoric in historical contexts in responding to political and ideological exigencies real or imagined in Mao's mind.

Having studied a full range of Mao's discourse, I have come to the conclusion that Mao's political rhetoric has been most influential in transforming and shaping China's modern history. It was instrumental in the defeat of Chiang Kai-shek, effective in instilling a Marxist-Leninist ideology of social change, and successful in inculcating so-called "proletarian consciousness" for the development of a new Communist person. Furthermore the myth created through Mao's discourse of hope provided a rhetorical vision for China's transformation from a Confucian society to a socialist country with a Communist ideology. Mao's rhetoric has empowered and given voice to many ordinary people while it has simultaneously oppressed and violated the human rights of millions of others.

Major Characteristics of Mao's Rhetoric

In my preface I raised the questions that motivated me to embark on this project: Why was Mao's rhetoric so powerful in persuading the Chinese people to follow him into the revolution, in controlling and transforming the minds of Chinese people? I hope my analyses of Mao's writings have provided some answers. These analyses demonstrate that Mao masterfully employed symbolic resources of Confucianism, Chinese classics, and radical versions of Marxism and Leninism. He used various rhetorical appeals and provided logical arguments and emotional appeals on why people should listen to, follow, and venerate him. He manipulated the desire of the Chinese people to engage in self-criticism in order to become a good person. He took advantage of historical opportunities and responded to exigencies with an interplay of an iron fist and soft schemes. He amplified hope and exaggerated fear regarding China's future. Mao's rhetoric was lofty and agitating; his use of language was clear, vivid, and forceful, using traditional Chinese rhetorical techniques of metaphor and analogies. He was a good storyteller, a teacher of Chinese history, and a demagogue for social change. He was a mythmaker and yet also a shrewd strategist. Through his moralistic and nationalistic rhetorical appeals, Mao consolidated his power, eliminated dissidents, vilified his enemies, and elevated himself to the status of a living god for the Chinese people.

I would argue that Mao's rhetorical effectiveness was squarely rooted in the period he lived in as well as based on the traditional Chinese expectations for leaders. For thousands of years in China people believed that if they had a good emperor or a good political leader, the country would be strong and life would be prosperous; great hope was placed on the individual leader rather than a social system. Mao presented himself as such a capable leader through his rhetoric, so people had faith in him. Moreover the Chinese education system for centuries had taught people not how to think critically but to follow authority obediently. Of course many people also followed Mao simply out of fear, especially after 1949 when Mao became the paramount leader of China. Oftentimes negative consequences of rhetoric are not recognized until disastrous actions have taken place and only in hindsight do people realize that they have been manipulated. Mao's case suggests that caution, critical thinking, and conscience are essential when people are being exposed to rhetoric with alleged lofty moral principles.

Three Stages of Mao's Rhetoric: A Diachronic Assessment

The trajectory of Mao's rhetoric and thought development can be summarized diachronically and synchronically. In a diachronic sense, Mao's rhetoric also can be divided into three stages. According to Yu Yingshi (2012), Mao's life can be divided into three stages. The first stage includes the years prior to 1921, before Mao participated in China's Communist movement. The second stage extends from 1921 to 1949, when Mao first became involved in and then led China's revolution. The third stage ranges from 1949 to 1976, when Mao died. In this last stage Mao's power in China was absolute and he had become increasingly dictatorial. In each stage his rhetoric was formulated and expressed according to his own assessment of situations and in response to his and the country's changing circumstances.

In the first stage (prior to 1921), Mao did not have a clear direction for his career path and ideological orientation. He was learning and absorbing ideas from a variety of Chinese and Western sources. But one thing is certain: Mao was rebellious in personality, as evidenced in his conflict with his father. Like some of his contemporaries, he was deeply concerned over the Chinese people's lack of national consciousness and about China's being humiliated by foreign powers. Mao's rebellious persona may have been the result of his father's beating him as a child, and his concerns for China may have come from his travels and books he read. Based on the selected pieces analyzed in chapter 1 ("Classroom Notes," "A Study of Physical Education," and "Marginal Notes to Friedrich Paulsen: *A System of Ethics*"), Mao embraced influences from traditional Chinese classics, from the modern thinking of the reformers, and also from Western ethics and progressive thinking. Mao was a patriot with a well-developed intellect and a passionate advocate for social change, eagerly searching for solutions to China's problems. He committed himself to the mission of saving China from humiliation and poverty. He was inspired by ancient Chinese heroes to become a sage or great man and expressed his desire to emulate them. His rhetoric was centered on advocating that Chinese people would build ethical characters with healthy bodies. Mao's philosophical orientation was more pragmatic, and his rhetorical style was characterized by clarity, advocacy, and argumentativeness.

In the second stage (1921–49) of his life, after Mao converted to communism, China went through the War of Resistance against Japan and then a civil war in which the Communists and the Nationalists fought for power to rule China. China also was transitioning from an imperial system to a modern state, which brought about change in the Chinese language from a formal, classical form to vernacular expressions. This change in language usage meant that a larger and more diverse audience had access to information, knowledge, and both spoken and written messages. In this stage Mao was an idealist and formed a utopian vision for China. Mao's rhetoric was characterized by revolutionary zeal and strategic thinking.

Once he had his own army in Jinggangshan, Mao continued producing messages about changing the face of China through a revolution using an armed force. Even at low points of his life when he was alienated and his army was weakened, Mao still confidently asserted that a "single spark can start a prairie fire" (Mao 1930/1967a, 117). His writing in this second stage was filled with optimism and encouragement, showcasing his well-honed skills of creating a rhetorical vision for a new China and his renowned ability to unite people from different sectors of life toward the common goal of building a strong, democratic, and prosperous China.

During this second stage Mao was unyielding on the battlefield and uncompromising in major negotiations. He displayed unqualified confidence in his rhetorical claim that power resided in the people of China, and he continued to support his assertions that the CCP was capable of leading China's revolution to victory. Using moral and patriotic appeals, Mao condemned Chiang Kai-shek and the United States and boosted the morale of his army, galvanizing public support for his party. Named by some as a military genius, he successfully maneuvered military operations when facing Chiang Kai-shek's series of onslaughts.

What distinguished Mao from other CCP military leaders of this time period was that he formulated and developed his own theories of revolution. He adopted a Marxist-Leninist ideology of dialectical materialism and class struggle. Mao appropriated Marxist-Leninist philosophical and political theories not only to address conflicts within the party but also to eliminate his opponents and his imagined ideological enemies. Mao preached empirical knowledge and maneuvered through contradictions to establish his credibility in Marxism-Leninism within the party. He called for social elites to serve the interests of the masses, turning the traditional Chinese hierarchical power structure on its head. He waved the flag of Marxism-Leninism as he constructed rhetorical strategies to classify the Chinese people into categories of good and bad, to elevate his reputation as the CCP's ultimate leader, and to unite the thoughts of intellectuals and party members through means of criticism and self-criticism under his guidance. Moreover, in his writings Mao admonished his party and party members to serve the interests of the Chinese people and to have qualities Mao described as well disciplined, engaging in plain living, and having class consciousness.

During this period Mao rose to power through his rhetorical acumen, his skilled use of military strategies, and, increasingly, the support of his party. By 1949 Mao had established himself as China's supreme leader and his revolutionary theories had become the guiding principles for the Chinese people. Mao's rhetoric in this period was filled with ethical, emotional, and rational appeals and was characterized by the use of narratives and metaphors, by redefinitions of key concepts, and by references to Chinese classics and common sayings. Mao used plain and metaphorical language to explain complicated ideas on issues of the people's concerns. Although he was trained in classical Chinese, Mao became adept at using vernacular Chinese to reach out to his audience and achieve a persuasive effect.

In the third stage (1949–76) of his life, Mao reigned as the paramount leader of China, but he was faced with internal and external pressure to consolidate his power and sustain the fruits of revolution. Internal pressure was exerted by resistance from pro-Nationalist individuals, criticism by intellectuals and some high-ranking party officials (although their criticisms may have been constructive and well intentioned), and criticism from the bourgeois class within the boundaries of the nation. External pressure mounted from the isolation and economic sanctions placed on China by the Western world, Nikita Khrushchev's betrayal of Stalin, and the deteriorating relationship between China and the Soviet Union as well as the uprisings in Poland and Hungary against their own Communist governments.[2] All these exigencies seemed to prove to Mao that Lenin's theory was accurate in that Lenin warned of continued class struggle between the proletariat and bourgeoisie after the Communists' takeover.

Janette Ai (2015) states, "Leninist ideas encouraged conflict, rebellion and struggle within Chinese society" (43). Mao had indeed put Lenin's ideas into practice in China. Mao's rhetoric in this period was filled with discourse of a "permanent revolution," which served as a constant reminder that class struggle indeed existed in a more insidious form. Mao argued that China would become a capitalist society, the ultimate evil form of society, and that people again would suffer from feudalism and colonialism if members of the proletariat did not exercise their dictatorship over class enemies. Guided by this logic and combined with his paranoia of being sabotaged, Mao launched a series of political campaigns to remold and reform the minds of the Chinese people with a particular target on intellectuals and on top-level party officials. Walder (2015) said it well: "Mao's diagnose led to a prescribed remedy that promised only continuing cycle of conflict and destruction" (341).

Mao's political campaigns as a remedy to his diagnosis reached a climax during the Cultural Revolution. The major means of thought reform imposed by Mao included criticism and self-criticism, actions that closely resembled the Confucian practices of self-cultivation. Although Mao repeatedly vowed to build a strong and prosperous China, his economic policies such as the Great Leap Forward and people's communes proved to be disasters as the result of his revolutionary fanaticism, his authoritarian leadership, and his lack of scientific knowledge. Although his insistence on attaining nuclear weapons for China boosted national pride—and the country built its infrastructure and industry base under his leadership—the living standards of Chinese people plummeted in the last ten years of Mao's reign. Mao's rhetoric at this stage was radical in his view of intellectuals and destructive as evidenced by the chaotic situations, persecutions, and human suffering his directives caused, especially during China's Cultural Revolution, which he launched in the name of continued class struggle and permanent revolution. Mao's social experiment failed miserably.

However, in this period Mao's rhetoric of nationalism and foreign policy may have benefited China. His foreign policy in his later years paved the way for the rapprochement between China and the United States and in general won more friends than foes in the world for China. His philosophical orientation seemed to move away from being doctrinaire toward pragmatism as he reappointed Deng Xiaoping to reinvigorate China's devastated economy toward the end of the Cultural Revolution.[3] The realm of Mao's rhetoric during this stage expanded from writings and speeches to conversations, letters, and directives.

Ross Terrill (1980) has concluded that "with all his faults, Mao gave China a new start, and gave the twentieth century a fascinating man of politics" (424). Despite the controversy over Mao among scholars and ordinary Chinese people, he had indeed united and transformed China into an independent nation. During his leadership and through his success in changing the thinking of the Chinese people, China had gone from a society centered on family to a society focused on recognizing itself as a nation and expressing national concern. Through Mao's rhetoric of *qiangguomeng* (the dream of a powerful nation), he promoted the dream of a strong China and worked to change China's image from "the sick man of Asia" to an image showing new citizens with so-called Communist morals in place: selflessness; sacrifice for the nation; loyalty to the party and Mao; and willingness to engage in criticism and self-criticism.

Major Rhetorical Themes of Mao's Rhetoric: A Synchronic Assessment

Mao's rhetoric fits the definition of transformative rhetoric as explained in the introduction. His rhetoric not only united Chinese people, moved China to a different social structure and institutional practice, and reshaped Chinese cultural habits and ideological beliefs, but it also had the power of instilling a new consciousness and new hope for the future. Specifically the transformative outcome of Mao's rhetoric can be seen in four recurring themes espoused in his speeches and writings: 1) the moral legitimacy of Marxism-Leninism; 2) the importance of serving the people; 3) the use of criticism and self-criticism; and 4) nationalism.

The first characteristic, the moral legitimacy of Marxism-Leninism, derives from Mao's claim that Marxism was the most correct and best-suited ideology to promote positive outcomes for the Chinese people. However, to make a foreign, Western, radical ideology acceptable in China, Mao had to present a convincing argument that Marxism was indeed applicable to China's situation. In 1938 Mao proposed "to apply Marxism concretely in China so that its every manifestation has an indubitably Chinese character" (Mao 1938/1967b, 299). In other words, Mao would reinterpret and adapt Marxism to the Chinese social and cultural context measured by the Chinese value system. This "sinification of Marxism" gave Mao the ideological legitimacy to lead the CCP and simultaneously allowed him to incorporate traditional Chinese values of hierarchy, loyalty, and self-cultivation, paving the way for his political persuasion.

Mao's writings show him to have been an ardent believer in the Marxist notion of class struggle. He was inspired by the Russian Revolution of 1917 and was a good student of Lenin, adhering to the Soviet doctrine of social transformation and proletarian dictatorship. Mao devoted his life to preaching and executing the Marxist theory of class struggle. He divided Chinese people into two classes after 1949: proletarian and bourgeois. The former class represented an advanced and correct consciousness and thus was entitled to control the nation using a dictatorship government, while the latter represented the bureaucratic, capitalist class that was believed to be morally defective and would inevitably be replaced by the former camp. This Marxist view of social change was one that, in Mao's words, "all other countries will inevitably take" (Mao 1937/1967a, 334).

In actuality Mao may never have systematically studied Marxism-Leninism. The only Marxist-Leninist concept that Mao applied and steadfastly adhered to was "class struggle." Under the banner of class struggle Mao polarized people, classifying them as friends or enemies. He stood vigilant against his external enemies (U.S. imperialism and Chiang Kai-shek) and his internal resistance (dissident intellectuals, some high-ranking party officials, and the bourgeois class within the boundaries of the nation). Guided by conspiracy theories and dualistic thinking, Mao constantly fought with real or imagined "class enemies" throughout his life. For example, he defeated Chiang Kai-shek's military force, wiped out private ownership of properties by landlords and capitalists, purged a number of top-level party officials, and accused many innocent intellectuals of being counter-revolutionaries. Mao increasingly used words of attack, dehumanization, and profanity to condemn U.S. imperialism and to criticize the Nationalists and Chiang Kai-shek, ultimately purporting that he (Mao) and his party, and not Chiang, had the moral legitimacy and were truly entitled to the "Mandate of Heaven" to rule China. Nevertheless, Mao's class-struggle framework implanted a polarized way of thinking into the Chinese mind, a polarization still evident in personal relationships and online discussions in post-Mao China. Accusations and verbal abuse among Chinese people in public and private settings are common. The traditional Chinese value of *zhongyong* 中庸 (the Doctrine of the Mean) has been abandoned by many Chinese growing up during Mao's era.

The second characteristic of Mao's rhetoric is his emphasis on "serving the people." Coming from a peasant family background, Mao claimed to be representative of the working class, a class comprising the majority of Chinese people. Throughout his writings Mao emphasized the message of "serving the people wholeheartedly," ordering party members and intellectuals to abandon their elitist attitudes and mingle with the masses. Mao called upon party members and intellectuals to learn from workers, peasants, and soldiers and to glorify those life experiences. He stated that "all our literature and art exist for the masses of the people, and in the first place for the workers, peasants and soldiers" (Mao 1942/1967c, 84). He devoted a number of his speeches and writings to explanations about how to serve people, how to connect with people, and how to use their language to identify with and persuade them. This concept of serving the people was a rhetorical strategy to ensure the "Mandate of Heaven" for governing, a concept rooted, in fact, in the Confucian tradition. Mencius, in particular, created the notion that those who win the hearts of people and practice benevolence "will be matchless in the Empire" (Lau 1970, 80).

Mao was keenly aware that he would not be able to win the revolution and lead the nation without support from the majority of the Chinese people. In many places in his writing Mao warned party members to be modest, endure hardship, be thrifty, and never separate themselves from the masses. The CCP members and leaders during Mao's era exhibited many of these qualities; corruption among officials was rare. In traditional Chinese culture, people were expected to serve their family members and friends; the "serving the people" doctrine required people to serve strangers, out-group members, and most important of all, other people of the same political class background. In Mao's period, the importance of doing things for the interest and welfare of others was strongly inculcated in people from childhood through adulthood. However, because the doctrine was politicized and then associated with the party's propaganda, it lost its rhetorical appeal in the post-Mao period.

The third characteristic of Mao's rhetoric is the employment of criticism and self-criticism as an approach to becoming a "new Communist person." Because of his literary talent and training in Chinese classics, Mao was, to a large degree, a Confucianist. A major component of Confucian teaching is self-cultivation, which is the rudimentary quality for maintaining a good family, building strong relationships with others, and making contributions to one's own country and subsequently to the rest of the world. Mao approached the idea of moral perfection by teaching how one could become a "new Communist person." The "new Communist person" was to be selfless, loyal to Mao and to the party, and willing to sacrifice for the country. The process involved a diligent study of moral exemplars, constant self-introspection, and a practice of criticism and self-criticism. Millions of party members, intellectuals, and ordinary Chinese people participated in criticism and self-criticism during countless political campaigns. In a typical session of criticism and self-criticism, intellectuals and party members were expected to denounce their so-called "selfish thoughts," "immoral behavior," and "erroneous views." They were to report how under Mao's guidance they would work hard to overcome their "ideological disease" and chart their development to becoming new Communist persons. Mao's hope was that by implementing constant criticism and self-criticism, people could develop their ability to self-correct and self-monitor their personal thought processes and also see the reformation of their consciousnesses. However, millions of Chinese people were deprived of their dignity and were forced to fabricate their purported wrongdoings as well as the wrongdoings of others. Lying for self-protection and betrayal of friends and family members became common behaviors. Such practices severely damaged traditional Chinese values of *cheng* 诚 (honesty) and yi 义 (justice and integrity).

The fourth characteristic of Mao's rhetoric was nationalism. Many Chinese people agree that Mao was a national hero. Like other Chinese heroes before him, Mao demonstrated his political ambition to eliminate a century of national humiliation brought on by unfair treaties and foreign military invasions as expressed in his early writings. Storytelling was one of the rhetorical techniques Mao used to construct Chinese nationalism. Mao reiterated throughout his writings and speeches that the Chinese people must strive for an independent, democratic, and prosperous China; to do so, Mao contended, China must follow a path of socialism and adopt the ideology of communism (Mao 1945/1967c, 229). Mao made this emotional plea: "All comrade commanders and fighters of our army! We are shouldering the most important, the most glorious task in the history of our country's revolution. We should make great efforts to accomplish our task. Our efforts will decide the day when our great motherland will emerge from the darkness into the light and our beloved fellow countrymen will be able to live like human beings, choosing the government they wish" (Mao 1945/1967d, 151–52). Mao's rhetoric of nationalism deepened Chinese people's resentment toward Western countries and Japan; it may have contributed to the sizable barrier between China and nations seeking peaceful solutions. For some Chinese people, such rhetoric firmly boosted Chinese national pride by generating a longing to restore China's glory of the past and by intensifying desires to exert more power in the world.

In foreign relations, Mao took a strong stand against the United States and later against the Soviet Union, refusing to be intimidated by U.S. sanctions or Soviet demands.[4] In his words, "China must be liberated, China's affairs must be decided and run by the Chinese people themselves, and no further interference, not even the slightest, will be tolerated from any imperialist country" (Mao 1949/1967d, 407). Mao even vowed that China would surpass the Western world in economy and military power (Mao 1958/1992b, 236). He expressed confidence that these goals would be reached and thus projected a bright future for the Chinese people. As Mao wrote on September 16, 1949, "Of all things in the world, people are the most precious. Under the leadership of the Communist Party, as long as there are people, every kind of miracle can be performed.... We believe that revolution can change everything, and that before long there will arise a new China with a big population and a great wealth of products, where life will be abundant and culture will flourish" (1949/1967d, 454). By embodying this unwavering optimism, Mao established himself as an admired leader and an inspiration to the Third World countries in acting against imperialism and colonialism.

At the same time, Mao was a strategist in foreign relations with the United States and the Soviet Union. By agreeing to meet with Nixon—a meeting that was historically significant—and paving the way for normalizing relations with the United States, Mao made his last efforts to rescue China's economy toward the end of his life. This gesture in his old age could also be interpreted as rhetoric of self-preservation that enhanced his own legacy. Mao's rhetoric of hope and promise and his use of emotional appeals engendered strong nationalistic sentiments among the Chinese and contributed to securing China a prominent place in the world.

Mao's Rhetorical Legacies in the Post-Mao Era: The Rhetoric of Deng Xiaoping, Jiang Zemin, and Hu Jintao

Mao died on September 9, 1976, bringing an end to the turbulent Cultural Revolution. New leaders of China faced the challenges of recovery from a devastated economy, demystification of Mao's godlike image, and the remapping of an ideological route for the party and for the country. The Chinese people were longing for stability and better lives. The succeeding leaders had to redefine the "rhetorical situation" and come up with rhetorical strategies to introduce the political and ideological transition. The CCP launched unprecedented reforms, which ultimately affected all areas of day-to-day life in China, particularly with regard to the economy and foreign policy. Each post-Mao leader crafted new linguistic formulations to legitimize the reform and consolidate the CCP's rule. Since Mao's death, China has seen four different regimes led by four different men.[5] Each top leader coined his own slogans and used rhetoric in ways that separated him from Mao, but each leader also appropriated different pieces of Mao's rhetoric to maintain political legitimacy—to be both a part of and apart from Mao's legacy.

For twenty-seven years (1949–76) under Mao's rule, China claimed to be a socialist country with a Communist ideology. By the end of the Cultural Revolution, China was in chaos and at the brink of economic collapse. The Chinese people were disillusioned about the Communist ideology and were uncertain about China's future. Deng Xiaoping, the first paramount leader in the post-Mao period, faced the rhetorical exigency of ideological crises and economic development. He was rhetorically challenged to fashion a fitting response that would bolster CCP legitimacy and also signal a quick economic recovery toward improving China's living standards and justifying the CCP's continued legitimacy. To that end, Deng (1981) coined the phrase "socialism with Chinese characteristics." The phrase was first used in July 1981 at a meeting with Jin Yong 金庸, a fantasy book writer and the head of a Hong Kong weekly journal, *Ming Bao*. The phrase signaled a departure from the Maoist utopian path within an acceptable framework of socialist norms. Deng justified this ambivalent yet strategic position by using a line made famous by Mao, "Practice is the sole criterion for measuring truth," implying that change is necessary to meet the imminent demands for a better life (Mao 1956/1977c, 316). Deng also emphasized that the change of direction was aligned with Mao's political ambition to build a strong, independent, and prosperous China.[6]

Deng spoke his loyalty both to Mao's ideological commitment to socialism and to his shared aversion to capitalism, although in practice, Deng encouraged borrowing funds and learning from capitalist countries in science, technology, investment, and management. Yet Deng asserted that a "capitalist system is profit-driven; it cannot rid itself of exploitation, pillage, and economic crisis" (Deng 1994b, 167). In another speech Deng reiterated that "China must adhere to socialism. Capitalism will not work in China. If China took the path of capitalism, its chaotic situation would never end; its poverty would never be changed" (Deng 1984/1993, 63). At this early stage of economic reform, many Chinese people still held Mao's belief that only socialism could guarantee equality and prevent exploitation. The fear of the evils of capitalism as created by Mao's discourse still lingered. Deng provided a fitting response to address the necessity for change, but he did not deviate much from Maoist ideals; he simply redefined "socialism." By employing the fear of capitalism and the rhetoric of promise for a better life, Deng sustained Mao's moral legitimacy of socialism and Communist rule while also sanctioning new practices of developing a market economy and promoting international trade as the new economic policy.

Deng's invention of the phrase "socialism with Chinese characteristics" is an example of language engineering, which Ji (2004) defines as "the attempt to change language in order to affect attitudes and beliefs" (3). The phrase is strategically ambiguous and rhetorically paradoxical, but it allowed pursuit of capitalist innovations and private ownership while retaining segments of state-owned economy and party control. The altered rhetoric challenged the Maoist dualistic philosophy of social systems and allowed for a practice of integrating opposing economic systems. In a significant way, Deng's use of this phrase rescued the CCP from its weakening mandate and reset the political agenda in China from one of ideological purity to one economically providing improvement of the material well-being of Chinese people.

Deng Xiaoping died in 1997, leaving China with a rapidly growing economy but also with increased corruption, mounting unemployment, environmental degradation, and a widening gap between the rich and the poor. Many businessmen and businesswomen who acquired new wealth from engaging in China's new market economy were recruited into the CCP, tying their business interests to those of the party. Some "princelings," children of high-ranking officials, held positions in government-run companies for natural resources and economic capitals and became China's new aristocracies.[7] The legitimacy of the CCP as a body of government meant solely for serving the masses was decidedly questioned. Jiang Zeming, Deng's successor, bore the burden of justifying the party's rule and appeasing the discontent. In doing so, Jiang proposed "Three Representatives" (三个代表) as the party's moral legitimacy (Jiang 2006, vol. 3). The party, he determined, represented 1) the demands for the development of advanced productive forces, 2) the forward direction of an advanced culture, and 3) the fundamental interests of the great majority of Chinese people. Jiang's rationale was first introduced in a speech on February 25, 2000, during a trip to Guangdong Province. However, the slogan did little to ameliorate the situation.

As the economic reform created accumulated wealth, the party had to represent itself as the vanguard of both the working class and entrepreneurs/capitalists. This duality signaled the changing nature of the party's original goals and its mission, which was to serve the peasants and the working class. At the same time, Jiang still rhetorically paid lip service to Marxist-Maoist ideology and continued to acknowledge his precedessors' rhetorical contributions. In his speech at the Sixteenth Party Congress, Jiang said, "Whatever difficulties and risks we may come up against, we must unswervingly abide by the party's basic theory, line, and program. We should persist in arming the entire party membership with Marxism-Leninism, Mao Zedong thought and Deng Xiaoping Theory, using them to educate our people" (Jiang 2001, 1).

In this context, Jiang's first two "representatives" served as code phrases for the party's legitimacy to continue with economic reform and Westernization. "Representing an advanced productive force" implied the party's determination to continue economic development. "Representing advanced culture" could be interpreted as a continued endorsement to embrace capitalistic elements in a socialist system. "Representing the vast majority of Chinese people" was appropriated from Mao's rhetoric of serving the people. In this sense, Jiang continued with Mao's rhetorical legacy of strong nation building and the promise of a better life for the Chinese people. The rhetorical style used by Jiang resembled the party's conventional clichés and catchy phrases in that it waved the flags of predecessors while justifying new moves. Jiang's political strategy aimed to rebuild the party's image to one of tireless adaptation to China's changing economic and social realities as well as expanding political support for the regime.[8] In doing so, Jiang allowed capitalists to become CCP members, subverting Mao's socialist doctrines and paving the way for the emergence and dominance of what Hong (2015) calls "power-capital economy," the power of the government officials linked with the wealthy class of the society in the "monopoly of the country's economic and political resources" (26).

Hu Jintao succeeded Jiang Zemin as the party's general secretary in November 2002 and became the third president of China in the post-Mao era. China's economy continued to boom under Hu's regime, paying a heavy price of increased disparity between rich and poor, rampant corruption among high-level party officials, and moral decline in the society. All these developments created nostalgia for Mao's era among many Chinese. In response to this rhetorical exigency, Hu made repeated references to the Confucian phrase "Putting People First" and stressed Mao's legacy of serving the people. In a speech celebrating the eighty-second birthday of the CCP, Hu expounded on this concept to party members: "Party officials at every level should solidly establish the mind-set of serving the people and the spirit of honesty to and responsibility for the people. Party officials must exercise their power for the people, build an emotional bond with the people, and seek benefits for the people. They must solve concrete problems for the people, make every effort to handle difficult situations for them, persistently do good deeds for the sake of the people, and always place the people's interests above everything else" (Hu 2003, 1).

Moreover in December 2002 Hu traveled to Xibaipo, Mao's revolutionary base, where he used both traditional and Maoist slogans to call for an "arduous struggle" and "plain living." Hu quoted Mao's "two musts": "[Party members] must keep the virtues of modesty, caution, humbleness, and calmness [and they] must continue to maintain the Party's tradition of plain living and arduous struggle" (Hu 2002, 1). Mao made these admonitions to party officials when he took over China in 1949. Hu's visit to Xibaipo sent a warning to officialdom about complacency and corruption among party members and showed his alignment with the Maoist call that the party's mission was to serve the people.

In his book *The Ideal Chinese Political Leader: An Historical and Cultural Perspective*, Guo (2002) notes, "In modern Chinese political thought, the notion of benevolent government is related to at least three central components: social equality, wealth of the people, and national greatness" (18). These three components comprised Mao's promises to the Chinese people when he founded the People's Republic of China. To build a strong and prosperous China had been the political ambition of several generations of Chinese leaders and had been the aspiration of the Chinese people. Hu's rhetoric of "Putting People First" was an effort to redirect priorities from economic growth at any price to developmental balance by encouraging entrepreneurship and cracking down on corruption. However, Hu's efforts were not successful. Problems of corruption and moral decline got worse. Xi Jinping succeeded Hu as China's fourth president after Mao, and Xi not only has upheld Mao's rhetorical legacies but also speaks like Mao.

Analysis of President Xi Jinping's Rhetoric

Since he took office as China's president in November 2012, Xi Jinping has won admiration from the majority of the Chinese people for his steadfast crackdown on corruption while communicating an image of being another authoritarian leader since Chairman Mao for his censorship on Internet use and unswerving opposition to Western democratic notions. Xi grew up in Mao's China and did not enjoy much privilege as the second generation of high-ranking officials. Xi's father, a high-ranking official and contemporary of Mao Zedong, was persecuted before and during the Cultural Revolution, and Xi had to go to a poverty-stricken village to labor for seven years when he was a teenager. Xi held a number of local and provincial leadership posts and experienced the transformation of China from Mao's era to the present period of economic reform. Because of his family background and his record of accomplishment, Xi is considered a good "princeling." Xi has delivered a number of speeches to domestic and international audiences in various contexts since he took office. He may not be considered a charismatic speaker, but he has the reputation of being calm, confident, and down-to-earth. Xi carries more political clout among the Chinese party officials than did his immediate predecessor, Hu Jintao, and appears more at ease in speaking his own mind. More importantly for my argument, it is striking to observe that Xi seldom utilizes his predecessors' political slogans, as would be expected within the tight protocols of CCP leaders; instead the only predecessor Xi references favorably with intensity and frequency is Mao Zedong.

I made this observation through reading and analyzing twenty-three of Xi's speeches from 2012 to 2013 on various occasions, ten speeches from 2008 to 2013 with a particular focus on party building, a speech commemorating Mao's 120th birthday on December 26, 2013, and a December 31, 2013, New Year's Eve address.[9] In these speeches Xi effectively drew from rhetorical resources left by Mao in constructing and communicating his messages. President Xi's Mao-like flavor certainly appealed to those Chinese audiences who were nostalgic for the Mao years. Textual evidence indicates that Xi not only appropriated Mao's rhetorical themes but also employed Mao's rhetorical styles in these speeches. Specifically Xi carried on Mao's rhetorical legacy by employing similar metaphors used by Mao, making references to Mao's quotes, and following Mao's storytelling techniques. It is useful to analyze those speeches by looking at three elements: the use of metaphors; references made to authoritative texts; and the telling of national stories.

Use of Metaphors

Using metaphors was a predominant feature of Mao's rhetoric, which was often elliptical, aphoristic, and literary; at the same time, Mao was famous for his blunt talk—oscillating between the two patterns was one of Mao's key rhetorical strategies. Xi has shared Mao's fondness for using metaphors and sometimes has used similar metaphors in addressing national visions and party building.

Dream metaphor. Xi has mentioned the "Chinese dream" in all his speeches; it is the predominant metaphor he uses, making it an archetype all over China. The "Chinese dream," as Xi defines it, "is about rejuvenation of China as a nation. It has been the greatest dream of Chinese people....History has taught us, every person's fate is closely linked to the future fate of the nation. Only when the nation is good can our lives be good" (Xi 2013a, 23). The "dream" is therefore a forward-looking wish for renewed greatness wrapped in the standard flag of Maoist nationalism. Xi's dream differs from the American dream, in which individual happiness is the primary goal and is premised on a good material life in a capitalistic society; in Xi's hands, the Chinese dream puts the nation first, invoking Mao's argument that individuals cannot be happy if their country is not strong and prosperous. Thus the dream metaphor has a Maoist discursive root and a nationalistic appeal to the Chinese people as the dream of building a strong nation was repeatedly stated by Mao in his writings before and after 1949. A typical line is "Our party aims to build a new China that is independent, free, democratic, united, prosperous and powerful" (Mao 1945/1977a, 229).

To avoid linking the Chinese dream with the American dream, Xi points out that "the realization of the Chinese dream depends on taking the Chinese road, reviving the Chinese spirit, and gathering China's strength" (Xi 2013a, 23). This statement implies that China will not follow the model of Western democracy and its value systems, for China has its own material and human resources to draw upon as it marches toward greatness. However, as Benjamin Bates (2004) points out, "Although metaphors do carry connotations for redefining reality, the use of a metaphor does not guarantee that it will hold in the long term" (460–61); when a national leader fails to act out the implication of a metaphor, it leads to "metaphor collapse" (461). Mao failed to deliver a democratic and prosperous China during his reign. Xi will carry the burden to guarantee the authenticity and actualization of the dream metaphor during his leadership.

Animal metaphor. Xi has also used with intensity the animal metaphor of the "tiger" and the "fly" in reference to corrupt party officials (Xi 2013a, 53). "Tigers" are high-ranking officials engaged in corruption, while "flies" are low-ranking officials who committed petty crimes. While the terms reentered Chinese discourse via Xi's speeches, they have become adopted as part of the CCP's "offialese"[10] wherein the metaphors are frequently used to express the government's determination to curb the problems of hedonism and corruption among party members. Such metaphors hearken back to Mao's era in 1951, when Mao launched two anticorruption movements known as the Three-anti Campaign and the Five-anti Campaign."[11] Those who were charged with corruption crimes were called "tigers" at the time. Thus the metaphor is nothing new to the Chinese people. Now the word has become a code word and metaphor for high-ranking party leaders who have been charged with corruption or economically related crimes.[12] In contrast to the representation of internal enemies as "flies" and "tigers," Xi has resuscitated the long-standing Confucian metaphor of the noble horse. For example, in one speech (2013b), he quotes Confucius: "Even four horses cannot catch it once gentlemen have made a promise" (Lun Yu 1992 12:124). The phrase is traditionally understood as describing a gentleman's noble quality to keep his promises, which, when rendered with honesty and vigor, outgallops even stallions. By using this metaphor, Xi signals to the Chinese people that he and his party are gentlemen—that they will keep their promises to bring a better life, in part by catching the flies and tigers who threaten to corrupt the state.

Hygiene metaphor. While Xi has used images of flies, tigers, and horses to speak about honor within the party, he also has used a wide range of metaphors about cleanliness to point to issues of moral behavior for party members. In one speech he told party members to "look at yourself in the mirror, groom your clothes, take a bath, and cure your disease" (Xi 2014a, 375). Xi explained that the mirror referred to the party constitution, and clothes referred to the party members' images. Looking in the mirror and adjusting their clothes require party members to examine themselves and monitor their own actions, as well as the actions of others. Taking a bath is to clean off any wrongdoings through Mao-style criticism and self-criticism; and curing the disease refers to helping corrupted officials return to good behavior, through either education or punishment. The acts of taking a bath and curing disease serve as warnings for disciplinary sanctions against party members' corruption. Xi's rhetoric clearly echoes one of Mao's famous lines about party corruption in which he said, "If a member of our Party acts in this way [being corrupt]...and his face is caked with the dust of bureaucracy, [he] needs a good wash in a basin of hot water" (Mao 1943/1967c, 158). In the same speech Mao observed, "As our faces are apt to get dirty, we must wash them every day; as the floor is apt to gather dust, we must sweep it every day" (160). For Mao, these references to cleaning the house and washing the body were meant to be folksy, agrarian indications that communism was a moral endeavor linked to long-standing, Confucian notions of honor and dignity. For Xi to so explicitly and repeatedly appropriate this rhetoric indicates that he, like Mao, sees his role as the party's and the nation's healer, literally as the figure who will wash the nation clean of its corruption.

Medicine metaphor. Xi's rhetoric of catching corrupt and dangerous animals and cleaning dirty bodies and dusty houses points to the central Maoist theme of self-criticism as a necessary means of rectifying party members. Xi has often described this Maoist tradition of engaging criticism and self-criticism as "good medicine" that can "prevent disease." In his words, "Medicine is bitter and does not sound good to the ears, but it is good for health," and he diagnoses the causes of party members' corruption as contracted "osteomalacia" and a "lack of calcium" (Xi 2012, 1–12). Much like those aspects of Xi's rhetoric addressed above, here too his language is based on careful invocations of Mao. For example, Xi quotes Mao a number of times about having a "correct attitude" toward criticism and self-criticism, stating that "party members must listen to any sharp criticism. Correct your actions if criticism applies; take a caution if criticism does not apply" (Xi 2013a, 59).

The rhetoric of criticism can shade into a paranoid, surveillance mode, such as when Mao said the following to party members in 1945: "Say all you know and say it without reserve"; "Blame not the speaker but be warned by his words"; and "Correct mistakes if you have committed them and guard against them if you have not." Mao had continued, "This is the only effective way to prevent all kinds of political dust and germs from contaminating the minds of our comrades and the body of our Party" (Mao 1945/1967c, 266–67). Likewise, Xi has asked non–party members to speak with honesty and courage, reflecting the voices of the masses and saying whatever they know and saying whatever they want to say (Xi 2013a, 59). In this sense, Xi appears to lean toward the same Maoist approach of mandatory criticism and self-criticism as ways to retain and legitimize control. As Cellia Hatton from the BBC News has noted, "China's current leader is clearly copying Mao Zedong's style, but he'll have to create his own solution to address the rampant corruption and disillusionment that was inconceivable in China's Communist heyday."[13]

References to Authoritative Texts

One of Xi's trademark rhetorical strategies is to situate his comments within the epic sweep of Chinese history, as Mao did. This strategy is evident in his many references to classical philosophical texts written by Confucius, Mencius, Xunzi, Han Feizi, Laozi, and Zhuangzi; to classical literary texts such as *Book of History* and *Book of Poems* and to assorted poems composed in the Tang and Song dynasties; and to the sayings from famous Chinese heroes as enshrined in classical Chinese texts. Moreover, Xi has supplemented his sense of China's historical grandeur with repeated references to Mao's sayings, thus folding Mao, who is usually thought of as offering a violent rupture in Chinese history, into the longer, seamless march of Chinese history. In Mao's and Xi's hands, that historical past points toward inevitable national greatness. As Xi (2013c) said in his speech commemorating Mao's 120th birthday, "Once the fate of China is in the hands of its people, China will be like the sun rising from the east that shines throughout the earth with its radiance." He said, "We Chinese have the spirit of fighting with our enemy until the end," and "we have the determination to be independent; we have the ability to stand high in the world." Just as Mao once predicted, so Xi (2013c) says that the "Chinese people have the will and competence to catch up and surpass the advanced countries in the world." Xi thus appropriates Mao's imagery, wraps it in a grand sense of China's future, and foretells an age when China will be strong, prosperous, and powerful.

In addition to referencing classical works in his speech, Xi has referred to Mao's sayings and his poetry. Particularly in the speech that commemorated Mao's 120th birthday, Xi (2013c) endorsed Mao as "a great Marxist, a great proletarian revolutionary, strategist, and theorist, a great patriot and a national hero.... [Mao is] a visionary political leader with a revolutionary belief and an extraordinary charisma...[who] has completely changed the destiny of Chinese people and has done immortal feats for China and for the Chinese people." Xi claimed that Mao's biggest contribution was to establish the People's Republic of China. Xi did not mention Mao's failures and mistakes during the Great Leap Forward and the Cultural Revolution. Instead, Xi pointed out that "we cannot lose the flag of Mao Zedong thought. If we lose it, we actually deny the glorious history of our party. We always will strive to uphold the flag of Mao Zedong thought." It has become a habit of Chinese leaders to use rhetorical resources of the past (classical Chinese works or Mao's legacy) to guide present behavior and future goals. Reglorifying Mao's contributions has served to obviate the mistakes and crimes he committed that caused the suffering and deaths of millions of Chinese people.

Xi grew up in Mao's China and is familiar with Mao's speeches, writings, and poems. In this speech commemorating Mao's birthday, Xi aimed at inspiring the audience to follow Mao's example and inherit his spirit by citing nine of Mao's poems throughout the speech to showcase Mao's political ambition, lofty sentiments, and heroic aspiration. Xi (2013c) referenced Mao's 1925 poem "Changsha" but rearranged the lines: "Mao Zedong is 'filled with student enthusiasm; / Boldly we cast all restraints aside; / Pointing to our mountains and rivers, / Setting people afire with our words." Xi cited Mao's question to the sky: "I ask, on this boundless land, / who rules over man's destiny?" Then Xi showed his own lofty spirit by citing Mao's line "How, venturing midstream, / we struck the waters, / And waves stayed the speeding boats." Citing this popular Mao poem indicated Xi's admiration for Mao and his determination to carry on Mao's ambition to build a strong China.

Further, to praise Mao for his resolve to overcome difficulty, his spirit of sacrifice, and his audaciousness to change the world for the better, Xi (2013c) cited other lines from Mao's poems: "Idle boast the strong pass is a wall of iron, / With firm strides we are crossing its summit" (Mao 1976, 32) and "Bitter sacrifice strengthens bold resolve, / Which dares to make sun and moon shine in new skies" (72). Many people of Xi's generation are familiar with Mao's poems and have been inspired by Mao's audacity and ambition. Xi's references to Mao's poems would evoke nostalgia for Mao and help boost the Chinese people's confidence and pride.

Xi (2013c) also quoted directly from Mao five times in this commemoration speech. The quotations were largely from two categories. The first category was inspirational, aiming to boost morale and national confidence, such as, "Once the fate of China is in the hands of its people, China will be like the sun rising from the east that shines throughout the earth with its radiance." Xi (2013c) quotes, "We Chinese have the spirit of fighting with our enemy until the end; we have the determination to be independent; we have the ability to stand high in the world.... Chinese people have the will and competence to catch up and surpass the advanced countries in the world." It seems that these words were intended to lift national pride and confidence, qualities that Mao wished to instill and that Xi appropriated to realize the Chinese dream under his own leadership. The words also invoked a competitive spirit to beat an opponent, a theme championed by Mao but which derived not from his Confucian background but from a Marxist intention for the lower class to struggle against the upper class. In this spirit, Xi (2013c) quoted Mao's saying "The future is bright, but the path is bumpy" as a cautionary reminder of the challenging tasks ahead and a justification to reduce expectations for a quick fix of China's problems.

The second category of quotations from Mao used by Xi concerned the role of the party in connection to the Chinese people. One of the present tasks facing the party is to reconnect to the Chinese population since many of its members have detached themselves from ordinary people. Xi (2013c) asked party members to study Mao's essays "Serve the People" (written in 1944) and "In Memory of Norman Bethune" (written in 1939). Xi cited Mao from "In Memory of Norman Bethune" inciting party members to become "noble-minded and pure," to become

198 The Rhetoric of Mao Zedong

"[men] with moral integrity and above vulgar interests, [men] who [are] of value to the people" (Mao 1939/1967b, 338). Further, Xi (2013c) quoted Mao's analogy about each party member's role among the people: "We Communists are like seeds, the people are like the soil. Wherever we go, we must unite with the people, take root and blossom among them" (Mao 1945/1967d, 58). Xi also referenced Mao's warning of not becoming like Li Zicheng[14] and keeping in mind Mao's "two musts": "The comrades must be taught to remain modest, prudent and free from arrogance and rashness in their style of work. The comrades must be taught to preserve the style of plain living and hard struggle" (Mao 1949/1967d, 374). Mao's "two musts" reminded party members to avoid excess and to act in the ways of the peasantry to earn the privilege of ruling the Chinese people.

As part of the commemorating speech, Xi took the opportunity to remind party members of Mao's legacy. Xi described the soul of Mao Zedong as having the three prongs of seeking truth from facts, "mass line,"[15] and national independence. Xi asserted that the party would continue to follow these core values in party building and in socialist development. Xi has often reiterated in his speeches that the party must stick to the "mass line" and work hard to win the hearts of people who are the ultimate arbitrators of the party's merits. He warns party members that if they distance themselves from ordinary Chinese people or place themselves above people, they will be abandoned by the masses and ultimately will lose their powers of governance. This "Mandate of Heaven" logic has been embedded in leadership philosophies since the inception of the Chinese imperial system, which Mao promulgated in his own writing.

Telling a National Story

In his writing, Mao often acted as a teacher of Chinese modern history. He repeatedly reminded his audience of the sufferings and struggles that Chinese people had experienced due to foreign invasion and unfair treaties imposed on China by Western powers. As was true of Mao's rhetoric as well, Xi's narrative of greatness has included a sense of struggle, victimization at the hands of foreigners, and heroic effort by the Chinese people. In one speech to party leaders, for example, Xi reviewed modern Chinese history since the Opium War: "After the Opium War, China had become a semi-colonial and semi-feudal society. Chinese history is a history of imperialist oppression, humiliation, and suffering. Almost all the imperialist countries in the world had invaded and bullied China.... They slaughtered Chinese people, forcing China to sign a series of inequitable treaties, sabotaging China's sovereignty, setting up their territories.... They extorted us to pay unfair reparation, pillaged our wealth, stole our treasures, and controlled China's economy. All these have brought unfathomable miseries to the Chinese people" (Xi 2013a, 241–42).

China's humiliating story did not end there, as Xi went on to list a series of resistances, reforms, and revolutionary movements all aimed at reclaiming Chinese dignity from a century of humiliation. These movements included the Taiping Rebellion, the Hundred Days' Reform, the Boxer Rebellion, the Revolution of 1911, and Mao's 1949 Revolution. Xi praised the leadership of the CCP during the Anti-Japanese War and the Chinese civil war and reminded his audience how many party members sacrificed their lives for the cause of creating an independent and prosperous China, culminating in the establishment of the People's Republic of China in 1949. This grand narrative of China's modern history was used as a recurring rhetorical strategy in Mao's writing. However, in his historical narrative, Xi skipped over the period of Mao's China and did not mention his mistakes, instead praising the party's leadership of post-Mao economic reforms. In this way the horrors of the Cultural Revolution were avoided and Mao's revolutionary communism was situated as part of the long, slow progress of China as a great, modern nation. This telling and retelling of China's history of victimization and triumphant resistance was a recurring theme in Mao's writings and much of contemporary Chinese rhetoric. Stephen Hartnett (2011) has called this rhetorical form "traumatized nationalism," arguing that it breeds resentment and hostility toward Western countries, fuels the determination to make China a strong military power, and stokes an aggressive sense of Chinese nationalism. Indeed, President Xi is an expert practitioner of the rhetoric of "traumatized nationalism," but he is also remarkably adept at invoking Confucian classics, folksy idioms, and a wide range of animal and nature metaphors, all while wrapping himself in the lineage of Mao's revolutionary communism, albeit switched now from an anticapitalist fervor to a strident form of Chinese nationalism.

In summary, Xi has employed metaphors similar to those used by Mao, referenced Chinese classics and Mao's sayings, and used narrative techniques similar to the rhetorical features employed by Mao in his speeches and writing to tell the national story of victimization. Through the appropriation and evocation of Mao, Xi not only has presented Mao favorably but also has presented his own Mao-like persona and rhetorical force, which have strongly appealed to those who have nostalgia for Mao's era and strong nationalistic sentiments. Moreover, Xi's use of various types of metaphors has made his speeches more interesting and relatable both to Chinese people and to international audiences. References to Chinese classics and culturally rooted discourse have enhanced Xi's ethos and served the political purpose of evoking patriotism and encouraging sacrifices for the nation. Xi has described himself as a scholar-politician, the traditional model of rulers likely to win the admiration and adherence of their people. Official Chinese media have praised him as an eloquent speaker (Cui, April 2, 2014).

Mao's Rhetoric and the Future of Chinese Official Discourse

Traditionally, Chinese official discourse was used in the imperial court in exchanges between the emperor and ministers on state issues, in proposals or arguments presented to the emperor in written or spoken form, in ritualistic state settings, and in government decrees or announcements. Within this highly structured imperial court context, the official Chinese language in ancient China was characterized by formality, courtesy, and conciseness. Such formal language was reserved for educated elites and government officials trained in the intricacies of Confucian teaching and Chinese classics. In contrast, ordinary Chinese people spoke the vernacular (*baihua*) or their local dialects (*fangyan*) in an informal manner wedded to a long-standing oral tradition.

Based on Link's (2013) observation, Chinese official language today has been influenced by Western grammatical structure as well as by the Japanese employment of a modern vocabulary beginning in the twentieth century.[16] The modern Chinese official language—in the forms of national news, political speeches, statements, propositions, and policy announcements—is structurally rigid and repetitive, using numbers, moral appeals, vagueness, and euphemisms as rhetorical techniques (Link 2013, 311–13). Schoenhals (1992) describes Chinese official language as "formalized language" in that it has its own formulaic jargon and is a restricted code for political and ideological dogma; he argues that such a formalized language has become a tool of coercion or a form of power in controlling and manipulating minds (14–22).

Calling it "officialese," Perry Link (2013, 13) claims that Chinese official language has become moralized, which is largely attributed to Mao's rhetorical influence. It is the belief in the Chinese tradition that proper use of language helps cultivate moral integrity and induce moral behavior. Mao appropriated this traditional belief for his purposes of achieving ideological unity. During Mao's years, speaking in line with party beliefs or referencing Mao's words was an indication of a moral person. During Mao's years, especially during the Cultural Revolution (1966–67), official language and private, vernacular language were supposed to be merged, as the Chinese people were expected to be politically correct, ideologically aligned, and linguistically enveloped within the CCP's discourse. As part of this Mao-led ideological and rhetorical consolidation, Chinese citizens were encouraged to fill their everyday language with quotations from Mao's *Little Red Book*. This Communist indoctrination was so complete that ordinary people were expected to use official and Maoist phrases to express their private thoughts in private settings such as in family conversations, personal diaries, and private letters. As this politicized language infiltrated every aspect of people's lives, many learned to monitor their choice of words, for they feared persecution if they said anything ideologically incorrect. As a result, people turned themselves into "thought police" (Orwell 1950, 2).

However, post-Mao official language and private language are separate. Official language is used by the government media outlets—newspapers, radio, political meetings, and speeches. Ordinary people no longer are bound to speak official language in private settings. Their expressions are colorful, humorous, and artistic. In contrast, Chinese official and political discourses still carry traces of "officialese" or formulaic jargons. As one of the most prominent leaders of the twentieth century, Mao Zedong exerted tremendous influence on Chinese official discourse used by subsequent Chinese leaders in the post-Mao regime. Typically, political leaders' speeches set the tone and jargon or set phrases for the official language, which is then regurgitated in other official or formal channels. Party officials are expected to use political jargons and set phrases from these speeches in all political and public situations to show conformity and loyalty to the CCP's leadership. These language practices resemble the practices called "Newspeak" in a society that George Orwell described in *Nineteen Eighty-Four*, where words and sentences were carefully crafted for political purposes and ideological correctness.

In the post-Mao period of economic and political reform, the CCP leaders have diverged from Mao's ideological dogmatism and have moved toward pragmatism, which is evident in the relaxed economic and foreign policies as well as in the more prevalent deradicalized rhetoric. However, the CCP still faces the challenge of addressing rhetorical exigencies of inequality, corruption, moral decline, and social unrest in the aftermath of reform, exigencies that threaten the legitimacy of CCP rule. As they manage their ideological shifts in response to these rhetorical exigencies, post-Mao leaders of China have often made references to Mao's discourse, attempting to bring to mind his legacy for the purposes of justifying the CCP's legitimacy; however, these leaders have been simultaneously breaking away from Mao's radical and utopian rhetoric while promoting their own drastic changes in actions and policies after Mao's death.

Drawing from Mao's rhetorical resources, these leaders, Deng, Jiang, Hu, and now Xi, carried on Mao's ideological discourse to maintain legitimacy of the CCP's rule over China. These leaders preached Mao's moral ideals of socialism, the political edifice of serving the people and building a strong nation. The leaders also continued to show concerns about the gap between the rich and the poor, to condemn corruption of party officials, and to tout self-cultivation through criticism and self-criticism to address the decline in faith regarding Communist ideals. Similar to Mao, four of these post-Mao top leaders used the official language for didactic purposes, characterized by giving instructions, explanations, and advice, especially when audiences included party members or officials. Similar to Mao, all these leaders ended their speeches with lofty slogans and promises. They inserted the political formulae of previous top leaders to show the continuity and mandate of the CCP's legitimacy. Metaphors, references to authoritative texts, and storytelling—all typical of Mao's rhetorical styles—have been strikingly evident in President Xi Jinping's speeches delivered to both domestic and international audiences. Mao's audaciousness has become the spiritual inspiration for the CCP, and Mao's rhetorical legacy remains as cultural and political resources from which subsequent Chinese leaders draw for guidance in government and party building.

However, post-Mao leaders' speeches deviated from Mao's rhetorical style in several aspects. First, they did not contain radical words and abandoned Mao's revolutionary ideology, particularly his divisive rhetoric of class struggle. Instead their speeches called for unity rather than division, harmony rather than conflict. In his speech delivered at the celebration of the fiftieth anniversary of Sino-French diplomatic relations in Paris, Xi remarked, "Napoleon Bonaparte once said that China 'is a sleeping lion,' and 'when China wakes up, the world will shake.' In fact, the lion of China has awakened, but what the world sees now is a peaceful, amiable, civilized lion" (Xi 2014b). This soft image of China is what post-Mao leaders have wanted to convey to the world.

Moreover, when they talked about China's modern history of humiliation, these leaders offered accounts of what has already happened, rather than attacking former colonizers and invaders. In a recent speech in commemoration of the seventieth anniversary of the victory of the Chinese people's War of Resistance against Japanese aggression and the world's anti-Fascist war, Xi did not dwell on China as a victim of the war as Mao had in the past. Instead his message celebrated the victory of the Chinese people and emphasized the importance of peace.[17] In this way the century of humiliation has given way to an age of expected greatness; Mao's nationalist aspiration has become Xi's "Chinese dream." Further, profanity has been absent in speeches, unlike in Mao's time, when it was occasionally used. Like Mao, these leaders were fond of using lofty statements, but their claims were less exaggerated and agitating than Mao's. While Mao employed many forms of persuasive devices ranging from rational argument to emotional appeal, speeches by leaders since Mao's time seemed to place more emphasis on ethos, especially when giving instructions and advice to party members.

One reason for these differences is that most of Mao's works were written prior to his reign over the CCP and China. He may have fashioned his rhetoric to contain elements of shock to draw audiences' attention and to establish himself as a well-articulated scholar and official, an inspiring leader. Post-Mao leaders, in contrast, already held power. They may have had less political need to elevate themselves and denounce their opponents; however, this difference between Mao and present leaders also may stem from personality or ideology differences. As evidenced from the analysis of President Xi's speeches, the future of Chinese official discourse used by post-Mao leaders will continue to draw from rhetorical resources in traditional Chinese literature, language arts, and cultural sayings, and it will continue to reference Mao as suited to the changing situation in China and China's relationship with the world.

With China now more open to the world and its people more exposed to a variety of rhetorical expressions from other sources, the rhetorical effects of official discourse have become more limited than they were historically. To many Chinese people, the formulaic nature of Chinese official discourse now seems too rigid and riddled with clichés. Observations from current conversations indicate that people have grown tired and cynical of "officialese" and are often put off by its emptiness. They regard the formulaic use of language as trite, commonplace, and banal, leading to a situation of "listening fatigue." Even among elites it has become common to hear of party officials texting, WeChatting, reading, or forwarding messages from their cell phones during party meetings, when they are purportedly diligently and even reverently listening to political speeches.

As the effectiveness of official discourse in today's China has drastically dwindled, Chinese people have begun to joke about revolutionary rhetoric or speak sarcastically about political jargon. People commonly deride the official discourse including Mao's widely employed sayings, making fun of the sayings and ridiculing the discourse and making the words humorous for comical effect in social and private settings. Perry Link (2013) has offered an example from his experience while he was visiting China. When someone brought food to the dinner table and jokingly said, "Serve the people," everyone laughed. Their laughter, Link suggests, occurred because "the Maoist slogan was highly incongruous, and therefore [it was] funny to insert it into such a relaxed and informal context" (238). In this sense, people employ what Burke calls "the comic frame" as a sarcastic critique to the fallibility within a rigid system (Burke 1959, 171).[18] In other words, by using official language for comic effect, both the speaker and the listener realize the incongruity between public discourse and private discourse and the relevance or irrelevance of the discourse for the situation. People may laugh to release tension and embarrassment embedded in the incongruity of the words as they are used in the present setting compared to the meaning they held in previous situations.

An example of sarcasm used with regard to official language occurred when President Hu Jintao's slogan of *hexie* 和谐 (harmony) was satirized as *hexie* 河蟹 (a river crab)—creating a pun because these Chinese words sound alike when they are pronounced but have completely different meanings. The Chinese artist Ai Weiwei implemented this homonym in his summer 2014 Brooklyn Museum exhibit by piling together a mass of fake river crabs as a form of mockery. The term *hexie*, meaning harmony, also has been cast with a negative meaning to suggest conforming to the party line, succumbing to political pressure, or surrendering one's dignity for the sake of protecting oneself. With the increasing use of the Internet and social media in China, such rhetoric of satire and ridicule challenges the power of official discourse. This new kind of rhetoric has emerged among the populace and may continue to grow as a form of empowerment for the Chinese people and resistance to the CCP.

Mao's political rhetoric had considerable power in transforming Chinese culture and in bringing about the success of the revolution by defeating Chiang's government in 1949. However, Mao's transformative rhetoric also inflicted great damage to Chinese society in terms of the economy, human dignity, and human relationships after 1949, destroying traditional Chinese cultural values in the process. Nevertheless, because of the tremendous impact of Mao's speeches and writings and nostalgia for Mao, Mao's sayings and his legacy still resound in everyday conversations and in online communications among many Chinese people. Chinese official discourse still harbors traces of abstractness, vagueness, lofty expressions, and empty promises. For the CCP to sustain its post-Mao legitimacy, Chinese leaders need to explore inventive ways of speaking. They need to expand their rhetorical repertoire and appeal to increasingly diverse and sophisticated domestic and international audiences. While they may find that appropriating Mao's rhetorical themes and styles is still useful for some political purposes, CCP leaders also face the challenge of breaking away from the formulaic jargon and Mao Zedong's legacy in order to engage in more responsive, civil, and effective rhetorical practices in reaching out to and having dialogues with the entire world.

Notes

Preface

1. The term "liberation," or *jiefang* 解放, is used in Mainland China to refer to the 1949 takeover from Chiang Kai-shek's Nationalist Party. The same event is referred to as "falling into the enemy's hands," or *lunxian* 沦陷, in Taiwan.

2. GDP growth in China 1952–2014, http://www.chinability.com/GDP.htm (accessed June 20, 2015).

3. The book is pocket-sized and contains a collection of Mao's sayings and aphorisms. It was originally compiled by Lin Biao for the People's Liberation Army.

4. The song can be found at http://v.youku.com/v_show/id_XMTY4MzM5NDg= .html (accessed June 25, 2013).

5. Mao wrote a poem in 1961 praising Chinese militia women; it reads, "How bright and brave they look, shouldering five-foot rifles. On the parade ground lit up by the first gleams of day. China's daughters have high-aspiring minds. They love the battle-array, not silks and satins." The poem popularized the image of young women who rejected their femininity and instead embraced masculine styles in clothing, hair, and demeanor. See Mao 1976, 77.

6. Another reason for my doubts about Mao was that my parents were persecuted during the Cultural Revolution, especially my father, who was almost beaten to death. I have recorded my family's suffering during this time in Lu 2004b.

Introduction

1. Since the 1980s China has become the world's fastest-growing economy as "its GDP has increased by an average of almost 10% a year for the past 30 years" (Woodall 2009, 61).

2. Agence France Presse, "China Marks Mao's Birth with Noodles and Songs," http://www.myrepublica.com/portal/index.php?action=news_details&news_id=66862 (accessed January 14, 2014).

3. Examples of such programs are "The Long March" and "In Praise of Yan'an," performed by highly popular Chinese actors.

4. Between 1951 and 1976, 250 million copies of the five volumes were printed. The sale of Mao's works declined significantly after Mao's death in September 1976 but has gone up since 1989, when Mao fever took place in China.

5. The caricature of "evil Mao" was mostly seen in the era immediately following 1949, when American sensitivities to communism were especially pronounced. For example, during the Cold War in the 1950s, the American media guru Henry Luce staged a

propaganda campaign against Red China in his magazines *Time, Life,* and *Fortune.* A representative example of the American anti-Maoist sentiment is found in the caption that accompanied Mao's portrait on the February 7, 1949, cover of *Time:* "The Communist Boss Learned Tyranny as a Boy." In the eyes of Americans, Mao was not only China's Hitler; he was also Stalin's and Lenin's ardent disciple, epitomizing the worst of the violence and brutality that had accompanied other authoritarian leaders around the world.

6. For example, in his 2005 review of their book, Andrew Nathan concluded, "It is clear that many of Chang and Halliday's claims are based on distorted, misleading or far-fetched use of evidence." Stuart Schram's review (2007) further pointed out inaccuracies in some of the book's accounts of Mao, while also noting their problematic reliance on sources that cannot be checked and claims that are based on speculation or circumstantial evidence.

7. Agnes Smedley and Anna Louise Strong, two other American journalists, gave favorable accounts of Mao throughout their journalistic writings on coverage of China. In their recent biography, *Mao: The Real Story* (2012), Alexander Pantsov and Steven Levine posit that Snow's sympathetic portrayal of Mao, in particular, struck a chord with Western leftist intellectuals and set the tone for subsequent positive depictions of Mao.

8. Western Mao studies began with Benjamin Schwartz's seminal publication *Chinese Communism and the Rise of Mao* (1951). Schwartz was among the first to use the oft-contended term "Maoism," and his work evoked a number of scholarly debates centered on Mao. Subsequently Stuart Schram published a series of books detailing Mao's life, speeches, and thought from the 1960s until his death in 1976; a number of other biographical publications also emerged during this time (e.g., Chen 1965; Paloczi-Horvath 1962; Payne 1950).

9. In China scholarly studies of Mao have largely conformed to the government's official assessment of him. This body of work can be divided into a number of different categories, each representing a unique perspective or community. The first group of studies on Mao comprises works produced by party intellectuals who held prominent positions in Chinese academic institutions such as the Chinese Academy of Social Science (中国社会科学院), the Chinese Center for Study of Party Documents (中央文献研究室), and the Office of Chinese Communist History (党史研究室). For example, Pang Xianzhi (逄先知), Gong Yuzhi (龚育之), Jin Chongji (金冲及), and Li Junru (李君如) wrote relatively academic treatments of Mao's life, his ideas, and his place in Chinese history. The most authoritative Chinese books on Mao are the two volumes of a biography of Mao Zedong, 1949–76 (毛泽东传), edited by Pang Xianzhi and Jin Chongqui and publishedin 1996 and 2003, respectively (Pang and Jin 2003). These two volumes endorse Mao as a national hero who made invaluable contributions to his nation by establishing the CCP, the People's Liberation Army, and a socialist Chinese government; moreover they offer high praise of Mao's writings. These latter volumes are said to be based on the historical documents of the Communist Party and Mao's original works, and they represent the party's official stance on Mao.

10. Some representative memoirs reflecting these perspectives include Quan Yanchi (权延赤) 2001; Chen Shiju (陈士榘) 1993; Chen Changjiang (陈长江) and Zhao Guilai 赵桂来) 1998; Shi Zhe (师哲) 1991; Guo Jinrong (郭金荣) 2009; and Li Rui (李锐) 2005a, 2005b. Mao Zedong's grandson Mao Xinyu, who currently is a major general in the

People's Liberation Army, has taken on the task of writing about his grandfather. He has thus far published several books on the subject; see, for example, Mao Xinyu 2003 爷爷毛泽东.

11. English publications that depict Mao in a negative light, such as Zhishui Li 1994; and Jung Chang and Jon Halliday 2005, are banned in China. In recent years a concerted effort has been made to translate Western books on Mao into Chinese. Terrill 1980, which was translated into Chinese, has sold well in China, and other Western scholars of Mao such as Benjamin Schwartz, Stuart Schram, and Maurice Meisner are referenced in China by writers seeking support for their depictions of "the good Mao." However, there is little evidence of any real scholarly exchange between Chinese and Western Mao studies experts.

12. The Chinese version of the document can be found at http://cpc.people.com.cn/GB/64162/71380/71387/71588/4854598.html (accessed August 15, 2013). The English version of the document can be found in *Beijing Review* 27 (July 1981): 6.

13. Mao wrote these words in his letter to Jiang Qing, his third wife. See Mao 1998a, 72.

14. To name a few: the analysis of President Lincoln's speeches in assuring support for the Civil War (Watson 2000); in the religious transformation of faith (Dufault-Hunter 2012); in the study of transformative rhetoric of African American leaders and scholars in black thought and movement (McPhail 1996; Powell 2004); and in Kayam 2014.

15. "Mao's Blood Revolution Revealed" 2013, http://www.youtube.com/watch?v=3EjxieKgvWY (accessed December 2013).

16. Although Mao held various positions within the party before 1943, none of these roles gave him actual power in the way that his chairmanship did. I argue, therefore, that his real influence over the CCP, and China more generally, began on March 20, 1943, when the politburo of the CCP named Mao as chairman of the CCP (thereby replacing Zhang Wentian, who had been the former leader of the CCP since 1935).

17. Some Chinese and Western scholars of Mao shared the view that Mao's five volumes of works reflect more of the collective wisdom of the party. In this sense, the authenticity of these texts is questioned, and it might be difficult to discern what deems to be Mao's original voice and what constitutes the party's collective thought. While I fully acknowledge the issue of originality of Mao's works, my analysis focuses largely on what is available and on the rhetorical capabilities and effects of the writings under Mao's name.

18. Chinese language is what is known as "high-context" language, in which the meanings of words are often ambiguous and allusive. See Hall "Context and Meaning" in his book *Beyond Culture*, 1976.

19. A number of scholars have debated both the originality and the proper construal of Mao's written works; along these lines, Cheek (2010) posits that Mao's writings are similar to biblical texts not simply in terms of their influence but rather because they are open to so many different interpretations. Although the influence of Mao's writings can be traced to the early 1940s in the Communist-occupied areas of Shanxi Province, there were also different versions of his essays and articles circulated in different regions. In 1949 the Central Committee of the Chinese Communist Party decided to form a committee to establish a unified version of Mao's works. The first four volumes were published in 1951, 1952, 1953, and 1960, respectively, with the fifth volume published in 1977. The

English versions of the first four volumes were published in 1967 (translated by a number of prominent scholars and translators including Jin Yueling 金岳霖 and Qian Zhongshu 钱钟书. It is believed, however, that Mao revised and changed some of his early speeches and essays before they were published in these official volumes. This adds weight to Wittfogel's (1960) argument that Mao modified certain sections of pieces such as "The Hunan Report" in order to suit the changing role of the CCP as China's ruling party.

20. It is well acknowledged by both Chinese and Western Mao scholars that most of Mao's writings were presumably done by Mao himself, but his secretaries Chen Boda, Hu Qiaomu, and Tian Jiaying—all of whom were top-notch party propagandists—edited, revised, and polished some of the works that were published under Mao's name. They even penned a few of Mao's articles by imitating Mao's style of writing. However, these articles were revised and approved by Mao before publication. Some articles, such as "The Present Situation and Our Tasks" 目前的形势和我们的任务, were in Mao's own spoken words but were written down by his wife Jiang Qing (Zhu Xiangqian 2007). Based on my own reading of Mao's complete works, Mao's writings prior to 1949 were more consistent in rhetorical themes and styles. Therefore my speculation is that Mao's works before 1949 were largely written by him with possible proofreading by his secretaries. His post-1949 writings may be more representative of the party's collective position. However, after 1957 Mao stopped writing lengthy articles and speeches. He issued only short directives or wrote letters. These short directives and letters were published as his works and were more likely written by him. During the Cultural Revolution, Mao's directives were issued more or less in spoken form rather than written; his foreign policies, in particular, were often revealed through his conversational remarks in meetings with foreign guests. While reading all of Mao's published works in Chinese, I examined the consistency within as well as the variations among Mao's rhetorical themes and styles from different periods of Mao's life.

1. Rhetorical Themes in Mao Zedong's Early Writings

1. For the English translation, see "Mao Zedong's Funeral Oration in Honor of His Mother," in Schram 1992, 419–420. In this oration Mao expressed his deep feelings toward his mother and highly praised her for being a kind-hearted and giving person who sacrificed her entire life for her family and helping others.

2. *The Three Character Classics* was written in the thirteenth century. The author is unknown. The booklet embodies the credo of Confucianism in simple and common language. It was written in the form of three Chinese characters and is easy to remember. This text is the first one that children learn to recite by heart and through which they learn Chinese characters and simultaneously Chinese morals and cultural values.

3. *The Thousand Character Classics* (千字文) is a Chinese poem used as a primer for teaching Chinese characters to children. It contains exactly one thousand unique characters. The author is Zhou Xingsi 周兴嗣, who served as a public servant for Emperor Liang Wu Di 梁武帝 (502–49) during the Southern and Northern dynasties (420–589).

4. See the English versions of Han Yu's essays "Essentials of the Moral Way," "Memorial on the Bone of Buddha," and "Edict of the Eighth Month" in defense of Confucianism and on his attacks on Daoism and Buddhism, in De Bary and Bloom 1999.

5. Kong Rong is one of the seven "Jianan" scholars (建安风骨 or 建安七子) who are known for their literary contributions during the East Han dynasty (22–220).

6. See Gong, Pang, and Shi 2009; Sun 1993.

7. Also known as *chu ci*, or Songs of the South, this is a collection of poems written by Qu Yuan. It was compiled by Liu Xiang in the Western Han dynasty (206 B.C.–24). The poems expressed the poet's patriotic sentiments, imagination, and emotion for his home state, Chu.

8. For example, Mao expressed his desire to save the country in many of his letters to his friends. The translated English versions of these letters are available in Schram 1992. For more discussion on the Chinese concept of jingshi zhiyong, see Chang 1996.

9. Each person is a well-known Chinese patriotic hero who devoted himself to the state and placed the interests of the people and state above his life and interests.

10. In a teacher-student relationship, Kang, the teacher, and Liang, the student, advocated a constitutional monarchy as opposed to revolution as a new form of government. They led the reform movement with the support of Emperor Guangxu but were stopped by Empress Dowager Cixi. Both Kang and Liang were prolific writers and social activists; both called for the preservation of traditional Chinese culture and Confucian values. Both were against the Westernization of China. Liang later deviated from his teacher and supported a radical and revolutionary approach to solve China's problems. He particularly advocated Chinese nationalism after his trip to Europe.

11. Known as the Second Guangzhou Uprising and led by Huang Xing, a leader of revolutionaries, this was aimed at a takeover of the Qing government but was instead crushed by the Qing army and resulted in the deaths of seventy-two revolutionaries.

12. The term "big-character essay" refers to an essay written in big characters and then pasted on a public wall for everyone to read. It is a traditional Chinese way of making a private thought public in order to draw public attention to an issue. The form was first invented by Deng Xi (545–501 B.C.E.).

13. The Wuchang Uprising took place in Wuchang, Hubei Province, when revolutionaries fought against the Qing government officials, which led to the 1911 revolution that overthrew the Qing dynasty and replaced it with the Republic of China (ROC).

14. Most of these books were translated by Yan Fu. See Schwartz 1964 for more information on Yan Fu's translation.

15. Mao passed up an opportunity to go to Europe and went to live in Beijing instead. He said to a friend in a letter that the reason he did not choose to go was that he wanted to learn more about China. Another possible reason was that he did not raise enough money for his overseas trip.

16. Most Mao scholars agree that Cai Hesen 蔡和森 was instrumental in persuading Mao to join the Communist Party and convert to communism. Cai was an active leader of the Chinese Communist Party and was executed in 1931 by the Nationalist Party.

17. Mao took notes for his classes and the newspapers he read. These notes were kept in his home village of Shaoshan. During the days of the "Mari Massacre" 马日事变 in Changsha (1927), when the Nationalists staged a killing spree of Communist members, Mao's relatives burned all his notes. This particular notebook was picked out from the fire by Mao's elementary tutor Mao Yuju 毛宇居, who kept it until 1949.

18. See Mao 1993; Sun 1993.

19. This saying is from Zhu Xi (1130–1200), the leading scholar of Neo-Confucianism 宋明理学, which flourished in the Song dynasty (960–1279). It was focused on rational aspects of Confucian ethics and metaphysics as a counterforce to Daoism and Buddhism, both of which are more interested in mysticism and the spiritual domain.

20. The quotation is from chapter 7, book 15 of Confucius's Lun Yu (*Analects.*), 1992.

21. Zhuge Liang (181–234) was a chancellor of the state of Shu Han during the Three Kingdoms period. He was well learned and had a noble spirit in serving his master and his people. Guan Zhong (720–645 B.C.E.) was a Legalist chancellor of the state of Qi. During his term of office, the state of Qi became much stronger as the result of his reforms. Fan Zhongyan (989–1052) was a prominent politician and literary figure in the Song dynasty in China. He was known for his famous saying "Bear the hardship and bitterness before others, enjoy comfort and happiness after others." Mao considered all of them as having sagelike qualities.

22. Yang Cangji received two doctoral degrees in philosophy, one from England and the other from Germany. His focus was on Immanuel Kant.

23. Paulsen's *System of Ethics* was translated from German to English by Frank Thilly. A Japanese scholar named 蟹江义丸 (Kanie Yoshimaru) translated the English version into Japanese. Cai Yuanpei translated the book into Chinese from the Japanese version.

24. See Foucault 1991; Mueller 1958.

25. Mencius's notion of *haoran zhiqi* 浩然之气 referred to the moral state of an individual. If a person had *haoran zhiqi,* he/she would emit positive energy in practicing humanity and defending justice. Mencius labeled those who demonstrated *haoran zhiqi* as *da zhangfu,* or true gentlemen. See Mencius, 1992, 60.

26. Chain reasoning was a characteristic of argumentation in ancient China. It was characterized by a sequence of cause-and-effect relationships; namely, the effect of a cause will become the cause that leads to another effect in a sequence of outcomes. See Lu (1998).

2. Mao Zedong's Theories of Rhetoric

1. Mao had a reputation for adapting Marxist Communist theories to China's situation. See Knight 1983.

2. "Pragmatism" (实用主义) is not a term used in traditional Chinese philosophy but is a translation from John Dewey's work on pragmatism. However, it is generally agreed that Chinese philosophical tradition concerns about the practical problems of human life as opposed to the supernatural form; it emphasizes practical applications rather than abstract theorization. From Confucian teaching to the concept of *jingshi zhiyong* (attending to issues in the real world and solving social problems) coined in the Ming dynasty, educated Chinese, or *shi,* are expected to become officials and bring real changes in society by putting their learning into a practice known as *rushi* 入世. See Chang 1996; Feng Youlan, 1994; Hajime Nakamura 1964, chap. 17; Zhai 2013.

3. Being the director of the CCP's delegation to the Comintern—an abbreviated name for the Communist international organization that was founded in 1919—in the Soviet Union and trained in the Soviet school, Wang Ming physically resided in Moscow and sent his commands to China, leading the CCP's revolution from 1931 to 1937. During this time Wang exerted much more authority than Mao both as the leader of the CCP and as a Marxist theorist. He was Mao's strong political rival; Mao disagreed with

Wang's dogmatic and bookish approach to military maneuvers, which resulted in multiple defeats by the Nationalists. Mao wrote "On Practice" to criticize Wang's dogmatism and to show that his own interpretation of Marxism was superior to Wang's. Mao successfully won the support of other CCP top leaders, and Wang Ming eventually was defeated in the power struggle.

4. It refers to the military retreat of the Red Army led by Mao Zedong and Zhu De to avoid the attack of the Nationalist army. They literally walked six thousand miles in harsh conditions between October 1934 and October 1935.

5. Mao favored peasant revolution, advocating for a military approach of encircling the cities from the rural areas. Original Marxist theory called for raising the consciousness of workers in the city. Lenin succeeded during the Russian Revolution by taking over the cities. In this sense, Mao deviated from Marx and Lenin.

6. Mao's use of the term "scientific" was loose. He did not refer to science as the scientific way of thinking (deductive or inductive reasoning). Rather, to him, Marx's view of knowledge/epistemology made more sense. Even to this day, CCP leaders use the word "science" to mean "the right way," e.g., Hu Jintao's slogan "Upholding the scientific perspective."

7. Deng Xiaoping appropriated Mao's view into a slogan, "Practice is the sole criterion of measuring truth," in legitimizing his economic reform in the 1980s.

8. The Communist Party and the Nationalist Party had been enemies. Once Japan waged war against China, the two parties attempted to form an alliance against the Japanese. A Delegation of Observation traveled to Yan'an to see if the Communist Party was prepared for the alliance and to discern if the CCP was enthusiastic and sincere about the alliance. While the Nationalist Party occupied the cities, the Communist Party's base was in rural areas with headquarters in Yan'an, Shanxi Province. Chiang's government refused to recognize the CCP as a legitimate political entity. A positive assessment by the Delegation of Observation of the CCP's success at forming this alliance was essential for achieving support and recognition from domestic forces and international allies.

9. Only with perfect knowledge will a person be able to accomplish sincerity (*cheng yi* 诚意). Only with the help of sincerity is one able to rectify one's heart (*zheng xin* 正心), and only with such a heart can man undergo self-cultivation (*xiu shen* 修身). Once cultivated, a man's family is brought into unison (*jia qi* 齐家), and when all families are in unison, a state can be governed (*zhi guo* 治国) in the right way. If all these steps are followed, there will be peace on earth (天下平). This notion was further refined and developed by Zhu Xi and Cheng Yi, two Neo-Confucianists, during the Song dynasty. See Chan 1989 on Zhu Xi and Neo-Confucianism.

10. Mao made a series of mistakes in his economic policies, in particular the policy of land, the people's commune, mass steel production, and the Great Leap Forward movement. See Yang 2008.

11. Li Da and Ai Siqi were scholars of Marxism in the 1920s. Both had written books on Marxism that Mao read. It is believed that Mao was indebted to them for learning and understanding Marxist-Leninist theories.

12. Mao referenced Lenin's works seven times in "On Practice" and thirteen times in "On Contradiction." The writings Mao referenced most from Lenin were "Hegel's Logic"

and "Let's Talk about Dialectics," from Vol. 55 of the Complete Collection of Lenin. The Chinese translation was published by the People's Press in 1990 in China.

13. The early version of the work was a speech delivered in the form of a lecture at the Anti-Japanese Military and Political College in Yan'an.

14. The 1942 rectification movement, the Anti-Rightest Movement in 1957, and the Chinese Cultural Revolution in 1966–76, to name a few.

15. Aristotle coined the term "enthymeme," which he defined as a rhetorical syllogism produced jointly by the speaker and the audience. It served to unite the speaker and the audience based on shared values and allowed the audience to engage in self-persuasion (Aristotle 1991, 40).

16. As "the bourgeois class" had become the class enemy, the category of bourgeois thought and behavior had been expanded and politicized. Any attempt to make money, any disagreement with the CCP, and even a person's choice of luxurious clothes, using perfumes, planting pot flowers, or having pets was considered "bourgeois."

17. The political opponents referred to were the 28 Bolsheviks, a group of young Communists trained in the Soviet Union and supported by the Comintern. Mao harshly criticized them for dogmatically applying Marxist-Leninist theories to China's revolution without considering China's situation.

18. Young intellectuals from urban areas flocked to Yan'an for the Yan'an spirit characterized by self-sacrifice, courage, selflessness, struggle, and diligence. See McDonald 2005.

19. The May Fourth Movement took place in 1919. It was marked by students' demonstrations protesting the Chinese government's concession to the Treaty of Versailles, which allowed Japan to claim Qingdao as its territory from Germany after World War I. In addition the movement, which was also known as the "New Cultural Movement," called for "science" and "democracy" in China. Most intellectuals who went to Yan'an were influenced by the spirit of this movement, which was characterized by freedom of expression, adherence to democratic ideals, and support for nationalistic sentiments.

20. Mao used the terms "the proletariat" and "the masses" interchangeably to refer largely to peasants. At this point in history, most party members and Red Army soldiers were peasants instead of industrial workers.

21. Mao gave a directive on May 7, 1968, calling for cadres to get reeducated in rural areas of China through hard labor. Since then 106 such labor camps under the name of "May Seventh Cadre Schools" were formed in eighteen provinces throughout China. Over ten thousand artists, writers, university professors, and middle-ranking officials were sent to work in these kinds of labor camps. These cadres also had to engage in political studies, criticism, and self-criticism after work.

22. One well-known story produced during the Yan'an period was "The White-Haired Girl." This story told how a peasant girl was exploited and ill-treated by a landlord. The girl hid herself in the mountains, and her hair turned white due to a lack of nutrition. The story was made into a movie and a ballad later and became one of the Communist classics.

23. "The spring snow" was a metaphor referring to elites with high taste, while "song of the rustic poor" was a metaphor used for ordinary people who had no taste for art and literature.

24. The best examples of meeting such standards are the eight Beijing operas produced during the Chinese Cultural Revolution under the supervision of Jiang Qing, Mao's wife.

25. Big-character posters or wall posters can be traced to the fifth century B.C.E., when Deng Xi, a lawyer, carved his views on judicial issues on bamboo slips and hung them on walls for the public to view. These have been means of communicating royal edicts, pronouncements, and orders between the emperor and his people. Over time it has become popularized and used by ordinary people for petitions. Mao reportedly wrote his first big-character poster when he was seventeen years old expressing his political views in support of Sun Yat-sen. See Lu 2004b for a more detailed description of its practices during China's Cultural Revolution.

26. Mao praised Lu Xun twice in this speech and asked writers and artists to learn from Lu Xun's sarcastic style in attacking counterrevolutionaries and from his fighting spirit in his writing.

27. The term "propaganda" carries negative connotations of brainwashing in the West, while in Chinese, especially in CCP discourse, it is a neutral term for disseminating information and educating the audience. There is a propaganda department at every level of the party apparatus.

28. In his study and translation of Chen Kui's (1128–1203) *Wen Ze* (文则), produced in the Song dynasty (960–1279), Kirkpatrick (2005) argues that based on Chen Kui's work, classical Chinese writers did use citations and references and that Chen Kui required writers to acknowledge the sources or persons they cited or referenced (127). I agree that classical writers used citations and referenced each other, but they did not have a system of using notes and bibliographies to indicate the sources of information until modern times.

29. John Dewey (1916) argued that humans are social beings and have common interests. They are interrelated and interacting with one another for mutual benefits and for strengthening democratic values. Dewey called this "a conjoint communicated experience," or "a mode of associated living" (87).

30. Hu Shi wrote "A Preliminary Discussion of Literary Reform," published in January 1917 in *New Youth*. He discussed eight types of speech that should be eliminated. The first one, "Write with substance," was the same as Mao's first indictment of "eight-legged" party writing, although the rest were different. There is no doubt that Mao was indebted to Hu Shi for the use of vernacular and effective language.

31. *Bangu wen* 八股文, or "eight-legged essay," was used as the standard writing style by the educated Chinese in imperial China. The style was divided into eight sections; effectively writing an eight-legged essay was required for the imperial examination after the Song dynasty.

32. It is possible that Mao's notion of audience adaptation was influenced by Chen Wangdao 陈望道, a contemporary of Mao and one of the leaders of the New Cultural Movement that promoted the use of vernacular language pioneered by Hu Shi. Chen wrote *Introduction to Rhetoric* (修辞学发凡) in 1932 after returning to China from his studies in Japan. In this book Chen treated rhetoric as a modification of terms and appropriate use of language. He provided different types of tropes and stylistic techniques in the book. Chen's focus was largely on stylistic elements of rhetoric in writing rather than on the persuasive and argumentative aspects of rhetoric.

3. Mao Zedong's Rhetorical Styles

1. It is believed that some of Mao's works were edited by his secretaries, such as Hu Qiaomu. Even though it is hard to say that Mao's written essays are representative of Mao's rhetorical style, there seems to be some consistency among Mao's early writings prior to 1949, before he had secretaries. I am mostly interested in analyzing the rhetorical effect and the impact of these early writings. See the introductory chapter for my explanation.

2. Mahayana Buddhism was brought to China from India around the first century of the Common Era. It became popular during the Tang dynasty (618–907 C.E.) as it was adopted by Tang emperors. Mahayana Buddhism emphasizes liberation from human suffering, accepting impermanence, and nonself. Its goal is to achieve enlightenment and nirvana through meditation, reading Buddhist sutra, veneration of Buddha, and participation in ceremonials and rituals.

3. An apagogic argument (reduction ad absurdum) disapproves a proposition by showing the absurdity of that position. This type of argument is commonly used in math and in Christian apologetics. This rhetorical technique was much favored by Han Yu in his defense of Confucianism and his denigration of Daoism and Buddhism.

4. Han Yu acted in response to the rhetorical style known as *pianwen* (骈文), passed on from the previous dynasties after the fall of the Han dynasty (206 B.C.E.–220 C.E.). The style required the paralleling of sentences by exactly the same number of words, harmony in sound and tones, and eloquence and embellishment in the choice of words. Han considered such a style empty in substance and impoverished in content. *Pianwen* was replaced by *guwen* for the civil service examination in the Song dynasty (960–1279).

5. Mao Sheng 毛胜 is a contemporary author who has written biographies of the CCP's top leaders. There is no evidence that the author is a relative of Mao Zedong.

6. Examples of these editorials can be found in *Mao Zedong zaoqi wengao,* published in 1990 in Hunan, China. The English translation of Mao's editorial comments can be found in Schram 1992.

7. Hu Shi studied under John Dewey at Columbia University in 1916. He was heavily influenced by Dewey's pragmatism. He introduced American pragmatism to China and appropriated the Chinese tradition of *jingshi zhiyong* (attending to the issues of the real world and solving social problems). He invited Dewey to China and translated Dewey's lecture in Chinese in 1919–21. Hu Shi and other New Cultural Movement activists considered classical Chinese to be a barrier to disseminating modern ideas. The shift to vernacular language would allow communication of ideas to reach more ordinary people, a practical approach to increase literacy and to induce social change.

8. Classical Chinese language is condensed in meaning and characterized by conciseness. It often omits the subject in a sentence and uses the reverse order of subjects, predicates, and objects as in the vernacular language. It tends to use functional words. The language presents on the page from right to left in a vertical fashion without punctuation. The meanings of words used in classical language depend heavily on linguistic and social contexts. Qian Xuantong wrote an essay in 1917 calling on scholars to use common, spoken language; to avoid using reverse order of sentences; to use punctuation; and to write from left to right in a horizontal manner. See Qian 论应用之文亟宜改良 2010 for information on the reform of expository writing. The essay was originally published in *New Youth* 3, no. 5, 1917.

9. It is not known if Mao was a true believer of Marxism or merely put on the clothes of Marxism in order to have an ideology with which to attract followers and in order to receive money from Stalin. It is possible that Mao thought much more like a strategist, compared to Karl Marx.

10. Retrieved from http://news.takungpao.com/history/wengu/2014–02/2312895.html (accessed September 15, 2013).

11. Here, Mao used another animal metaphor to boost the morale of his army: "Liu Tsung-yuan's description of 'The Donkey in Kweichow' also contains a valuable lesson. A huge donkey was brought to Kweichow and the sight of him rather frightened a small tiger. But in the end this huge donkey was devoured by the small tiger. Our Eighth Route and New Fourth Armies are the Monkey King or the small tiger, and they are fully capable of dealing with the Japanese demon or donkey. Now it is imperative for us to do a little changing and make ourselves smaller but sturdier, and then we shall be invincible" (Mao 1942/1967c, 101). This metaphor illustrated that even though Mao's army was small in size, it could still win over the Japanese. The original story comes from Liu Zhongyuan (773–819), a member of the literati from the Tang dynasty.

12. After the civil war, an effort failed to establish a coalition government. When Chiang lost control of northern China to the CCP, both the United States and the Soviet Union supported the idea of dividing China into south and north, setting up Chiang Kai-shek to rule the south and Mao to control the north. Mao disagreed. In 1949 Chiang's government made one last attempt to negotiate with the CCP for a dual rule for China, proposing the Yangtze River as the dividing line, with the CCP ruling north of the Yangtze and the Nationalists ruling south of the Yangtze. The proposal was rejected by Mao; Chiang Kai-shek retreated to Taiwan.

13. After the speech delivered by Madame Chiang to the U.S. Congress on February 18, 1943, the United States began to have sympathy for China and started to supply China with materials through Burma. The United States also provided a volunteer air force known as the "Flying Tiger," under the command of Claire Lee Chennault, to help China with air defense against Japan. China received some help at the beginning of the war, but substantial support from the Soviet Union did not come until 1946 during China's civil war. Mao broke relationships with the Soviet Union after Nikita Khrushchev denounced Stalin for his personal cult and brutal rule of the Soviet Union at the Soviet Communist Party's 20th Congress in February 14, 1956.

14. Until 1987, when I went to the University of Oregon to study rhetoric, I did not know that the United States had supported China during the Anti-Japanese War. I learned this from Henry Rust, a member of my host family in Eugene, Oregon, who told me this information and showed me pictures from when he was in the U.S. Air Force during World War II. His unit was dispatched to China, and his job was to transport medical supplies by plane to China from the United States.

15. According to Young (1991), Lenin coined the term "counterrevolutionary" to label those who disagreed with the Soviet Communists (139).

16. "Permanent revolution" was initially a Marxist concept meaning a proletarian strategy in protecting its class interests. The concept was developed by the Soviet Marxist Leon Trotsky to mean socialist revolution in less developed countries. Mao took the concept even further to mean a never-ending revolution as long as class difference or

class struggle exists in a society. In Mao's belief, the bourgeois class or counterrevolutionaries would always want to take the social, economic, and political power back from the proletarians.

17. See examples of the use of such language during the Cultural Revolution in Lu 2004b.

18. Retrieved from http://caochangqing.com/gb/newsdisp.php?News_Idaho=530 (accessed December 15, 2013).

4. Mao Zedong's Rhetoric of Class Struggle

1. Mao did not read German; he read Karl Marx's works that were translated from German to Russian and then from Russian into Chinese by Chinese scholars. Some of Marx's works were translated from German to Japanese and then from Japanese to Chinese.

2. China at the time had not developed its proletariat class yet as it was still largely an agrarian society with little national industry. Peasants constituted 70–80 percent of CCP party members (Gao 2004).

3. In December 1930 the Futian Battalion's leaders rebelled against Mao, who was the leader of the Red Army at the time. The mutiny failed. Under the command of Mao, seven hundred army officers were arrested and executed. These actions were followed by the Sufan (cleaning out hidden counterrevolutionaries) movement within the party, escalating the purge against so-called members of the Anti-Bolshevik League. Within a few years about seventy thousand army soldiers and officers had been killed. Not until 1956 did Mao admit that these actions were mistakes and that all those killed were innocent. See 戴向青、罗惠兰 Dai and Luo 1994.

4. Because it lagged behind in economic development and specifically lagged behind in the development of means of production, China did not follow the social pattern seen in Europe in which a burgeoning class of proletariat emerged. To this point China had not generated large numbers of workers and laborers who would have constituted the proletariat class. Mao recognized that the bifurcated relationship between the Chinese bourgeoisie and the proletariat had never existed in Chinese history. The two classes emerged only after foreign powers opened and began to operate factories in China. Mao considered a section of peasants and handcraft workers as the precursors of the Chinese proletariat (Mao 1939/1967b, 310).

5. The targets of Sufan or the Campaign to Suppress Counter-Revolutionaries were the remnants of the Nationalist Party who were accused of various types of sabotage and spying against the new Communist government. Millions were executed and arrested. The death toll varies from source to source. According to Goldhagen 2009, the most recent study on the campaign, roughly ten million were killed from 1949 to 1953. In Gao Hua's (2004) source, one million people were imprisoned and five hundred thousand people were killed.

6. As mentioned before, the targets of Sufan were identified as enemies of the CCP.

7. Mao feared that bureaucracy and corruption would grow among party officials as they began to receive privileges. He called upon nonparty members, particularly public intellectuals, to voice their concerns and help the party identify and correct their mistakes. On April 28, 1956, Mao proposed to "let one hundred flowers bloom in the arts; let

one hundred schools of thought contend in academics" at the meeting of the CCP extended politburo. In his writing Mao endorsed "one hundred flowers bloom and one hundred schools of thought contend" as the guiding principle for the development of art and science (Mao 1956/1977c, 433).

8. Mao instigated the Anti-Rightist Movement in 1957. The main targets of the movement were intellectuals who had criticized Mao and the CCP's leadership and who had expressed favorable views on capitalism and the Western democratic system. The movement lasted for two years, during which 550,000 people were labeled as rightists and were persecuted, imprisoned, or sent to labor camps. Mao's endorsement of "letting one hundred flowers bloom and one hundred schools of thought contend" has been viewed as a trick to "draw out snakes from the caves"—to reveal the true identity of "counterrevolutionaries." But some scholars argue that this claim needs to be substantiated with more evidence (e.g., Leese 2011; Shen 2012).

9. Number nine was the lowest socioeconomic class in the Yuan dynasty (1271–1368). "Stinking" refers to the arrogance of the educated elites. During the Cultural Revolution, intellectuals ranked number nine in the order of class enemies; numbers one to eight were landlords, rich peasants, counterrevolutionaries, criminals, rightists, traitors, spies, and capitalists.

10. Peng first wrote a private letter to Mao with these criticisms in June 1959. Mao circulated the letter at the Eighth Plenum of the Eighth Central Committee of the CCP held in Lushan. Mao had an open debate with Peng. After the debate Mao accused Peng of being the leader of an "anti-party clique" and dismissed him from his position as defense minister. Peng wrote another letter, known as the "80,000 words letter," to Mao and the politburo continuing to criticize Mao's Great Leap Forward economic policy. Peng was deprived of political participation and was put under house arrest until 1965.

11. Mao chose to ally with the Soviet Union in his foreign policy, but when Nikita Khrushchev became the Soviet party secretary after Stalin's death, the relationship between China and the Soviet Union deteriorated due to a serious disagreement in ideology, socialist practices (e.g., the role of communes), and international relations. Beginning in 1960 China and the Soviet Union began to attack one another verbally. Mao believed that the Soviet Union under Khrushchev's leadership had renounced the Marxist-Leninist Communist ideology and had taken a capitalistic path. Mao started calling Khrushchev a revisionist and used the word "revisionism" to refer to the socialism practiced in the Soviet Union.

12. The Chinese translation of John Foster Dulles's speech can be found in Du Lesi 1959.

13. Mao considered the American "peaceful evolution" to be an ideological conspiracy to undermine the absolute control of Communist regimes. It had been Mao's fear that some Communists "were not conquered by enemies with guns ... but cannot withstand sugar-coated bullets" (Mao 1949–1967d, 374).

14. Retrieved from http://blog.rbc.cn/html/28/528–291.html (accessed January 30, 2014).

15. Mao equated revisionism with capitalism and the bourgeoisie, as it meant supporting Khrushchev's criticism of Stalin, opposing the ideology of class struggle, and spreading bourgeois ideas.

16. Mao made such a call in his essay "Talks at the Yanan Forum on Literature and Art." Mao believed that there was no such thing as art for art's sake. Mao contended that art and literature must represent the life experiences of the proletarian class and must be used as weapons to destroy the class enemy (Mao 1942/1967c).

17. Some of these films are "Never Forget," "Grab the Seal," "Li Shuang Shuang," "The Youth," and "Along the Jiangan River."

18. Mao's private conversations with his family members had been published at his new directives.

19. Since 1956 Mao had been worried that China would take the path of capitalism in economic development, the bourgeois ideology (code words for Western democracy and the Western way of life). But Mao had to concede to economic development led by Liu Shaoqi and Chou En-lai. Mao was concerned that a capitalistic China would lead to economic disparity and economic crisis (Qian 2012, 79).

20. Mao wrote and published his big-character poster titled "Bombing the Headquarters: My Big-Character Poster" in the *People's Daily* on August 5, 1966. The poster declared Mao's demarcation from Liu Shaoqi and identified Liu and Deng Xiaoping as the biggest class enemies in China.

21. For example, Liu Shaoqi, the president of China, was accused of being a traitor, a scab, and a counterrevolutionary. He was denounced in public, imprisoned and tortured, and finally died of multiple injuries and infections.

22. Mao issued a directive on May 7, 1966, to send intellectuals and party officials (cadres) to labor camps known as "May Seventh Cadre Schools" to do manual labor and undergo ideological reeducation during the Cultural Revolution.

23. The concept of the "banality of evil" was coined by Hannah Arendt in her book *Eichmann in Jerusalem: A Report on the Banality of Evil*. It was evil not by intention but by blindly following a set of language rules that brought disaster to other people and humanity.

24. The Khmer Rouge, a radical Maoist and Marxist-Leninist Cambodian Communist Party, ruled Cambodia from 1975 to 1979, during which over two million Cambodians were executed or starved to death under the name of counterrevolutionary crimes. See Depaul and Pran 1997.

25. Stalin launched the Great Purge campaign in the Soviet Union in 1936–38, accusing and executing many Russian officials, intellectuals, and artists for their so-called counterrevolutionary crimes. See Conquest 1990.

26. In his meeting with officials of the CCP Central Committee, Deng Xiaoping (1980) showed his open defiance of Mao regarding class struggle: "Revolution requires class struggle, but revolution cannot be just class struggle. Revolution of productivity is also a type of revolution; it is the most important and most fundamental type of revolution from a historical perspective" (313).

27. Lu and Simons (2006) characterized post-Mao transitional rhetoric as "dilemma-laden" because Chinese leaders had to balance pragmatic agendas and idealistic views, between hardliners of Mao's followers and reform-minded entrepreneurs, and between internal demands and external/international pressures. In response to such rhetorical exigency, Deng coined the term "socialism with Chinese characteristics" to justify China's seemingly inconsistent ideological orientation—an authoritarian society with a market economy—in the view of Western observers.

28. The World Bank reports on China's annual GDP can be found at http://data
.worldbank.org/indicator/N.Y..GDP.MKTP.KD.ZG (accessed May 20, 2014).

29. By 2013 China ranked twenty-ninth in the world among countries that had the
greatest inequality in income according to a report of the World Development Index (retrieved from http://www.infoplease.com/world/statistics/inequality-income-expenditure
.html [accessed May 20, 2014]).

5. Mao Zedong's Rhetorical Construction of a New Communist Person

1. According to Munro (1977), the new Soviet man was "a goal-oriented activist,
conscious of future tasks and able to introduce changes in himself and in his material
environment by pursuing them" (14).

2. The saying is from "Great Learning" 大学, one of the Confucian classics; see Wu
1990, 1–17.

3. Based on Confucian values of the "Three Cardinals" 三纲 (ruler guides subject,
father guides son, and husband guides wife) and the "Five Constant Virtues" 五常 (benevolence, righteousness, propriety, knowledge, and sincerity) as well as the Daoist
notion of "wuwei" 无为 (nonaction).

4. Confucius's notion of *renren* did not include women. He actually despised
women, calling them *xiaoren*, or base persons.

5. This view was held as well by other prominent intellectuals during China's republic period (1911–49). Scholars and educators such as Cai Yuanpei 蔡元培, Ye Qisun 叶
企孙, and Li jinhui 黎锦晖 all believed that China could be changed only when its people were changed and that the only way to change people was through education. They
advocated for "saving China through education" 教育救国.

6. Mao outlined three kinds of people. The first consisted of the sages who had
mastered the ultimate principles, in this case philosophy and ethics. The second kind
consisted of the worthies who had mastered some of the ultimate principles. The third
kind of people included the fools who knew nothing about ultimate principles. A sage
was an exceptionally wise and virtuous person such as Confucius, who was knowledgeable on the universe and human affairs and who also had a vision for the future.

7. Mao's view on ethics was much influenced by his teacher and father-in-law, Yang
Cangji (see chapter 1).

8. Mao contradicted himself when he advocated a democratic government for China's future in his negotiations with the Nationalists. I believe that his early view of
individual moral perfection was genuine but that his rhetoric for a democratic government was a rhetorical strategy meant to win the support of the majority of the Chinese
people.

9. Mao never gave a clear definition of "proletarian consciousness," and China never
had a significant number of workers whom Marx would have identified as the proletarian
class. Mao's followers were largely peasants, so the term "proletarian consciousness"
was more like a code for "loyalty to the CCP."

10. "Three Rules of Discipline and Eight Points for Attention" had been modified a
couple of times. The final version provided these directions: "Obey commands in all
actions; do not take anything from the masses; and submit everything captured." The
"Eight Points of Attention" advocated that the Army "be soft spoken; engage in fair

trade; return what is borrowed; compensate for what is damaged; do not curse and beat people; do not damage crops; do not seduce women; and do not abuse captives."

11. The Chinese word for "intellectual," or *zhishi fenzi* 知识分子, was loosely used to refer to the educated. The education level could range from high school to doctorate. The old term for "intellectual" was *shi* 士, the lowest rank of aristocracy in imperial China. These individuals were well educated in the arts, literature, and military knowledge. They did not produce anything. Their jobs were to assist higher ranking officials regarding government and military affairs.

12. To a great extent, Mao's prediction proved true as witnessed by the rampant corruption among party officials once economic reform was under way. The CCP's image of representing the working-class people was severely tarnished by its corruption.

13. The first rectification movement occurred in Yan'an in 1942 during the Anti-Japanese War. The second occurred in the midst of civil war. The third occurrence was a series of rectification campaigns in the 1950s.

14. After Zhang Guotao departed from Mao's troops, his military force was defeated by the local forces. He finally joined Mao's army in Yan'an but lost his power as one of the party leaders. He lived in Canada during his later years.

15. Leon Trotsky (1879–1940) was a Soviet Marxist and revolutionary leader. Because of his anti-Stalinism stand, he was removed from power and was deported by Stalin. He was assassinated in Mexico. Nikolai Bukharin (1888–1938) was a top Soviet politician and theorist who was expelled from the poliburo because he opposed Stalin's collectivization. He was arrested and executed in 1938. Chen Tu-hsiu or Chen Duxiu (1879–1942) was a co-founder of the CCP and the CCP's general secretary from 1921 to 1927. He criticized the Comintern, denounced Stalin, and opposed Mao about relying on peasants as the primary force and also opposed Mao about the rejection of the bourgeoisie for China's revolution. Chen was expelled from the CCP in 1929 and died of an illness in 1942.

16. Such a type of moral rhetoric was not restricted to Communist China. President Ronald Reagan referred to the Soviet Union as the "evil empire" in his anti-Communist rhetoric. President George W. Bush named Iraq, Iran, and North Korea as the "axis of evil" in his antiterrorism rhetoric.

17. In 1951 the CCP announced its decision to form cooperatives among Chinese peasants. China's cooperatives were modeled after the Soviet experience in that peasants put their lands and resources together for agricultural production. Mao considered cooperatives as socialist structures and vehicles moving down the path toward communism. The purposes of cooperatives were supposedly to maximize the benefits for peasants and bring about higher productivity.

18. Mao used "people" and "masses" interchangeably and oftentimes combined the two words, such as *renmin qunzhong* 人民群众 (people, masses).

19. Liu Shaoqi, another top CCP leader who eventually was persecuted to death during the Cultural Revolution, delivered a series of lecture to the students of Yan'an Marxism-Leninism Institutes in 1939 in order to interpret Mao's ideas of why and how the CCP members should mingle with the masses. The lectures were published in the CCP newspaper "Liberation" and titled "How to Be a Good Communist" (论共产党员的修养). It was a required reading during the Rectification Campaign in 1942 and was published by the People's Press in China as a booklet for all CCP members. The English

version of the text can be found at https://www.marxists.org/reference/archive/liu-shaoqi/
1939/how-to-be/ (accessed July 20, 2015).

20. Mount Tai is located in Shandong Province and is the highest and largest mountain in China.

21. There has been a debate about whether Lei Feng was a real person or was fabricated for political purposes. In post-Mao China, Lei Feng became a laughingstock and the subject of cynicism among young people. For more readings on Lei Feng, see Edwards 2010.

22. Pan Xiao was the pen name on a letter published in *China Youth* in May 1980. In the letter the author argued that everybody has self-interest; even when they do things for others, the author argued, people have motives derived from their own interests, suggesting that being selfish is a part of human nature. This letter evoked a huge debate among the Chinese, who had been taught during Mao's years that a person could eradicate his or her selfishness by emulating Communist role models and becoming a new Communist person.

23. *How I Changed My Thought* was published in 1950. The book contains articles of self-criticism from top intellectuals such as Pei Wenzhong 裴文中, Zhang Zhizhong 张治中, Luo Changpei 罗常培, Xiao Gan 萧干, Li Ziying 李子英, and Xie Fengwo 谢逢我 (Hu 2007, 33).

24. See Lu 2004b for more examples of criticism and self-criticism during the Cultural Revolution.

25. There was a designated "political studies" time in every work unit and school during the Cultural Revolution. In these "political studies" sessions, people would study (often read aloud) Mao's works and quotations or read current newspapers, followed by criticism and self-criticism rituals. Many people voluntarily engaged in self-criticism in their diaries.

26. In the Chinese language, *xin,* or heart, is used to refer to mind or thought.

27. Kenneth Burke discussed this process of rebirth in several of his other works. See Foss, Foss, and Trapp 1991, 194–97, for further explanations and references.

28. The translation of "self-styled" is a bit awkward. A more accurate translation should be "complacency."

29. During the Cultural Revolution (1966–76), millions of cadres were removed from their leadership posts and publicly humiliated by their subordinates. Workers, peasants, and students verbally assaulted and humiliated them, tyrannized them, and even in some cases physically abused them.

30. Despite Mao's tireless efforts to promote plain living, many CCP officials became corrupt and lived luxurious lifestyles in post-Mao China.

31. Intellectuals such as Liu Bingyan 刘宾雁, Fang Lizhi 方励之, Li Zehou 李泽厚, Wang Ruowang 王若望, and Liu Xiaobo 刘晓波 publicly spoke out criticizing the government and demanding democracy in China. Unfortunately they were either put into prison or had to exile overseas for their dissident views.

32. The term "the exquisite egocentric person" 精致的利己主义者 was coined by Qian Liqun, a professor from Peking University. In his explanation, the characteristics of the exquisite egocentric person include being "highly intelligent, conventional, and sophisticated. They are good at presenting themselves, know how to cooperate with

others, and take advantage of the system to achieve their personal goals." Qian expressed his views on the concept at a local symposium on May 3, 2012, retrieved at http://news.sina.com.cn/c/2012–05–03/040724359951.shtml (accessed May 3, 2015).

6. Mao Zedong's Rhetorical Constructions of Chinese Nationalism

1. The movement was considered extreme and violently radical. According to Chinese and Western scholars, the movement halted the progress of China's modernization (Luo, Fuhui, et al. 1996, Zhao 2004).

2. The Twenty-One Demands were stipulations made of China by Japan on January 18, 1915. The demands would greatly extend Japanese control of Manchuria and of the Chinese economy. The Chinese people responded with a spontaneous, nationwide boycott of Japanese goods.

3. In the chapter "hequ shu" 河渠书 (Book of Records), in Sima 1993, 141.

4. Even the ancient Chinese used the term *tianxia* 天下 (the world), but the term does not carry the meanings of "country" or "nation" 国家. The term refers to the imperial family, the Chinese race, and Chinese culture (Liang 1987, 166).

5. The "Chinese GDP in 1820 was nearly 30 per cent higher than that of Western Europe and its Western offshoots combined" (Angus Madison, "World Economy: A World Perspective," retrieved from http://pratclif.com/economy/china/chinahistory.htm [accessed May 30, 2014]). China's GDP dropped substantially as a result of the Anti-Japanese War and civil war in the 1930s and 1940s. By 1950 it accounted for just 4.5 percent. It steadily increased in the first few years of Mao's era and then fell again during the Cultural Revolution (1966–76). Since the government launched economic reform in the early 1980s, China has been experiencing an impressive growth spurt in the past thirty-five years. It now has the third-highest GDP in the world, behind the United States and Japan. See http://www.wisegeek.com/how-has-chinas-gdp-changed-over-time.htm (accessed May 30, 2014).

6. The "Five Cardinal Relationships" came from Confucian doctrine. They included the relationships between superior and subordinate, between father and son, between husband and wife, between elder brother and younger brother, and between friends. To Confucius, a society would be orderly and harmonious if individuals respected the hierarchy in these relationships and acted according to each of these positional roles. In doing so, a person would cultivate his/her virtues of humanity, benevolence, and goodness.

7. Chinese cultural characteristics or traits of character included 1) sanity, 2) simplicity, 3) love of nature, 4) patience, 5) indifference, 6) old roguery, 7) fecundity, 8) industry, 9) frugality, 10) love of family life, 11) pacifism, 12) contentment, 13) humor, 14) conservatism, and 15) sensuality (Lin 1938, 41).

8. Cai Heseng, Mao's classmate, went to France and was converted to Marxism. Cai and Mao corresponded through those years, during which Mao was introduced to communism, political thought about class struggle, and the notion of a proletarian dictatorship. Cai was the most influential person in Mao's conversion to Marxism.

9. Shang Yang (390–338 B.C.) was a statesman of the Qin Kingdom. There he proposed and put into practice numerous reforms, which made Qin a powerful state.

10. See Chang 1997.

11. Mao's works might not have directly reached a large audience before 1949, but his writings were often published in newspapers and circulated among the educated Chinese or reading audiences. This educated, reading audience garnered support for the CCP and promoted the idea to set aside domestic infighting with the Nationalist army and instead form an alliance against the Japanese invasion.

12. Because Chinese is a high context language, Mao omitted some parts in the chain (for information on the chain reasoning process, see endnote 26 in chapter 1) for the audience to fill in. The complete chain for this quote should be as follows: "if things were not done this way, the revolution will fail, [if the revolution fails,] the people will suffer, [if the people suffer,] the country will be conquered."

13. Chiang launched five extermination campaigns on the CCP in hopes of eradicating the Communist army, but he failed to accomplish his goal in the first four campaigns because of Mao's skillful use of guerrilla warfare. The Communist army was defeated in the fifth extermination campaign because the army did not adopt Mao's strategies, which forced the army to start the Long March.

14. Ironically the Western concept of democracy became the new common hegemonic symbol for the construction of a nationalistic identity for the Chinese. Mao's demands sounded more like those of the political dissidents of contemporary times in China.

15. The Double Tenth Agreement is also known as the Summary of Conversations between the Representatives of the Nationalist Party and the Communist Party of China. It was agreed to on October 10, 1945, after negotiations between the two parties mediated by Patrick Hurley, then U.S. ambassador to China. The agreement stated that the CCP acknowledged Chiang's Nationalist Party as the legal government while the Nationalist Party in return recognized the CCP as a legitimate opposition party.

16. More recent evidence has shown that the Nationalist army under Chiang's leadership rather than the Communist army under Mao's leadership was the main military force in the resistance against Japan. However, in the speech that commemorated the seventieth anniversary to end the war against Japan, President Xi Jinping praised the Chinese people for their spirit and deeds during the war but gave little acknowledgment of the decisive role of the Nationalist army. For the English translation of Xi's speech, see http://www.scmp.com/news/china/policies-politics/article/1854943/full-text-xi-jinping-military-parade-speech-vows-china (accessed September 4, 2015).

17. John Leighton Stuart was born in China in 1876. He was the president of Yanjing University (now Peking University) before he was appointed as U.S. ambassador to China in 1946.

18. The report was titled *United States Relations with China* and was published by the U.S. State Department on August 5, 1949. It reviewed the American involvement in China between 1844 and 1849 and proposed an end to aiding the Nationalist Party due to its corruption. The report also verbally attacked the CCP and refused to recognize the CCP as an upcoming, legitimate government.

19. The strong national discourse was repeated in several of Mao's speeches. On September 21, 1949, Mao delivered an opening speech at the First Plenary Session of the Chinese People's Political Consultative Conference entitled "The Chinese People Have Stood Up." In the speech Mao declared that the "Chinese people, comprising one quarter

224   *Notes to Pages 152–155*

of humanity, have now stood up. The Chinese have always been a great, courageous and industrious nation; it is only in modern times that they have fallen behind. And that was due entirely to oppression and exploitation by foreign imperialism and domestic reactionary governments.... From now on, our nation will no longer be a nation subject to insult and humiliation. We have stood up. Our revolution has won the sympathy and acclaim of the people of all countries. We have friends all over the world" (Mao 1949/1977c, 16–17). The phrase "the Chinese people have stood up" was used in Chinese political discourse beginning in 1949 to boost nationalism as well as the image of Mao as the savior of China from its weak and miserable past.

20. When the People's Republic of China was founded in 1949, the Soviet Union agreed to aid China technologically in the development of a nuclear industry. However, in June 1959 the USSR refused to provide relevant information as it had previously promised. Moreover, the Soviet Union recalled all technicians and advisers from China. In July 1960 Chairman Mao Zedong called on Chinese scientists to rely on their own efforts and develop China's atomic bomb within eight years. Retrieved from http://www.china .org.cn/english/congress/228244.htm (accessed May 12, 2014).

21. Chiang Kai-shek retreated to Taiwan after being defeated by the CCP's army. The Taiwan government, still called the Republic of China, signed the Sino-American Mutual Defense Treaty with the United States in 1954. The United States provided military assistance to Taiwan until 1979, after China formally established diplomatic relations with the United States. However, despite new diplomatic relations with the People's Republic of China, the United States and Taiwan signed the Taiwan Relations Act, which requires the United States to intervene militarily if the PRC attacks or invades Taiwan. This agreement still stands.

22. One may say that Mao's rhetoric was visionary as in the past sixty years China has gained economic strength, which has developed with increasing speed during the last thirty years. Ironically the rapid development has not been the result of a socialist system. China has increasingly become more capitalistic in terms of value orientation and consumption behavior since the economic reforms in the 1980s. Social progress in areas of social justice, civil rights, and equity has been hindered. See Hong 2015.

23. On April 7, 2008, as the Olympic torch relay passed through Paris, it was met with thousands of protesters from France and elsewhere in Europe in support of the autonomy of Tibet and demanding the essence of human rights from the Chinese government. Jin Jing, a young female handicapped athlete in a wheelchair, protected the torch when a protester attempted to grab it. This instance angered the Chinese people, who considered it humiliating to China and who blamed the French government for allowing it to happen. On April 19 Chinese people from several cities took to the streets to denounce calls for Tibetan independence and to boycott Carrefour, a French chain supermarket in China.

24. The military parade summoned twelve thousand troops, two hundred aircraft, and dozens of tanks and missiles. At the time of the parade, China's stock market plunged 40 percent and the economy slowed down. September 3 has been claimed as a national holiday to commemorate the victory in China. This is the day after the Japanese army surrendered to Allied forces in 1945.

25. See Xing Lu's articles on the rhetorical analyses of these books: "A Burkean Analysis of China Is Not Happy: A Rhetoric of Nationalism" (2012); and "A Rhetoric of Nationalism and Anti-Americanism in China Can Say No" (1999).

26. Yu argues that Chinese nationalism is not only built on the hatred of foreign powers such as the United States; it is also embedded in the nation's psyche that foreign countries such as Japan and the United States are far more advanced than China. This is evidenced by many Chinese nationalists who condemn the United States while sending their children to study there. See Yu, Yingshi 余英时. Minzhu yu minzu zhijian 民主与民族主义之间 (Democracy and Nationalism), http://history.sina.com.cn/his/zl/2013-08-08/113051184.shtml, 2013 (accessed June 4, 2014).

7. Rhetoric of Mao Zedong's Foreign Policy

1. "Third World" terminology is Mao's assignation and will be discussed later in the chapter.

2. The speech was delivered at the first session of the preparatory meeting for the Eighth National Congress of the Chinese Communist Party.

3. After the publication of the book, many young people traveled to Yan'an, Mao's revolutionary base, to join the revolution. Even some foreign doctors, reporters, and writers came, including a group of Indian doctors and various other international aid workers. Among them, Dr. Dwarkanath Kotnis is well remembered by the Chinese people in a memorial to him in Shijiazhuang, the capital of Hebei Province. He came to Yan'an and met Mao Zedong; he treated many Chinese patients and Chinese soldiers and died in 1942 in China at the age of thirty-two.

4. Owen Lattimore (1900–1989) was accused of being a Soviet spy during McCarthyism. The charge was later dismissed. He wrote *The Inner Asian Frontiers of China* (1940) and taught Chinese history at the University of Leeds in England. See Ho 2005.

5. The cinematic portrayal and print publications of the "Chinaman" in the United States were filled with stereotypes, prejudice, and racism. The popular show *Fu Manchu,* which aired over a decade later in the United States, depicted the Chinese man as full of trickery, evil, and ruthlessness against white people. See Lee 1999; Choy, Choy, and Hom 1994.

6. However, Mao's request was denied (Cohen 2000, 146).

7. Initially Hurley had Mao sign a "Five-Point Draft Agreement" that allowed the CCP and the Nationalists to share power. Mao was extremely pleased and thanked President Roosevelt for his support for a democratic China. However, when Hurley presented the agreement to Chiang Kai-shek, Chiang refused to sign and called for the CCP army to be under Nationalist control. Mao was infuriated by the counterproposal and refused to sign. Hurley's mediation failed, and China lost its chance to have a two-party system for its government.

8. Some Western scholars hold the view that Mao had sent friendly gestures and had expanded his desire to be recognized by the United States but was ignored and rejected by the U.S. government, which lost the opportunity to form a working relationship with the CCP and planted the seed for a deteriorating Sino-American relationship with Mao's regime in the 1950s and 1960s.

9. Mao made this remark in his interview with the U.S. journalist Anna Louise Strong in August 1946.

10. "Paper tiger" (纸老虎) is a literal translation of an ancient Chinese saying whose origin is not clear. It has been used in classical writings as well as in the writings by other Communist leaders (e.g., Cai Heseng, Yun Daiying, Deng Zhongxia) before Mao used it. The metaphor refers to something that appears to be threatening, like a real tiger, but is actually weak and easily defeated as it is made of paper.

11. This political action is known as the "lean-to-one-side" policy in that a CCP-led China would lean to the side of the Soviet Union and the socialist countries against Western capitalism and imperialism. Mao signed a Sino-Soviet alliance in 1950. For the background and consequences of this policy, see Shen and Li 2011.

12. After China was defeated in the Boxer Rebellion, a peasant uprising to drive foreigners out of China in 1900, the Qing Empire had to pay an indemnity in fine silver to the eight nations involved, including the United States. Under President Theodore Roosevelt's administration, the United States used the indemnity to set up the Boxer Indemnity Scholarship Program for Chinese students to study in the United States. From 1909 to 1929 about thirteen hundred Chinese students received these scholarships. Many of them became prominent scholars and leaders who were pioneers in China's modernization.

13. In 1948 Korea was divided into North Korea, a Communist state aligned with China and the Soviet Union, and South Korea, which was supported by the U.S. government. When North Korea crossed the border to invade South Korea, the United States sent its troops to Korea along with the United Nations allied forces. When the U.S. force fought its way close to the Yalu River, on the Korea-China border, China was threatened, so Mao sent the Chinese voluntary army to war in support of North Korea. The war ended with a permanent division between the two Koreas.

14. Mao issued a political report on April 28, 1969, denouncing the U.S. occupation of Taiwan and America's invasion of other countries and calling for the Chinese people to prepare themselves for a U.S. invasion. In fact, since 1949 Mao had been paranoid about a U.S. invasion, especially fearing that America would use nuclear bombs against China. In the 1960s the Chinese people were on the alert, digging air-raid shelters and participating in air-raid drills.

15. After Richard Nixon was elected president of the United States in 1968, he ordered the bombing of Cambodia because he believed that country would help Vietnam Communists fight the war with the United States. The fierce bombing campaigns swept through the Cambodian countryside until 1973. The scale of this bombing was unprecedented. See Kiernan 1989.

16. On April 4, 1971, a U.S. Ping-Pong team player at a tournament in Japan made a mistake and boarded a bus carrying the Chinese Ping-Pong team. The two teams ended up exchanging gifts, and the U.S. team expressed interest in visiting China. Their message reached Mao, who decided to invite the U.S. Ping-Pong team to visit China. Both U.S. leaders and Chinese officials were surprised by Mao's decision. On April 10, 1971, the U.S. Ping-Pong team visited China, miraculously changing U.S.-China travel policies, a change that has remained in place since that time.

17. Moreover, Nixon's commitment to peace resonated with the strong desire for peace among the U.S. public, which was weary from the Vietnam War. Another appeal

that Nixon employed was his rhetoric of change in international relations. In his foreign policy report of February 1971, Nixon stated, "The world has changed. Our foreign policy must change with it. We are prepared to establish a dialogue with Peking" (Bostdorff 2002, 44). The American people's acceptance of Nixon's visit to China also was bolstered by Nixon's unassailable reputation as an anti-Communist crusader, a position that helped shield him from suspicions that he was yielding to a Communist state.

18. "Turtle egg," a cursing phrase in the Chinese language, refers to someone who has no morals and who commits evil acts.

19. Xiao Duojie (2011) wrote about a number of political cases in which Mao manipulated between yin and yang in that he said one thing but acted in an opposite way or in his private rhetoric contradicted his public rhetoric.

20. These principles were enunciated in the preamble to the Agreement on Trade and Intercourse between the Tibet Region of China and India, which was signed in Peking on April 29, 1954.

21. Mao demanded that the U.S. military withdraw from Taiwan and that the United States recognize only one China, the PRC.

22. On October 4, 1957, the Soviet Union successfully launched Sputnik 1, the world's first artificial satellite. On November 3, 1957, Sputnik 2, or Prosteyshiy, was the second spacecraft launched into orbit. The two satellite launches surprised the world, demonstrating Soviet advancement in science and technology and initiating the space age. "They" in this context refers to the United States and its Western allies.

23. No specific names for the publication of the conversation are given in the original source.

24. Robert F. Williams was an American civil rights leader and author. Facing criminal charges and threats to his life by a lynch mob in the United States, he and his wife first exiled to Cuba and then went to China. He stayed in China from 1965 to 1969 for political asylum. Bloom and Martin (2013) wrote, "Mao was deeply impressed with Williams and saw common cause in the struggle for black liberation in the United States and the global struggle against imperialism" (33).

25. Mao was often referenced by radical African American civil rights leaders such as Malcolm X, Huey Newton, and Robert Williams. His *Little Red Book* was used as a source of inspiration for the Black Panther Party. For more information on how Mao influenced African American political leaders and the civil rights movement, see Rhodes 2007.

26. Mao wrote a letter to his wife Jiang Qing in July 1966 saying that he was disappointed to see that "only a few parties in the world, among over a hundred parties, believed in Marxism and Leninism. Marx and Lenin have been torn down. What will happen to us?" (Mao 1966/1998a, 72). This remark revealed Mao's fear for his own fate living in a world operating on a different ideology from Marxism and also his sense of isolation and disillusion regarding world communism.

27. Two million Cambodians were killed by the Khmer Rouge (also known as Angkar) government at sites known as the Killing Fields.

28. Maoism had also influenced Europe and the developed world on a different scale; see Alexander 2001.

Conclusion: Mao Zedong's Rhetorical Legacy Lives On

1. China's GDP growth rate was 10.7 percent in 1966 when Mao launched the Cultural Revolution, and the GDP rate became -1.6 percent in 1976 when he, along with the political movement, died. See http://www.chinability.com/GDP.htm (accessed July 14, 2014).

2. The U.S. government refused to recognize the legitimacy of the People's Republic of China and imposed political isolation and economic sanctions against China in the 1950s and 1960s.

3. The CCP's assessment of Mao was issued in "The Resolution of the Sixth Plenum of the 11th Central Committee of the Communist Party of China" in June 1981. The document acknowledged that Mao made serious mistakes when launching the Cultural Revolution and criticized his policies as inappropriate for China's realities and development. In it Mao was hailed as "a great Marxist and a great proletarian revolutionary, a stunning strategist and theorist.... His contributions to the Chinese revolution far outweigh his mistakes. His merits are primary and his errors secondary." The English version of the document can be found in *Beijing Review* 27, no. 6 (July 1981).

4. The Soviet Union demanded to increase its own military defense by placing equipment for surveillance of shared coastal lines in China's territory. Mao refused. Further ideological rifts intensified the conflict between the two Communist countries. In 1960 the Soviet Union cut all economic aid to China and broke off its relationship with China as a Communist ally.

5. Hua Guofeng was appointed by Mao as the chairman of the CCP before his death. Hua was the top leader in China for two years and then was forced to step down by Deng Xiaoping's liberal clan. Soon after the Third Plenum of the Chinese Communist Party in 1978, China ended the system of lifelong tenure for the top leadership office. Now the top leadership changes every ten years.

6. Deng Xiaoping was brought down by Mao during the early stage of the Cultural Revolution and was accused of being the number two capitalist running dog after Liu Shaoqi, Mao's appointed successor before the Cultural Revolution. Deng was known for his saying "No one cares if a cat is white or black as long as it can catch mice," implying that the ideological path that China took to repair the economy did not matter as long as the economy grew.

7. The "princelings," also translated as the Crown Prince Party, were the sons and daughters of high-ranking Chinese Communist officials. The term was derogatory as princelings received benefits and privileges earned not by their own merits but by the connections and influence of their parents. Many princelings held influential positions in business and government.

8. See further discussion on this point in Wang and Zheng 2003.

9. Xi's speeches were possibly penned by his secretaries or ghost speech writers, as it is suspected was the case for some of Mao's writings. But it is more likely that the main ideas and style of these speeches were Xi's own choices. Also see Agence France Presse, "China Marks Mao's Birth with Noodles and Songs," http://www.myrepublica .com/portal/index.php?action=news_details&news_id=66862 (accessed July 30, 2015).

10. Perry Link (2013) coined the term to refer to Chinese official and political discourse that has been moralized and become formulaic jargon.

11. The Three-anti Campaign was launched in 1951 and was aimed at anticorruption, antiwaste, and antibureaucracy. The Five-anti Campaign followed in 1952 and targeted antibribery, antitheft of state property, anti–tax evasion, anticheating on government contracts, and antistealing of state economic information. The campaigns appeared to address moral and economic issues but were directed toward wealthy capitalists and political dissidents.

12. Since Xi took office, a large number of "tigers" (provincial and central-level party officials) have been charged with various kinds of crimes along with Bo Xilai (a former member of the Political Bureau of the Central Committee of the CCP and secretary of the CCP, Chongqi branch) and Zhou Yongkang (a former member of the Politburo Standing Committee of the CCP and secretary of the Central Political and Legislative Committee), who stood at the top of the list. See Badkar 2014.

13. Cellia Hatton from BBC News, "Can Xi Jinping's Mao-Style Clean-up Campaign Revive Public Trust?," http://www.bbc.com/news/world-asia-china-24296365 (accessed August 15, 2015).

14. Li Zicheng (1606–45) rebelled against and finally overthrew the Ming dynasty in 1644. He established the Dashun dynasty in 1645 and became the emperor. However, his army was defeated after forty days, and he was killed in 1645. The cause of the defeat is still unclear. Rumor says that Li's death was due to the corruption of ministers. The dynasty's short-lived rule has become a history lesson for the succeeding rulers of China.

15. "Mass line" means serving the masses and relying on the masses. The term has constituted the CCP strategy to mobilize the masses for political and economic campaigns and movements. According to Ai 2015, 43, Mao borrowed this idea from Lenin.

16. Japan first borrowed Chinese characters and infused them into their own language in ancient times. Western-educated Japanese scholars translated Western texts into Chinese characters during the nineteenth and early twentieth centuries. Chinese scholars introduced and incorporated these characters with modern concepts, and the ideas trickled back into Chinese language. On this topic, see Howland 2002.

17. For the English translation of the speech, see http://www.scmp.com/news/china/policies-politics/article/1854943/full-text-xi-jinping-military-parade-speech-vows-china (accessed September 5, 2015).

18. Burke explains that the comic frame is a method that is "neither wholly euphemistic, nor wholly debunking—hence it provides the charitable attitude towards people that is required for purposes of persuasion and co-operation, but at the same time maintains our shrewdness concerning the simplicities of 'cashing in'" (Burke 1959, 166). The comic frame allows the critic to analyze how people cope with dilemmas and how to reconcile tensions within a given context. It presents a worldview that emphasizes fallibility and individuals' needs to be creative within the rigid system.

Bibliography

English Sources

Ai, Janette. 2015. *Politics and Traditional Cultures: The Political Use of Traditions in Contemporary China.* Hackensack, N.J.: World Scientific.

Alexander, J. Robert. 2001. *Maoism in the Developing World.* Westport, Conn.: Praeger.

An, Jiang. 2013. "Mao Zedong's 'Three Worlds' Theory: Political Considerations and Value for the Times." *Social Science in China* 34: 35–57.

Anderson, Benedict. 1991. *Imagined Communities: Reflection on the Origins and Spread of Nationalism.* London: Verso.

Apter, David E., and Tony Saich. 1994. *Revolutionary Discourse in Mao's Republic.* Cambridge, Mass.: Harvard University Press.

Arendt, Hannah. 1963. *Eichmann in Jerusalem: A Report on the Banality of Evil.* New York: Penguin Group.

Aristotle. 1941. "Metaphysics: Topics." In *The Basic Works of Aristotle,* edited by Richard McKeon, 689–934, 187–206. New York: Random House.

Aristotle. 1991. *Aristotle on Rhetoric: A Theory of Civic Discourse.* Translated by George Kennedy. New York: Oxford University Press.

Aune, James Arnt. 1999. "Cultures of Discourse: Marxism and Rhetorical Theory." In *Contemporary Rhetorical Theory: A Reader,* edited by John Louis Lucaites, Celeste Michelle Condit, and Sally Caudill, 539–51. New York: Guilford Press.

Avraham, Eli, and Anat First. 2003. "I Buy American: The American Image as Reflected in Israeli Advertising." *Journal of Communication* 53: 282–99.

Badkar, Mamta. 2014. "China's President Has Only Begun to Take Down the Tigers and Swat the Flies in His Historic Corruption Crackdown." http://www.businessinsider .com/chinas-corruption-crackdown-2014-7 (accessed August 15, 2015).

Bakhtin, Mikhail. 1973. *Marxism and Philosophy of Language.* Translated by Ladislav Matejka and I. R. Titunik. New York: Seminar Press.

Bandyopadhyaya, Jayantanuja. 1973. *Mao Tse-Tung and Gandhi: Perspectives on Social Transformation.* Bombay, India: Allied Publishers.

Bates, R. Benjamin. 2004. "Audiences, Metaphors, and the Persian Gulf War." *Communication Studies* 55: 447–63.

Beer, Francis A., and Robert Hariman. 1996. "Realism and Rhetoric in International Relations." In *Post-Realism: The Rhetorical Turn in International Relations,* ed. Francis A. Beer and Robert Hariman, 1–34. East Lansing: Michigan State University Press.

Bianco, Lucien. 1973. *Origins of the Chinese Revolution, 1915–1949.* Stanford, Calif.: Stanford University Press.

Billig, Michael. 1996. *Arguing and Thinking.* 2nd ed. Cambridge: Cambridge University Press.

Birth, Cyril. 1960. "Fiction of the Yenan Period." *China Quarterly* 4: 1–11.

Bitzer, Lloyd. 1968. "The Rhetorical Situation." *Philosophy and Rhetoric* 1 (Winter): 1–14.

Bizzell, Patricia, and Bruce Herzberg, eds. 1990. *The Rhetorical Tradition: Readings from Classical Times to the Present.* Boston: St. Martin's Press.

Bloom, Joshua, and Waldo E. Martin Jr. 2013. *Black against Empire: The History and Politics of the Black Panther Party.* Berkeley: University of California Press.

Bostdorff, Denise M. 2002. "The Evolution of a Diplomatic Surprise: Richard M. Nixon's Rhetoric on China, 1952–July 15, 1971." *Rhetoric & Public Affairs* 5: 31–56.

Burke, Kenneth. 1984. *Permanence and Change: An Anatomy of Purpose.* Berkeley: University of California Press.

Burke, Kenneth. 1959. *Attitudes toward History.* Berkeley: University of California Press.

Burke, Kenneth. 1966. *Language as Symbolic Action: Essays on Life, Literature, and Method.* Berkeley: University of California Press.

Burke, Kenneth. 1968. *Counter-Statement.* Berkeley: University of California Press.

Burke, Kenneth. 1969. *A Rhetoric of Motives.* Berkeley and Los Angeles: University of California Press.

Buruma, Ian. 2005. "Divine Killer." *New York Review of Books,* February 24, pp. 18–25.

Butterfield, Rya. 2012. "Rhetorical Forms of Symbolic Labor: The Evolution of Iconic Representations in China's Model Worker Awards." *Rhetoric & Public Affairs* 15: 95–126.

Cabestan, Jean-Pierre. 2005. "The Many Facets of Chinese Nationalism." *China Perspectives* 59. Translated from the original French by Michael Black. http://chinaperspectives.revues.org/2793 (accessed June 15, 2014).

Calhoun, Craig. 2007. "Nationalism and Culture of Democracy." *Public Culture* 19: 151–73.

Callahan, William. 2004. "National Insecurities: Humiliation, Salvation, and Chinese Nationalism." *Alternatives* 29: 199–218.

Chan, Wing-tsit. 1989. *Chu Hsi: New Studies.* Honolulu: University of Hawaii Press.

Chan, Wing-tsit. 2002. *Source Book in Chinese Philosophy.* Westport, Conn.: Greenwood.

Chang, Changfu. 2002. "The Problem of the Public: John Dewey's Theory of Communication and Its Influence on Modern Chinese Communication." In *Chinese Communication Studies: Contexts and Comparisons,* edited by Xing Lu, Wenshan Jia, and D. Ray Heisey, 47–64. Westport, Conn.: Ablex.

Chang, Hao. 1996. "The Intellectual Heritage of the Confucian Ideal of Ching-Shih [jingshi]." In *Confucian Traditions in East Asian Modernity: Moral Education and Economic Culture in Japan and the Four Mini-Dragons,* edited by Tu Wei-Ming, 72–91. Cambridge, Mass., and London: Harvard University Press.

Chang, Iris. 1997. *Rape of Nanking: The Forgotten Holocaust of World War II.* New York: Basic Books.

Chang, Jung, and Jon Halliday. 2005. *Mao: The Unknown Story.* New York: Knopf.

Cheek, Timothy. 2008. "The Multiple Maos of Contemporary China." *Harvard Asia Quarterly* 2, nos. 2–3 (Spring–Summer): 14–25.

Cheek, Timothy. 2010. "Mao: Revolution and Memory." In *A Critical Introduction to Mao,* edited by Timothy Cheek, 3–30. Cambridge: Cambridge University Press.

Cheek, Timothy, and Eugene Wu. 1989. *The Secret Speeches of Chairman Mao.* Cambridge, Mass.: Harvard University Press.

Chen, Jerome. 1965. *Mao and the Chinese Revolution.* London: Oxford University Press.

Chen, Jerome. 1969. *Mao.* Englewood Cliffs, N.J.: Prentice-Hall.

Choy, Philip, P. L. Dong Choy, and M. K. Hom. 1994. *The Coming Man.* Hong Kong: Joint Publishing.

Chu, Godwin C. 1977. *Radical Change through Communication in Mao's China.* Honolulu: University of Hawaii Press.

Cohen, Warren I. 2000. *America's Response to China: A History of Sino-American Relations.* 4th ed. New York: Columbia University Press.

Confucius. 1997. *The Analects of Confucius.* Translated by Simon Leys. New York: W. W. Norton.

Conquest, Robert. 1990. *The Great Terror: A Reassessment.* London: Hutchinson.

Cook, C. Alexander. 2010. "Third World Maoism." In *A Critical Introduction to Mao,* edited by Timothy Cheek, 288–312. New York: Cambridge University Press.

Crosswhite, James. 2013. *Deep Rhetoric: Philosophy, Reason, Violence, Justice, Wisdom.* Chicago and London: University of Chicago Press.

De Bary, William Theodore, and Irene Bloom, comps. 1999. *Sources of Chinese Tradition.* 2nd ed. Vol. 1. New York: Columbia University Press.

Depaul, Kim, and Dith Pran. 1997. *Children of Cambodia's Killing Fields: Memoires by Survivors.* New Haven, Conn.: Yale University Press.

Dewey, John. 1916. *Democracy and Education: An Introduction to the Philosophy of Education.* New York: Macmillan.

Dewey, John. 1973. *John Dewey: Lectures in China, 1919–1920.* Translated by R. Clopton and T. Ou. Honolulu: University of Hawaii Press.

Dewey, John. 1981 (1925). "Experience, Nature, and Art" In *John Dewey: The Later Works, 1925–1953,* vol. 1, edited by Jo Ann Boyston. 266–294. Carbondale: Southern Illinois University Press.

Dikotter, Frank. 2010. *Mao's Great Famine: The History of China's Most Devastating Catastrophe, 1958–62.* London: Bloomsbury.

Dufault-Hunter, Erin. 2012. *Transformative Power of Faith: A Narrative Approach to Conversion.* Lanham, Md.: Lexington Books.

Edwards, L. 2010. "Military Celebrity in China: The Evolution of 'Heroic and Model Servicemen.'" In *Celebrity in China,* edited by Elaine Jeffreys and Louise Edwards, 21–44. Hong Kong: Hong Kong University Press.

Esherick, W. Joseph. 1995. "Ten Theses on the Chinese Revolution." *Modern China* 21: 45–76.

Fairbank, John. 1972. "The New China and the American Connection." *Foreign Affairs* 51: 31–43.

Fairbank, John. 1976. "The Chinese Patters." In *Comparative Communism: The Soviet, Chinese, and Yugoslav Models,"* edited by Gary Bertsch and Thomas W. Ganschow, 55–64. San Francisco: W. H. Freeman.

Farrell, B. Thomas. 1993. *Norms of Rhetorical Culture.* New Haven, Conn.: Yale University Press.

Feigon, Lee. 2002. *Mao: A Reinterpretation.* Chicago: Ivan R. Dee.

Fitzgerald, John. 1995. "The Nationless State: The Search for a Nation in Modern Chinese Nationalism." *Australian Journal of Chinese Affairs* 33: 75–104.

Fogel, Joshuass. 1987. *AiSsi-chi's Contribution to the Development of Chinese Marxism.* Cambridge, Mass.: Harvard University Council on East Asian Studies.

Foss, K. Sonja, A. Karen Foss, and Robert Trapp. 1991. *Contemporary Perspectives on Rhetoric.* 2nd ed. Prospect Heights, Ill.: Waveland.

Foucault, Michel. 1991. *Discipline and Punish: The Birth of a Prison.* London: Penguin.

Foucault, Michel. 1998. *The History of Sexuality: The Will to Knowledge.* London: Penguin.

Frank, David. 2000. "The Mutability of Rhetoric: Haydar 'Abd al-Shafi's Madrid Speech and Vision of Palestinian-Israeli Rapprochement." *Quarterly Journal of Speech* 86: 334–53.

Frank, David. 2009. "The Prophetic Voice and the Face of the Other in Barack Obama's 'A More Perfect Union' Address." *Rhetoric and Public Affairs* 12: 167–94.

Frey, Lawrence R., Carl H. Botan, and Gary L. Kreps. 1991. *Investigating Communication: An Introduction to Research Methods.* Englewood Cliffs, N.J.: Prentice-Hall.

Friedman, Edward. 1993. "A Failed Chinese Modernity." *Daedalus:* Vol. 122, 1–17.

Friedman, Edward. 1994. "Democracy and 'Mao' Fever." *Journal of Contemporary China* 3: 84–95.

Friedman, Edward. 1995. *National Identity and Democratic Prospects in Socialist China.* Armonk, N.Y.: M. E. Sharp.

Friedman, Edward. 1997. "Chinese Nationalism, Taiwanese Autonomy and the Prospects of a Larger War." *Journal of Contemporary China* 6: 5–32.

Garrett, Mary. 1991. "Asian Challenges." In *Contemporary Perspectives on Rhetoric,* edited by Sonja Foss, Karen Foss, and Robert Trapp, 295–306. Prospect Heights, Ill.: Waveland.

Garrett, Mary. 1993. "Classical Chinese Conceptions of Argumentation and Persuasion." *Argumentation & Advocacy* 29: 105–15.

Gellner, Ernest. 1983. *Nations and Nationalism.* Ithaca, N.Y.: Cornell University Press.

Goh, Evelyn. 2005. *Constructing the U.S. Rapprochement with China, 1961–1974: From "Red Menace" to "Tacit Ally."* Cambridge: Cambridge University Press.

Goldhagen, J. Daniel. 2009. *Worse than War: Genocide, Eliminationism, and the Ongoing Assault on Humanity.* New York: Public Affairs.

Gries, Hays Peter. 2004. *China's New Nationalism: Pride, Politics and Diplomacy.* Berkeley: University of California Press.

Grossberg, Lawrence. 1979. "Marist Dialectics and Rhetorical Criticism." *Quarterly Journal of Speech* 65: 235–49.

Guo, Yingjie. 2004. *Cultural Nationalism in Contemporary China: The Search for National Identity under Reform.* London and New York: Routledge Curzon.

Guo, Xuezhi. 2002. *The Ideal Chinese Political Leader: An Historical and Cultural Perspective.* Westport, Conn.: Praeger.

Hall, Edward T. 1976. *Beyond Culture.* New York: Anchor Books.

Harding, Harry. 1992. *A Fragile Relationship: The United States and China since 1972.* Washington, D.C.: Brookings Institution.

Hartnett, Stephen J. 2011. "Google and the 'Twisted Cyber Spy' Affair: US Chinese Communication in an Age of Globalization." *Quarterly Journal of Speech* 97: 411–34.

Havel, Vaclav. 1986. *Living in Truth: Twenty-two Essays Published on the Occasion of the Award of the Erasmus Prize to Vaclav Havel.* Edited by Jan Vladislav. London: Faber and Faber.

Hegel, G. W. F. 1989. *Phenomenology of Spirit.* Translated by A. V. Miller. Atlantic Highlands, N.J.: Humanities Press International.

Hobsbawm, Eric. 1992. *Nations and Nationalism since 1780: Programme, Myth, and Reality.* Cambridge: Cambridge University Press.

Hong, Zhaohui. 1998. "The Role of Individuals in U.S.-China Relations, 1949–1972." In *Image, Perception, and the Making of U.S.-China Relations,* edited by Li Hongshan and Hong Zhaohui, 345–64. Lanham, Md.: University Press of America.

Hong, Zhaohui. 2015. *The Price of China's Economic Development: Power, Capital, and the Poverty of Rights.* Lexington: University Press of Kentucky.

Howland, Douglas. 2002. *Translating the West: Language and Political Reason in Nineteenth-Century Japan.* Honolulu: University of Hawaii Press.

Hu, Shi. 2000. "A Preliminary Discussion of Literary Reform" and "A National Speech of Literary Quality." In *Sources of Chinese Tradition.* 2nd ed. Vol. 2. Translated by Wing-Tsit Chan and compiled by William Theodore de Bary and Richard Lufrano, 357–60, 361–63. New York: Columbia University Press.

Hughes, E. Richard. 1968. *The Invasion of China by the Western World.* New York: Barnes & Noble.

Hughes, R. Christopher. 2005. "Interpreting Nationalist Texts: A Post-structuralist Approach." *Journal of Contemporary China* 14: 247–67.

Ip, Hung-Yok. 2010. "Mao, Mao Zedong Thought, and Communist Intellectuals." In *A Critical Introduction to Mao,* edited by Timothy Cheek, 169–95. New York: Cambridge University Press.

Jensen, Vernon. 1992. "Values and Practices in Asian Argumentation." *Argumentation & Advocacy* 28: 155–66.

Ji, Fengyuan. 2004. *Linguistic Engineering: Language and Politics in Mao's China.* Honolulu: University of Hawaii Press.

Johnson, Chalmers. 1962. *Peasant Nationalism and Communist Power: The Emergence of Revolutionary China.* Stanford, Calif.: Stanford University Press.

Kaplan, Robert B. 1966. "Cultural Thought Patterns in Intercultural Education." *Language Learning* 16: 1–20.

Karl, Rebecca. 2010. *Mao Zedong and China in the Twentieth-Century World: A Concise History.* Durham, N.C., and London: Duke University Press.

Karnow, Stanley. 1972. *Mao and China: From Revolution to Revolution.* New York: Viking.

Kau, Michael Y. M., and John Leung, eds. 1986. *The Writings of Mao Zedong, 1949–1976.* Armonk, N.Y.: M. E. Sharpe.

Kayam, Orly. 2014. "Transformative Rhetoric: How Obama Became the New Face of America, a Linguistic Analysis." *Journal of Language and Cultural Education* (online journal) 2: 233–50.

Kelley, Robin D. G., and Betsy Esch. 1999. "Black China and Black Revolution." *Souls* (Fall): 6–41.

Kennedy, A. George. 1980. *Classical Rhetoric and Its Christian and Secular Tradition from Ancient to Modern Times.* Chapel Hill: University of North Carolina Press.

Kennedy, A. George. 1991. *Translator's Introduction to Aristotle on Rhetoric: A Theory of Civic Discourse.* Oxford: Oxford University Press.

Kiernan, Ben. 1989. "The US Bombardment of Cambodia, 1969–1973." *Vietnam Generation* 1 (Winter): 4–41.

Kincaid, D. Lawrence. 1987. "Communication East and West: Points of Departure." In *Communication Theory: Eastern and Western Perspectives,* edited by D. Lawrence Kincaid, 331–40. San Diego, Calif.: Academic Press.

King, Peter. 2004. *One Hundred Philosopher: The Life and Work of the World's Greatest Thinkers,* NY: Barron's Educational Series.

Kirkpatrick, Andrew. 2002. "Chinese Rhetoric through Chinese Textbooks: Uniquely Chinese?" In *Chinese Communication Studies: Contexts and Comparisons,* edited by Xing Lu, Wenshan Jia, and D. Ray Heisey, 245–60. Westport, Conn.: Ablex.

Kirkpatrick, Andrew. 2005. "China's First Systematic Account of Rhetoric: An Introduction to Chen Kui's *Wen Ze.*" *Rhetorica: A Journal of the History of Rhetoric* 23: 103–52.

Kirkpatrick, Andrew. 2012. "Yin and Yang Rhetoric and the Impossibility of Constructive Dissent in China." *African Yearbook of Rhetoric* 3: 37–48.

Kissinger, Henry. 2011. *On China.* New York: Penguin.

Kluver, A. Randy. 1996. *Legitimating the Chinese Economic Reform: A Rhetoric of Myth and Orthodoxy.* Albany: State University of New York Press.

Knight, Nick. 1983. "The Form of Mao Zedong's 'Sinificant of Marxism.'" *Australian Journal of Chinese Affairs* 9 (January): 17–33.

Knight, Nick. 1990. "Introduction: Soviet Marxism and the Development of Mao Zedong's Philosophical Thought." In *Mao Zedong on Dialectical Materialism,* edited by Nick Knight, 3–83. Armonk, N.Y.: M. E. Sharpe.

Knight, Nick. 2005. *Marxist Philosophy in China: From Qu Qiubai to Mao Zedong, 1923–1945.* Dordrecht: Springer.

Lakoff, George, and Mark Johnson. 1980. *Metaphors We Live By.* Chicago and London: University of Chicago Press.

Laozi. 1982. *Dao De Jing.* Translated by D. C. Lau. Hong Kong: Chinese University Press.

Lee, G. Robert. 1999. *Orientals: Asian Americans in Popular Culture.* Philadelphia: Temple University Press.

Leese, Daniel. 2011. *Mao Cult: Rhetoric and Ritual in China's Cultural Revolution.* Cambridge: Cambridge University Press.

Levenson, Joseph. 1959. *Liang Ch'i-ch'ao and the Mind of Modern China.* Cambridge, Mass.: Harvard University Press.

Li, Shuang. 1970–72. Personal diaries.

Li, Zhisui. 1994. *The Private Life of Chairman Mao.* Translated by Hung-Chao Tai. New York: Random House.

Lifton, Robert J. 1957. "Brainwashing in Perspective." *New Republic,* May 13, 21–25.

Lin, Yutang. 1962. *My Country and My People.* London: Heinemann.

Link, Perry. 2013. *An Anatomy of Chinese: Rhythm, Metaphor, Politics.* Cambridge, Mass.: Harvard University Press.

Liu, Yawei. 1998. "Mao Zedong and the United States: A Story of Misperceptions, 1960–1970." In *Image, Perception, and the Making of U.S.-China Relations*, edited by Li Hongshan and Hong Zhaohui, 189–232. Lanham, Md.: University Press of America.

Lu, Xing. 1998. *Rhetoric in Ancient China: Fifth to Third Century B.C.E.* Columbia: University of South Carolina Press.

Lu, Xing. 1999. "A Rhetoric of Nationalism and Anti-Americanism in China Can Say No." *Intercultural Communication Studies* 53: 163–76.

Lu, Xing. 2004a. "The Red Sun Shines Again: Resurrection of Mao's Legacy in China." Paper presented at the 90th National Communication Association Annual Convention, Chicago, November 11–14.

Lu, Xing. 2004b. *Rhetoric of the Chinese Cultural Revolution: The Impact on Chinese Thought, Culture, and Communication.* Columbia: University of South Carolina Press.

Lu, Xing. 2012. "A Burkean Analysis of China Is Not Happy: A Rhetoric of Nationalism." *Chinese Journal of Communication* 5: 194–209.

Lu, Xing. 2015. "Comparative Rhetoric: Contemplating on Tasks and Methodologies in the Twenty-First Century." *Rhetoric Review* 34: 266–73.

Lu, Xing, and Herbert W. Simons. 2006. "Transitional Rhetoric of Chinese Communist Party Leaders in the Post-Mao Reform Period: Dilemmas and Strategies." *Quarterly Journal of Speech* 92: 262–86.

Lucaites, John Louis, Celeste Michelle Condit, and Sally Caudill, eds. 1999. *Contemporary Rhetorical Theory: A Reader.* New York: Guilford Press.

Lynch, Michael. 2004. *Mao.* London: Routledge.

MacFarquhar, Roderick. 1974. *The Hundred Flowers Campaign and the Chinese Intellectuals.* New York: Octagon Books.

MacFarquhar, Roderick. 2010. "Perspective 2: Mao Zedong." In *A Critical Introduction to Mao,* edited by Timothy Cheek, 332–52. Cambridge: Cambridge University Press.

Mao, Luming. 2003. "Reflective Encounters: Illustrating Comparative Rhetoric." *Style* 37 (Winter): 401–25.

Mao, Zedong. 1967a. *Selected Works of Mao Tse-Tung.* Vol. 1. Beijing: Foreign Language Press.

Mao, Zedong. 1967b. *Selected Works of Mao Tse-Tung.* Vol. 2. Beijing: Foreign Language Press.

Mao, Zedong. 1967c. *Selected Works of Mao Tse-Tung.* Vol. 3. Beijing: Foreign Language Press.

Mao, Zedong. 1967d. *Selected Works of Mao Tse-Tung.* Vol. 4. Beijing: Foreign Language Press.

Mao, Zedong. 1976. *Mao Tse-Tung Poems.* Beijing: Shangwu yinshu guan chubanche.

Mao, Zedong. 1977. *Selected Works of Mao Tse-Tung.* Vol. 5. Beijing: Foreign Language Press.

Margolin, Jean-Louis. 1999. "China: A Long March into Night." In *The Black Book of Communism: Crimes, Terror, Repression,* edited by Stéphane Courtois and translated by Jonathan Murphy and Mark Kramer, 463–547. Cambridge, Mass.: Harvard University Press.

Marx, Karl. 1906. *Capital: A Critique of Political Economy.* Edited by Friedrich Engels. New York: Modern Library.

Marx, Karl. 2013 (1848). *The Communist Manifesto.* Edited by Frederic L. Bender. 2nd ed. New York: W. W. Norton.

Marx, Karl, and Friedrich Engels. 1972. *The German Ideology.* Edited by C. J. Arthur. New York: International Publishers.

Marx, Karl, and Friedrich Engels. 1998 (1948). *The Communist Manifesto.* Introduction by Martin Malia. New York: Penguin Group.

McDonald, Di. 2005. *Revolution: China, a Student Handbook.* Collingwood, Victoria: History Teachers Association of Victoria.

McGee, Michael. 1980. "The Ideograph: A Link between Rhetorical and Ideology." *Quarterly Journal of Speech* 66 (February): 1–16.

McGee, Michael Calvin. 1999. "Text, Context, and the Fragmentation of Contemporary Culture." In *Contemporary Rhetorical Theory: A Reader,* edited by John Louis Lucaites, Celeste Michelle Condit, and Sally Caudill, 65–78. New York and London: Guilford Press.

McPhail, Mark L. 1996. *Zen in the Art of Rhetoric: An Inquiry into Coherence.* Albany: State University of New York Press.

Meisner, Maurice. 1977. *Mao's China: A History of the People's Republic.* London: Collier Macmillan.

Meisner, Maurice. 1982. *Marxism, Maoism, and Utopianism: Eight Essays.* Madison: University of Wisconsin Press.

Meisner, Maurice. 1989. "The Deradicalization of Chinese Socialism." In *Marxism and the Chinese Experience: Issues in Contemporary Chinese Socialism,* edited by Afir Dirlik and Maurice Meisner, 341–61. Armonk, N.Y.: M. E. Sharp.

Melvin, Sheila. 2012. "Commemorating Mao's Yan'an Talks." The Great Flurishing, Arts-journal Blog. http://www.artsjournal.com/china/2012/05/commemorating-maos-yanan-talks (accessed November 7, 2013).

Michael, Franz. 1977. *Mao Tse-Tung & the Perpetual Revolution: An Illuminating Study of Mao Tse-Tung's Role in China and World Communism.* Hauppauge, N.Y.: Barrons Educational Series.

Milosz, Czeslaw. 1953. *The Captive Mind.* New York: Knopf.

Mosher, S. 1990. *China Misperceived: American Illusions and Chinese Reality.* New York: Basic Books.

Moskalev, Alexei. 2003. "Doctrine of the Chinese Nation." *Far Eastern Affairs* 31: 64–82.

Mueller, Gustav E. 1958. "The Hegel Legend of Thesis-Antithesis-Synthesis." *Journal of the History of Ideas* 19: 411–14.

Mueller, Ralph. 2010. "Critical Metaphors of Creative Metaphors in Political Speeches." In *Researching and Applying Metaphor in the Real World,* edited by Graham Low, Alice Deignan, Lynne Cameron, and Zazie Todd, 321–32. Amsterdam: John Benjamins.

Munro, Donald J. 1977. *The Concept of Man in Contemporary China.* Ann Arbor: University of Michigan Press.

Nakamura, Hajime. 1964. *Ways of Thinking of Eastern Peoples.* Honolulu: University of Hawaii Press.

Nathan, Andrew. 2005. "Jade and Plastic." *London Review of Books* 27, no. 22: 17.

Nixon, R. 1971. Televised speech to the nation. http://blog.nixonfoundation.org/2010/07/7-15-71-rn-accepts-invitation-to-china (accessed May 5, 2014).

Nixon, Richard. 1978. *The Memoirs of Richard Nixon.* New York: Crosset & Dunlap.

Northrop, Filmer S. C. 1944. "The Complementary Emphases of Eastern Intuitive and Western Scientific Philosophy." In *Philosophy East and West,* edited by Charles A. Moore, 168–234. Princeton, N.J.: Princeton University Press.

Oliver, Robert. 1971. *Communication and Culture in Ancient India and China.* Syracuse, N.Y.: Syracuse University Press.

Orwell, George. 1950. *Nineteen Eighty-Four.* New York: Signet Classic.

Paloczi-Horvath, George. 1962. *Mao Tse-Tung: Emperor of the Blue Ants.* London: Secker & Warburg.

Pantsov, Alexander, and Steven Levine. 2012. *Mao: The Real Story.* New York: Simon and Schuster.

Payne, Robert. 1950. *Mao Tse-Tung, Ruler of Red China.* New York: Henry Schuman.

Perelman, Chaim, and Lucy Olbrechts-Tyteca. 1969 (1958). *The New Rhetoric: A Treatise on Argumentation.* Translated by John Wilkinson and Purcell Weaver. Notre Dame, Ind.: University of Notre Dame Press.

Perlmutter, David. 2007. *Picturing China in the American Press: The Visual Portrayal of Sino-American Relations in Time Magazine, 1949–1973.* Lanham, Md.: Lexington Books.

Plato. 1977. *Phaedrus and Letters VII and VIII.* Translated by Walter Hamilton. London: Penguin Books.

Plato. 1981. *The Republic of Plato.* Translated by Francis Macdonald Cornford. London: Oxford University Press.

Powell, Gerald A. 2004. *A Rhetoric of Symbolic Identity: An Analysis of Spike Lee's X and Bamboozled.* Whitewater: University of Wisconsin-Whitewater Press.

Pye, Lucian. 1968. *The Spirit of Chinese Politics: A Psychocultural Study of the Authority Crisis in Political Development.* Cambridge, Mass.: MIT Press.

Raphals, Lisa. 1992. *Knowing Words: Wisdom and Cunning in the Classical Traditions of China and Greece.* Ithaca, N.Y., and London: Cornell University Press.

Rhodes, Jane. 2007. *Framing the Black Panthers: The Spectacular Rise of a Black Power Icon.* New York and London: New Press.

Rintz, W. A. 2010. "The Failure of the China White Paper." *Constructing the Past* 11, issue 1, article 8.

Rowland, Robert C., and David Frank. 2002. *Shared/Conflicting Land Identity: Trajectories of Israeli Palestinian Symbol Use.* East Lansing: Michigan State University Press.

Schell, Orville. 1977. *In the People's Republic: An American's First View of Living and Working in China.* New York: Random House.

Schell, Orville, and John Delury. 2013. *Wealth and Power: China's Long March to the Twenty-first Century.* New York: Random House.

Schram, Stuart. 1983. *Mao Zedong: A Preliminary Reassessment.* Hong Kong: Chinese University Press.

Schram, Stuart. 1984. "Mao Studies Retrospect and Prospect." *China Quarterly* 97: 95–125.

Schram, Stuart. 1989. *The Thought of Mao Tse-Tung.* Cambridge, Mass.: Cambridge University Press.

Schram, Stuart. 2007. "Book Review of Mao: The Unknown Story." *China Quarterly* 189: 207–208.

Schram, Stuart, ed. 1975. *Chairman Mao Talks to the People: Talks and Letters, 1956–1971.* Translated by John Chinnery and Tieyun. New York: Pantheon Books.

Schram, Stuart, ed. 1992. *Mao's Road to Power: Revolutionary Writings 1912–1949.* Vol. 1. New York: M. E. Sharpe.

Schrift, Melissa. 2001. *Biography of a Chairman Mao Badge: The Creation and Mass Consumption of a Personality Cult.* New Brunswick, N.J.: Rutgers University Press.

Schoenhals, Michael. 1992. *Doing Things with Words in Chinese Politics.* Berkeley: Center for Chinese Studies, University of California.

Schurmann, Franz, and Orville Schell, eds. 1967. *Communist China.* London: Penguin Books.

Schwartz, Benjamin. 1951. *Chinese Communism and the Rise of Mao.* Cambridge, Mass.: Harvard University Press.

Schwartz, Benjamin. 1960. "The Legend of the 'Legend of Maoism.'" *China Quarterly* 2: 35–42.

Schwartz, Benjamin. 1964. *In Search of Wealth and Power: Yan Fu and the West.* Cambridge: Oxford University Press.

Selden, Mark. 1971. *The Yenan Way in Revolutionary China.* Cambridge, Mass.: Harvard University Press.

Shen, Zhihua, and Danhui Li. 2011. *After Leaning to One Side: China and Its Allies in the Cold War.* Washington, D.C.: Woodrow Wilson Center Press.

Sheng, M. Michael. 1998. "Mao's Ideology, Personality, and the CCP's Foreign Relations." In *Image, Perception, and the Making of U.S.-China Relations,* edited by Li Hongshan and Hong Zhaohui, 169–88. Lanham, Md.: University Press of America.

Short, Philip. 1999. *Mao: A Life.* New York: A John Macrae/Owl Book.

Siao-Yu. 1959. *Mao Tse-Tung and I Were Beggars.* New York: Syracuse University Press.

Smith, H. Arthur. 1894. *Chinese Characteristics.* New York: Fleming H. Revell.

Snow, Edgar. 1938. *Red Star over China.* New York: Grove.

Spence, Jonathan. 1999. *Mao Zedong: A Penguin Life.* New York: A Lipper/Viking Book.

Stuckey, Mary. 2013. *The Good Neighbor: Franklin D. Roosevelt and the Rhetoric of American Power.* East Lansing: Michigan State University Press.

Tang, Xiaobing. 1996. *Global Space and the Nationalist Discourse of Modernity: The Historical Thinking of Liang Qichao.* Stanford, Calif.: Stanford University Press.

Tang, Zongli, and Bing Zuo. 1996. *Maoism and Chinese Culture.* New York: Nova Science.

Terrill, Ross. 1980. *A Biography of Mao.* New York: Harper & Row.

Townsend, James. 1996. "Chinese Nationalism." In *Chinese Nationalism,* edited by Jonathan Unger, 1–30. Armonk, N.Y.: M. E. Sharpe.

Vladimirov, Peter. 1975. *The Vladimirov Diaries: Yenan, China, 1942–1945.* Garden City, N.Y.: Doubleday.

Wakeman, Frederic. 1973. *History and Will: Philosophical Perspective of Mao Tse-Tung's Thought.* Berkeley: University of California Press.

Walder, Andrew G. 2015. *China under Mao: A Revolution Derailed.* Cambridge, Mass.: Harvard University Press.

Wander, Philip. 1997. "The Rhetoric of American Foreign Policy." In *Cold War Rhetoric: Strategy, Metaphor, and Ideology,* edited by M. J. Medhurst, R. L. Ivie, P. Wander, and R. Scott, 153–84. East Lansing: Michigan State University Press.

Wang, Ban. 1997. *The Sublime Figure of History: Aesthetics and Politics in Twentieth-Century China*. Stanford, Calif.: Stanford University Press.

Wang, Gungwu, and Yongnian Zheng. 2003. "Embracing the Capitalists: The Chinese Communist Party to Brace Itself for Far-Reaching Changes." In *Damage Control: The Chinese Communist Party in the Jiang Zemin Era*, edited by Wang Gungwu and Yongnian Zheng, 365–76. London: Eastern Universities Press.

Wang, Minmin. 2000. "Mao Zedong's Talks at the Yenan Forum on Literature and Art." In *Chinese Perspectives in Rhetoric and Communication*, edited by D. Ray Heisey, 179–95. Stamford, Conn.: Ablex.

Wasserstrom, N. Jeffrey. 1996. "Mao Matters: A Review Essay." *China Review International* 3 (Spring): 1–21.

Watson, Martha. 2000. "Ordeal by Fire: The Transformative Rhetor of Abraham Lincoln." *Rhetoric & Public Affairs* 3: 33–49.

Williams, Robert. 1967. "The Great Conspirator's Conspiracy." *Crusader* 9 (July): 1.

Wittfogel, Karl. 1960. "The Legend of 'Maoism.'" *China Quarterly* 1: 16–34.

Womack, Brantly. 1982. *The Foundations of Mao Zedong's Political Thought, 1917–1935*. Honolulu: University of Hawaii Press.

Woodall, Pam. 2009. "The Dragon Still Roars." *Economist: The World in 2010*, November 13. http://www.economist.com/node/14742408 (accessed June 17, 2016).

Wu, Lengxi. 1996 (1995). "Inside Story of the Decision Making during the Shelling of Jinmen." In *The Cold War in Asia*, edited by Jian Chen and James Hershberg, 208–15. Washington, D.C.: Woodrow Wilson International Center for Scholars.

Xi, Jinping. 2012. "Remarks by Vice President Biden and Chinese Vice President Xi at the State Department Luncheon." http://www.whitehouse.gov/the-press-office/2012/02/14/remarks-vice-president-biden-and-chinese-vice-president-xi-state-departm (accessed July 10, 2014).

Xi, Jinping. 2013. Speech at the Opening Ceremony of the Boao Forum for Asia (English translation). http://english.boaoforum.org/mtzxxwzxen/7379.jhtml (accessed July 5, 2014).

Xiao, Yanzhong. 2010. "Recent Mao Zedong Scholarship in China." In *A Critical Introduction to Mao*, edited by Timothy Cheek, 273–87. Cambridge: Cambridge University Press.

Yang, Jisheng. 2008. *Tombstone: The Great Chinese Famine: 1958–1962*. Translated by Jian Guo. New York: Farrar, Straus and Giroux.

Yang, M. Michelle. 2011. "President Nixon's Speeches and Toasts during His 1972 Trip to China: A Study in Diplomatic Rhetoric." *Rhetoric & Public Affairs* 14: 1–44.

Young, John Wesley. 1991. *Totalitarian Language: Its Nazi and Communist Antecedents*. Charlottesville and London: University Press of Virginia.

Yu, Frederick T. C. 1972. "Communication and Politics." In *Communist China: A System-Functional Reader*, edited by Yung Wei, 275–82. Columbus, Ohio: Charles E. Merrill.

Yu, Ying-shih. 1993. "The Radicalization of China in the Twentieth Century." In *China in Transformation*, edited by Tu Wei-Ming, 125–50. Cambridge, Mass.: Harvard University Press.

Zhang, Mei. 2000a. "Official Role Models and Unofficial Responses: Problems of Model Emulation in Post-Mao China." In *Chinese Perspectives in Rhetoric and Communication*, edited by D. Ray Heisey, 67–86. Stamford, Conn.: Ablex.

Zhang, Mei. 2000b. "Raising the Social Status of Intellectuals and Prescribing Ideal Behavior for Chinese Citizens: Press Images of Model Intellectuals under Economic Reform." In *Beyond Public Speeches and Symbols: Explorations in the Rhetoric of Politicians and the Media*, edited by Christ'l De Landtsheer and Ofer Feldman, 147–64. Westport, Conn.: Praeger.

Zhang, Wenxian, comp. 1986. *Mao Zedong: Biography, Assessment, Reminiscence.* Beijing: Foreign Language Press.

Zhao, Suisheng. 1997. "Chinese Intellectuals' Quest for National Greatness and Nationalistic Writing in the 1990s." *China Quarterly* 152: 725–45.

Zhao, Suisheng. 2004. *A Nation-State by Construction: Dynamics of Modern Chinese Nationalism.* Stanford, Calif.: Stanford University Press.

Zheng, Yonnian. 1999. *Discovering Chinese Nationalism in China: Modernization, Identity, and International Relations.* Cambridge University Press.

Chinese Sources

Ba, Jin 巴金. 1987. *Sui xianglu* [随想录] (A Collection of Reflections). Beijing: Life, Reading & New Knowledge.

Cao, Changqing 曹长青. 1992. "Yuyan baoli" 语言暴力 (Language of Violence). http://caochangqing.com/gb/newsdisp.php?News_Idaho=530 (accessed October 30, 2013).

Chen, Changjiang 陈长江, Zhao Guilai 赵桂来. 1998. *Mao Zedong's zuihong shinian: Jiwei tuizhang de huiyi* [毛泽东最后十年：警卫队长的回忆] (A Memoir of Mao Zedong's Guard: The Last Ten Years). Beijing: Chinese Communist Party School Press.

Chen, Danqing 陈丹青. 2007. *Duoyu de sucai.* [多余的素材] (Residual Materials). Guangxi, China: Guangxi Normal University Press.

Chen, Duxiu 陈独秀. 1987. "Duiri waijiao de genben zuie" 对日外交的根本罪恶 (The Evil in the Foreign Relations with Japan). In *Duxiu wencun* [独秀文存] (Duqiu's Writings). Hefei People's Press.

Chen, Duxiu 陈独秀. 1993. "Wangguo pian" 亡国篇 (Destruction of Nation). In *Chen Duqiu zhuzuo qian* [陈独秀著作选] (Selected Works of Chen Duxiu). Shanghai: Shanghai People's Press.

Chen, Shiju 陈士榘. 1993. *Cong Jianggangshang dao zhongnanhai: Laojiangjun huiyi Mao Zedong* [从井冈山走进中南海：老将军回忆毛泽东] (From Jianggangshang to Zhongnanhai: A Memoir of an Old General). Beijing: Chinese Communist Party School Press.

Chen, Shuliang 陈书良. 2009. *Liang Qichao wenji* [梁启超文集] (The Collection of Liang Qichao). Beijing: Yanshan Press.

Chen, Wangdao 陈望道. 1932. *Xiucixue fafuan* [修辞学发凡] (Introduction to Rhetoric). Shanghai: Big River Books.

Confucius. 1992. *Lun Yu* [论语] (The Analects). Compiled by Gong Cheng Yi 勾承益 and Li Yadong 李亚东. Beijing: China Books.

Du, Lesi 杜勒斯 (John Foster Dulles). 1959. "Zai yige bianhua zhe de shijie zhong de yuanze he zhengce" 在一个变化着的世界中的原则和政策 (Principles and Policies in a Changing World). In *Du Lesi yanlun xuanji* [杜勒斯言论选辑] (Selected Speeches of Dulles). Beijing: World Knowledge Press.

Dai, Xiangqing, and Luo Huilan 戴向青、罗惠兰. 1994. *AB tuan yu futian shibian shimo* [AB 团与富田事变始末] (AB Regiment and Futian Uprising). Henan, China: Henan People's Press.

Deng, Xiaoping. 1981. Yu jinyong de tanhua 与金庸的谈话 (Talk with Jin Yong). http://theory.people.com.cn/GB/49150/49152/7542100.html (accessed May 23, 2014).

Deng, Xiaoping. 1993. *Deng Xiaoping wenxuan* [邓小平文选] (Selected Works of Deng Xiaoping). Beijing: People's Press.

Feng, Chenglue 冯成略. 2007. *Mao Zedong sixiang yu qiye guanli* [毛泽东思想与企业管理] (Mao Zedong's Thought and Corporate Management). Beijing: Zhongyang wenxian chubanche.

Feng, Youlan 冯友兰. 1994. *Feng Youlan qianji* [冯友兰选集] (Selected Writings of Feng Youlan). Compiled by Tu Youguang 涂又光. Tianjing, China: Tianjing People's Press.

Fu, Lei 傅雷. 1992. *Fu Lei jiashu* [傅雷家书] (Letters of Fu Lei). Beijing: Life, Reading, New Knowledge, and Three Alliance Books.

Fu, Sinian 傅斯年. 1919. "Zhongguo gou he zhonguoren" 中国狗和中国人 (Chinese Dogs and Chinese People). *Xin qingnian* [新青年] (New Youth). Vol. 6, 67.

Gao, Hua 高华. 2000. *Hongtaiyang shi zenyang shengqide: Yan'an zhengfeng de lailongqumai* [红太阳是怎样升起的：延安整风的来龙去脉] (How Does the Red Sun Rise: The Story of Yan'an's Rectification Movement). Hong Kong: Chinese University Press.

Gao, Hua 高华. 2004. *Shenfen he chayi: 1945–1965 nian zhongguo shehui de zhengzhi fenxi* [身份和差异：1945–1965 年中国社会的政治分析] (Status and Differences: Political Analysis of Chinese Society in 1945–1965). Hong Kong: Hong Kong Chinese University.

Gao, Hua 高华. 2010. *Geming niandai* [革命时代] (The Era of Revolution). Guangzhou, China: Guangdoing People's Press.

Gong, Yushi, Xianzh Pang, and Zhongquan Shi 龚育之, 逄先知, 石仲泉. 2009. *Mao Zedong de dushu shenghuo* [毛泽东的读书生活] (Mao Zedong's Life as a Reader). Beijing: Live, Reading, New Knowledge, and Three Alliance Press.

Guo, Jinrong 郭金荣. 2009. *Zuojin Maozedong zuihong suiyue* [走进毛泽东最后岁月] (The Last Days of Mao's Life). Beijing: Chinese Communist Party's History Press.

He, Xin 何新. 2004. *Lun wenhua da geming yu maozedong wanqi sixiang* [论文化大革命与毛泽东晚期思想] (On the Cultural Revolution and Mao Zedong Thought in His Late Years). http://wenku.baidu.com/view/63c7970090c69ec3d5bb757a.html (accessed June 17, 2013).

He, Yi 何以. 2010. *Mao Zedong's qingqu* [毛泽东的情趣] (Mao Zedong's Interest). Beijing: China Central Documents Press.

Ho, Zhihong 霍志宏. 2005. "Fenghuang shanglu: Youpeng zi yuanfang lai—Ji 1937 nian zhi 1938 nian Mao Zedong zai yan' an huijian zhongwai renshi" [凤凰山麓：有朋自远方来 1937 年至 1938 年毛泽东在延安会见中外人士] (Phoenix Mountain: Friends from Far Away—Records of Mao Zedong's Meeting with the Chinese and Foreigners in Yan'an from 1937 to 1938). *Zhonghua hun* [中华魂] (Chinese Soul) 12. http://www.globalview.cn/ReadNews.asp?NewsID=6481 (accessed October 15, 2013).

Hong, Bing 洪兵. 2010. *Mao Zedong zhanlue zhihui yu xiandaihua shanzhan* [毛泽东战略智慧与现代化商战] (Mao Zedong's Strategies and Wisdom in Modern Business War). Beijing: Chinese Academy of Social Science Press.

Hu, Jintao. 2002. "Zai xibanpo de jianghua" 在西半坡的讲话 (Speech at the Visit of Xibanpo). *People's Daily,* December 9, 1.

Hu, Jintao. 2003. "Zai zhongguo gongchandang jiandang 82 zhounian de jianghua" 在中国共产党建党 82 周年的讲话 (Speech at the 82nd Birthday of the Chinese Communist Party). *People's Daily,* July 2, 1.

Hu, Jintao. 2012. "Shibada zaijing kaimu Hu jingtao zuo baogao" 十八大在京开幕 胡锦涛作报告 (Hu Jintao's Speech at the 18th Party Congress). November 8. http://china.caixin.com/2012-11-08/100458021_all.html#page9 (accessed May 15, 2013).

Hu, Jintao. 2005. "Zai shengbuji zhuyao lingdao ganbu tigao goujian shehui zhuyi hejie zhehui nengli yantaoban shang de jianghua" 在省部级主要领导干部提高构建社会主义和谐社会能力专题研讨班上的讲话 (Speech at the Seminar on Improving the Ability of Provincial Leaders in Building a Socialist Harmonious Society). http://www.china.com.cn/chinese/news/899546.htm (accessed August 19, 2013).

Hu, Ping 胡平. 2007. *Rende qunhua, duobi yu fanpan* [人的驯化、躲避与反叛] (Slave the People, Avoidance and Rebellion). Hong Kong: Asian Science Press. Online version.

Hu, Shuzhong 胡曙中. 1993. *Yinghan xiuci bijiao yanjiu* [英汉修辞比较] (Contrastive Studies of Chinese and English Rhetoric). Shanghai: Shanghai Foreign Languages and Education Press.

Jiang, Zemin. 2001. "Jiang Zemin zai dang de shiliu da daibiao dahui shang de jianghua" 江泽民在党的十六大代表大会上的讲话 (Jiang Zemin's Speech at the 16th Party Congress). *People's Daily,* August 9, 1.

Jiang, Zemin. 2006. *Jiang Zemin wenxuan* 江泽民文选 (Selected Works of Jiang Zemin). vol. 3 Beijing: People's Press.

Lenin, L. Vladimir 列宁. 1984 (1897). "E-guo shehui minzhu zhuyizhe de renwu" 俄国社会民主主义者的任务 (The Task of Russian Socialist Democrats). In *Liening quanji* [列宁全集] (Complete Collection of Lenin), translated by Central Compilation and Translation Bureau, 2:426–49. Beijing: People's Press.

Lenin, L. Vladimir 列宁. 1985a (1919). "Guanyu yong ziyou pingdeng kouhao qipian renmin" 关于用自由平等口号欺骗人民出版序言 (On the Deception of People through the Slogans of Freedom and Equality). In *Liening quanji* [列宁全集] (Complete Collection of Lenin), translated by Central Compilation and Translation Bureau, 36:359–63. Beijing: People's Press.

Lenin, L. Vladimir 列宁. 1985b (1918). "Quan e zhongyang zhixing weiyuanhui huiyi" 全俄中央执行委员会会议 (The Meeting of Russian Central Executive Committee). In *Liening quanji* [列宁全集] (Complete Collection of Lenin), translated by Central Compilation and Translation Bureau, 34:223–56. Beijing: People's Press.

Lenin, L. Vladimir 列宁. 1985c (1918). "Wuchanjieji geming he pantu kaociji" 无产阶级革命和叛徒考茨基 (Proletarian Revolution and Traitor Kautsky). In *Liening quanji* [列宁全集] (Complete Collection of Lenin), translated by Central Compilation and Translation Bureau, 35:229–327. Beijing: People's Press.

Lenin, L. Vladimir 列宁. 1986a (1920). "Guanyu gongchan guoji dierci daibiao dahui de jiben renwu de tigang" 关于共产国际第二次代表大会的基本任务的提纲 (Proposal on the Basic Task of the Second Congress of the Comintern). In *Liening quanji* [列宁全集] (Complete Collection of Lenin), translated by Central Compilation and Translation Bureau, 39:179–91. Beijing: People's Press.

Lenin, L. Vladimir 列宁. 1986b (1919). "Wuchanjieji zhuanzheng shidai de jingji he zhengzhi" 无产阶级专政时代的经济和政治 (The Economy and Politics in the Era of Proletarian Dictatorship). In *Liening quanji* [列宁全集] (Complete Collection of Lenin), translated by Central Compilation and Translation Bureau, 37:263–77. Beijing: People's Press.

Li, Pengcheng 李鹏程. 1993. *Mao Zedong yu zhongguo wenhua* [毛泽东与中国文化] (Mao Zedong and Chinese Culture). Beijing: People's Press.

Li, Rui 李锐. 2005a. *Li Rui tan Mao Zedong* 李锐谈毛泽东 (Li Rui Talking about Mao Zedong). Hong Kong: Shidai guoji chuban youxian gongsi.

Li, Rui 李锐. 2005b. *Mao Zedong zaonian dushu shenghuo: Qia tongxue shaonian* [毛泽东早年读书生活: 恰同学少年] (Mao Zedong's Reading Life in His Early Years). Shenyang, China: Thousand Volumes.

Li, Zehou 李泽厚. 1986. *Zhongguo gudai sixiang shilun* [中国古代思想史论] (History of Chinese Ancient Thought). Beijing: People's Press.

Li, Zehou 李泽厚. 2008. *Zhongguo xiandai sixiang shi* [中国现代思想史] (Modern History of Thought in China). Beijing: Three Alliance Press.

Li, Zhisui 李志绥. 1994. *Mao Zedong siren yisheng huiyilu* [毛泽东私人医生回忆录] (The Private Life of Chairman Mao). Taipei: Shibao wenhua shubanshe.

Liang, Qichao 梁启超. 1935. *Yinbingshi wenji* [饮冰室合集] (Collected Essays from the Ice-driner's Studio). Vol. 1. Shanghai: Shanghai Wenhua Jinbushe.

Liang, Shuming 梁漱溟. 1987. *Zhongguo wenhua yaoyi* [中国文化要义] (The Essence of Chinese Culture). Hong Kong: Joint Publishing.

Liang, Xiaosheng 梁晓声. 1998. *Yige hongweibing de zibai* [一个红卫兵的自白] (Confession of a Red Guard). Xi'an, China: Shaaxi Tourism.

Link, Perry 林培瑞. 1999. *Ban yang suibi* [半洋随笔] (Notes across the Ocean). Taipei: Sanmin shuju.

Mao, Sheng 毛胜. 2011. "Mao Zedong ruhe pingjia Liang Qichao" 毛泽东如何评价梁启超 (How Mao Zedong Evaluates Liang Qichao). http://news.xinhuanet.com/theory/201107/27/c_121726946_3.htm (accessed January 15, 2013).

Mao, Xinyu 毛宇新. 2003. *Yeye Mao Zedong* [爷爷毛泽东] (Grandfather Mao Zedong). Beijing: National Defense University Press.

Mao, Zedong 毛泽东. 1977. *Mao Zedong xuanji* [毛泽东选集], 第五卷 (Selected Works of Mao Zedong). Vol. 5. Beijing: People's Press.

Mao, Zedong 毛泽东. 1995. *Mao Zedong zaoqi wengao* [毛泽东早期文稿] (Mao Zedong's Early Writings). Hunan, China: Documentaries of the Chinese Communist Party.

Mao, Zedong 毛泽东. 1991. *Mao Zedong xuanji* [毛泽东选集], (Selected Works of Mao Zedong). 2nd ed. Vol. 3. Beijing: People's Press.

Mao, Zedong 毛泽东. 1992a. "Zai Chengdu huiyi shang de jianghua tigang" 在成都会议上的讲话提纲 (The Synopsis of the Speech in Chengdu). In *Jianguo yilai Mao Zedong wengao* 建国以来毛泽东文稿 (Writings of Mao since 1949). Vol. 7, 108–20. Bejing. Central Documentation Press.

Mao, Zedong 毛泽东. 1992b. "Dui zhongguo bada zhengzhi baogao gao de piyu he xiugai" 对中共八大政治报告稿的批语和修改 (Remarks and Revision of the Political Report at the Eighth Chinese Communist Party Congress). In *Jianguo yilai Mao Zedong wengao* 建国以来毛泽东文稿 (Writings of Mao since 1949). Vol. 6, 136–64. Beijing: Central Documentation Press.

Mao, Zedong 毛泽东. 1992c. "Beijianzhe zui chongming, gaoguizhe zui yucun" 卑贱者最聪明，高贵者最愚蠢 (The Humble is the Most Intelligent, the Noble is the Most Stupid). In *Jianguo yilai Mao Zedong wengao* 建国以来毛泽东文稿 (Writings of Mao since 1949). Vol. 7, 236–38. Beijing: Central Documentation Press.

Mao, Zedong 毛泽东. 1992d. "Wei yinfa dulesi yanshuo congni" 为印发杜勒斯演说重拟 (Redraft in the publication of Dulles' Speech). In *Jianguo yilai Mao Zedong wengao* 建国以来毛泽东文稿 (Writings of Mao since 1949). Vol. 7, 606–07. Beijing: Central Documentation Press.

Mao, Zedong 毛泽东. 1992e. "Zai sulian zuigao suweiai qingzhu shiyue geming sishi zhounian huishang de jianghua" 在苏联最高苏维埃庆祝十月革命四十周年会上的讲话 (Speech at the 40th Anniversary Celebration of Soviet Union's October Revolution). In *Jianguo yilai Mao Zedong wengao* 建国以来毛泽东文稿 (Writings of Mao since 1949). Vol. 6, 615–24. Beijing: Central Documentation Press.

Mao, Zedong 毛泽东. 1996a. "Jiejian riben, guba, baxi, agenting fanghua daibiaotuan shide tanhua" 接见日本，古巴，巴西，阿根廷访华代表团时的谈话 (A Conversation at the Meeting with Delegation from Japan, Cuba, and Argentina during their Visit to China). In *Jianguo yilai Mao Zedong wengao* 建国以来毛泽东文稿 (Writings of Mao since 1949). Vol. 9, 187–89. Beijing: Central Documentation Press.

Mao, Zedong 毛泽东. 1996b. "Tong aerjiliya linshi zhengfu zongli abasi tanhua yaodian" 同阿尔及利亚临时政府总理阿巴斯谈话要点 (Main points in the Conversation with Primer Abbas of Temporary Government from Algeria). In *Jianguo yilai Mao Zedong wengao* 建国以来毛泽东文稿 (Writings of Mao since 1949). Vol. 9, 296–99. Beijing: Central Documentation Press.

Mao, Zedong 毛泽东. 1996c. "Tong yafei waibin de tanhua" 同亚非外宾的谈话 (A Conversation with Visitors from Asia and Africa). In *Jianguo yilai Mao Zedong wengao* 建国以来毛泽东文稿 (Writings of Mao since 1949). Vol. 9, 477–78. Beijing: Central Documentation Press.

Mao, Zedong 毛泽东. 1996d. "Zhichi meigou heiren fandui zongzhu qizhi douzheng de shengming" 支持美国黑人反对种族歧视斗争的声明 (Declaration in Support of American Blacks in their Fight against Racial Discrimination). In *Jianguo yilai Mao Zedong wengao* 建国以来毛泽东文稿 (Writings of Mao since 1949). Vol. 10, 355–38. Beijing: Central Documentation Press.

Mao, Zedong 毛泽东. 1996e. "Zhongguo renming jianjue zhichi banama renmin de aigouzengyi douzheng" 中国人民坚决支持巴拿马人民的爱国正义斗争 (Chinese People's Unwavering Support to the People of Panama in their Struggle of Patriotism). In *Jianguo yilai Mao Zedong wengao* 建国以来毛泽东文稿 (Writings of Mao since 1949). Vol. 11, 6–7. Beijing: Central Documentation Press.

Mao, Zedong 毛泽东. 1996f. "Zhonggou renmin zhichi riben renmin weida de aigou douzheng" 中国人民支持日本人民伟大的爱国斗争 (Chinese People Support Japanese People in Their Great Patriotic Fights). In *Jianguo yilai Mao Zedong wengao* 建国以来毛泽东文稿 (Writings of Mao since 1949). Vol. 11, 9–11. Beijing: Central Documentation Press.

Mao, Zedong 毛泽东. 1996g. "Guanyu zhichi gangguo renmin fangdui meiguo qinlue de shengming" 关于支持刚果人民反对美国侵略的声明 (On the Declaragion of Supporting People of Congo against American Invasion). In *Jianguo yilai Mao Zedong wengao* 建国以来毛泽东文稿 (Writings of Mao since 1949). Vol. 11, 247–48. Beijing: Central Documentation Press.

Mao, Zedong 毛泽东. 1996h. "Zhichi duominijia renmin fandui meiguo wuzhuan qinlue de shengming" 支持多米尼加人民反对美国武装侵略的声明 (Declaration of Supporting Dominican People's Opposition against American Armed Invasion). In *Jianguo yilai Mao Zedong wengao* 建国以来毛泽东文稿 (Writings of Mao since 1949). Vol. 11, 365–68. Beijing: Central Documentation Press.

Mao, Zedong 毛泽东. 1998a. "Gei jiangqing de xin" 给江青的信 (The Letter to Jiang Qing). In *Jianguo yilai Mao Zedong wengao* 建国以来毛泽东文稿 (Writings of Mao since 1949). Vol. 12, 71–75. Beijing: Central Documentation Press.

Mao, Zedong 毛泽东. 1970/1998b. "Quanshijie renmin tuanjie qilai, dabai meiguo qinluezhe jiqi yiqie zougou" 全世界人民团结起来，打败美国侵略者及其一切走狗 (United, the People of the World, Defeat American Invaders and all Their Running Dogs). In *Jianguo yilai Mao Zedong wengao* 建国以来毛泽东文稿 (Writings of Mao since 1949). Vol. 13, 96–98. Beijing: Central Documentation Press.

Mao, Zedong 毛泽东. 1998c. "Tong sudan zhengfu youhao daibaiotuan tuanzhang mahagubu tanhua jiyao" 同苏丹政府友好代表团团长马哈古卜谈话纪要 (Minutes of the Conversation with Mahgoup, the Head of Sudan Government Friendship Delegation). In *Jianguo yilai Mao Zedong wengao* 建国以来毛泽东文稿 (Writings of Mao since 1949). Vol. 13, 105–7. Beijing: Central Documentation Press.

Mao, Zedong 毛泽东. 1998d. "Huijian sinuo de tanhua jiyao" 会见斯诺的谈话纪要 (Minutes of the Conversation with Snow). In *Jianguo yilai Mao Zedong wengao* 建国以来毛泽东文稿 (Writings of Mao since 1949). Vol. 13, 163–81. Beijing: Central Documentation Press.

Mao, Zedong 毛泽东. 1998e. "Tong kawengda, bumaiding tanhua neirong de tongbao" 同卡翁达，布迈丁谈话内容的通报 (Release on the Conversation with Kaunda and Boumediene). Vol. In *Jianguo yilai Mao Zedong wengao* 建国以来毛泽东文稿 (Writings of Mao since 1949). Vol. 13, 379–82. Beijing: Central Documentation Press.

Mao, Zedong 毛泽东. 2012. *Yu waiguo shounao ji jizhe huitan lu* [毛泽东与外国首脑及记者会谈录] (Recordings of Mao Zedong's Conversations with Foreign Leaders and Correspondents). Beijing: Taihai.

Pang, Xianzhi 逄先知, and Jin Chongji 金冲及. 2003. *Mao Zedong Zhuang* [毛泽东传] (Biographies of Mao Zedong). Vols. 1 and 2. Beijing: Zhongyang wenxian chubanshe.

Qian, Liqun 钱理群. 2012. *Mao Zedong shidai he hou Mao Zedong shidai 1949–2009* [毛泽东时代和后毛泽东时代] (The Mao Zedong Era and Post-Mao Zedong Era, 1949–2009). Taiwan: Lianjing chuban shiye youxian gongsi.

Qian, Xuantong 钱玄同. 2010. "Lu yingyong zhiwen ji yi gailiang" 论应用之文亟宜改良 (On the Reform of Expository Writing). In *Qian Xuantong wenxian* [钱玄同文选] (Selected Works of Qian Xuantong), edited by Wenguang Lin 林文光. Chengdu, Sichuan, China: Sichuang chuban jituan. http://baike.baidu.com/view/3984695.htm (accessed September 10, 2013).

Quan, Yanchi 权延赤. 2001. *Zouxia shentan de Mao Zedong* 走下神坛的毛泽东 (Mao Zedong Walking Down from the Altar). Inner Mongolia, China: Inner Mongolian People's Press.

Shanghai Mao Zedong Thought and Practices Studies Committee 上海毛泽东思想理论与实践研究会. 1993. *Mao Zedong—Zou ziji de lu* [毛泽东－走自己的路] (Mao Zedong—Take Our Own Road). Shanghai: Shanghai Academy of Social Science Press.

Shen, Zhihua 沈志华. 2012. "Mao Zedong 1957 nian zhengfeng bingfei yinse chudong 毛泽东 1957 年整风并非引蛇出洞 (Mao Zedong's 1957 Rectification Campaign Is Not Pulling Snakes out of Caves). Wen Shi 文史 (Literature and History), January 2. http://epaper.qingdaonews.com/html/lnshb/20120102/lnshb361245.html (accessed October 5, 2013).

Sima, Qian 司马迁. 1993. *Shi ji* [史记] (Records of History). Edited by Teng Ren 腾人. Beijing: Beijing Broadcasting Institute Press.

Sun, Baoyi 宋宝义. 1993. *Mao Zedong dushu shengya* [毛泽东读书生涯] (The Reading Life of Mao Zedong). Taiwan: Guojicun wenku shudian.

Tao, Wenzhao 陶文钊, ed. 1999. *Zhongmei guanxi shi: 1949–1972* [中美关系史: 1949–1972] (History of China-U.S. Relations). Shanghai: People's Press.

Wang, Subai, and Sheheng Zhang 汪澍白, 张慎恒. 1983. *Mao Zedong zaoqi zhexue sixiang tanyuan* [毛泽东早期哲学思想探源] (Philosophical Thoughts of Mao Zedong in His Early Years). Beijing: China's Academy of Social Science Press.

Wu, Enpu 乌恩溥, ed. 1990. *Sishu yizhu* 四书译注 (Four Classics). Jilin, China: Jilin Classics Press.

Wu, Qichang 吴其昌. 2009. *Liang Qichao Zhuan* [梁启超传] (Biography of Liang Qichao). Beijing: Dongfang Press.

Xi, Jinping 习近平. 2012. "Jinjin weirao jianchi he fazhan zhongguo tese shehui zhuyi" 紧紧围绕坚持和发展中国特色社会主义 (Closely Centered around Adherence and Developing Socialism with Chinese Characteristics). In *Shibada fudao duben* 十八大辅导读本 (18th Party Congress Study Book), 1–12. Beijing: People's Press.

Xi, Jinping 习近平. 2013a. "Dang de shibada yilai xi jinping tongzhi de zhongyao jianghua huibian" 党的十八大以来习近平同志的重要讲话 (Important Speeches of Comrade Xi Jinping since the Party's 18th Congress). Compiled by the Office of Communist Youth Association of Fujian Province. http://www.fjrtvu.cn/gqtw/ (accessed April 10, 2014).

Xi, Jinping 习近平. 2013b. "Jinian Mao Zedong danchen 120 zhounian de jianghua" 纪念毛泽东诞辰 120 周年的讲话 (Speech Commemorating Mao Zedong's 120th Birthday Anniversary). http://www.asianews.it/news-en/Xi-Jinping:-Mao-was-not-a-god-,-but-his- spirit-...-29901.html (accessed January 10, 2014).

Xi, Jinping 习近平. 2013c. "Xi Jinping jieshou jinzhuan guojia meiti lianhe caifang shi de tanhua" 习近平接受金砖国家媒体联合采访的谈话 (Talk by Xi Jinping at the alliance media interview by BRICKS countries), March 19. http://www.fmprc.gov.cn/mfa_chn/gjhdq_603914/gjhdqzz_609676/jzgj_609846/xgxw_6 09852/t1022932.shtml (accessed April 15, 2014).

Xi, Jinping 习近平. 2014a. "Xijinping zai zhongfa jianjiao 50 zhounian jinian dahui shang de jianhua" 习近平在中法建交50周年纪念大会上的讲话 (Speech by Xi Jinping at the 50th anniversary of China-France diplomatic relations), March 27. http://news.qq.com/a/20140328/003294.htm (accessed April 1, 2014).

Xi, Jinping 习近平. 2014b. "Zhunque bawo dangde qunzhong luxian jiaoyu shijian huodong de zhidao sixiang he mubiao yaoqiu" 准确把握党的群众路线教育实践活动的指导思想和目标要求 (Guiding Principles and Goal Requirements for Accurately

Executing the Party's Mass Line Education Practice Activities). In *Xi jinping tan zhiguo lizheng* [习近平谈治国理政] (Xi Jinping Talks about Governing), 373–80. Beijing: Foreign Language Press.

Xiao, Duojie 萧铎洁. 2011. "Fanyunfuyu Mao Zedong" 翻云覆雨毛泽东 (Turning Clouds and Reversing Rain in Mao Zedong). http://www.zmw.cn/bbs/thread-119983-1-1.html (accessed April 30, 2014).

Xu, Yuanhong 徐元鸿. 2013. "Mao Zedong kaichuangle yidai wenfeng" 毛泽东开创了一代文风 (Mao Zedong Created a New Style). http://dangshi.people.com.cn/n/2013/1217/c85037-23866064.html (accessed February 9, 2014).

Yan, Fu 严复. 1986. *Yan Fu Ji* [严复集] (Collection of Yan Fu). Edited by Wang Shi 王栻. Beijing: China Books.

Yang, Jisheng 杨继绳. 2000. *Zhouguo shehui ge jieceng fenxi* [中国社会各阶层分析] (Analysis of Social Stratification in China). Hong Kong: Three Alliance Company.

Yi, Yan 易严. 1998. *Mao Zedong yu Lu Xun* [毛泽东与鲁迅] (Mao Zedong and Lu Xun). Shijiazhuang, Hebei, China: Hebei People's Press.

Yi, Zhongtian 易中天. 2007. *Diguo de zhongjie* [帝国的终结] (The End of Imperial China). Shanghai: Fudan University Press.

Yu, Hua 余华. 2011. *Shige cihui li de zhongguo* [十个词汇里的中国] (China in Ten Words). Taiwan: Maitian Press.

Yu, Xilai 喻希来. 2009. "Liang Qichao: Zhongguo minzuzhuyi de dianjiren" 梁启超: 中国民族主义的奠基人 (Liang Qichao: The Founding Father of Chinese). http://bbs.tianya.cn/post-no01-24987-1.shtml (accessed September 30, 2013).

Yu, Yingshi 余英时. 2012. "Dai tianxia de guangun—Mao Zedong yu zhongguo shi" 打天下的光棍－毛泽东与中国史 (Bachelor Conquering the World). *Minzhu zhongguo zazhi* [民主中国杂志] (Magazine of Democratic China). http://minzhuzhongguo.org/ArtShow.aspx?AID=25310 (accessed June 4, 2014).

Zhai, Yuzhong 翟玉忠. 2013. *Zhengming: Zhongguoren de luoji* [正名：中国人的逻辑] (Rectification of Names: Chinese People's Logic). Beijing: Central Compilation and Translation Press.

Zhou, Shizhao 周世钊. 1961. "Maozhuxi qingnian shiqi keku xuexi de jige gushi" 毛主席青年时期刻苦学习的几个故事 (A Few Stories of Studying Hard of Chairman Mao in His Youth). *Hebei Daily* [河北日报], October 13, 4.

Index

Shi Ji (Records of History) (Sima Qian), 141
Shi Jing (*Book of Poetry*), 85
Shimonosek, Treaty of, 139
Short, Philip, 3
Sima Guang, 19
Sima Qian, 126–27, 141
Sino-American Mutual Defense Treaty, 165, 166
Smedley, Agnes, 158, 206n7
Smith, Adam: *The Wealth of Nations*, 22, 140
Smith, H. Arthur, 142–43
Snow, Edgar, 8, 69, 99, 140, 158, 206n7; as intermediary between the U.S. and China, 167–68, 177; *Red Star over China*, 3, 157
Snow, Helen Forster, 158
social change: contradiction as impetus for, 48–52; Marxist-Leninist theories of, 40, 50–51; Mao's views on, 35, 36–37, 99–100. *See also* class struggle, Mao's rhetoric relating to
Socrates, 27
Soviet Union: China's shift away from, 172–73, 188, 217n13; China's shift toward, 162; as example of "positive" art and literature, 59, 68; rhetoric of, 92; satellites launched by, 227n22. *See also* Marxist-Leninist ideology
Spencer, Herbert: *The Study of Sociology*, 22, 140
Stalin, Joseph, 43, 83; bloody purge of, 105; *History of the Communist Part of the Soviet Union, Short Course*, 40
Steele, A. T., 161
Stein, Gunther, 158
Strange Tales of Liao Chai, 50
Strong, Anna Louise, 150, 158, 206n7
Stuart, John Leighton, 150, 223n17
Stuckey, Mary, 143
Sufan movement, 100–101, 216n7
Sun Baoyi, 40
Sun Yat-sen, 21–22, 88, 96–97, 115, 135, 141; and the nationalist movement, 146, 147, 148, 150, 154

Sunzi (*The Art of War*), 28, 82
symbols: as used in Mao's political rhetoric, 9–10

Taiwan, 166
Tang, Zongli, 99
Tao Te Ching. See Dao De Jing
Tao Yuanming, 35
"terministic screen," 85
Terrill, Ross, 38, 184
Third World countries: Mao as influence in, 176–77, 178
thought crimes, 101–2
thought reform: evolving into witch hunts, 136; as ongoing goal of Mao, 121–22, 124
Thousand Character Classics, 17, 208n2
Three Character Classics, 17, 208n2
Three Worlds Theory: as articulated by Mao, 14, 175–77
Tianjin, Treaty of, 139
tianming (mandate from heaven): as moral justification for rule, 149, 186
Trotsky, Leon, 215–16n16
Truman, Harry, 162
truth and knowledge: Mao's theories on, 41–47; practice as aspect of, 42–44, 45–46; as response to indigenous Chinese philosophy, 44–46; two-stage process of, 44
Twenty-Four Histories, 17

United States: anti-China sentiment in, 164; China's hostility toward, 150, 153–54, 156, 157, 160–64; Chinese stereotypes in, 225n5; Mao's private efforts to reach out to, 166–68, 177–78; Mao's rhetoric directed at, 14, 160–61, 162–64, 165–66, 167, 170–71, 172–73, 177; policy toward China, 105, 157; as potential ally of China, 159–60, 169–70; as supporter of the Nationalist Party, 160–61; and support for China during the Anti-Japanese War, 83, 158, 163